WOODROW WILSON CENTER SERIES

In face of the facts

Other books in the series

Michael J. Lacey, editor, *Religion and Twentieth-Century American Intellectual Life*

Michael J. Lacey, editor, *The Truman Presidency*

Joseph Kruzel and Michael H. Haltzel, editors, *Between the Blocs: Problems and Prospects for Europe's Neutral and Nonaligned States*

William C. Brumfield, editor, *Reshaping Russian Architecture: Western Technology, Utopian Dreams*

Mark N. Katz, editor, *The USSR and Marxist Revolutions in the Third World*

Walter Reich, editor, *Origins of Terrorism: Psychologies, Ideologies, Theologies, States of Mind*

Mary O. Furner and Barry Supple, editors, *The State and Economic Knowledge: The American and British Experiences*

Michael J. Lacey and Knud Haakonssen, editors, *A Culture of Rights: The Bill of Rights in Philosophy, Politics, and Law— 1791 and 1991*

Robert J. Donovan and Ray Scherer, *Unsilent Revolution: Television News and American Public Life, 1948–1991*

Nelson Lichtenstein and Howell John Harris, editors, *Industrial Democracy in America: The Ambiguous Promise*

William Craft Brumfield and Blair A. Ruble, editors, *Russian Housing in the Modern Age: Design and Social History*

Michael J. Lacey and Mary O. Furner, editors, *The State and Social Investigation in Britain and the United States*

Hugh Ragsdale, editor and translator, *Imperial Russian Foreign Policy*

Dermot Keogh and Michael H. Haltzel, editors, *Northern Ireland and the Politics of Reconciliation*

Joseph Klaits and Michael H. Haltzel, editors, *The Global Ramifications of the French Revolution*

René Lemarchand, *Burundi: Ethnic Conflict and Genocide*

James R. Millar and Sharon L. Wolchik, editors, *The Social Legacy of Communism*

James M. Morris, editor, *On Mozart*

Continued on page following index

In face of the facts

Moral inquiry in American scholarship

Edited by
RICHARD WIGHTMAN FOX and
ROBERT B. WESTBROOK

WOODROW WILSON CENTER PRESS

AND

CAMBRIDGE
UNIVERSITY PRESS

PUBLISHED BY THE PRESS SYNDICATE OF THE UNIVERSITY OF CAMBRIDGE
The Pitt Building, Trumpington Street, Cambridge CB2 1RP, United Kingdom

CAMBRIDGE UNIVERSITY PRESS
The Edinburgh Building, Cambridge CB2 2RU, United Kingdom   http: //www.cup.cam.ac.uk
40 West 20th Street, New York, NY 10011–4211, USA   http: //www.cup.org
10 Stamford Road, Oakleigh, Melbourne 3166, Australia

© The Woodrow Wilson Center International Center for Scholars 1998

First published 1998

Printed in the United States of America

Typeset in Sabon

*Library of Congress Cataloguing-in-Publication Data
is available*

*A catalogue record for this book is available from
the British Library*

ISBN 0 521 62133 X   hardback

WOODROW WILSON INTERNATIONAL CENTER FOR SCHOLARS

The Center is the living memorial of the United States of America to the nation's twenty-eighth president, Woodrow Wilson. Congress established the Woodrow Wilson Center in 1968 as an international institute for advanced study, "symbolizing and strengthening the fruitful relationship between the world of learning and the world of public affairs." The Center opened in 1970 under its own board of trustees, which includes citizens appointed by the president of the United States, federal government officials who serve ex officio, and an additional representative named by the president from within the federal government.

In all its activities the Woodrow Wilson Center is a nonprofit, nonpartisan organization, supported financially by annual appropriations from Congress and by the contributions of foundations, corporations, and individuals.

WOODROW WILSON CENTER PRESS

The Woodrow Wilson Center Press publishes books written in substantial part at the Center or otherwise prepared under its sponsorship by fellows, guest scholars, staff members, and other program participants. Conclusions or opinions expressed in Center publications and programs are those of the authors and speakers and do not necessarily reflect the views of the Center staff, fellows, trustees, advisory groups, or any individuals or organizations that provide financial support to the Center.

Woodrow Wilson Center Press
Editorial Offices
370 L'Enfant Promenade, S.W., Suite 704
Washington, D.C. 20024-2518
telephone: (202) 287-3000, ext. 218

Contents

Acknowledgments

The editors wish to thank the editorial staff of the Woodrow Wilson Center Press for their expert assistance. Joseph Brinley, director of the Press, has our special gratitude for shepherding the manuscript through the approval process. At the Woodrow Wilson International Center for Scholars, James Morris and Michael Lacey took a decisive interest in this project from the start, and Morris was instrumental in arranging the funding for the conference in May 1995 that gave birth to the book. Based outside the usual corridors of academia, thinkers such as Morris and Lacey play an indispensable part in American intellectual life, and we salute their pivotal role in convening this group of scholars. Our effusive thanks go also to Susan Nugent of the Woodrow Wilson Center, who organized the details of the conference and then performed word-processing heroics by combining these ten essays into a single, coherent manuscript. Her gracious labor informs every page of this book.

In face of the facts

Introduction

Moral inquiry in American scholarship

RICHARD WIGHTMAN FOX and
ROBERT B. WESTBROOK

The phrase "moral inquiry" is bound to give some readers a start. Moral inquiry will suggest the morals squad, the righteous fervor of self-appointed judges, the closed-mindedness of petty dispositions and pinched spirits, the restoration of Victorian constraint after nearly a century of ever-expanding openness, exposure, and toleration. Moral inquiry implies moralism and poses a menace to a modern ethic of live-and-let-live pluralism. Ironically, many critics of such open-ended pluralism will themselves find fault with "moral inquiry," since it implies that human deliberation is supposed to settle moral questions—questions better left to faith, revelation, or the dictates of unchanging natural law. Bitterly opposed to one another, both camps agree that the moral life, as they see it, is only threatened by the intrusions of inquiry.

The coupling of "moral inquiry" with "scholarship" will also cause some readers to recoil. In their view the terms are mutually exclusive since scholarship should be based upon the dispassionate pursuit and assessment of fact, not preaching or even deliberating about values. Modern scholarship has been premised, they will say, upon the repudiation of earlier generations' joining of moral zealotry with supposedly scientific but actually parochial investigation. To speak of moral inquiry in the same breath with scholarship is especially risky in this day and age, some will add, because partisan appeals to "political correctness" of both the right- and left-wing varieties are liable to divert universities from the free pursuit of the truth. Inquiry and scholarship, as they see it, are only undermined by the concerns of the moral life.

What the fearful and wary on all sides here share is the conviction that facts and values can and should be sealed off from one another and that scholarly inquiry—and scholarly institutions such as universi-

1

ties—will traffic only in the former. Insofar as scholars examine the moral life, they should ask only "how do we (or they) live?" (a question of fact) not "how should we (or they) live?" (a question of value). And they should resist any temptation to ask whether the first sort of question might bear some relation to the second, for it does not and cannot.

This common view of the university as a haven for disinterested truth-seeking and of the scholar as a pursuer of facts, not a professor of values, still reigns throughout much of academia in the United States. But it has recently come under criticism—and not only from politicized forces of the left and right, each of which aspires to supplant value-neutrality with an ideological alternative of its own. Dissatisfaction with the fact-value split is growing even among those with scant desire to take sides in the "culture wars" that wrack contemporary America.

A quick tour of some recent American intellectual history suggests the sources of this disenchantment. A generation ago scholars in many disciplines in the social sciences and humanities were united in a commitment to common "scientific" methods and goals: to conduct research and come to verifiable truths about an ever-proliferating range of topics. Researchers were to be detached, dispassionate; objectivity depended on impersonality and neutrality. Political, religious, social, or moral concerns were to be kept at bay lest they contaminate the professional sifting of evidence. Much sport was made of the genteel amateurs of the nineteenth or early twentieth centuries who routinely injected their historical, literary, or sociological works with sentimental hopes about the moral advance of civilization and with celebratory gestures about the greatness of this nation or that great leader. Modern-day scholars by contrast checked their beliefs and values at the academy's door.

In the 1950s and 1960s this ideal of impassive value neutrality came under fire—first by a few pundits on the right (William Buckley Jr.'s *God and Man at Yale* was the key document), and then by many on the left, including many professors.[1] Not only did the critics observe the failures of academics to abide by the positivist, "objectivist" ideal, but

---

[1] *God and Man at Yale* was published in 1951 by Regnery. The "anti-textbooks" published by Pantheon were a pivotal expression of the left-wing academic assault on the "liberal" ideal of value neutrality. See, for example, Theodore Roszak, ed., *The Dissenting Academy* (1968), Berton J. Bernstein, ed., *Towards a New Past: Dissenting Essays in American History* (1968), and Philip Green and Sanford Levinson, eds., *Power and Community: Dissenting Essays in Political Science* (1970).

they also questioned the ideal itself. No scholarship, they argued, was disinterested, least of all the prevailing wisdom, much of which thinly disguised a liberal ideology serving powerful interests beneath a veneer of disinterestedness. Since every perspective was interested, the argument went, every scholarly work should explicitly embrace its own position and expose those of others.

Yet few of these critics were relativists. They considered their own values, whether grounded in the truths of Christian revelation or Marxist history, superior to all others. Such critics assaulted the fact-value distinction by raising their own values to the status of objective, disinterested, "foundational" fact—an approach that remains characteristic of conservative critics of the academy. Ideological unmasking and the "hermeneutics of suspicion," of both the right- and left-wing varieties, were applied to others but not to one's own position.

In the past two decades we have witnessed the crumbling in some quarters of this campaign to have one's cake and eat it too. In our own time, under the influence of a postmodern sensibility and a declining faith in social progress and shared civic commitment, scholars have turned more and more to the view that all knowledge—including their own—is perspectival and that since each perspective is a product of discrete historical forces and particular interests, no perspective can ultimately be deemed superior to any other. The new catchwords are "localism," "particularity," "situatedness," "positionality," whereas "objectivity," "universality," and "cosmopolitanism" draw a yawn at best and more typically elicit a look of amazed condescension, as if to say "right-minded thinkers gave those up years ago." If earlier left- and right-wing critics questioned the value-neutrality of liberal academics while fashioning their own values into facts, the current critical tendency, particularly in the humanities, is to reduce all facts to incommensurable and competing values, and consequently to diminish moral deliberation to little more than a struggle for power. Ironically, such postmodernism has brought us full circle to renewed skepticism about the capacity of scholarly inquiry to address ethical questions, a skepticism as thoroughgoing as that of earlier positivists.

Some scholars, however, have sought to recast moral inquiry by sustaining the logical distinction between facts and values while refusing to banish values from scholarship. These scholars are unhappy with the fact-value split that still holds sway in American social science and with the erasure of the distinction between them that reigns in many humanities disciplines. They aim not to abandon the logical differentiation between facts and values nor to reduce one to the other but rather to foster the traffic between facts and values and hence between scholarly inquiry and moral judgment. Often calling on the forgotten legacy of pragmatists such as Charles Peirce, William James, and John Dewey, they have followed Dewey in abandoning the "quest for certainty" while resisting wholesale skepticism. And they have affirmed the fallible yet still "warranted" assertions that might provide a link between inquiry and moral deliberation. Fruitful inquiry, such scholars argue, is attuned to the moral dimension in all inquiry, and astute moral judgment is alert to the estimate of causes and consequences and to the appreciation of the fabric of lived experience that only inquiry can provide. Inquiry cannot free itself of values, and moral judgment without inquiry is impoverished. Not only does the moral life have nothing to fear from scholarly inquiry and scholarly inquiry nothing to fear from the moral life, but both are the richer for their marriage.

This latter view is gaining ground in American scholarship. Amidst the battles over postmodernism in colleges and universities and the struggles over a more general crisis of values in the wider public realm, scholarly work has emerged that places itself between or, better yet, beyond claims to moral certainty on the one hand and positivist and postmodernist moral skepticism on the other. Although we are both historians, we have done enough piecemeal reading across the artificial boundaries that separate one scholarly community from another to identify scholars in other disciplines who have neither exiled moral concerns from their scholarship, nor treated every exercise of the moral imagination as a power play.

Longstanding though this interest was for us, it took on particular intensity after the untimely death in early 1994 of our friend Christopher Lasch. His writing was exemplary of the sort of moral inquiry we had in mind. So with a friend equally bereft by Lasch's death, Jean Bethke Elshtain, we gladly accepted the generous invitation of the Woodrow Wilson International Center for Scholars to put together a conference that would assess the scope and character of moral inquiry in contemporary American scholarship. The essays in this volume are the product of that conference, which took place in May 1995. In addition to the contributors to this book, other incisive commentators, critics, and troublers of the intellectual peace attended the conference: Casey Blake, Fred Dallmayr, Thomas Haskell, Stanley Hauerwas, Amelie Rorty, and Joan Tronto.

We asked each of the contributors to describe and assess the course of moral inquiry in his or her discipline and invited them to situate their own work in relation to that story. We tried to cast our net widely, but we could not accommodate every relevant discipline, or treat the full international context of contemporary scholarly life.[2] This selectivity, and the happenstances that affect any effort to persuade a bunch of busy people to get together, led inevitably to some regrettable omissions. Most regrettable perhaps is the absence of an essay on the work being done at the intersection of biology and ethics, work that has attracted the interest not only of scholars but of a wider public audience.[3] Nonetheless, we managed to arrange for contributions on philosophy, political theory, public policy analysis, psychology, history, literary criticism, anthropology, religious studies, sociology, and legal theory. Anyone familiar with the unforeseeable forces shaping collective projects like this one will understand why we are tempted to draw upon a formulation of Richard Nixon and accept the responsibility for the disciplinary omissions, but not the blame.

Each of the chapters that follow offers readers its own particular riches, and we will not attempt to summarize those here. Nor can we—with the contentious, sometimes heated, exchanges that marked the conference still ringing in our memories—begin to suggest that the contributors share a consensus about the nature, purposes, and virtues of moral inquiry. Some of them (Alan Wolfe is perhaps the clearest example) have moved but a modest distance, and even then cautiously, from the ruling assumptions of value-free science. Others, like Joan Williams, are closer to postmodernist skepticism. These differences are sometimes explicitly aired in the essays, a debate we have encouraged. But despite their differences, the contributors occupy common ground worth noting, common ground that points to the promise of moral inquiry that is interdisciplinary—must be interdisciplinary—if it is to realize its possibilities.

[2] We are well aware that the "American" of our subtitle is often one of those "thick evaluative" adjectives to which Elizabeth Anderson directs our attention in her chapter. In describing the scholarship of our contributors as "American," we intend not to claim it as a peculiarly local knowledge but only to mark "where it is coming from" in the most literal geographical sense and to suggest that some of the moral concerns that animate the essays have a particularly American cast.

[3] See, for instance, two widely discussed recent efforts to bring Darwinism back into ethical discourse: Daniel Dennett, *Darwin's Dangerous Idea: Evolution and the Meanings of Life* (New York: Simon and Schuster, 1995); and Robert Wright, *The Moral Animal: Evolutionary Psychology and Everyday Life* (New York: Pantheon, 1994).

We have given pride of place to Elizabeth Anderson's essay because we think it provides a philosophical charter for interdisciplinary moral inquiry that all of our contributors would endorse. As Anderson notes, the fact-value split institutionalized itself in the academy as a divide between the human sciences, which were assigned the realm of fact, and philosophy, which patrolled the precincts of value. (It did so, that is, after the heyday of logical positivism, in which even philosophy was banned from this neighborhood.) Once we call the fact-value split into question, as Anderson does, we can dispute as well the institutional division of labor between philosophy and the human sciences. In a complaint echoed by Jean Elshtain, Marion Smiley, and Owen Flanagan, Anderson criticizes the renewal of substantive moral inquiry in philosophy marked by the 1971 publication of John Rawls's *Theory of Justice* for committing philosophy to an excessively abstract conception of the enterprise, a conception that preserved what Flanagan terms "Kant's dogma" separating normative ethics from the empirical investigation of the particulars of concrete moral lives.[4] As Anderson says, "this conception of moral inquiry preserves the fact-value dichotomy because it takes empirical inquiry into the facts and experiences of living up to the ethical norms embodied in actual social practices as irrelevant to the justification of the moral principles that 'apply' to these practices, and because it assumes that the actual state of these practices has nothing to do with whether the norms they embody are reasonable or apt."

Against this abstract, disembodied form of moral inquiry, Anderson offers an alternative "pragmatism," which accepts the logical distinction between facts and values yet argues for an evidential (and hence defeasible) connection between them.[5] For pragmatists, she says, "empirically grounded knowledge and forms of understanding bear upon the justification of ethical principles themselves. The most important source of empirical knowledge relevant to ethical justification comes from our experiences in living out the lives our ethical principles prescribe for us. We might find life in accordance with the principles we *think* are valid to be deeply unsatisfactory, to pose problems that are intolerable and irresolvable in terms of those very principles. Or we might find lives lived

[4] John Rawls, *A Theory of Justice* (Cambridge, Mass.: Harvard University Press, 1971).
[5] In an academic culture now filled with competing and often incompatible "neopragmatisms," Anderson's neopragmatism has the rare virtue of being consistent with the arguments of the pragmatisms of James and Dewey.

in accordance with fundamentally different principles to be profoundly attractive or appealing. This is different from having the armchair intuition that one approves of such lives. . . . The evidence pragmatists care about is gathered not from armchair reflection, which takes place from an observer's point of view, but from living the lives themselves from the point of view of agents." Consequently, such philosophers will be terribly interested in the portraits of moral lives that those in the human sciences can offer them, and those engaged in humanistic and social scientific inquiry who offer such portraits are making an invaluable contribution to moral inquiry. Thus Anderson's subversion of the fact-value split and her pragmatist conception of moral inquiry "urges us to view social, scientific, humanistic, and ethical inquiry as interconnected aspects of a joint enterprise."

The sort of interdisciplinary moral inquiry that Anderson's argument authorizes would find particular riches in what one might call the "narrative disciplines"—such as ethnography, history, literary criticism— since they are especially given to the collection and analysis of those stories that illuminate the moral life. One might well generalize Karen Brown's judgment about ethnography and argue that such moral inquiry requires "a significant collection of rigorous, dense [stories] that give sustained attention to morality as a key component of culture." And it requires stories near to and far from our own experience: stories from Alan Wolfe's middle-class American suburbanites (whose moral lives we all too often presume to know and to judge from our armchairs), as well as stories from Brown's Vodou priestess and Jane Kamensky's Puritans. Needless to say, Wayne Booth's Shakespeare will weigh in as well.[6] A wide-ranging and open-ended moral inquiry convinced of the evidentiary value of such stories requires scholars—ethnographers, historians, and critics—capable of journeying for a time to that destabilizing "boundary" that Robert Orsi so eloquently describes: "an in-between orientation, located at the intersection of self and other, at the boundary between one's own moral universe and the moral world of the other . . . ground that belongs completely neither to oneself or to the other but that has come into being between them, precisely because of the meeting of the two." For it is here alone, as Orsi says, that "one

---

[6] As this implies, interdisciplinary moral inquiry rests not only on the work of those who collect, retell, and analyze such stories, but also on that of those who tell them in the first place: novelists, playwrights, autobiographers, memoirists, filmmakers, songwriters, and so forth.

comes to know something about the other and about oneself through relationship with the other."

In addition to hopes for interdisciplinary moral inquiry, our contributors share a common aversion to moralizing, which might be characterized as moral judgment untethered from responsible moral inquiry. Moral inquiry does not preach or press evidence into the service of pre-established arguments. None of these authors is in quest of—let alone in possession of—moral certainty, unassailable moral prescriptions, or algorithms capable of generating knockdown moral arguments. The purpose of moral inquiry, as they see it, is to enrich moral deliberation, not preempt it. Sometimes—as Marion Smiley's essay suggests most forcefully—all we might reasonably ask of moral inquiry is a clearer, better set of questions to work with as we struggle to shape our common moral life. At the same time, none of these authors is given to thoroughgoing skepticism about the role of reason in the moral life; they all occupy what Kamensky terms a "capacious middle ground" between certitude and wholesale doubt.

In short, this is a gathering of scholars given to what Flanagan nicely terms "unconfident moral confidence." Not all the contributors might agree with the criteria that Booth, following David Hume, lays out for sound moral reasoning, but all, we think, would see themselves in Booth's characterization of Hume: "Radically skeptical about all hard and certain proof, even in so-called scientific matters, and especially skeptical about decisive demonstration of moral and religious conclusions, he nevertheless always distinguishes those who make their practical or rhetorical claims carelessly from those who use a rational discourse to pursue common ground."

"Unconfident confidents" cannot blink moral conflict, and none here does. We think all would agree with Elshtain that moral inquiry must struggle "to find ways to deal with a multiplicity of moral claims that must be adjudicated both within ourselves and within our societies, and to do so in a way that does not presuppose a final harmony of purposes, ends, virtues, and identities." The intractable moral divides that afflict modern American culture and politics loom large in these essays. No one here suggests that moral inquiry can solve these conflicts, though no one—even those who focus on the most intractable of disputes—presumes that it cannot at least clarify them. For example, Joan Williams, who speaks of "incommensurable" moral perspectives abroad in American life, hopes that "ever-shifting points of potential translation and convergence" can still foster "a process of mutually respectful social negotiation across incommensurability, leading to shifting alliances that will depend for their success on how well we understand what really matters to groups of people with whom we profoundly disagree."

We have every reason to believe, having been witness to conversations among our contributors, that each of them would make particular moral arguments that would elicit conflict with other members of the group. But we are equally convinced that all abide by at least one common moral commitment and that is to inquiry itself and to a community of inquiry in search of truths at once provisional and shared. Far from a neutral, value-free assortment of procedures, inquiry is a morally laden set of practices. As John Dewey observed, inquiry is "absolutely dependent for logical worth upon a moral interest: the sincere aim to judge truly."[7] Readers must judge for themselves whether the chapters that follow judge truly; but none may doubt their aim.

---

[7] John Dewey, "Logical Conditions of a Scientific Treatment of Morality" (1903), in *The Middle Works of John Dewey* (Carbondale: Southern Illinois University Press, 1977), 3:19.

1

Pragmatism, science, and moral inquiry

ELIZABETH ANDERSON

Of all the academic disciplines, philosophy is perhaps the one that most fully embraces the legitimacy of moral inquiry as part of its enterprise. The attempt to avoid ethical judgments has long been rationalized by various local arguments within the other disciplines—in anthropology, by a methodological commitment to ethical relativism; in literary studies, by the modernist repudiation of didacticism in art and art criticism; in economics, by the pretense that criteria of welfare that take individual preferences as given and incomparable are morally neutral. But these local arguments can all trace their roots to a philosophical dichotomy between facts and values. If Anglo-American philosophy can claim moral inquiry as a proper part of its mission, this is largely because it conceives of the academic division of labor as assigning responsibility for discovering the empirical facts to the natural and social sciences, while it works on a priori truths and value judgments. Philosophy no less than the other disciplines operates under the shadow of the fact-value dichotomy, even when it accepts the legitimacy of moral inquiry.

Of course, during the heyday of logical positivism, even philosophy regarded substantive moral inquiry as an illegitimate enterprise. The most philosophy could do was to delineate the meaning of moral terms, not determine when, if ever, they truthfully or reasonably applied. Two events in 1971 dramatically revived philosophical inquiry into substantive moral issues: the publication of John Rawls's *A Theory of Justice* and the launching of the journal *Philosophy and Public Affairs*.[1] But the

I would like to thank Fred Dallmayr, Jean Elshtain, Amelie Rorty, Marion Smiley, Alan Wolfe, and Robert Westbrook for their comments and criticisms of this chapter.
[1] John Rawls, *A Theory of Justice* (Cambridge, Mass.: Harvard University Press, 1971).

terms on which academic moral inquiry was revived demonstrate the continuing power of the fact-value dichotomy over its character.

The explosion of "applied ethics" that these two events initiated reflected the very top-down, a prioristic conception of moral inquiry that the term suggests. One begins with fundamental moral principles or "intuitions," perhaps systematized into a "theory" such as utilitarianism or contractarianism, which supplies a formula for right action. And then one "applies" these principles or intuitions or formulas to the "facts" of a case. This conception of moral inquiry preserves the fact-value dichotomy because it takes empirical inquiry into the facts and experiences of living up to the ethical norms embodied in actual social practices as irrelevant to the justification of the moral principles that "apply" to these practices, and because it assumes that the actual state of these practices has nothing to do with whether the norms they embody are reasonable or apt.[2] Thus, in the voluminous mainstream philosophical writing on abortion, one rarely hears testimony about the varied experiences of women who have been denied access to a safe abortion, or who have had an abortion, about the impact of legalized abortion on sexual mores and the status of women and children, or about the socially contested meanings of motherhood and their connections to religious convictions. The situation is no different for the other issues that have attracted widespread philosophical attention, such as affirmative action, euthanasia, the death penalty, state paternalism, and the legal enforcement of morality. Empirical evidence may be accepted as relevant to the question of how to apply an ethical principle but almost never to the question of whether the ethical principle is justified in the first place.

Instead, the justification of ethical principles has tended to take either a foundationalist or a narrowly coherentist form. In foundationalist projects, philosophers use metaphysical considerations about the nature of personal identity, or abstract theories of practical reasoning, or metaethical theories about the meaning of moral claims to justify basic moral principles.[3] In coherentist projects, philosophers play off intuitions (pretheoretical moral opinions accepted in conditions of calm reflection)

---

[2] Marion Smiley also identifies these assumptions as key weaknesses in applied ethics. See her chapter in this volume.

[3] See, for example, Derek Parfit, *Reasons and Persons* (Oxford: Clarendon Press, 1984); John Harsanyi, "Morality and the Theory of Rational Behavior," in *Utilitarianism and Beyond*, ed. Amartya Sen and Bernard Williams (Cambridge: Cambridge University Press, 1982), 39–62; and R. M. Hare, *Moral Thinking* (Oxford: Clarendon Press, 1981).

about general moral principles against intuitions about particular cases until they reach "narrow reflective equilibrium."[4] This is the point where the principles one accepts give reflectively acceptable answers to the particular cases one has considered, and one's intuitions about what should be done in particular cases can be accounted for by acceptable ethical principles. Coherentist projects, unlike foundationalist ones, acknowledge that justification is a two-way street, that views about particular cases have a bearing on the warrant of general ethical principles. But the views that matter in most instances of coherentist methodology are the views one accepts in calm, practically removed, armchair reflection, not the views one accepts in the light of one's experience in living according to rival principles. Moreover, both foundationalist and narrow coherentist projects typically adopt a monological methodology. In other words, they offer a technique of justifying ethical principles usable by one mind working alone. Dialogue with others forms no inherent part of the methods employed to justify ethical conclusions.

What is worse, the principal theories employed in "applied ethics"—utilitarianism/consequentialism/cost-benefit analysis in one family, and Kantianism/contractarianism in the other—fail a fundamental pragmatic test: we just do not know how to embody them effectively in our lives. These theories purport to offer principles that cannot be justified by particular empirical facts, since they are supposed to be true in all possible worlds or valid for all rational beings. This aspiration rescues moral principles from contingency at the cost of abstracting them so far from particular situations that we do not know how to apply them in a determinate fashion. Kantian/contractarian theories are notoriously difficult to "get right." Despite recent extraordinary advances in Kantian casuistry[5] and contractarian theorizing, they are far from being able to offer detailed prescriptions in the complex cases that people actually confront. The Kantian/contractarian hope that moral disputes could be settled by reducing them to problems of rational choice under constraint has foundered on the controversies that beset the theory of rational choice itself. For example, John Rawls, John Harsanyi, and David Gauthier all accept the contractarian doctrine that the right principles of distributive justice are those that free, equal, and self-interested rational

[4] See, for example, Frances Kamm, *Morality, Mortality* (New York: Oxford University Press, 1993).
[5] See, for example, Barbara Herman, *The Practice of Moral Judgment* (Cambridge, Mass.: Harvard University Press, 1993).

persons would consent to under fair or "morally neutral" conditions.[6] Yet their theories support conflicting principles of distribution largely because they appeal to competing, controversial principles of rational choice.

Coherentist deontological methods, which do not subsume the diversity of moral intuitions under a single master principle such as the categorical imperative, suffer from practical difficulties too. They invite conversation-stopping appeals to opinions about bizarre cases, in which people often have little confidence, as a means to settle real problems. Thus, Judith Jarvis Thomson urges us to judge the morality of abortion by teasing out intuitions about whether it would be all right for a woman to kill "people seeds" that invaded her apartment, if people grew like plants from wind-born seeds.[7] Yet we might well hesitate to draw conclusions from such weird analogies, if we thought that our views about the responsibilities of parenthood and the scope of private property rights might change dramatically under such different conditions of human reproduction.

Theories in the consequentialist camp suffer from similar difficulties, despite their pretenses to the contrary. Cost-benefit analysis offers the only genuinely quantitative consequentialist method for generating determinate rankings among detailed, complex alternatives. But its ability to generate results hangs on assumptions most people reject—for example, that the worth of endangered species can be reduced to a monetary equivalent, or that risks one finds worthwhile when voluntarily chosen are equally acceptable when imposed by others.[8] Other forms of direct consequentialism lead to absurd and outrageous results, suggesting, for instance, that it would be all right to torture or enslave people if only enough people were entertained heartily enough by such actions. To avoid such horrors, consequentialist theories must resort to sophisticated forms of indirection such as rule and motive utilitarianism and "self-effacing" consequentialism, in which people are directed not to believe the theory that justifies their actions.[9]

Moreover, in responding to objections from commonsense morality,

---

[6] John Rawls, *A Theory of Justice,* John Harsanyi, "Morality and the Theory of Rational Behavior," and David Gauthier, *Morals by Agreement* (Oxford: Clarendon Press, 1986).

[7] Judith Jarvis Thomson, "A Defense of Abortion," *Philosophy and Public Affairs* 1 (1971): 47–66.

[8] For further discussion, see Elizabeth Anderson, *Value in Ethics and Economics* (Cambridge, Mass.: Harvard University Press, 1993), ch. 9.

[9] Parfit, *Reasons and Persons*, 43.

indirect consequentialist theories must appeal to remote effects, slippery slopes, and other dubious contingencies that undermine their claim to provide a standard of conduct distinct from nonconsequentialist intuitions. For example, it is a commonplace of rule utilitarianism that one should not murder one person to harvest her organs, even if doing so would save five (happier) lives, because the advantages of murdering whenever this maximizes happiness are outweighed by the general distress people would suffer from the fear that they might be murdered for this purpose. Yet rule utilitarians have never produced empirical data to support their confidence in this calculation. It appears to be rooted instead in commonsense nonconsequentialist moral intuitions. Consequentialist prescriptions are thus either intolerable, or parasitic upon nonconsequentialist moral intuitions.

Ironically, neither of the two dominant methods in applied ethics followed Rawls's own conception of justification. He did not regard his a priori argument that rational self-interested persons in fair conditions would choose his principles of justice as the complete justification for them. Rather, he insisted that moral claims be vindicated in *wide* reflective equilibrium. This is a state that incorporates consideration not just of armchair ethical intuitions but knowledge of what the human sciences can tell us about the character of lives in regimes regulated by the moral principles under investigation. Part III of his *Theory of Justice* was devoted to showing (1) that what we know about human moral development was consistent with the expectation that people could live up to the principles of justice he recommended, and (2) that people would find their lives in societies regulated by the principles of justice to be satisfactory, congruent with the successful pursuit of their conceptions of the good. Rawls took for granted that people's experiences in living up to (or trying to live up to) particular moral principles provide evidence relevant to the justification of those principles. Alas, the extraordinarily high level of abstraction at which Rawls prefers to argue tends to obscure the pragmatic elements in his work.

A PRAGMATIST VIEW OF ETHICAL INQUIRY

I shall argue that pragmatism offers the key to breaking out of the impasses in moral inquiry imposed by the fact-value dichotomy. The enforcement of this dichotomy by disciplinary self-definitions has worked to the detriment of both philosophical moral inquiry and humanistic/

social scientific inquiry. On the part of philosophy, it has led to serious neglect of the importance of evidence and experience to the justification of ethical principles. On the part of the human sciences, it has led to a failure to reflect on what it takes to justify the ways they classify phenomena.

Pragmatism urges us to view social scientific, humanistic, and ethical inquiry as interconnected aspects of a joint enterprise. Ethical inquiry is a quest for forms of self-understanding by which we can lead our lives in ways that meet our own standards for excellence or success. These standards evolve in response to the facts we learn about ourselves, and forms of understanding we develop for ourselves, in leading our lives— facts and self-understandings that it is the project of the humanities and social sciences to explore. In regarding ethical and humanistic/social inquiry as a joint enterprise, pragmatists display one of the hallmarks of their philosophy: a skepticism of philosophical dichotomies. The pragmatist W. V. O. Quine attacked numerous philosophical dichotomies: analytic-synthetic, theory-observation, metaphysics-science.[10] Pragmatists since Quine—notably Hilary Putnam and feminist empiricists such as Lynn Nelson—have returned to the older pragmatists John Dewey and William James in deconstructing the one philosophical dichotomy Quine left untouched: that between fact and value.[11]

Pragmatic moral inquiry differs from its two main rivals—foundationalist theory and narrow coherentist theory—in the uses it makes of the evidence, theories, and forms of self-understanding developed by humanistic and social scientific inquiries. Foundationalists typically seek ethical principles that are valid in all possible worlds and/or that apply to all rational beings. This requires that fundamental ethical truths be expressed at a level that abstracts from all the particularities of human existence. The principle of utility and Kant's categorical imperative express abstractions of this sort. If our basic ethical principles are this abstract, and if they are justified by a priori considerations, then empirical facts and theories cannot figure in the justification of ethical principles but only in their application to particular ethical problems. Narrow coherentists allow that intuitions about particular cases of

---

[10] W. V. O. Quine, *From a Logical Point of View*, rev. ed. (New York: Harper and Row, 1963).

[11] Hilary Putnam, *Reason, Truth, and History* (Cambridge: Cambridge University Press, 1981); and Lynn Nelson, *Who Knows? From Quine to a Feminist Empiricism* (Philadelphia: Temple University Press, 1990).

moral choice figure in the justification of ethical principles. But the intuitions about particulars that matter for narrow coherentists are all conceived as expressing purely ethical opinions, couched in the language of "ought"; they are not seen as empirically grounded opinions. Thus, for coherentists, too, empirical facts and understandings figure only in the application of ethical principles, not in their justification.

For pragmatists, however, empirically grounded knowledge and forms of understanding bear upon the justification of ethical principles themselves. The most important source of empirical knowledge relevant to ethical justification comes from our experiences in living out the lives our ethical principles prescribe for us. We might find life in accordance with the principles we *think* are valid to be deeply unsatisfactory, to pose problems that are intolerable and irresolvable in terms of those very principles. Or we might find lives lived in accordance with fundamentally different principles to be profoundly attractive or appealing. This is different from having the armchair intuition that one approves of such lives. Such intuitions are accessible to narrow coherentists. The evidence pragmatists care about is gathered not from armchair reflection, which takes place from an observer's point of view, but from living the lives themselves from the point of view of agents.

For example, in his youth, John Stuart Mill accepted Jeremy Bentham's one-dimensional hedonistic conception of happiness as the sole measure of value for all things. His Benthamite utilitarian principles were consistent, coherent, and in reflective equilibrium with his intuitions about what to do in particular cases. Mill's doubts about the adequacy of Bentham's philosophy grew not from any conflicts it posed with other moral intuitions but from the fact that living his life in accordance with Benthamite maxims caused him to fall into an intractable depression for which Bentham's philosophy offered neither relief nor explanation. Where narrow coherentism would have vindicated Mill's Benthamite convictions, Mill took his experiences in living out Bentham's philosophy as evidence that his conception of happiness was fundamentally impoverished. His rejection of Benthamism was pragmatic. He took the crucial evidence relevant to the justification of moral principles to come from what it is like to live the life they prescribe.[12]

[12] For further discussion of Mill's pragmatic rejection of Benthamism, see Elizabeth Anderson, "John Stuart Mill and Experiments in Living," *Ethics* 102 (1991): 4–26. Mill's objection to Bentham's theory was not that following it led to unhappiness. Bentham's theory could accommodate this by recommending indirect strategies to hap-

Pragmatic ethical justification thus depends on fine-grained, subject-centered descriptions of actual human experience and conduct. People describe what it is like to live their lives in accordance with ethical principles in terms that *matter* to them, in heavily value-laden terms; for example, they talk about betrayal, respect, dignity, alienation, and trust. This fact shapes the character of pragmatic ethical inquiry in three ways. First, pragmatists avoid appeal to ethical principles that reside at too high a level of abstraction from the particulars of human experience. They do not attempt to articulate or justify ethical principles supposed to be true in all possible worlds or valid for all rational beings. Pragmatic ethical principles are contingent, reflecting the circumstances of culture, locality, and history. Second, pragmatists conduct their ethical inquiries hand-in-hand with empirical investigations into the particular features of the institutions, practices, and predicaments real agents participate in, construct, and confront. Third, pragmatists justify their recommendations contextually. They see the quest for livable ethical principles as arising from concrete practices and predicaments, situated in particular historical and cultural contexts. Justification is addressed to the agents in these contexts and works by demonstrating the practical superiority of the proposed solution to the finite, concrete alternatives imagined at the time. The result is a form of ethical inquiry that sticks closely to the facts of particular social practices and the experiences of those participating in them, that lies closer to social criticism than to metaphysical speculation or armchair moralizing.

HOW EXPERIENCE CAN PROVIDE EVIDENCE FOR MORAL CLAIMS

Pragmatic moral inquiry, as I have described it, seems to fly in the face of the fact-value dichotomy. Yet pragmatists do not deny the bare logical distinction between asserting that P exists and asserting that P ought to exist. Rather, they criticize two claims that are thought to follow from this distinction. First, it is claimed that facts or experience have no evidential bearing on intrinsic value judgments and hence are irrelevant to

---

piness. Rather, Mill took his experience as evidence that Bentham's evaluative categories were impoverished, that they failed to mark intrinsically important distinctions of worth, such as between higher and lower pleasures. He took the empirical facts of his depression to figure in a moral critique, not just of Bentham's means, but of his ends, his basic conception of happiness. This is the distinctively pragmatic feature of his argument.

the justification of noninstrumental practical principles.[13] To attempt to logically deduce "ought" from "is" is to commit the naturalistic fallacy. Second, it is claimed that ethical principles cannot be relevant to the justification of social scientific theories. What actually exists is entirely independent of what ought to exist. To permit moral or political concerns to figure in the justification of social scientific theories is to guide belief by wishful thinking or partisan political interests rather than by the evidence.

I shall argue, in response to these objections, that there are domains of human experience equally relevant to the justification of moral principles and the justification of empirical accounts of human affairs. These are domains described in terms of so-called thick evaluative concepts, which combine factual and evaluative judgments.[14] Experiences couched in these terms provide the crucial empirical evidence for ethical judgments. At the same time the classification of phenomena in humanistic and social scientific inquiry is and ought to be based on thick evaluative concepts, and the justification for using some classifications rather than others must combine normative and empirical considerations.

Thick evaluative concepts include concepts such as "cruel," "humiliating," "courageous," "dignified," and "graceful." They are contrasted with the "thin" ethical concepts—"good," "bad," "right," "wrong," and "ought"—because they have quite specific empirical subject matters. Certain facts have to obtain for the thick evaluative concepts to apply. An act cannot be cruel unless it expresses an intention to make some creature suffer. One's conduct is not dignified if one bows and scrapes before others. These evaluative concepts threaten the fact-value dichotomy because they simultaneously play a factual and an evaluative role in discourse, feeling, and conduct. From "this act is cruel" we are entitled to infer both that the act has a particular factual character and that we have a reason to condemn and discourage it.[15]

---

[13] This claim must be confined to intrinsic value judgments and noninstrumental practical principles. Everyone admits that factual evidence about an object's causal powers is relevant to the claim that it is instrumentally good, and to the validity of instrumental practical principles of the form, "if you intend to bring about x, you ought to do y."

[14] See Bernard Williams, *Ethics and the Limits of Philosophy* (Cambridge, Mass.: Harvard University Press, 1985).

[15] I say that the fact that an act is cruel gives us *a* reason to condemn it. I do not say that it gives us a conclusive reason to condemn it, or even that it gives us most of what we need to know to tell whether we ought to condemn it. Alan Wolfe's complaint in this volume that such thick descriptions do little to inform the moral assessments of acts is thus misguided. To be sure, one thick description of an act is not enough to tell us how

Against this last claim, R. M. Hare has urged that thick evaluative concepts can be analyzed into logically distinct factual and evaluative components.[16] The descriptive features of "cruel" must be separated from the moral condemnation that usually attends the description. Thus, one is logically free to accept the claim that an act is cruel while rejecting the normative implications thought to follow from it. Hence, we are not *logically* entitled to infer that we have a reason to condemn an act, just because we know it is cruel. To make this inference is to commit the naturalistic fallacy, to mistakenly suppose that the meaning of "good" is reducible to some value-neutral property.

Hare's analysis is logically correct; it follows from the conceptual distinction between "*x* exists" and "*x* ought to exist." But it is irrelevant to the question of what we are entitled to infer in moral argument. Consider the logically analogous fact-perception dichotomy. There is a conceptual distinction between "*x* exists" and the report "I see *x*," where *x* is an object that exists independent of the mind. Hence, one is always *logically* entitled to reject the usual inference from the report "I see *x*" to "*x* exists."

However, if one insists on rejecting this inference without offering reasons to doubt the evidence of one's senses, one simply is not engaged in empirical inquiry. Similarly, if one insists on rejecting the usual normative inferences licensed by thick evaluative judgments without offering reasons to doubt, for instance, that cruelty is bad, one simply is not engaged in ethical inquiry. In both cases the entitlement to infer one claim from another is not logical but evidential. And both forms of inquiry are constitutively structured by substantive presuppositions about evidential connections—that sensory perception provides evidence about mind-independent objects; that what engages people's interests or arouses their favorable responses provides evidence about what is good. One who rejects these presuppositions is not engaged in empirical or ethical inquiry, respectively, however much one utters meaningful sentences about mind-independent objects or the good.

For pragmatists, the connection between ethical experiences couched

---

to assess it. But the sum total of all acceptable thick descriptions gives us virtually all the information we can have and need to have to pass judgment on an act. As I stress later in this chapter, this implies not that all moral controversy is closed once we have gathered all such information, but only that it is very seriously constrained by such information.

[16] R. M. Hare, "Descriptivism," in *Essays on the Moral Concepts* (London: Macmillan, 1972), 55–75.

in thick evaluative terms and moral judgments is evidential, not logical. The only evidence, and very good evidence indeed, that something is good is that people do in fact value it; they experience it in favorable terms, find it appealing, take an interest in it. Evidence is, of course, defeasible. If we find ourselves valuing something because of circumstances we judge to distort our evaluative perspectives, we discount our experiences as unreliable. If people take up an interest in obeying a cult leader only because they have been subject to abuse, coercion, or brainwashing, their expression of interest in obedience to the cult leader does not count as evidence that such obedience is good. Pragmatists thus regard facts about human experience and motivation as providing empirical evidence for claims about what is good, right, and just. Since evidence is defeasible, to assert an evidential link between facts and values is not to assert a conceptual reduction. Thus, pragmatists commit no naturalistic fallacy when they cite facts as evidence for evaluative claims.

Pragmatists are particularly interested in thick evaluative concepts because these are typically the terms in which the human experiences relevant to evaluating intrinsic value judgments are framed. Insofar as we experience the world and ourselves in terms of thick evaluative concepts, we reach beyond instrumental goods to our conceptions of our final ends and interests. A person who experiences her actions and feelings in terms of "sinfulness," "humility," and "holiness" has constituted a conception of the good quite distinct from a person who experiences her actions and feelings in terms of "injustice," "dignity," and "decency." Once a given set of thick concepts constitutes our experiences, these experiences count as evidence for or against particular ethical recommendations concerning final goods. Consider the Christian, thick conceptual discourse in which "humility" is contrasted with "arrogance." In this discourse, from the empirical fact that an action is humble, it follows that it is worthy of praise and emulation. Actions of this sort are intrinsically good, in that they express humans' proper appreciation of their sinfulness in relation to God's glory and goodness. Consider, by contrast, the Enlightenment discourse in which "humility" is contrasted with "dignity." In this discourse, the fact that an action is humble tends to count against its being performed or praised. Actions of this sort are intrinsically unworthy because they express a degrading conception of one's self-worth.

The meaning of a given thick concept is established in relation to others. Christian humility cannot be fully grasped apart from notions of sinfulness, God's glory, and the like. The evaluative import of a given thick concept is likewise established in relation to the field of alternatives that it helps constitute. Once theism is rejected, one loses the conceptual ground for regarding Christian humility as a virtue. It then can reflect only a superstitious bowing down to earthly authorities no better than oneself, once these persons' claims to have their authority delegated to them by God or grounded in a great chain of being are undercut. A person might think that she is free to evaluate something falling under a thick concept favorably or unfavorably, when she considers it in isolation. She could just go "pro" or "con" for humility. But once the field of feasible alternatives is defined, formidable obstacles arise to reversing the usual evaluative connotations of a thick concept.[17] Once one reconceives Christian humility as a superstitious slavishness, as one must once one rejects the Christian's own conceptual alternative—defining one's actions in relation to God—there is no conceptual space left for representing good-making qualities in (Christian) humility. For claims about what is good must be capable of being backed up by reasons, or considerations of their good-making qualities, which we have seen need to be plausibly linked to things that can sensibly arouse a favorable response in us. But superstition and slavishness, understood as such, rightly arouse only contempt.

These facts show that "humility" does not mean the same thing, or even have the same extensions, in Christian and Enlightenment moralities. For "humility" does not have the same opposites in the two discourses. Enlightenment "dignity" is not the same concept as Christian "arrogance," but with a favorable evaluative judgment attached. Rather, the actions that Christians bundled together under the common vice-term "arrogance" are divided in egalitarian Enlightenment thought between virtuous "dignified" actions and still vicious "arrogance"—where the latter is now taken to mean, not humans (mis)taking themselves to be better than the place God assigned to them, but some humans (mis)taking themselves to be intrinsically superior to other humans, and hence entitled to dominate them.

If this reasoning is sound, then the question of what is good and right

---

[17] See Charles Taylor, "Neutrality in Political Science," in *Philosophy and the Human Sciences* (Cambridge: Cambridge University Press, 1985), 58–90.

is largely answered by articulating the field of thick evaluative concepts in terms of which we ought to describe, discriminate, and experience ourselves and the world. The question then becomes: on what grounds can we determine whether one discursive field or another better articulates the range of alternatives?

Pragmatists argue that our experiences in living our lives in terms of different thick conceptual fields offer crucial evidence that bears upon whether we have adequately defined and described our alternatives. We will experience things going wrong with our lives if we lump together under one vice dispositions that should be divided between distinct virtues and vices. We will confront problems that cannot be solved within the terms our thick concepts offer us. Sometimes the causal explanation of why we experience things going wrong with our lives will be that our thick evaluative classifications are confused, or leave out normatively important phenomena, or include others that do not do all the work they purport to do, or are related in undermining ways that our classifications do not admit. If we reworked the terms in which we lead our lives, we might be able to overcome or ameliorate these problems.

Thus, John Stuart Mill managed to overcome his youthful depression in part by revising his conception of the good—most importantly, by acknowledging the roles his emotions and imagination played in signifying qualitative, hierarchical distinctions among pleasures. This successful revision showed that Bentham was wrong to distrust the emotions and to lump higher and lower pleasures together.[18]

The question of whether we have an adequate system of normative classification thus depends on causal claims. Empirical inquiry and observation are needed to support causal claims. Therefore, empirical inquiry and observation are relevant to the justification of our normative classifications, and hence of our practical ethical principles.

HOW CLASSIFICATION IN THE HUMAN SCIENCES IS A NORMATIVE ENTERPRISE

I shall now defend the converse thesis, that normative considerations are relevant to the justification of the empirical classifications in humanistic and social scientific inquiry. I believe this is true because these disciplines

[18] See Anderson, "John Stuart Mill."

ought to classify phenomena in terms of their relations to human interests and values.[19] There are two reasons for this.

First, a fundamental aim of many of these disciplines is to guide policies to promote human interests and values. They cannot do this if they classify phenomena out of relation to these interests and values. This point applies as much to applied natural sciences such as medicine and horticulture as to policy-oriented human sciences such as economics. Medicine classifies organisms living in the human body into pathogenic and nonpathogenic; horticulture classifies plants into crops and weeds. These classifications explicitly track human interests in health and in useful plants. The point of classifying living things in these ways is to guide technological development—drugs that selectively kill the pathogens, agricultural techniques that favor crop growth and discourage weeds. We classify heterogeneous organisms in these ways so that we can take up a common practical and evaluative response to them. In the policy-oriented social sciences, too, theoretical classifications typically track human interests and values. Economics investigates the causes of employment and interest rates, because human plans depend on these variables. Sociology investigates the nature and causes of social stratification because humans care about inequality. These sciences could not effectively guide practice if they did not classify phenomena in relation to human interests.

The second reason why humanistic and social scientific inquiry ought to classify phenomena in relation to human interests and values reaches beyond direct policy applications and covers non-policy-oriented humanistic inquiry. The subject matter of humanistic and social scientific inquiry is ourselves. This fact has inescapable practical implications. As Charles Taylor has emphasized, it is part of our nature as self-interpreting, deliberative beings that we must act on our understandings of who we are.[20] Thus, to propose that we understand ourselves in certain terms is to propose that we embody these terms in our practices.

[19] By "human interests and values," I do not mean exclusively the interests humans take in themselves—that is, human welfare. Humans take an intrinsic interest in other things besides themselves, including animals, ecosystems, and inanimate natural objects and artifacts. And we often rightly care about these things, independently of any relation they may bear to human welfare. For example, we may find them wonderful and awe inspiring, and valuable on that account, even when they pose a threat to human welfare, as volcanoes sometimes do. I thus endorse the view that we ought to care about other things besides ourselves and to conduct inquiry with these concerns in mind.
[20] Charles Taylor, "What Is Human Agency?" in *Human Agency and Language* (Cambridge: Cambridge University Press, 1985), 58–90.

If social scientific and humanistic inquiry proposes to offer terms of
self-understanding, this cannot but have practical consequences, however much some researchers may want to avoid responsibility for their
explanations.

If humanistic and social scientific inquiry ought to classify phenomena
in terms of their relations to human interests and values, then these
forms of inquiry are, and ought to be, value laden. Advocates of the
value-neutrality of science concede that human interests may properly
influence the context of scientific discovery. Most importantly, interests
may direct our inquiry toward some subjects and away from others. But
they insist that human interests be kept out of the context of justification.
Interests may tell us where to look but not what we shall find when we
look there. This distinction cannot be sustained if my normative claim
is true. Interests ought to tell us not only where to look, but also the
terms in which we describe what we find there. Empirical inquiry will
shape our conception of our interests, and it will also tell us what things
fall under the classifications set by our interests. To justify the use of a
system of classification in humanistic and social scientific inquiry, it is
not enough to show that the classification meets morally neutral empirical criteria. One must also show that the classifications are appropri-
ately related to human interests and values.

Against these arguments stands the dominant tradition in the philosophy of science. This tradition raises the second challenge that the fact-
value dichotomy poses to pragmatic moral inquiry. This is the claim that
ethical judgments are irrelevant to the justification of scientific theories.
What exists is entirely independent of what ought to exist. The classifications of objects in empirical inquiry—the types of objects empirical
inquiry finds in the world—are or ought to be defined entirely independently of human interests and values.

This claim could be interpreted either as a fact or as a norm. As a
factual claim, it offers a particular picture of the relation of cognition
to desire. In this picture the mind first cognizes a value-neutral world,
already classified into discrete packages defined independent of any relation to human interests. It then responds with various "pro" or "con"
attitudes toward these intrinsically value-neutral classifications. The classical empiricists offered a picture like this in which human experience of
the world is fundamentally described in terms of a value-neutral field of
colors, shapes, sounds, smells, temperatures, and textures. Different bundles of these qualities then cause desire and aversion in us. But what we

care about does not shape our initial classification of objects into different kinds.

This picture plainly fails to capture the phenomenology of human experience. We experience the world not as fields of discrete sensory qualities but in terms of "middle-sized dry goods"—cars, houses, trees, and so forth. Insofar as we experience things as artifacts, we already conceive of them in relation to human interests and not just as value-neutral entities: a thing does not count as a chair if it cannot serve as a place for creatures like us to sit.

We also experience the world and ourselves in terms of thick evaluative concepts. Here again, our ethical interests drive the classification of actions into different virtues and vices.[21] It is not as if we grasp already naturally classified types of intrinsically value-neutral actions, and then respond to them with approval or disapproval. Rather, we decide to classify heterogeneous actions (putting all of our eggs in one basket, acting like there is no tomorrow, leaping before we look) under the same thick concept ("imprudence") because of the common favorable or unfavorable relation these actions bear to particular human interests (in this case, to our self-interest). We classify them together so that we can sensibly take up a common evaluative response to them. So the claim about the independence of empirical classifications from values, interpreted as a fact about the terms in which we experience the world, is false.

If this claim is to hold up, then, it must be interpreted as a norm: empirical inquiry *ought* to classify phenomena independent of the relations they bear to human interests and values. This norm is thought to explain the success of modern physics, chemistry, and astronomy compared with the failures of their anthropocentric scholastic and hermetic counterparts. As long as humans divided the heavens on the assumption that they were the center of cosmic attention (and rotation), certain astronomical phenomena, such as the phases of Venus, were inexplicable. According to this story, the natural sciences could not progress until they classified phenomena in ways that bore no systematic relation to human interests and values.

This normative lesson is often expressed in terms of a story about natural kinds. In this view nature divides itself into kinds independent

---

[21] Williams, *Ethics and the Limits of Philosophy*, 141–2; and Putnam, *Reason, Truth, and History*, 154.

of human interests. Phenomena may be grouped together into natural kinds if and only if they have common causes or effects—that is, if and only if there exist causal laws connecting each of the phenomena in the group to phenomena in some other group. But the causal laws of the universe exist independently of human interests; the universe does not care about us. The project of natural science is to discover the language nature uses to classify itself, and thereby the laws nature uses to govern itself. This project can succeed only if we set aside our own anthropocentric classifications and read the book of nature in the language of nature itself.

John Dupré has made the most important arguments against this story about natural kinds.[22] A norm for scientific practice should be rejected if the actual, highly successful sciences we have repudiate it. Dupré argues that the various natural sciences, particularly sub-branches of biology, adopt crosscutting classifications shaped by the varied interests of researchers, not dictated by the natures of the objects studied. We have seen that this is true in medicine and horticulture. The metaphysical picture of nature that underwrites this scientific practice is one of disorder, multiplexity, and contingency. Nature is not reducible to a few fundamental variables and eternal deterministic laws. Rather, a spectacular variety of intersecting, nonreducible classifications supports contingent and changing causal regularities.

Whether or not Dupré's picture can succeed for the seemingly less anthropocentric natural sciences of physics and astronomy, it does fit the practices and findings of the social sciences very well. In highly heterogeneous disciplines such as psychology and sociology, the variables studied are crosscutting and mutually irreducible even within subfields. Consider, for instance, the crosscutting ways socioeconomic classes are defined: by income, occupational status (blue/white/pink collar), "cultural capital," relation to the means of production, and so forth. There is no reason to doubt that many regularities found in these fields are causal and genuine, yet they often vary over time. Even the causal regularities studied by economics, the most conceptually unified of the social sciences, depend upon historical contingencies. Before the invention of double-entry bookkeeping and probability theory, merchants and fin-

---

[22] John Dupré, *The Disorder of Things* (Cambridge, Mass.: Harvard University Press, 1993).

anciers had little idea of their overall financial position or exposure to risk. So they could not effectively adjust their actions to the goal of profit maximization. Thus, those regularities of economics that depend upon firms maximizing their profits, however causally sound they may be today, apply to the world only because of contingent events exogenous to economic theory.

The fact that classifications in the social sciences are designed to track human interests rather than interest-independent natural kinds does not preclude empirical investigation into the causes and effects of items in these classes. To be sure, the regularities such sciences generally find are complex and contingent. Phenomena classified in these ways have heterogeneous and contingent causes and effects. But this makes for no principled obstacle to systematic empirical investigation. Nor does it set the social sciences on a lower plane than the natural sciences. The facts are no different in natural sciences such as population biology. Whether a gene promotes an individual organism's reproductive success often depends on its prevalence in the general population. Game-theoretic models demonstrate that propensities to "altruism" typically enhance reproductive success in individuals that live in populations in which this trait prevails, but reduce it in individuals that live in populations containing few reciprocators. Thus, the causal powers we ascribe to a genetic disposition for "altruism"—whether we say that it promotes or frustrates individual reproductive fitness—depend on contingent features of the environment that are at least partly exogenous to biological theory.

There are no fundamental value-neutral "natural kinds" in the social sciences that give us a unique set of explanatory categories. The categories we choose to describe ourselves are not given to us by the nature of human beings as such. We cannot distinguish between the "real" categories and the "unreal" categories by appeal to the ability of the "real" ones to figure in causal explanations or laws. This is because for every concept that could figure in such explanatory or descriptive statements, there are other concepts in its neighborhood that could figure equally well. Consider, for example, the relation of the gross national product (GNP) to "CGNP," which I shall define as the market value of all goods and services produced by the nation's economy whose names begin with the letter "C." Just as we find a genuine causal regularity between GNP and total employment, we will find a genuine causal regularity between CGNP and total employment. Why not study CGNP then? The reason is that CGNP is a silly concept. There is no point to paying attention to it; it is not interesting. Which distinctions we choose to employ in our theories is not a function of fundamental ontology but a function of our practical interests.

The classifications in the humanities and social sciences, if they are to yield knowledge worth having, ought to be expressed in thick evaluative terms. Recall that a concept is thickly evaluative if (1) its application is guided by empirical facts; (2) it licenses normative inferences; and (3) interests and values guide the extension of the concept (that is, what unifies items falling under the concept is the relation they bear to some common or analogous interests or values). Therefore, these classifications require both a normative and an empirical justification.[23] They must set terms of self-understanding that it makes sense to adopt, and they must be able to sustain empirically adequate theories.

But does the first requirement have anything to do with the second? Is there something about normatively unjustified theoretical classifications that makes them unable to sustain empirically adequate theories? As a pragmatist, I believe that normatively unjustified thick evaluative terms contain empirical defects, the exposure of which helps us understand why they are unjustified. These defects can be of various sorts: they can confuse phenomena that are fundamentally different, pose false distinctions among phenomena that are fundamentally similar, represent a partial truth as the whole truth about some matter, offer a misleading or distorted representation of some phenomenon, promise more than they can deliver, or misrepresent what secures the causal generalizations they support. I shall argue that these empirical defects are inextricably normative defects. They make our lives go badly when we adopt empirically inadequate thick evaluative concepts to understand ourselves.

---

[23] Hilary Putnam defends a similar claim about scientific classifications. He argues that science seeks not just any truths, but relevant or significant truths, and that relevance or significance can be judged only in relation to human interests. See Putnam, *Reason, Truth, and History*, 137–8, 201–2. Putnam's argument is incomplete, however, in light of Philip Kitcher's epistemic analysis of significant scientific truth in *The Advancement of Science* (New York: Oxford University Press, 1993). Advocates of the value-neutrality of science may concede that purely epistemic values, internal to science, are relevant to the determination of the facts; and that political, moral, and cultural values taken from the social context in which people operate may guide how they classify phenomena for practical purposes. The controversial question is whether these "contextual" values should guide how phenomena are classified in scientific research. See Helen Longino, *Science as Social Knowledge* (Princeton, N.J.: Princeton University Press, 1990).

EMPIRICAL-NORMATIVE CRITICISM
IN HISTORY AND ECONOMICS

Let me first illustrate the joint operation of empirical and normative inquiry in an easy case. Consider the narrative history of Nazi Germany. It would be absurd to try to tell this history while avoiding thick evaluative descriptions of Nazi practices that condemn them. The history of Nazi Germany is a history of aggression, oppression, murder, slavery, violence, and brutality. To try to represent the actions of Nazi Germany in ostensibly value-neutral terms (to say, for instance, that the Nazis merely "entered" Poland rather than that they invaded it) is to mislead by grotesque euphemism.[24] Given the decision to describe the Nazi occupation of Eastern Europe in a discursive field structured by such thick evaluative concepts as justice and freedom, the facts of Nazi behavior leave no serious room for characterizing their actions as other than oppressive. And these thick evaluative descriptions of Nazi behavior have explanatory power. They explain why the millions of Eastern Europeans who hated Stalin and dreaded Soviet rule, even those who initially welcomed Nazi occupation, refused to join Hitler when the tide turned against Germany, despite their knowledge that Stalin would take over when Hitler left. You cannot make loyal allies out of people you murder, exploit, and enslave.[25] This causal claim, couched in thick evaluative terms, is as sound as any claim known in the social sciences.

But why not tell the history of Nazi Germany in the Nazis' own thick evaluative vocabulary of racial purity, national glory, and the like? This would be morally monstrous, of course. But the moral monstrosity is not unconnected to the fact that the Nazis' self-understandings are also deeply fraudulent, based on falsehoods down to the very core. This is not to claim that Nazi classifications could not sustain true causal generalizations. Nazi explanatory/evaluative categories are not empirically empty; we know only too well that the Nazis fixed elaborate empirical criteria for the application of racial classifications. And given that these

---

[24] Leo Strauss, *Natural Right and History* (Chicago: University of Chicago Press, 1953).
[25] The historian Paul Johnson put the matter aptly in *Modern Times* (New York: Harper and Row, 1983), 380. Explaining why Hitler did not take effective advantage of the hatred of Eastern Europeans and Russians for Stalin by recruiting them in a campaign of liberation on the Eastern front, Johnson observed that "Hitler was not in the business of liberation. Like Stalin, he was in the business of slavery."

categories were embodied in Nazi laws and public policies, phenomena classified in these terms had profound causal consequences.

The trouble is that racial categories do not figure in true causal claims for the reasons the Nazis supposed. The concept of race figures in some true historical explanations but not as what it purports to be—namely, a natural-kind biological classification. It figures rather as a social construction designed to sustain an oppressive system by falsely passing itself off as having a biological justification. And understanding this fact about how racial classifications figure in social explanations is crucial to seeing why racist institutions are fraudulent. The fraud is inseparable from the injustice. There might have been a natural biological hierarchy of races, such that the lower orders actually were incapable of self-government, and such that interbreeding would cause the degeneration of all admirable capacities in the higher orders. If such Nazi claims of scientific racism had been true, then egalitarian democracy would not have been a viable or just system of social order, and some features of the Nazi regime, such as the Nuremburg laws prohibiting miscegenation, might have been justified. If these claims had been true, then miscegenation would have been morally on a par with deliberately inducing birth defects in fetuses. Racism is wrong in part because these claims are false and because in general racist classifications can never deliver on everything they promise.

It is perhaps too easy to illustrate the joint operation of moral and empirical judgments in historical accounts of Nazism. But what about the conduct of social science when it deals with more ordinary phenomena? We rarely find overt appeal to moral virtues and vices as causes or effects of phenomena investigated by most social sciences. Nevertheless, human interests and values shape the classifications we use there. These classifications, although they do not refer to specifically moral characteristics, are thick evaluative concepts in the sense defined above. Consequently, their use in the social sciences needs to be justified from an ethical as well as an empirical point of view.

Consider, for example, the system of national income accounting in economics, which yields the GNP, an aggregate measure of a nation's annual production of goods and services. National income accounting serves both an empirical and a normative function. Empirically, it defines the scope of macroeconomics and provides measures of the key variables in its models of the economy. Normatively, it is designed to guide policy by defining a worthwhile goal—namely, economic growth, as measured by GNP. This goal is normatively justified on the broadly utilitarian ground that increases in total production yield increases in total welfare.

But the concept of GNP has been subject to searching empirical and normative critiques. I shall mention one developed by Marilyn Waring.[26] She criticizes the sexism inherent in economists' definitions of the scope of the economy. National income accounting is based on a conceptual distinction between production and consumption activities. Where does production end and consumption begin? As a first approximation, economists define the scope of the economy to coincide with the scope of market exchange. GNP measures the aggregate market value of goods produced for sale in a nation. But economists have found this first approximation unsatisfactory, especially for nations with relatively undeveloped markets, in which a large proportion of food, housing, and other goods is produced directly for consumption rather than for sale. They therefore impute a market value to various unmarketed domestic production activities associated with subsistence agriculture, home construction, and the like.

Which of these household activities do economists choose to count as productive? In practice, economists have defined the "production boundary" in such societies by imposing an obsolete, Western, androcentric conception of the household on them. They assume that households consist of a productive primary producer, the husband, who supports a wife engaged in "housework," which is assumed to be economically unproductive or part of leisurely "consumption" (whose?). "Housework" has no clear definition in societies where most production takes place within the household. So economists apply the concept of "housework" to whatever productive activities a society conventionally assigns to women. Thus, women's unmarketed labor in these societies counts as productive only if men usually perform it too, whereas men's unmarketed labor is usually counted in the national income statistics regardless of its relation to women's labor.[27] The result is that in Africa, where women do 70 percent of the hoeing and weeding of subsistence crops, 80 percent of crop transportation and storage, and 90 percent of water and fuel collecting and food processing, these vital activities rarely appear in the national income accounts.[28]

---

[26] Marilyn Waring, *If Women Counted* (San Francisco: HarperCollins, 1990).
[27] Ibid., 74–87.
[28] Ibid., 84.

The exclusion of women's unpaid labor from GNP calculations is objectionable on interdependent empirical and normative grounds. Empirically, GNP measurements make women's unpaid contributions to the economy invisible. This is not to say that GNP statistics are false. But they are misleading in presenting only a partial truth as if it were the whole. And they confusedly project an obsolete, sexist, Western middle-class ideal of the household—in which the husband proves his manhood by earning enough to consign his wife to leisure, consumption, and the unpaid labor of child-rearing and housekeeping—onto societies in which women are essential to agricultural production and enjoy less leisure than do men.[29] Yet in order to mount these empirical objections, one must already accept a broader conception of what the economy is and what work is than economists' conception of it. What considerations can justify drawing the boundaries of the economy in one place rather than another?

Purely epistemic criteria, such as those that underwrite the belief in natural kinds, will not do. GNP is an aggregate composed of heterogeneous elements with heterogeneous causes and effects. *Any* arbitrary collection of products and services produced by human beings, such as my absurd CGNP, would equally well display causal regularities with other economic variables. The considerations that justify drawing the boundaries of GNP and other economic variables where they are cannot be found in some value-neutral conception of nature but only in the relation of these variables to human interests. And the normative implications of taking economists' definitions of GNP to guide our thinking about the

[29] Although economists from Adam Smith on have regarded domestic work as unproductive, the classic economic interpretation of the gendered ideal of separate spheres was articulated by Thorstein Veblen in *The Theory of the Leisure Class* (New York: Macmillan, 1899). Jean Elshtain objects that my description of the Western middle-class conception of the household offers a jaundiced view of the ideal of separate spheres for men and women. The ideal was meant to free women from wage labor so that they could engage in the honorable domestic tasks of child-rearing and household maintenance, not to leave them in idleness. Elshtain accepts too much at face value the claims of separate spheres advocates that they honored women's domesticity. Consider how the meaning of gender ideologies is informed by the realities of race and class. Prosperous members of the middle and upper classes delegated domestic tasks to hired servants, who were often members of despised racial and ethnic groups. One hardly expresses honor for a form of labor by delegating its performance to servile and despised classes, or by using the fact that they engage in that labor as an excuse for depriving them of basic rights of citizenship or access to public opportunities. Nor can one, without an exercise of doublethink, fully honor women for performing such labor if one despises men for engaging in it. Gender ideology offers a rich field for exploring the extraordinary capacities of human beings to simultaneously idealize and degrade people.

economy are devastating to women's interests. It encourages people to believe that what women do is of no account.

Hence, economic policies aimed at GNP growth disregard the costs to women's welfare and women's productivity of allocating productive resources away from them to cash-generating activities that in poor countries are usually dominated by men.[30] Water diverted from a common well to privately irrigated cash crops grown by men may increase GNP but force every village woman and her daughters to spend two extra hours a day fetching water from more distant wells for drinking, cooking, and washing. This not only taxes women's and girls' limited energy and time but also increases infant mortality rates to the extent that infants who are suffering from diarrhea cannot get promptly rehydrated. Moreover, a key variable influencing women's share of household resources is their ability to generate outside income.[31] Yet policies to increase GNP often exacerbate women's economic dependence on their husbands by favoring measures that increase the productivity and wages of men's work at the relative expense of women's productivity. These policies make women and their daughters worse off even when GNP increases, by threatening their access to adequate nutrition, health care, and safety.

Thus, economists' focus on GNP as the measure of economic production is normatively defective because it neglects the economic contributions and interests of women. We need a measure of the economy that is justified from the standpoint of everyone's interests, not just from the standpoint of men's interests. Waring argues that this would require counting women's unpaid labor as part of the economy and taking measures to ensure that women's productivity is encouraged rather than ignored, as present policies oriented to GNP growth do. Because there are compelling normative reasons for economists to pay attention to the contributions of women's unpaid labor, we are justified in saying that present measures of GNP are empirically inadequate: they mislead in presenting a partial picture of the economy as if it were the whole. Because women's unpaid labor is both arduous and indispensable, it is an insulting distortion to represent their activities as leisurely and unproductive. Getting an empirically adequate understanding of the scope of

[30] Waring, *If Women Counted*, ch. 9.
[31] Amartya Sen, "Gender and Cooperative Conflicts," in *Persistent Inequalities*, ed. Irene Tinker (Oxford: Oxford University Press, 1990), 123–49.

the economy is inseparable from getting a normatively adequate understanding of its scope.

Empirical theories have consequences of their own. In adopting social scientific theories as our forms of self-understanding, and in applying these theories to practical problems of the day, we *make* certain empirical regularities true of ourselves that would otherwise not be true. For example, suppose the central banking system of a nation adopts a policy of tightening credit whenever the growth of GNP exceeds a certain specified rate. We can define GNP in various ways, depending on where we decide to draw the production boundary. As we have seen, this boundary is informed by practical interests—for instance, by the ways we value the forms of labor assigned to women.

By adopting a sexist theory of the production boundary, which refuses to count women's domestic labor as part of the GNP, we can make it true of our society that what women do at home will have very little effect on the availability of credit. By adopting an alternative definition of the production boundary that includes women's domestic labor, we can make a different empirical regularity true of our society, one that establishes a causal connection between women's activities and the availability of credit. In this way our practical, value-laden choices influence what social scientific theories will be true of us, just as the theories we adopt will influence our practical, value-laden choices. Since the facts about ourselves are facts we, in part, make through our interested choices and self-understandings (they are, in part, "socially constructed"), the decision to accept a social scientific theory of ourselves can never be justified on what are taken to be purely value-neutral, empirical grounds alone but must also be justified in terms of our practical interests.

HOW PRAGMATIC MORAL INQUIRY WORKS

Pragmatists characterize the search for normatively adequate terms of self-understanding as a search for empirically adequate terms of self-understanding. So far we have seen how normative considerations can be used to criticize empirical theories. But how do we use empirical inquiry to aid our normative quest?

Think of theories in the humanities and social sciences as maps of our social world that help us navigate our ways through it. All maps are simplifications of reality; they leave out most of the features of the world.

If they did not, they would be too confusing to read. We do not say on account of these simplifications that these maps are empirically inadequate. They are empirically inadequate only if they leave out normatively significant features of our social world, or if they misplace or misdescribe them in ways that confuse and mislead us. When we use the map to plan a route, and find that it leads us someplace we do not want to be, then we say the map misrepresents reality because it has failed to adequately represent the *normatively important* facts. But what facts we consider normatively important can change, once we are informed of new facts. Europeans got along all right with maps that omitted the New World, until they found out about it.

Let me illustrate the pragmatic uses of empirical inquiry with a particularly striking argument developed by Lynn Sanders.[32] Sanders criticizes a traditional conception of deliberation in democratic theory. Democracies need mechanisms for allowing critical reflection to influence which policies are adopted. This is the principal justification for representative democracy over direct democracy—only relatively small, dedicated legislative bodies have the time, resources, and internal structure to sustain deliberation. But in some schools of democratic theory, deliberation involves much more than this. It fits into a discursive field where the alternatives to rational deliberation are described as yielding to irrational emotion, factionalism, and demagoguery. Historically, these were the charges that conservatives made against democracy as such.

Sanders shows that some democrats (including Benjamin Barber, Robert Bellah, Donald Downs, and Robert Reich) have met the charge that democracy leads to demagoguery, factionalism, and irrationality, not by repudiating conservatives' representations of the field of alternatives, but by arguing that democracy could avoid the bad alternatives by incorporating deliberative norms into its institutions. These norms demand that interlocutors speak in moderate tones and terms, appeal to common interests, and strive for consensus.

How do these prescriptions work in practice? Sanders exposes some disturbing facts about conversational dynamics in the American jury, our best working model of a deliberative citizen body. Social scientific studies of mock juries find that race, class, and gender inequalities strongly influence the structure of deliberation. Whites, professional and managerial persons, and men speak more often and are more likely to be chosen

---

[32] Lynn Sanders, "Against Deliberation," *Political Theory* (forthcoming).

as forepersons than are people of color, poor or working-class persons, and women, respectively. Even after controlling for the content of what is said, their concerns and vocabulary more often set the agenda, their observations are more likely to be taken seriously, and their arguments are more likely to be accepted.

These facts fit into a pattern of distorted political discussion that has been documented by other scholars. William Chafe shows how, during the civil rights movement, white North Carolineans exploited norms of civility in deliberation to suppress the legitimate grievances blacks had against segregated schools and public accommodations.[33] Given the polite deliberative norm that political claims should be moderate and consensus-seeking, and whites' power to define the discursive field against which claims were tested for moderation, the white North Carolineans managed to cast their own infinitesimal gestures toward token integration as the moderate position, against which the positions of the National Association for the Advancement of Colored People and the Ku Klux Klan were represented as equal and opposite extremes. Given the polite deliberative norm to stay calm and unemotional, and the power to define as emotional any assertive speech, whites managed to cast out as irrational and illegitimate the claims of blacks who defied the caste system, and they singled out the deferential voices of their black domestic servants, who dared not speak out for fear of losing their jobs, as the true spokespersons for their race.

Thus, the conception of deliberation embodied in influential schools of democratic theory, in conjunction with facts about our actual experiences in deliberation, yield substantively undemocratic deliberative processes in which some voices are ignored, discounted, or dismissed because of race, gender, or class status. To accept "polite" norms of deliberation under present conditions is to subvert one's own democratic commitments to the political equality of citizens. The "polite" conception of deliberation promises more than it can deliver: as embodied in our actual practices, it misrepresents discussions that meet its norms as more democratic than they really are. This empirical inadequacy is simultaneously a normative failure.

Sanders proposes to remedy this situation by adopting a new conception of political discussion, which she calls "testimony." It recognizes the need for those in power to learn how to listen to those with less

[33] William Chafe, *Civilities and Civil Rights* (New York: Oxford University Press, 1980).

power, in the emotional, unmoderate, and particularistic terms and tones in which the latter sometimes understand their own grievances.[34] Her critique of the ideal of deliberation does not claim that it is bad in all possible worlds, only that it is premature for our social world. Her remedy does not claim to be valid for all rational beings, but something to be tested in practice to see whether it helps us better realize our democratic ideals. While it cannot replace deliberation, it may well serve as a prerequisite to doing it well under present conditions. It is an exemplary case of pragmatic inquiry, in which empirical research and normative critique go hand in hand, mutually shaping the terms in which we understand ourselves.

Pragmatism holds out the prospect of overcoming obstacles to moral inquiry posed by the dominant conceptions of the fact-value dichotomy. It does so by enlisting moral and political philosophy in a common project with social and humanistic studies. Both try to come to terms with our lives—that is, to offer terms of self-understanding that simultaneously meet criteria of empirical adequacy and successfully guide practice.

I have argued that the bare logical distinction between "is" and "ought" poses no serious theoretical obstacles to this project. In his chapter in this volume, Alan Wolfe complains that while I may have overcome the philosophical scruples against joining moral with scientific inquiry, I have not confronted the political objections to such an enterprise. Scientists ought to strive for value-neutrality out of respect for the

---

[34] In his chapter in this volume, Alan Wolfe criticizes the idea of testimony for supposedly requiring that we take the stories of our fellow citizens "as necessarily true or real." This is a plain misreading, as should be evident from the courtroom context from which the idea is borrowed: jurors are duty bound to pay attention to testimony, not to regard it as absolute truth. Testimony is designed to get people for the first time to listen respectfully and take seriously what others say, not to get them to believe whatever they are told. More seriously, Jean Elshtain expresses the worry that testimony that focuses on the aggrieved mental states of the oppressed may be less persuasive than a recounting of objective facts. She is right to oppose the view that politically and legally redressable harms should be measured by the degree of emotional distress they cause. People are entitled to redress on the grounds that their rights have been violated or their persons treated disrespectfully, regardless of how wounded this makes them feel. Still, testimony confined to objective facts may fail to convey how disrespectful certain behaviors are to those who do not "get it." Instead, testimony can convey *interpretations* of behaviors. For example, a female employee might explain why she sees it as sexist, not polite, for an executive to use profanity when addressing the men in a business meeting, while always turning to her to apologize when he does so. In behaving this way, the executive treats profanity as necessary to convey important business concerns, and women as too delicate to hear it, and thereby implies that women employees are not really up to the demands of the job, and not properly part of his audience.

"fragility of truth." "Doing justice to subjects, intervening descriptive accounts with political and ideological ones," and affirming scientists' moral obligations to condemn evil practices "all interfere with fulfilling" the scientist's obligation "to try to understand the real world," he writes.

Ironically, Wolfe takes the political case for insisting that science be value-neutral to be based on "the notion that an open society must value the possibility of falsification in political, as well as scientific, beliefs." But if he really believed, as pragmatists do, that moral and political beliefs are just as subject to critical revision in light of the empirical evidence as scientific beliefs are, then he would have no grounds for thinking that scientists compromise the search for truth in expressing value judgments in their theories or methods. Do physicians compromise the search for medical truths in doing justice to their patients, intervening descriptive accounts of physiological processes with evaluations of their implications for the well-being of their patients, and affirming medical researchers' moral obligations to criticize practices that endanger health? Wolfe expresses distrust of ethnographers who pursue their inquiry with such moral aims in mind as the eradication of cruelty. Strangely, he suggests that inquiry devoted to eliminating cruelty will preclude critical reflection on whether or not the things the ethnographer wants to eliminate really are cruel. By parallel reasoning, Wolfe should distrust physicians who pursue clinical research with the aim of eradicating disease, on the ground that this aim will interfere with their ability or willingness to determine whether a given target of research really is a disease, or whether the treatment is worse than the disease.

Wolfe's real political objections to value-laden inquiry are based on the idea that to affirm a value judgment is to close one's mind, to insist on a foregone conclusion, and to ignore the facts. In other words, he thinks that value judgments can only be dogmatically affirmed, not based on evidence and arguments. This thought depends on the nihilist, emotivist, and subjectivist metaethical doctrines that underwrite the conventional construal of the fact-value dichotomy. But the fact-value distinction does not track the inquiry-dogma distinction. Moral and factual inquiry alike entail a commitment to revise one's beliefs in light of the evidence. Moral and factual judgments alike can be held dogmatically. Science, as a form of inquiry, must reject dogmatism to retain its integrity. This requirement, which pragmatists embrace, does nothing to undermine the pragmatic case for joining moral with scientific inquiry.

The really formidable obstacles to pragmatic inquiry are institutional.

The self-conceptions of the academic disciplines embody mislead-ing ideas about the implications of the distinction between "is" and "ought." As a result, scholars are poorly equipped to conduct pragmatic inquiry. Philosophers are typically untutored in empirical inquiry; social scientists are unused to subjecting their theoretical concepts to normative scrutiny. In holding knowledge of the other disciplines to be irrelevant to their own, scholars misunderstand what it takes to do their own jobs well. To clear the way for pragmatic inquiry, we need to study human-istic and social scientific inquiry as social practices, whose terms of self-understanding may misrepresent what we are actually doing in them.[35] Despite the official academic division of labor, scholars on both sides of the fact-value dichotomy need to engage work on the other side to suc-ceed in their own tasks.

[35] See Charles Taylor, "Social Theory as Practice," in *Philosophy and the Human Sciences* (Cambridge: Cambridge University Press, 1985), 91–115.

2

Political theory and moral responsibility

JEAN BETHKE ELSHTAIN

The story of the revival of moral inquiry in political theory is, in large part, an account of the fate among political scientists of political theory itself. The rising and falling, waxing and waning, of the fortunes of political theory—an unabashedly normative enterprise—goes a long way toward alerting us to how political science takes up, or manages to avoid or evade, certain moral questions, including the relationship between our theories and our practices, between freedom and responsibility, and between the political actor and the ordinary citizen.

Political theory in the American academy involves the stitching together of certain texts. Those of us who teach political theory know the drill. Inevitably we offer undergraduate courses in political theory or philosophy entitled "Ancient and Medieval Political Theory" and "Modern Political Theory." Modern political theory usually begins with Machiavelli and takes the student and instructor through Karl Marx and John Stuart Mill. Perhaps he or she gets into the twentieth century at the end of the term. Ancient political theory is primarily a reading of Plato and Aristotle. Medieval thinkers get, at best, a cursory nod. Indeed, "religious thinkers," for the most part, are excised. American political thought is a separate course and is sometimes not even placed within the realm of political theory but seen instead as a task for "Americanists."

The story of how political theory is defined is a story of contestations *within* political theory. What texts are in, what are out? Academic political theory is also a story of debates about how to interpret canonical texts.[1] But whatever their disagreements about such matters, political

---

[1] Thus, one finds Straussians pitted against non- or anti-Straussians. Straussians follow the interpretive mode and method of the late Leo Strauss. Other major contenders at

theorists come together to engage in a contest of another sort, one that pits political theory against dominant trends in political science.[2] That debate is a necessary backdrop to the rethinking of moral inquiry under way in the American academy and to the nature of that rethinking.

When I was studying political theory as a graduate student of political science, I learned the necessity of a commitment to neutral, scientific objectivity. Values were expunged as a central feature of political study. The ideal was a value-free enterprise with the values of the researcher bracketed as "biases" and the values of research subjects reduced to calculations of opinions, attitudes, and preferences that were not themselves of great epistemological value. This ideal guided an enterprise called behaviorism or behavioralism. It was an undertaking whose assumptions and objectives included the presumption that there are discoverable uniformities in political behavior, that these regularities are akin to the laws of physics, and that they provide the grounding for explanatory theories in political science that are verifiable (or falsifiable) empirically and have predictive value. This enterprise, according to its enthusiasts, shared the scientific rigor of its counterparts in the physical and natural sciences.[3]

In order for political science to take on this particular status, it was necessary utterly to separate ethical evaluation from empirical explanation. A wedge was driven between so-called descriptive and so-called

---

the moment include postmodernists and Habermasians. But there is great variety in interpretive styles.

[2] I would be loathe to give the impression of a war unto death here, and certainly many political theorists and political scientists have maintained diplomatic relations throughout the years. Few political theorists disdain empirical research altogether; rather, it is a particular epistemology that precludes so-called "normative" questions that draws their fire. The discussion that follows is about this debate and should not be construed as an attack on empirical research per se.

[3] What is at stake, then, is a reductive scientism. It is also important to note that the American, academic appropriation (at least in political science departments) of the positivist tradition was, for the most part, philosophically naive. The great positivist thinkers—Ludwig Wittgenstein (if he really belongs here, a disputed matter), Sir Alfred Jules Ayer, Hempel, and others—would scarcely recognize what behavioralism did to positivism as a philosophical tradition that aimed to protect certain moral commitments by taking them out of disputations over "the facts of the matter." They were, in other words, insulating moral commitment from both ideology and religion. But, in the process, moral norms themselves took a beating and got ever more "privatized." For a *locus classicus* of the behavioralist revolution, see David Easton, "The Current Meaning of 'Behavioralism' in Political Science," in *The Limits of Behavioralism in Political Science*, ed. J. C. Charlesworth (Philadelphia: American Academy of Political and Social Science, 1983). Easton is one of the makers of the behavioralist triumph in political science—and one of its most intelligent spokesmen.

evaluative or normative statements. The goal of behavioralist explanation was neither the understanding of human beings and their social and political world, nor the interpretation of that world of self and others, but the construction of verifiable hypotheses with the power to predict. In order to predict, one needed behavioral regularity that followed an inexorable logic; behavior, in other words, must be caused. Confidence in law-like generalizations within political and social life, then, presupposed a logic of explanation that assumed the possibility of prediction.

The aim here was to strip away the "apparent" complexities of political life and action and to get rid of anything untidy. Then, and only then, could one engage in a search for law-likeness in political life. The problem with all this lies not in the hope to discover norms or rough-and-ready rules and conventions that govern and guide political life—any good political analyst aspires to this—but in a tremendous over-confidence in prediction lodged in a series of reductionistic premises about human life and politics. Thus, all resonant themes and moral issues must be expunged from view before the analyst begins work, or contested issues may be incorporated but in an anemic way, as the "biases" one brings to one's research.

Within the epistemological presumptions of behavioralist political thinking, to describe and to evaluate, to state what is and to state what ought to be, are two entirely separable activities. Those who mixed the two activities were considered fuzzy-minded, impressionistic, and incapable of rigorous analysis. A bifurcation, then, between descriptive and evaluative statements was essential to behavioralist inquiry. Laborers in the mainstream vineyard assumed that except in so-called analytic statements, which entail a nonfalsifiable correspondence between subject and predicate by definition (for example, "all married women are wives"), the political analyst was presented with a problem of establishing a relationship between subject and predicate that could be explored and adjudicated in thorough empirical investigation. The investigation that ensued would demonstrate—or so the assumption went—a correlation between the subject of the statement and its predicate.

The nearer the investigator came to a correlation of 1.0, the closer he or she was presumed to be to the truth and the greater the power of the statement, couched as a hypothesis, to predict. The researcher was required to reduce or to bracket ambiguity, imprecision, complexity, and ambivalence, in order to come as close as possible to symmetry between naming (the subject) and meaning (the predicate that expresses the truth of the statement). The result was a simplistic verificationist theory of meaning, one in which meaning is ground so fine—a predicate carrying a very lightweight truth—that it is stripped of the power to persuade or to compel.

The theory of meaning embedded in mainstream behavioralist political inquiry claimed as a central presumption that the meaning of synthetic statements (for example, "all married women are happy") is exhausted once a relationship between the subject and predicate has been established via correlations. Yet even before such tests begin, the hypothesis has been impoverished by the reduction of rich, reactive terms central to human social relationships (such as "happiness") to a series of stipulative definitions. In the words of Charles Taylor, "The profound option of mainstream social scientists for the empiricist conception of knowledge and science makes it inevitable that they should accept the verification model of political science. . . ." This means, in turn, that a study of our civilization in terms of its inter-subjective and common meanings is ruled out. Rather, this whole level of study is made invisible.[4]

Early challenges to this position came on a number of different fronts. For example, thinkers such as Peter Winch, Charles Taylor, Steven Lukes, Julius Kovesi, and Alasdair MacIntyre questioned the coherence of the verificationist theory of meaning from a number of alternative perspectives. In *Moral Notions* (1967), Julius Kovesi offered an especially compelling critique of the presumptions undergirding behavioralist political inquiry. He argued that those presumptions necessarily yielded normative implications for persons and for politics, for there is no such thing as "mere" description. Description, Kovesi insisted, is always from a point of view and hence is always evaluative: it cannot help but be moral in some sense, or secrete moral notions and ideas.[5] We describe situations on the basis of those aspects of the situation we deem relevant or important. In this way we are always in a world of interpretation, for we are always evaluating under a certain description. Thus, the most important contrast is not between description and evaluation, but between "description from the moral point of view as opposed to other points of view."[6] Kovesi argued that description always served a pur-

[4] Charles Taylor, "Interpretation and the Sciences of Man," *The Review of Metaphysics* 26 (1971): 33.
[5] Julius Kovesi, *Moral Notions* (London: Routledge and Kegan Paul, 1967), 63.
[6] Ibid.

pose. That purpose may, and often does, remain hidden from view—embedded in a series of tacit prior commitments the analyst or researcher has not acknowledged and therefore sees no need to defend.

The behavioralist reaction to some of these early challenges was to reaffirm even more vehemently the separation between description and evaluation, between statements of fact and statements of value. In the behavioralist world, values were presumed, first, to be rationally indefensible and, second, to be related to facts and descriptions in much the way that clothing and accoutrements are related to an unadorned department store mannequin. A window decorator begins with such an unadorned mannequin and dresses or undresses it as he or she sees fit. In much the same way, the behavioralist would have the political analyst dress up the objective facts with values. These facts, like so many immobile, silent mannequins, remained unaltered beneath such window dressing.

By contrast, a link between political inquiry and moral imperatives was explicitly presumed by classic theorists in the history of political thought. Political theorists raised challenges to behavioralism by focusing on moral dilemmas demonstrating the ways in which the bifurcation between description and evaluation simply did not work. For example, imagine that a group of people are gathered around listening to a description of a brutal event in which young children are tortured systematically by sadistic adults. The account is replete with details of the desperate cries of the children and the cold cruelty of their torturers. One of those who hears this tale of terror and tragedy is a behavioralist political scientist who accepts the dichotomy between description and evaluation. He insists, once the speaker has recounted the tale in all its graphic horror, that the group now be queried as to whether the actions of the torturers are to be approved or not.

Would such a demand make sense? Remember, this situation was characterized by the speaker on the basis of those aspects considered relevant. These included the details of the suffering of children at the hands of torturers, described as brutal and sadistic. The *description* of events constituted an evaluation from what Kovesi called the moral point of view. A person devoid of a moral perspective would have described these events in different language—in language not designed to arouse in the listener compassion, sorrow, moral indignation, and outrage. Kovesi, and other critics of behavioralism, then, gestured toward a world of "thick" moral concepts, a world in which morality is not slathered like butter on bread but is there in the baking of the bread itself as a constituent ingredient. They reminded us of the dense imbrication of moral notions and responses with something that seems as "mere" (as in "mere description" or "mere rhetoric") as the words we use to describe and the words we use to persuade.

If we place these considerations within the context of contemporary political inquiry, we find that those analysts who adopt a moral point of view from which to describe and thereby evaluate political reality, characterize social reality in language very different from that deployed by analysts who presume they have at their disposal a neutral language of description. For the former, precisely the obverse of the behavioralist claim obtains: we evaluate the world *through* our descriptive notions. In Kovesi's language, "moral notions describe the world of evaluation."[7]

Behavioralist presumptions floated into moral theory as well. Those who adhered to the view that moral notions, opinions, biases, and beliefs could be stated apart from description and research methods and findings; that such notions are rationally indefensible; and that they can be bracketed after they have pushed the researcher toward certain questions, adopted tacitly a theory known as *emotivism*. Emotivism is an account of moral notions compatible with behavioralist presumptions. The emotivist holds that terms of moral evaluation such as *good* or *bad* are purely emotive; that is, these terms stand "for nothing whatever" and merely "serve as an emotive sign expressing our attitude . . . and perhaps evoking similar attitudes in other persons."[8]

According to the emotivist, that which we call *good* depends on our values or biases. Should you commend a course of action to me as good, you are merely recounting your biases or tastes—none of which comprises an evaluation for which reasons can be adduced and given. Should my own taste happen to concur with yours, I will likely accept the commendation. But suppose, a critic might challenge, I am confronted with a moral dilemma. One day I find myself sequestered with a sadist who delights in lighting a fire to tails of captured stray dogs. Wishing to draw me into the enterprise of maltreating and abusing animals, this person tells me, "It is good to torture helpless creatures and to make them feel pain." Why is it good? Because this individual feels it to be. He "feels

---

[7] Ibid., 161.
[8] Quoted in W. H. Hudson, *Modern Moral Philosophy* (Garden City, N.Y.: Doubleday, 1970), 125.

good" when engaging in the torture of animals and thus commends these actions to others so that they, too, might feel good.

How am I to respond to these claims? I could try to get out of the problem by declaring the puppy torturer a psychopath whose views must perforce be ignored. But perhaps the torturer's behavior betrays no sign of irrationality. Indeed, the person is calm and cool throughout. All that is left me, if I am a consistent emotivist, is the reply: "Well, you have your opinion as to what is good, and I have mine. Personally, I do not feel it is good to torture animals. My feelings are different from yours, so why don't we agree to disagree, and I'll leave now, if it's all the same to you."

Emotivists presume that no epistemologically valid argument for or against a social structure or set of social arrangements could be formed from a moral point of view that requires powerful terms—injustice, fairness, exploitation, discrimination—just in order to *describe* the situation. The emotivist might oppose obnoxious practices, but this would be taken as his "bias." To the extent my biases matched up with his, we would have political agreement. The emotivist or value-neutralist insists that he does endorse values, but these are, by definition, indefensible rationally.

Critics of emotivism argue that the difficulties presented by questions of bias or values cannot be dealt with simply by admitting to one's biases and claiming that one has set them aside for the purpose of research. This response does not touch the heart of the matter, namely, an epistemology that requires severing fact from value in the first place. The difficulty, then, is more complex and fundamental by far than any charge, or embrace, of bias. It is that every explanatory theory of politics supports a particular set of normative conclusions. To proffer an explanatory theory, the analyst must adopt a framework that sets the boundaries of the phenomena to be investigated. Some factors of social life will be incorporated and others will be expunged from view before research begins. The framework compels choices, affirms some interests, excludes others, and precludes seeing the political world under an alternative characterization.[9]

---

[9] Portions of the material discussed thus far, including several of the examples, appeared in my piece, "Methodological Sophistication and Conceptual Confusion: A Critique of Mainstream Political Science," in *The Prism of Sex: Toward an Equitable Pursuit of Knowledge*, ed. J. Sherman and E. Beck (Madison: University of Wisconsin Press, 1980), 229–52.

The history of intensive epistemological contestation I have just surveyed offers the reader insight into arguments that pitted advocates of behavioralism against political theorists.[10] Political theorists were the most likely members of departments of political science to be philosophically trained and, as well, to be engaged explicitly with politics and ethics, including questions of politics and moral responsibility. Several books published in the early 1970s helped to set political theory on a new and more self-assured course. One was political theorist Sheldon Wolin's *Politics and Vision*, and the second was philosopher John Rawls's *A Theory of Justice*.[11] Wolin's accomplishment was to put before us a rich tradition of political theory and to show the deep and abiding questions it raises about freedom, responsibility, justice, order, equality, and political action itself. Rawls's work made much the bigger impact, in part because he offered up a powerful antidote to both behavioralism and the thin, ethical theory of emotivism with which it had been associated. But the Rawlsian strategy was to revitalize moral inquiry at a very lofty level. Playing on the well-established metaphor of the social contract, Rawls posited an original position in which essentially noumenal beings generated principles of justice behind a veil of ignorance.[12] Enshrouded in a veil of ignorance, beings stripped of historic time and place, denuded of concrete information and knowledge, would opt for social arrangements in which the difference between the least and most well-off was optimally minimal. (*Why* such beings would move in this direction was not clear, unless one built in a specific moral psychology, but the veil of ignorance prohibits such specificity.)

Rawls's project spawned a renewal of public ethics. Quickly, subfields emerged, including so-called discourse ethics or communicative ethics of the sort associated with Jürgen Habermas.[13] In the meantime, continental philosophy made huge inroads into American political theory, and one began to hear such words as antifoundationalism, postmodernism, and poststructuralism. Indeed, some have even suggested that we have

---

[10] Rational choice theory is now the dominant mode embraced by those committed to one form or another of emotivism. The models to which rational choice practitioners aspire are drawn from grand macroeconomic theories.

[11] Sheldon Wolin, *Politics and Vision* (Boston: Little, Brown, 1970); and John Rawls, *A Theory of Justice* (Cambridge, Mass.: Harvard University Press, 1971).

[12] Thanks to Fred Dallmayr for his helpful suggestions in this regard.

[13] An early, important text was Jürgen Habermas, *Legitimation Crisis* (Boston: Beacon Press, 1973).

come full circle, for in the most extreme forms of postmodernism, ethics is once again depleted or forsaken as central to our understanding of politics. Interestingly enough, the primary political category for most postmodernists is "power" rather than "justice." In reducing all of life (not just all of politics) to a series of power plays, some postmodernists, indebted variously to a left-wing Nietzcheanism, Michel Foucault, and a no-doubt narrow reading of Jacques Derrida, reproduce the ardent claims of founders of modern political science who insisted that politics was about "who gets what, where, and when" *tout court* and that larger issues of freedom, justice, and fairness were so much icing on the cake of the "real stuff" of power.

Strong postmodernists tend to see human beings as "wholly constructed" creatures with no substantive identity or deeply textured inner life, hence beings who bear an uncanny resemblance to the thin selves tugged and pulled by external forces featured in the old behaviorism. I cannot survey the whole of this terrain. Instead, I will focus on a critical shortcoming in the revitalization of moral inquiry in political theory— namely, its emergence as a terribly abstract enterprise tied to what I call the *heroic temptation*—a temptation that has long been a part of the tradition of political theory.[14]

Heroic political theorists have often taken as their task clearing away the debris of the old and making room for a brand new and much better, if not perfect, way of life. Consider Plato's ideal city, Rousseau's perfect republic where the general will reigns supreme, Marx's classless society, and Mill's happy realm of rational, liberal choosers. For them, the political enterprise was a matter of remaking the world as it is into a world that is to come: a world to be made radically different and much better. One difficulty with political theory whether as a systematic plan for overcoming the old in favor of the new, or as a "few simple maxims" (Mill's phrase) that would, if followed, usher in a cleaned-up social and political universe—was that it tended to make day-to-day, humanly possible work look rather boring. This work appeared distinctly unheroic, hence not particularly interesting and not something to be sustained by human agents and interpreted and understood by political theorists.

The heroic urge is a systematizing or simplifying temptation—a desire

---

[14] Rawls, with his grand, systematic theorizing, or macroeconomic theory, for that matter, perhaps belongs in this camp.

to bring all of social and political life under the umbrella of a grand schema or fixed set of criteria. It is this tendency that separates a political philosopher such as Rawls from a political theorist such as Wolin. Rawls, the philosopher, aims to abstract from the concrete and the particular in order to establish tradition and context-free norms or rules to which any disinterested person might subscribe. Wolin, the political theorist, while not abandoning the aspiration for commonalities or "the universal," claims that our understandings are tradition-dependent and that political theory and action cannot be made to subscribe to a few ahistorical norms, no matter how elegantly couched. To call the one approach "monistic" and the other "pluralistic" would be to oversimplify, of course, but these terms do designate the tendencies embodied in the positions I here associate with Rawls and Wolin, respectively.

Isaiah Berlin is another important political theorist who has urged theorists to forsake the ground of systematicity (and ideology). He warned of the dangers inherent in visions of perfect freedom, or equality, or "positive liberty" that turn on naive views of a perfectible human nature and utopian claims about the perfectibility of political life. When I was in graduate school in the late 1960s, it was fashionable to make light of these warnings, and Berlin was accused of being a faint-hearted compromiser with the status quo. But Berlin understood that debates about moral claims can never be settled definitively in a political world. Part of what it means to recognize moral claims is to recognize the contestability of those claims.[15] As John Gray put it:

Berlin uttered a truth, much against the current of the age, that remains thoroughly unfashionable and fundamentally important. . . . [He] cuts the ground from under those doctrinal or fundamentalist liberalisms—the liberalism of Nozick or Hayek no less than of Rawls or Ackerman—which suppose that the incommensurabilities of moral and political life, and of liberty itself, can be smoothed away by the application of some theory, or tamed by some talismanic formula. . . . It is in taking its stand in incommensurability and radical choice as constitutive features of the human condition that Berlin's liberalism most differs from the Panglossian liberalisms that have in recent times enjoyed an anachronistic revival. Unlike these, Berlin's is an agonistic liberalism, a stoic liberalism of loss and tragedy. For that reason alone, if there is any liberalism that is now defensible, it is Berlin's.[16]

[15] Isaiah Berlin's most recent statement of his basic insights appears in *The Crooked Timber of Humanity* (New York: Vintage, 1992).
[16] John Gray, "The Unavoidable Conflict," *Times Literary Supplement*, 5 July 1991, 3.

Although I am not primarily concerned with debates about, or within, liberalism, Berlin's basic contention—that moral conflict cannot be smoothed away—is vital, and it is either overlooked or glossed over in much political thought.

As the end of this bloodiest of all centuries approaches, political theorists are struggling to deal with a multiplicity of moral claims that must be adjudicated both within ourselves and within our societies, and to do so in a way that does not presuppose a final harmony of purposes, ends, virtues, and identities. We *must* have something in common, if human beings are to hold together a way of life as an ongoing and relatively humane enterprise. But to try to forge too overweening a unity out of human plurality is to fall into the heroicizing mode, on the level of theory, and, all too often, to promote one version or another of anti-democratic politics, on the level of practice.

Two exemplary thinkers and political actors illustrate the approach to moral inquiry and political theory I have in mind as an alternative to abstract systematicity, on the one hand, and antinominian refusal to make any strong moral claims, on the other. They are the philosopher, playwright, and current president of the Czech Republic, Václav Havel, and the American reformer and social thinker Jane Addams.

Havel begins by rejecting ideology and the heroic and utopian urgency it bears when he writes: "The idea of manufacturing a paradise on earth did not triumph, and it will be very difficult now for it to do so. Such a notion could only feed the arrogant minds of those who are persuaded that they understand everything, that there are no longer any higher, mysterious institutions above them, and that they can give directives to history." Havel recognizes that our practices can never be made perfect any more than our theories can explain all that wants explaining or help us to understand all that requires understanding. Nevertheless, he insists that it is the very murkiness and ambiguity of the world that demands our very best effort, an effort he describes as a commitment to live in truth.[17]

That commitment for Havel is inescapably shaped by a modern loss of metaphysical certainties coupled with an equally sure and certain insistence on our continuing need for a "higher horizon," for "a transcendental or super-personal moral authority which alone can check the

---

[17] Václav Havel, *Toward a Civil Society* (Prague: Nakladatelstvi Lidove Novinyi, 1994), 23.

human will to power, an anthropocentric arrogance that threatens the human 'home.' "[18] Havel insists that one must begin from the bottom, from the humbly respected boundaries of the natural world, rather than from behind a veil of ignorance where one enacts a project of justice as a noumenal moment.

A primary challenge to all posttotalitarian, postideological political thought and action is to avoid what Havel calls "pseudo-ideological thinking," thinking of the sort that separates the words we use from the realities they purport to describe, leading to what he calls "evasive thinking." He offers a wonderful example of this tendency—a tendency to disarticulate words from concrete referents, to leapfrog too quickly from the particular to the universal. A stone window ledge has come loose, fallen from a building, and killed a woman. The response of the communist regime (mired in ideological thought, of course) is to assure everyone that window ledges "ought not to fall" but look, after all, at the wonderful progress we have made in so many areas and, what is more, we must always think about mankind itself and "our prospects for the future." A second window ledge falls and kills someone else. There is another flurry of reports about the overall prospects for mankind—rosy, as it turns out, as socialism spreads and workers' states proliferate! In the meantime, ledges fall and particular people in real local places are killed. The prospects of mankind are, Havel warns, "nothing but an empty platitude if they distract us from our particular worry about who might be killed by a third window ledge, and what will happen should it fall on a group of nursery-school children out for a walk."[19] Language, and not only language, is degraded if hollow platitudes deflect our attention from concrete worries and dangers.

Where the ideologist mystifies and a certain sort of universalist tries to unify, the thinker and actor devoted to what Havel calls "politics without cliché" tries to demystify and diversify, to look at the messy, complex realities of *this* situation, here and now, as that which requires our attention and calls forth our very best and clearest attempts at thick description laden with moral notions. Politics is a sphere of concrete responsibility. Its antithesis is an all-purpose, grandiose leap into the universal that too easily promotes a vapid (because unbounded) "responsibility" for everything everywhere. A politics beyond cliché is also

---

[18] Václav Havel, "Home," *New York Review of Books*, 5 December 1991, 49.
[19] Václav Havel, *Open Letters* (New York: Knopf, 1991), 11.

one in which the political theorist and political actor refuses what Havel calls a "messianic role," an avant-garde arrogance that knows better and knows more than anyone else. The authentic political hope, by contrast, draws us away from systems that do our thinking for us and heroes that do our acting for us to what Havel calls a politics of "hope and reality." His hope is that human beings, in taking responsibility for a concrete state of affairs, might "see it as their own project and their own home, as something they need not fear, as something they can—without shame—love, because they have built it for themselves.[20]

Seventy years before Havel's writings first became available to English-speaking readers, Jane Addams penned her classic American autobiography, *Twenty Years at Hull-House*.[21] Interestingly, Addams's reputation as a writer and thinker plummeted rather sharply, even before her death, and there has been no revival of it. She is not a "systematic" thinker. She relies on stories and parables. These and other criticisms put her beyond the ken of political theory. But her work bears another look as an example of political theory as the morally aware and concrete activity I here endorse. Addams understood that political and social life cannot be written about save from one's own standpoint. That standpoint, however, need not be confined: it could radiate from a particular point (say, her father's den in Cedarville, Illinois) to a wider world beyond (the Italy of Giuseppe Mazzini). She describes her deep fellowship with her father and her dawning understanding when he explained why his visage, at a particular day, was particularly solemn: Mazzini had died. Young Jennie Addams protested that Mazzini was not even an American! Then her father explained his sorrow and did so in a way that afforded her intimations, even a "solemn realization, of a genuine relationship" made possible with strangers—strangers who become part of a loose community of international fellowship. Her father helped her to understand through analogy by comparing the American abolitionist struggle to Italians fighting Hapsburg oppression.[22]

Addams argues that we are called into the moral life through bonds of affection when we are children—not through abstract formulas and nostrums. We seek to imitate an "adored object." We struggle to live

[20] Václav Havel, *Summer Meditations* (New York: Knopf, 1992), 128.
[21] Jane Addams, *Twenty Years at Hull-House* (New York: New American Library, 1981). The original edition was published in 1910).
[22] Ibid., 21.

up to expectations. We seek companionship and fellowship. Hopefully, the circles of fellowship widen as we grow. But this is always done through example and by moving from the particular toward the universal without losing the tethering to the particular in the process. Hers is a dense, thick moral theory that relies heavily on stories and descriptive power to bear the moral point, so to speak. Stories are intrinsic to her method of social diagnosis: This is a method that enabled her to combine empirical observation—telling the facts—with strenuous moral lessons and claims. Let one example suffice:

I recall one snowy morning in Saxe-Coburg, looking from the window of our little hotel upon the town square, that we saw crossing and recrossing it a single file of women with semicircular heavy wooden tanks fastened upon their backs. They were carrying in this primitive fashion to a remote cooling room these tanks filled with a hot brew incident to one stage of beer making. The women were bent forward, not only under the weight which they were bearing, but because the tanks were so high that it would have been impossible for them to have lifted their heads. Their faces and hands, reddened in the cold morning air, showed clearly the white scars where they had previously been scalded by the hot stuff which splashed if they stumbled ever so little on their way. Stung into action by one of those sudden indignations against cruel conditions which at times fill the young with unexpected energy, I found myself across the square, in company with mine host, interviewing the phlegmatic owner of the brewery who received us with exasperating indifference, or rather received me, for the innkeeper mysteriously slunk away as soon as the great magnate of the town began to speak. . . . It was doubtless in such moods that I founded my admiration for Albrecht Dürer, taking his wonderful pictures, however, in the most unorthodox manner, merely as human documents. I was chiefly appealed to by his unwillingness to lend himself to a smooth and cultivated view of life, by his determination to record its frustrations and even the hideous forms which darken the day for our human imagination and to ignore no human complications. I believed that his canvases . . . were longing to avert that shedding of blood which is sure to occur when men forget how complicated life is and insist upon reducing it to logical dogmas.[23]

The complexity of these passages is stunning. The word portrait Addams paints, unforgettable. One sees the bowed over women, their faces and hands laced by scalding brew as they make their way, tediously, laboriously, back and forth, on a snowy wintry day in Saxe-Coburg. All this for beer! One peers head-on at a bitter process, and from this defining moment one is catalyzed to protest *and* to thought,

---

[23] Ibid., 73–5.

to philosophic reflection that refuses to take refuge in the excising comforts of systematicity.

In giving up God-likeness and mastery, Havel and Addams hold on to the vitality of the moral act in the here and now. This, I would argue, is the form an authentic revitalization of moral inquiry in political theory would take. Political thinking in the American academy has suffered from the penury and niggardliness of behavioralism and its various offspring, as well as from an overly grand tradition of political and ethical theorizing. It has suffered from the fact that political theory as a tradition has been constituted and reconstituted through a set of nigh unvarying texts. But studying political theory and moral inquiry from the ground up shifts the terrain and leads us into a realm in which we refuse to freeze history and politics into categories that yield "narratives of closure." These are narratives—theories—in which everything is known in advance, all the categories are specified, and all the possibilities are laid out. A genuine revival of moral inquiry shifts us away from narratives of closure to narratives of possibility capable of entering into and helping us to see the vitality and importance of everyday life. We begin to see the connection of small events to wider streams of life and thought.

Michael André Bernstein in his book *Foregone Conclusions* writes against apocalyptic history: "Beliefs, ideas, values and people are tested best in the daily, routine actions and habits of normal life, not in moments of extraordinary crisis, and because foreshadowing can only point to a single, inerrantly dramatic, rather than typical, quotidian resolution, it must privilege the uniquely climactic over the normative and repeatable."[24] By foreshadowing, Bernstein means reading the past from the standpoint of a present moment and seeing everything as leading almost inevitably to that moment. Hence, his retelling of an old Russian joke during the Brezhnev era. Question: "What is the great world historical event of 1875?" Answer: "Vladimir Ilych Lenin turned 5!" There is a way in which political theory has given shape and form to events, precisely through a kind of foreshadowing of the past, or at least particular highly dramatic moments within it, leading to the promise of a new and more glorious present. It is very difficult to give up this frame of mind. It is, if anything, even more difficult to offer up a defense of the quotid-

---

[24] Michael André Bernstein, *Foregone Conclusions* (Berkeley: University of California Press, 1994), 89.

ian. To quote Bernstein again, "The kind of ethics for which I am contending can better be enacted than formalized, and any adequate description must itself contain sufficient local depth and resonance to make vivid the lived world in which particular actions take place."[25]

Now that the dust has settled on the behavioralist and antibehavioralist debates, now that foundationalism and antifoundationalism have been rehearsed and re-rehearsed, perhaps we will be open to a humbler and more political enterprise. Some will argue that to offer up the very best sense one can of particular voices, moments, movements, not in a still life, but in the stream of life, is to lose political *theory* altogether. But I think it just may be the way for political theory to find itself and to embrace a new identity as we enter the next century. This would lend support to a politics of experimentation, but from deep seriousness of purpose; a politics of wariness and skepticism that nevertheless encourages and even requires faith, trust, and hope. Such a revival of moral inquiry strips the political theorist herself of any privileged role in the discussion. But that is all right. One engages then as a citizen among citizens, a neighbor among neighbors, a friend among friends.

Havel argues that a central task of political philosophy for our time lies in recognizing what has happened at this century's end for what it is. What has happened is the definitive collapse of an attempt to rebuild human society on some overarching *Weltanschauung*. What has been undermined is the comforting myth that we have transparent and direct instructions and relations. Europe, Havel argues, has entered the long tunnel at the end of the light. One might say the human race has entered the long tunnel at the end of the light. The problems that lie before it could not be more exigent and will not be dealt with in a lightning flash. One must continue to think political thoughts and to do political deeds, not knowing how the story ends, nor with any finality who or what is its author. The last word shall be Havel's:

Genuine politics, politics worthy of the name, and in any case the only politics that I am willing to devote myself to, is simply serving those close to oneself: serving the community, and serving those who come after us. Its deepest roots are moral because it is a responsibility expressed through action, to and for the whole, a responsibility that is what it is—a "higher" responsibility, which goes out of a conscious or subconscious certainty that our death ends nothing, because everything is forever being recorded and evaluated somewhere else, some-

[25] Ibid., 121.

where "above us," and what I have called "the memory of Being," an integral aspect of the secret order of the cosmos, of nature, and of life, which believers call God and to whose judgment everything is liable. Genuine conscience and genuine responsibility are always, in the end, explicable only as an expression of the assumption that we are being observed "from above," and that "up there" everything is visible, nothing is forgotten, and therefore earthly time has no power to wipe away the pangs brought on by earthly failure: our spirit knows that it is not the only one that knows of these failures. If there is to be a minimum chance of success, there is only one way to strive for decency, reason, responsibility, sincerity, civility, and tolerance: and that is decently, reasonably, responsibly, sincerely, civilly, and tolerantly.[26]

With these words, Havel reminds us that the task of political theory is inseparable from a project of ethical formation in and through which what is created is the free responsible citizen who honors the complexity of the moral universe yet who finds a way to create and to sustain both homes and homelands amid contingency and flux.

[26] Václav Havel, "Paradise Lost," *New York Review of Books*, 9 April 1992, 6–7.

3

Moral inquiry within the bounds of politics;
or, A question of victimhood

MARION SMILEY

Political science departments were for many years not a friendly place
to pursue moral arguments about policy issues. Indeed, such arguments
were often rejected outright on the grounds that they violated the scientific spirit of the discipline. But in recent years many political science
departments have begun to make room for normative discourse about a
host of controversial issues, ranging from abortion to welfare policy to
nuclear war. Moreover, those departments with the financial resources
to do so have frequently sponsored, if not wholly supported, interdisciplinary programs devoted to the study of ethics and public affairs. I
laud the revival of moral inquiry in these departments and hope that it
continues. But I worry about the form that such inquiry now takes—
applied ethics—and suggest below how we might replace it with a more
integrated and pragmatic approach to the formulation of moral concepts. I begin by sketching very briefly what I take to be the flaws of
applied ethics in the field of ethics and public affairs. I illustrate these
flaws by focusing on a set of arguments that employs the concept of
moral responsibility to talk about a variety of worldly harms. I then
establish an alternative framework for arguing about moral responsibility in two contemporary political controversies. The first concerns who
is morally responsible for racial violence in U.S. society. The second
concerns whether battered women are responsible for the violence that
they inflict on their abusers.

THE FLAWS OF APPLIED ETHICS

Although those who participate in the field of ethics and public affairs do not begin with a shared moral theory, they do share a sense of two things that they can contribute to the policymaking process. The first is to evaluate particular policies on the basis of criteria derived from a general moral theory (for example, utilitarianism or Kantianism). The second is to draw out the implications of a particular moral value (for example, rights or equality) for a designated policy arena. Both projects are often heralded as at least partly practical in that they move us beyond pure moral philosophy into the realms of social and political practice. But neither project requires us to know much about society or politics. Indeed, both assume that we can get our moral values straight—and embody them institutionally—without knowing anything about the structure of our particular community at all.

Where do these assumptions come from? How can they be explained? Two things become obvious from a glance through the most frequently cited journals in the field. The first is simply that the field of ethics and public affairs is not really interdisciplinary after all. Instead, it places one particular discipline—moral philosophy—at the center of our attention. While historians, sociologists, and policy analysts may find themselves quoted in the literature, they are quoted only for illustrative purposes, not for any knowledge about morality that they might provide. Likewise, scholars from these disciplines might be asked to participate in normative debates about, say, abortion or the welfare state. But they are expected to make their arguments within the framework of prevailing moral theories rather than from their perspectives as historians, sociologists, or policy analysts.

Second, the moral theories that now prevail—and that are placed at the center of normative debate about policy issues—generally view morality as having its source outside of social and political practice. Indeed, much of contemporary moral philosophy tries to move us out of the realm of social and political practice—where mere contingency reigns—and into the realm of pure rationality—where we can learn moral truth uncontaminated by worldly considerations. Hence, we should not be surprised to discover that social and political knowledge is not at a premium in discussions of ethics and public affairs. Nor should we be surprised when we are told to leave both sorts of knowledge behind—either by moving behind a veil of ignorance or by viewing ourselves as pure noumena.

CONCEPTS OF MORAL RESPONSIBILITY
AND THEIR CONSEQUENCES

What has this view of morality meant for the study of ethics and public affairs? First of all, it has meant that we are at a loss when asked, "Why do you begin with moral concept X or value Y in discussing policy Z?" Since we cannot acknowledge the extent to which our choice of moral values and concepts is shaped by either practical considerations or prior moral commitments, we are forced to fall back on conventional judgments about which values and concepts are appropriate to particular policies and practices. In discussing federal welfare policy, for example, we assume that we should invoke the principle of distributive justice, and we ignore questions of personal autonomy and citizenship. Not surprisingly, our reliance on convention, especially in its politically charged form, is hard to justify in light of the ostensibly nonpolitical nature of morality itself.

Moreover, such a reliance on convention may—and often does—lead us to ignore important developments in our social and political world, developments that may require us to revive moral values and concepts such as personal responsibility and citizenship that we have neglected in recent years. In many cases we will simply need to shift our focus to values and concepts that are more relevant to the public issues now before us. In other cases we will need to reformulate these values and concepts.

Take, for instance, the concept of rights. In U.S. society activities that were once unregulated—for example, those pertaining to family life— are now regulated, and the boundaries between private and public spheres are more porous than ever. Yet many of us continue to formulate rights in the absolutist language of the nineteenth century. Hence, unlike our colleagues in legal theory,[1] we are not able to argue coherently about rights as they are actually structured in our community. Instead, we are pushed farther and farther into the realm of abstraction, where rights are analyzed as moral attributes rather than as phenomena to be realized in practice.

Since the field of applied ethics requires us to apply our moral values and concepts to social and political life, we might expect to be dragged

---

[1] See, for example, Cass Sunstein, *After the Rights Revolution: Reconceiving the Regulatory State* (Cambridge, Mass.: Harvard University Press, 1990).

back to earth. But we are not. Instead, we are told to apply our moral values and concepts to particular policies and practices as if the logic of application is inherent in the value or concept itself. In other words, we are told to draw out the logical implications of the value or concept for a particular policy or practice without exploring the policy or practice in any detail.[2] But surely some sort of knowledge about the policy or practice in question is necessary if we are to ensure a proper fit between it and the value or concept that we have invoked.

In the case of welfare assistance, for example, we presumably need to know something about the role that welfare plays in our society and the priority that we attach to particular goods before we can think about what a just distribution might look like. (How else can we decide where justice, as distinct from benevolence, is relevant, or what particular goods are to be distributed justly?) Not surprisingly, we often incorporate such knowledge—rough as it is—into our application process and, by doing so, enable ourselves to embody the value of justice in practice. But we do so on a fairly low level—not having studied the relevant institutions and practices. Hence, our arguments are frequently dismissed as ill-informed or beside the point by those who act in public.

What kind of knowledge—besides that of moral philosophy—would we need if we were to render our moral arguments about public affairs relevant to the formulation of a moral public policy? Certainly, we would need to know about the relevant institutions and practices associated with the policy in question, but that kind of social and political knowledge would not be enough. We would also need to know much more than we now do about our own moral practices. In particular, we would need to know about the sorts of moral judgments that we make as community members, where these judgments come from, and why they differ on occasion among community members. Likewise, we would need to know what sorts of moral concerns community members bring to bear on particular policies and how they prioritize their values. For without such knowledge we would not be able as community members to participate in moral controversies about, say, abortion or capital punishment. Nor would we be able to persuade others within our community of the soundness of a particular argument or course of action.

---

[2] Two very interesting exceptions are Andrew Altman, "Pragmatism and Applied Ethics," *American Philosophical Quarterly* 20 (1983): 227–35; and A. Edel, E. Flower, and A. O'Connor, *Critique of Applied Ethics* (Philadelphia: Temple University Press, 1994).

Since most of those in the field of ethics and public affairs want to contribute to moral argument in public life, they would be well advised to take popular moral arguments seriously, if only to find out how their own arguments might be rendered more persuasive. But the possibility of persuading others is not the only reason to take these arguments seriously. Nor is it the most important. In my discussion of moral responsibility, I suggest two further reasons for doing so. The first is that the moral judgments that we make in practice are, in and of themselves, crucial to the fabric of our political community. Hence, they need to be understood and evaluated as part of communal practice. The second is that by exploring the normative assumptions that ground these judgments, we are able to contribute not only to communal practice but to moral philosophy as well.

In particular, by exploring the various normative assumptions that ground our moral judgments in practice, we can broaden our understanding of the moral values and concepts that moral philosophers now place at the center of their attention. In the case of moral responsibility, philosophers in recent years have narrowed their focus almost exclusively to a discussion of free will and determinism. But an analysis of our judgments of moral responsibility in practice reveals that moral responsibility is not just about free will. Instead, it is about free will as shaped by, among other things, standards of fairness, social roles, conceptions of communal boundaries, and norms of victimhood. If we want to develop an adequate concept of moral responsibility—one that will enable us to talk about the moral responsibility of individuals not just for their own character but for external harm as well—and argue openly about moral responsibility in practice, we will have to construe moral responsibility as shaped in part by these and other worldly phenomena.

TWO CASES

What are our judgments of moral responsibility in the cases of race riots and battered women? What is it that we disagree about in these two cases? In both cases we disagree about who is responsible for harm. But the location of our disagreement is somewhat different. In the case of race riots, such as those in Los Angeles after the Rodney King verdict, we disagree about whether or not particular individuals or groups can be held causally responsible for the violence. Although some of us are willing to hold the all-white jury (or the federal government or the rioters themselves) causally responsible for the violence, others are not. In the case of battered women who inflict violence on their batterers, we generally assume a direct causal connection between, say, the shooting of a gun and the death of a man. Hence, we generally agree on the causal responsibility of the woman's act for the harm in question. But we do not agree on whether the woman can be excused from responsibility for the violence by virtue either of the mental instability caused by the battering or the self-defense implicit in her violent act.

In the case of the race riot as in the case of battered women, we make a dual judgment: first, whether the harm is a consequence of the individual's actions, and second, whether the individual caused her own actions to the extent that we can blame her for the harm. Likewise, when we disagree about who is responsible for harm, we disagree about one or both of these judgments—that is, about either the causal connection that exists between the individual and harm, or the control that the individual was able to exert over her own actions. In the case of urban riots, we disagree about whether or not particular individuals or groups can be held causally responsible for harm. In the case of battered women, we disagree about whether or not a particular sort of mental impairment excuses individuals from blame.

RESPONSIBILITY AND BLAME

How are we to decide who was—or is—responsible in these cases? The course followed most frequently by moral philosophers is to apply the concept of moral responsibility as ideally construed. Hence, those writing on the moral responsibility of battered women might ask, "Did individual X herself cause—freely will—her actions?" "Did she know what she was doing?" "Was she in control of herself?" Likewise, we see the notion of free will invoked in this context being interpreted not as part of a social practice (for example, that of blaming) but as a fact about the essence of individuals, a fact that is supposed to be independent of the contingencies that contribute to our own judgments of blameworthiness.

The analysis of the race riot proceeds on superficially different grounds. Here we are told to ask not "Did individual X himself cause—freely will—his own actions?" but "Is individual X, Y, or Z the primary cause of harm?" Although the arena of responsibility (external harm rather than an individual's own action) has changed, the structure of the analysis is the same. In both cases we are presented with ideal causal relations that are supposed to be inherently moral and independent of our social practice of blaming or any particular interests or perspectives that we might invoke to locate causal responsibility in one place rather than another.

Yet neither set of causal relations is either inherently moral or independent of social and political practice. Indeed, those now writing on the two cases inadvertently incorporate many of these practices into their analysis of moral responsibility. Nevertheless, they frame their analysis with a more abstract notion of moral responsibility in mind, one that requires them to insist on the complete independence of moral responsibility from all worldly considerations. I explore this notion in much greater depth elsewhere and view it as a distinctly modern construction.[3] Suffice it to point out here that the concept of moral responsibility that they invoke rejects any connection between moral responsibility and our own practical judgments of blameworthiness.

Joel Feinberg provides one of the clearest definitions of the modern concept of moral responsibility in the following passage:

A stubborn feeling persists even after legal responsibility has been decided that there is still a problem—albeit not a legal problem—left over: namely, is the defendant really responsible (as opposed to "responsible in law") for the harm? This concept of real theoretical responsibility distinct from a practical responsibility "relative to the purposes and values of a particular community" is expressed very commonly in the language of "morality"—*moral* obligation, *moral* guilt, *moral* responsibility.[4]

Since moral responsibility is ostensibly independent of all practical considerations, it must be not only absolute but precisely decidable. Likewise, it must be purely factual rather than dependent on the discretion of a worldly (or even otherworldly) judge. Like all matters of "record," moral responsibility must be "read off the facts or deduced from

[3] I distinguish the modern concept of moral responsibility from its classical and Christian counterparts in *Moral Responsibility and the Boundaries of Community: Power and Accountability from a Pragmatic Point of View* (Chicago: University of Chicago Press, 1992). I focus on the ostensible independence of the modern notion of blameworthiness from our social practice of blaming.

[4] Joel Feinberg, *Doing and Deserving* (Princeton, N.J.: Princeton University Press, 1970), 30. For a very interesting treatment of moral blameworthiness in the context of other sorts of blameworthiness, see Peter French, "Senses of 'Blame'," *Southern Journal of Philosophy* 14 (1976): 443–5.

them: there can be no irreducible element of discretion for the judge, if his judgments are to have the stamp of superior rationality."[5]

What kind of factual judgment is moral responsibility? Since it requires that individuals have caused that for which they are being blamed, it is in some respects a scientific judgment. But it cannot be construed as value-neutral, since it embraces within itself a moral judgment about the individual in question: that she is morally blameworthy for having brought about harm. Hence, we might want to talk about it as a morally charged sort of causation or judgment of moral agency.

William Frankena captures the conflation of causation and blameworthiness when he writes:

> Saying that X was responsible for Y seems, at first, to be a causal, not a moral, judgment; and one might, therefore, be inclined to say that "X was responsible for Y" simply means "X caused Y," perhaps with the qualification that he did so voluntarily, unintentionally, etc. But to say that X is responsible for Y is not merely to make a causal statement of a special kind. . . . It is to say that it would be right to blame or otherwise punish him.[6]

By conflating causation and blameworthiness into one moral fact about persons, we are able to use a single term—moral responsibility—to cover both causation and blameworthiness together. But in doing so we create two very formidable tasks for ourselves, tasks that our classical and Christian predecessors were able to avoid by viewing blameworthiness not as an aspect of causation per se, but as relative to the standards of an external blamer (the community and God, respectively). The first task is to show how individuals can be understood as blameworthy outside of a relationship between them and an external blamer—that is, simply by having caused something bad. The other is to show how they can be in control over such causation itself to the extent required by moral blameworthiness. (If they do not cause their own actions, how can they—as distinct from their environment—be morally to blame?)

Both tasks are very difficult, if not impossible, to accomplish.[7] But

---

[5] Feinberg, *Doing and Deserving*, 31.
[6] William Frankena, *Ethics* (Englewood Cliffs, N.J.: Prentice-Hall, 1963), 56.
[7] Endless debates have ensued over the possibility of free will. See J. J. C. Smart, "Free Will, Praise and Blame," *Mind* 70 (1961): 291–306. It is still one of the most convincing refutations of free will construed as contra-causal freedom. Although most of those now participating in the free will versus determinism controversy have chosen to replace free will construed as contra-causal freedom with a "softer" notion of free will that is compatible with determinism, very few have gone on to ask what this softer notion of free will means for the possibility of moral blameworthiness. Indeed, very few "soft deter-

even if we could accomplish them, we would have a construal that would be of limited use in addressing the case of the race riot or battered women. For these cases are about the moral responsibility of individuals for both their own actions and for external states of affairs.[8] Among other things, "moral luck"—and the precariousness of worldly events that the term was originally intended to capture—rule out the sort of control that individuals would have to have over external harm if they were to be held responsible for it.[9] Although individuals might be understood to control their own actions, or at least their own intentions, they cannot be understood to control the conditions under which they act in the world. Nor can they be understood to control the use to which others might put their actions. In this context Tom Nagel concludes, "from the point of view that makes responsibility dependent on control, this precariousness seems absurd."[10]

Joel Feinberg goes even further. He refers to the "senselessness" of invoking the concept of moral responsibility to talk about the causal relations between individuals and external harm. According to Feinberg, while we might want to continue talking about individuals as morally responsible for their own actions, we would be wise to give up talking about them as morally responsible for external states of affairs. According to Feinberg, "if we are rational," we will admit that "moral responsibility for external affairs makes no sense and argue that moral responsibility is restricted to the inner world of the mind, where the agent rules supreme and luck has no place."[11]

---

minists" ever get back to the question of blameworthiness at all. An important exception here is Peter Strawson. See his discussion of free will in *Freedom and Resentment* (London: British Academy, 1974).

[8] Although the moral responsibility of individuals for external harm is part of everyday discourse, most philosophers—for reasons I explain later—focus primarily on the moral responsibility of individuals for their own actions. There are, of course, exceptions. See, for example, John Harris, *Violence and Responsibility* (London: Routledge, 1980); John Casey, "Actions and Consequences," in *Morality and Moral Reasoning* (London: Methuen, 1971); and Dennis Thompson, *Political Ethics and Public Office* (Cambridge, Mass.: Harvard University Press, 1987).

[9] According to Tom Nagel, "moral luck" refers to both the element of contingency in an individual's actions and the fact that we nevertheless persist in scrutinizing such actions from a moral point of view. He writes, "When a significant aspect of what someone does depends on factors beyond his control, yet we continue to treat him in that respect as an object of moral judgment, it can be called moral luck." See Tom Nagel, "Moral Luck," in *Mortal Questions* (Cambridge: Cambridge University Press, 1979), 32–3.

[10] Ibid., 33.

[11] Feinberg, *Doing and Deserving*, 32.

Both Nagel and Feinberg are correct to question the wisdom of applying the modern concept of moral responsibility to external states of affairs. (I try elsewhere to explain why such wisdom also fails in the case of moral responsibility for actions.)[12] At the very least, their arguments suggest that we do not now discover moral responsibility for external harm in the way that we frequently suppose we do, and that trying to improve our judgments by translating the modern concept of moral responsibility into a set of worldly criteria will not work. But should we leave the concept of moral responsibility behind in practice simply because our philosophical understanding of it is antipractical?

Instead of leaving the concept of moral responsibility behind altogether in discussions of worldly harm, I believe that we should reconstruct the concept as part of two closely related social and political judgments. The first of these judgments is that harm is the consequence of a particular individual's action. The second is that the individual is worthy of our blame. Both judgments, I suggest, are grounded in a variety of norms that we share—however differently we may sometimes interpret them—as members of a particular community. Moreover, these norms are often buried in our judgments and difficult to discern. Hence, we need to tease them to the surface before we can examine their place in our moral judgments. I do so below by focusing on those judgments of causal responsibility and blameworthiness that differ from one another most blatantly.

How can we understand our judgments of causal responsibility in cases of external harm? As Nicholas Haines and others have made clear, causal responsibility is not just about causation; it is about accountability as well.[13] When we hold each other causally responsible for external harm we do not simply display an array of possible causes that are somehow independent of our practical goals. Instead, we choose the point in a causal chain where we want to stop and ask for an accounting. If we find the cause represented by this point to be primary, we go on to hold it causally responsible for the harm. Judgments of causal responsibility require us not only to locate various causes but to stipulate which among them is primary. Likewise, if we are ever to understand

---

[12] Marion Smiley, "A Question of Responsibility," *Midwest Studies in Philosophy* 1994 (Minneapolis: University of Minnesota Press, 1995), 15–36.
[13] Nicholas Haines, "Responsibility and Accountability," *Journal of Philosophy* 30 (1955): 141–51.

our judgments of causal responsibility, we will need to know what "primacy" means in this context and how we discover it.

LOS ANGELES RACE RIOTS

The case of the 1992 Los Angeles riots is instructive here. An all-white suburban jury found three white policemen not guilty of beating up a black man, Rodney King, even though most of those who viewed the relevant videotapes—a large chunk of the U.S. population—concluded otherwise. A riot ensued in the mostly black neighborhood of South Central Los Angeles, where protests against the verdict—and against "white justice"—were heard in the midst of much violence. If the verdict had come down differently, the riots would probably not have occurred. Hence, observers across the political spectrum were willing to hold members of the jury partly responsible for the violence that occurred.

But not all participants in the controversy were willing to do so. Some argued vigorously that juries cannot be expected to think about the consequences of their verdicts for society at large, and that the jury in the Rodney King case could therefore not be held causally responsible for the riots. Interestingly enough, many of those who held the jury partly responsible agreed with the claim that juries cannot be expected to think about the consequences of their verdicts for society at large. But they added that all juries can be expected not to be racist, an addition that enabled them to support their original conclusion that members of the jury were indeed at least partly responsible for the riots.

Jury members were, of course, not the only ones blamed for the Los Angeles riots. The rioters themselves were the focus of much attention. But there was not a lot of agreement on whether they could be held causally responsible for the riots. Since the rioters physically perpetrated the violence, it is difficult not to see a very direct causal connection between them and the riots. Indeed, the two are so closely tied up with one another that it is not clear where the distinction between them begins. But exculpators of the rioters frequently chose to see the riots as a rebellion against injustice or to argue that the rioters were driven to violence by the racism of the larger community. Some black activists went further. They argued not only that members of the South Central Los Angeles black community should have rioted or rebelled, but that if they had not done so, they could now be held causally responsible for perpetuation of white supremacy.[14]

Very few observers were willing in the end to excuse the rioters entirely from responsibility. But many participants in the controversy did argue that while the rioters were causally responsible for what happened, so were a variety of other groups, including the Los Angeles police, the federal government, and white racists throughout society. The police were to blame because they did not carry out the standard requirements of their job.[15] The federal government was to blame because of its failure to remedy inner city problems. (*The Progressive* said the L.A. riots were the administration's fault "for not providing adequate jobs or health care or education for all Americans so that everyone—black and white— could hope for a decent life.")[16] White racists were to blame because of their general oppression of blacks and their legitimation of a racist police force and jury.[17]

Of course, observers disagreed vehemently about which individuals or groups could be held morally responsible. Black leaders such as Al Sharpton blamed the white establishment for the riots on the grounds that white racism was the primary cause of black anger. ("It is white racists who are causally responsible for the looting of those stores.")[18] Charles Murray, author of *The Bell Curve*, argued on the contrary that whites cannot be blamed for the Los Angeles riots because racism is no longer a significant factor in blacks' lives. "The present problems of the black community owe more to black behavior than to white oppression. . . . To blame whites is to blame victims."[19] Murray's contention here is a self-conscious reversal of the claim by many black leaders that to blame blacks for the Los Angeles riots is to blame victims.

In dispute also is the contention that the federal government is to blame for the riots. Vice President Dan Quayle denied federal responsibility and attributed the riots to "the breakdown in family structure, personal responsibility and social order."[20] Marlin Fitzwater, press sec-

---

[14] For a discussion of the various positions that black leaders took on responsibility for the Los Angeles riots, see "Black and White," *Newsweek*, 18 May 1992, 28–39.

[15] See, for instance, Eugene Methvin, "How to Hold a Riot," *National Review*, 8 June 1992, 32–5.

[16] "Blame the Poor," *The Progressive*, July 1992, 8.

[17] See, for example, Andrew Hacker, *Two Nations: Black and White, Separate and Hostile* (New York: Scribner's, 1992).

[18] Al Sharpton, quoted in "Black and White," *Newsweek*, 33.

[19] Charles Murray, "Causes, Root Causes and Cures," *National Review*, 8 June 1992, 32.

[20] Dan Quayle, quoted in "Blame the Poor," 8.

retary to President George Bush, went one step further and argued not only that the federal government cannot be blamed but that the Los Angeles riots were the result of Lyndon Baines Johnson's Great Society.[21] Roger Wilkins, civil rights activist, disagreed. Wilkins argued that the Great Society was a model that the Bush administration should have followed and that by shirking its responsibilities to end racism and poverty, the Bush administration rendered itself vulnerable to blame for the riots.[22]

CAUSAL RESPONSIBILITY

All of these judgments are based on a causal analysis of racism in general and the Los Angeles riots in particular. But they are not purely factual judgments. Nor could they be, since in our efforts to decide where responsibility lies, we inevitably bring various expectations to bear on the causal connections that we locate between a moral agent and harm. Most of these expectations concern whose job it is in society to prevent certain kinds of harm. If one thinks that jury members are supposed to prevent race riots, then one is more likely to hold jury members responsible for violence in cases where they hand down incendiary verdicts. Likewise, if one thinks that the federal government is supposed to alleviate poverty in society, or that poor people are not supposed to loot under any circumstances, then one is likely to hold one or the other responsible.

In many cases the expectations that we have of particular individuals come out of a practical analysis of who can best prevent the sorts of harm in question. But even such analyses are not immune from normative scrutiny, since they are filtered through expectations concerning whom we can expect to devote attention to a particular problem. In most cases the latter sort of expectation involves a sense not only of who can best prevent harm, but also of who can reasonably be expected to put her projects aside and do something for someone else.

Roger Wilkins thinks that white Americans can be expected to pay more taxes in order to alleviate racism and poverty among persons of color. Charles Murray does not. What explains the differences between

---

[21] Marlin Fitzwater, quoted in "How to Hold a Riot," 33.
[22] Roger Wilkins, "Don't Blame L. B. J.'s Great Society," *The Progressive*, June 1992, 16–18.

them? Among other things, they disagree about how much white racism has hurt blacks and about how much good can be done now by federal government intervention. But it is not only a prior causal analysis that leads them to differ about how much whites can be expected to do to alleviate racism and poverty, since they both derive their views from normative judgments about communal boundaries. Murray makes clear that "whites should no longer be guilt-tripped into thinking that blacks are necessarily part of their community of concern."[23] Wilkins, like almost all civil rights leaders of his generation, writes of the "community of mankind" in his discussions of causal responsibility.[24]

The point here is that our expectations that individuals will and should act to prevent harm rise substantially when the individuals are acting as members of their community. This point was driven home by the Crown Heights riots in New York in 1991. In the Crown Heights case a van carrying Hasidic Jews ran over and killed a black youth. Disagreement about whether the Hasidic driver intentionally ran over the black youth, Gavin Cato, and about whether the Hasidic entourage chose not to save Cato's life by instructing its private ambulance not to pick him up, was quickly coupled with normative disagreement about whether members of one community can be expected to care about the well-being of members of another. Not surprisingly, those who included "ethnic outsiders" in their community of concern were more likely than exclusivists to find themselves—and their ethnic community—causally responsible for at least some of the difficulties that they did nothing to prevent.[25]

In the case of race riots, we usually focus on groups of people. In other cases, such as that of black rappers who perform songs with sexist and racist lyrics, we think about causal responsibility in individualistic terms. But we still bring social expectations to bear on our judgments

---

[23] Murray, "Causes, Root Causes and Cures," 32.

[24] Wilkins, "Don't Blame L. B. J.'s Great Society," 17.

[25] The Crown Heights riots have been scrutinized in many different contexts. For a discussion between blacks and members of the Hasidic community about causal responsibility, see "Side by Side, Apart: The Difficult Search for Racial Peace in Brooklyn," *U.S. News and World Report*, 4 November 1991, 44–54. For an argument about why we should not take perspectives—as distinct from facts—seriously in judging causal responsibility for the Crown Heights riots, see "Crown Depths," *New Republic*, 16 August 1993, 7–8. It is argued there (p. 8) that by focusing on perceptions instead of facts, the "Report to the Governor on the Disturbances in Crown Heights" becomes an "intellectual and political abdication of responsibility." In my view both facts and perceptions have to be taken into consideration.

of causal responsibility. Here these expectations derive from our divergent normative judgments about the role of "artist" or the "black artist." Although some of us believe artists have a responsibility to consider the social consequences of their art, others do not. (As critics point out, a double standard is often invoked when dealing with black artists who, for a variety of reasons, are more likely to be ascribed social responsibilities than are their white counterparts.)[26] Hence, we differ widely about the causal responsibility of rap artists for the sexist and racist attitudes expressed among members of their listening audience.

What about moral blameworthiness? In most cases we tend to blame those whose actions or omissions we deem causally responsible for harm. But we do so only because we assume that the second condition of moral responsibility—free will—can be met. On what basis do we decide whether an individual's will was free in the sense required by moral blameworthiness? Although we may take all sorts of consequences into consideration when arguing about which excuses are valid to invoke in discussions of free will, we do not generally rely on a consequentialist understanding of free will itself. Instead, we ask straightforwardly, "Could the individual have done otherwise than she actually did?" Moreover, in doing so, we often assume that we are asking about contra-causal freedom or, in other words, about the ability of an individual to transcend both physical and social determinism.

But as Kant himself was willing to acknowledge, human beings are not capable of discovering contra-causal freedom in the world. Hence, the notion of free will that we require of them in practice must be a notion of relative control over their decisions to act. What sorts of control are relevant to the notion of free will that we invoke in discussions of moral responsibility? How much control must be present? The case of battered women who respond violently is instructive here.

BATTERED WOMEN

The major disagreement in this instance, which concerns the moral responsibility of individuals for their own actions, centers on whether a battered woman could have done otherwise than she actually did. If she could have refrained from violence, she is assumed to have freely willed

---

[26] For an interesting discussion of this phenomenon, see Elizabeth Wartzel, "Fight the Power," *The New Yorker*, 28 September 1992, 110–3.

her actions. These assumptions are made uniformly throughout both moral and legal debate.

In the case of battered women who shoot their abusers while their abusers are asleep, most observers agree both that the women in question were, at the time of action, seriously hindered by years of battering and that they could have physically walked away from their abusers at that point. But observers disagree about two related aspects of the notion of free will deemed relevant to moral responsibility. One is the amount of control that the individuals could have been expected to exert over themselves. The other is whether—given the life situations of these women—they could reasonably have been expected to walk away from their abusers. Both of these issues appear to be—and are often portrayed as—factual controversies. But the controversies themselves do not involve factual disagreements per se or at least not purely factual judgments. Instead, they involve competing judgments about the battered women's syndrome and more purely normative expectations that we impose on battered women and, as it turns out, on all women as a group.

Although psychological studies of particular battered women are undoubtedly important, they are often accompanied by normative judgments concerning the status of women as victims in society and whether such a status is healthy. In the case of Claudette Berdis, a battered woman who seriously abused her own children, psychiatrists claimed outright that our society

has conditioned women to accept that they are to serve men. Ms. Berdis has been robotized by living with a lout. As a victim, her human responsibilities collapsed and she became putty in his hands. This diminished entity could scarcely be held accountable for victimizing another.[27]

Such claims are not at all uncommon and accompany most pleas that employ the battered women argument. Yet they are not acceptable to all. In some cases, such as the Berdis case, skeptics argue that the woman in question was not really incapable of taking control over her life. But skeptics do not necessarily reject the battered women argument in general. Indeed, the prosecutor in the Berdis case contended that the defendant's plea was an insult to women in the community who were really battered to the point of losing all self-esteem. In other cases the obliteration of self-esteem is acknowledged by all parties to be complete, but

[27] Quoted in Jean Elshtain, "Battered Reason," *New Republic*, 8 October 1992, 28.

disagreement arises over the relationship between self-esteem and free will. Advocates of the battered women defense assert that the loss of self-esteem undercuts free will. Critics of that view hold that even the most degraded battered women are free agents and hence responsible persons.

How can those who sympathize with battered women and who acknowledge the complete loss of self-esteem that results from some cases of battering deny the validity of the battered women argument in discussions of moral responsibility? Two sets of claims about free will and battered women become central here. One has to do with the choices of women to enter abusive relationships and concerns how far back in a person's life we should go in establishing that person's control and hence responsibility. The other has to do with the social meanings that we attach to the term "victimhood" and the fairness of blaming individuals who are oppressed in society. Both sets of claims illustrate the extent to which we bring normative assumptions about the appropriateness of particular behaviors to bear on our judgments of free will.

At what point in an individual's life do we locate control? A battered woman may lack control over her life, but she may have once freely chosen the abusive relationship in which she is now trapped. Hence, she should, according to critics, be held morally responsible for her present actions. The argument here is similar to the one used in cases in which alcoholism, drug addiction, and gambling are seen as freely chosen conditions. In these cases it is often acknowledged that although, say, cocaine psychosis is a bona fide psychosis, it cannot excuse addicts from moral responsibility since it results from a voluntary act, the taking of cocaine. In response to their critics, those who invoke cocaine psychosis as an excuse do not dispute the presence of control associated with the initial choice to take cocaine. Instead, they claim that prior actions have no bearing on the present actions of a self who is without control.[28]

The same sort of controversy over prior selves arises in the battered women case. How far back should we go in locating control? Even if a battered woman is not now able to control her will, was she not once able to do so? Should we simply forget that she freely chose to enter an abusive relationship, or should we take that choice into consideration as a sign of her free will? Do women ever freely choose to enter abusive

---

[28] For a discussion of the controversy surrounding cocaine psychosis as a volitional excuse, see Stephanie Goldberg, "Fault Lines," *ABA Journal* 80 (1994): 42.

relationships, or is their choice necessarily the result of prior abuse and/
or socially determined patterns of behavior? Does the image of battered
women as victims translate into the image of all women as victims?

THE QUESTION OF VICTIMHOOD

Interestingly enough, many of the answers offered to these questions
have just as much to do with the projected consequences of victimization
talk on women in general as they do with the particular women in question. Indeed, much of the disagreement about whether battered women
should be treated as morally responsible for their actions has focused on
what the label "victim" does to women as a group. The same holds true
for the black rage excuse. Although discussion of that excuse is just
beginning, it has so far centered on whether or not using "black rage"
to excuse particular blacks from moral responsibility will lead to the
conclusion that blacks in general are less than fully autonomous beings
and hence ill prepared for full citizenship.

Not surprisingly, the debate is most heated among feminists, who
have the greatest stake in the matter. Proponents of the battered women
defense—as well as feminists such as Catherine MacKinnon—argue that
women are victims in society and that by acknowledging their diminished responsibility we underscore their abuse and make claims on the
state for remedy. As Lenore Walker writes, "only by portraying women
as unfree now can we hope to undo that which has so victimized them
in the past: male domination."[29] Other feminists, equally concerned
about the empowerment of women, worry about the very claims of victimhood itself—both because it potentially reinforces the picture of
women as debased, deformed, and incapable of autonomy, and because
it assumes a gendered theory of responsibility that might backfire on
women. As Jean Elshtain writes about the Berdis case, "it demonstrates
how pernicious a difference argument can become when taken to extremes. Women cease to be viewed as responsible human agents."[30]

How much control we ascribe to particular battered women is thus
a matter of both free will and what we see as happening in society when
we equate the obliteration of self-esteem with diminished responsibility.

---

[29] Lenore Walker, *Terrifying Love: Why Battered Women Kill and How Society Responds*
(New York: Harper and Row, 1989).
[30] Elshtain, "Battered Reason," 29.

Most of the concerns expressed in this context have to do with victimization. But on other occasions the concerns are with what victimization talk may cover up. Nan Hunter, an activist for battered women, argues that the victim status that accompanies claims of diminished responsibility may not only backfire on women and perpetuate stereotypes of helpless creatures but also hide the real causes of battering. "Women-as-victim is a cultural script that evokes sympathy without challenging the hierarchical structure of patriarchy. It is a kind of melodrama that doesn't lead to any change in the conditions that cause victimization," she writes.[31] Hunter now advises battered women to assert their free wills against the system.

All of this suggests that the extent of control required by free will is associated, at least in part, with the extent to which participants in the debate want to see individuals identified with victimhood. But what about the seemingly factual judgments concerning whether a battered woman could have—physically, as opposed to psychologically—done otherwise than she did? What, in other words, about those judgments concerning whether she could have left her abuser, judgments that are equally important to questions of moral responsibility? On the surface, these judgments appear to be made simply by asking questions like: "Could she have gotten away from her abuser?" ("Was he, for instance, sleeping at the time?") "Did she have any place to go?" But very quickly, the argument turns to more open-ended questions about what it is reasonable to expect from battered women. Since many battered women choose to attack their abusers when they are asleep or otherwise disarmed, we ask: "Was the threat such that a reasonable person could have formulated and carried through another plan of action?" Under what conditions can we reasonably expect a battered woman to leave her abuser? Among other things, we need to know what other possibilities existed.

In the Berdis case the prosecution—and many commentators—argued that the defendant could have called her family or others to help take care of her children, even if she was compelled to stay with her husband. "She thus had choices," writes Elshtain, "and she chose, on some level, to destroy her child."[32] But in other cases the choice to leave an abuser

---

[31] Nan Hunter, as quoted in Tamar Lewin, "Feminists Wonder if It Was Progress to Become 'Victims'," *New York Times*, 10 May 1992, 6.
[32] Elshtain, "Battered Reason," 28.

is not as available as it might at first appear to be. Since to leave might
bring on worse violence in the long run and in any case, if children are
involved, the financial backing of a spouse, even an abusive one, might
be necessary, we need to ask: "Could the battered woman in question
be expected to leave?"

As things now stand, when confronted with such circumstances, most
feminists argue that "leaving is too high a price to expect women to
pay."[33] Others disagree. Who is to decide on the reasonableness of a
price to pay? Is there an objective criterion to be found? Although discerning reasonableness may involve scrutinizing the facts of the situation—"What really were her other options?" "How likely was her
abuser to retaliate?"—factual inquiry cannot alone tell us how much
abuse is "too much." For, as the present state of disagreement over
battered women and responsibility demonstrates, what is "too much"
abuse for some is "not enough" for others.

How might we deal with these differences? The most common response is to argue that one position is correct. In my view no such
argument is persuasive. Instead, I have tried to show that the judgments
of moral responsibility that we make in practice are based on a variety
of social norms that we use to locate the causes of both harm and free
will. Moreover, I have suggested that we set out to locate such causes
in the first place—when moral responsibility is an issue—because we are
concerned to blame someone for harm or, in other words, because we
are participants in the social practice of blaming. Hence, we cannot view
our judgments of moral responsibility as independent of our own place
in this practice. We must instead become conscious of the goals and
norms that we—and those who disagree with us—bring to bear on our
causal judgments.

What would it mean to argue openly with one another about moral
responsibility in cases of race riots or battered women? In my view it
would not involve applying an ideal concept of moral responsibility to
the two cases. Instead, it would involve articulating—and then evaluating—the various normative assumptions that we now incorporate into
our judgments of causal responsibility and blameworthiness. In particular, we would need to discuss what expectations we should have of
particular individuals, how we should interpret their social roles, who
should belong to their community of concern, and how we should deal

---

[33] Nancy Gibbs, " 'Til Death Do Us Part," *Time*, 18 January 1993, 42.

with the label "victim." Moreover, we would have to come to terms with how these normative assumptions ground our understanding of the facts of the situation.

In doing so, we would inevitably challenge the view of moral responsibility as a purely factual matter. But we would not deny the importance of factual inquiry. Indeed, we would still need to ask a variety of factual questions if we wanted to evaluate our judgments of responsibility in the two cases at hand, questions such as: "What effect did the jury's verdict really have on the population of South Central Los Angeles?" "To what extent has white racism undermined the ability of Los Angeles blacks to survive and prosper?" "Do rap songs really lead to violence against women and white policemen?" "Would particular battered women be subjected to further violence if they ran away from their abusers?" "Can a battered women's syndrome be demonstrated?"

While our answers to these questions might simply confirm our present views, they might also change our judgments of moral responsibility in important ways. In the case of racial riots, we might change our minds about how great a difference, say, federal government assistance would make to the alleviation of racism and poverty. If we did change our minds about the federal government in this context, we might also change our minds about where to stop in the causal chain of events that led up to the riots. We might conclude, for instance, that responsibility actually lies with the rioters themselves rather than with government. In the case of battered women, we might come to see that physical battering destroys willfulness to a much greater extent than we realized before. Or we might become convinced that battering is not a syndrome but rather a set of external pressures from which women can reasonably be expected to distance themselves.

EXPECTATIONS OF THE INDIVIDUAL

Such factual analysis could never be sufficient, since our judgments about whether a particular individual's will is free depend partly on our expectations of the individual. At the very least, we need to examine the expectations that we often unselfconsciously incorporate into our judgments of causal responsibility and free will. In some cases these expectations are openly stated even if they are not actually focused upon. Charles Murray and Roger Wilkins have vastly different expectations of virtually all those potentially responsible for the Los Angeles riots: the jury, the federal government, the rioters themselves, the Los Angeles police, and the "White Establishment." In other cases, participants in the debates are less forthcoming about the normative expectations of individuals embodied in their causal judgments, and these expectations need to be made explicit.

The case of battered women provides a very good example of how hidden expectations can hold us back from arguing openly about moral responsibility. Since those who disagree about the battered women's defense tend to focus on whether battering obliterates free will, they often fail to notice that the question is not "Is individual X's will free from external determination?" but "How much control do individuals need to exert over themselves before their will can be characterized as free (in some obviously less absolute sense than contra-causal freedom)?" The latter formulation is necessary because we are never completely free from external determination. The question thus becomes what sorts of control we are focusing on and measuring when we deem an individual's will free in the sense relevant to moral blameworthiness.[34]

Since the notion of control in question is thought to be registered in the absence of a valid excuse, we might profitably begin with these excuses and the conditions under which we construe them as valid. In most cases we examine the bad behavior and look for the degree of control that was present. But there are obviously cases in which we both agree that individuals are totally out of control and deny the validity of their excuses. In the case of drug and alcohol abuse, for example, many among us assert that the individual could have controlled her behavior early on. Moreover, we make clear that we feel comfortable in our expectations that she should have controlled her behavior at that point. To be sure, such assertions rest partly on scientific beliefs about the mental capacities of individuals to control their own psychological processes. (We are not willing to blame the insane.) But they also rest on a variety of cultural beliefs about where to draw the line on self-indulgence.

Although we do not generally blame the insane for their actions, seventeenth-century Puritans did, believing that if such individuals "really tried" they could overcome their compulsive behavior.[35] Likewise,

---

[34] This formulation allows for the possibility that we may have different notions of free will in mind in different contexts and asserts the necessity of being context specific.

[35] For an excellent discussion of this phenomenon, see H. W. Schneider, *The Puritan Mind* (Ann Arbor: University of Michigan Press, 1959).

while many of us are not now willing to accept excuses based on "stress," others are willing not only to accept them but to incorporate them into the legal system. How can we explain the differences between us? Psychological theories may keep some of us apart, but two other differences appear to be more relevant. One concerns how much of an individual's environment we can expect her to resist. The other concerns the levels of self-control we feel we can expect the individual to attain in stressful situations.

Both differences are clear in the debates now surrounding the responsibility of African-Americans for the lack of economic initiative in the black community. Black liberals, such as Benjamin Hooks, and black conservatives, such as Thomas Sowell, claim to agree on the pressures that confront those living in dire poverty. But they disagree on how far African-Americans can go in using such pressures to assign responsibility for their own impoverishment. Hooks places the blame on the system that takes initiative away from blacks.[36] Sowell places it squarely on the shoulders of African-Americans themselves.[37] Hooks and Sowell incorporate different norms of behavior into their analyses of the constraints that face poor blacks and come up with very different opinions about blameworthiness.

OPEN ARGUMENT

By clarifying these expectations and exposing them to view, we can create a framework for open argument about responsibility. But could we ever evaluate particular judgments of moral responsibility on the basis of these expectations? What would it mean to do so in discussions of free will? Among other things, we would have to ask a variety of questions about what kind of practice of blaming we want to endorse. Should we be strict or compassionate in particular situations? How far should we go in excusing wrongful actions? How much psychological control should we expect individuals to exert over their own wills in situations of great stress? How far back in the individual's history should we go in locating a choice that we consider free? How much abuse should we expect individuals to take?

---

[36] See Benjamin Hooks's arguments in *Go Tell It!* (New York: National Association for the Advancement of Colored People Press, 1979).

[37] Sowell develops this position in *Compassion versus Guilt and Other Essays* (New York: Morrow, 1987); and *A Conflict of Vision* (New York: Morrow, 1987).

In the case of causal responsibility, we would have to decide what individuals should be expected to do in society to prevent harm. Should juries be expected to ask about the effects of their verdicts on race relations in a particular community? Should police officers be expected to enter into situations in which they may be shot? Should middle-class taxpayers be expected to finance government efforts to alleviate poverty? Should poor people be expected not to loot stores as a form of rebellion? Should rap singers be expected to constrain their art for the sake of communal harmony?

How could we possibly argue about these questions? We would probably want to begin by raising a series of practical questions about our various—and often conflicting—expectations of individuals. Is our system of justice really served by expecting jurors to consider the social consequences of their verdicts? Are government projects the answer to poverty and racism? If not, what is? Does the battered women defense perpetuate an image of women in general as victims? Does it challenge the hierarchical systems of power that subordinate women as a group? Does it lead to self-indulgence and irresponsibility on the part of those who use it? Will our acceptance of it lead to the deaths of many men?

Such practical analyses are important when we argue about moral responsibility in cases where our normative judgments differ. But such analyses can never be construed as neutral with respect to whose interests are at stake. In the cases of both causal responsibility and free will, our judgments of responsibility necessarily raise questions of fairness. Would it be fair to expect those who have been treated in a racist manner to refrain from rebellion when those who are racist go unpunished? Would it be fair to expect middle-class taxpayers to financially support those who do not have jobs? Would it be fair to expect battered women to take abuse if batterers go free? Would it be fair to excuse battered women from blame and not excuse alcoholics and drug addicts? If we excuse alcoholics and drug addicts from blame, are we being fair to those who have tried to live a responsible life and who may end up being the victims of alcohol- or drug-related crimes?

In our efforts to resolve—or at least argue about—questions of fairness, two sorts of discussions have to take place. The first and most obvious concerns our standards of fairness themselves. Do we want to equate fairness with equality? Could we possibly do so, given that individuals do not find themselves in the same life situations? (Although some "individuals" find themselves susceptible to battering or racist treatment, other "individuals" do not.) Do we want to replace the term "individuals" in the two cases under discussion with "men" and "women," "blacks" and "whites"? Can we do so while maintaining the equation of fairness with equality? Or do we need to embrace a theory of fairness that places "difference" at the center of our attention?[38]

Although such a discussion might not lead us to change our minds about fairness, it has led others to do so in a variety of race- and gender-based cases.[39] Moreover, even if such a discussion did not change our judgments of responsibility, a second sort of discussion about fairness might lead us to do so—namely, one concerning the consistency with which we apply our principles. Have we, in our discussions of free will, distinguished between different sorts of excuses on the basis of race or gender even though we explicitly hold to a gender- and race-blind theory of fairness? Are we willing to indulge some individuals and not others, even though their situations are the same? Can we consistently accept the battered women's excuse and not the black rage excuse?

Questions of consistency and fairness are more easily discussed in the context of claims about free will than they are in the context of claims about causal responsibility. Although individuals are all supposed to have free will as human beings, they occupy many different roles in society and as such can be expected to do very different things to prevent harm. At the very least, we need to ask about the fairness of our configuration of social roles, a configuration that grounds many of our judgments of causal responsibility. Are we placing too much of a burden on some individuals? Are we being unfair to police officers in expecting them to risk their lives? Are we taxing the wealthy too much in our efforts to alleviate poverty? Are we being unfair to blacks and other persons of color in expecting them to carry the burden of fights against racism?

The distribution of labor in these cases needs to questioned on grounds of both fairness and utility, but neither discussion will be sufficient. As the race riot case demonstrated, whom we can expect to sacrifice how much in order to help others is just as much a matter of communal boundaries as it is a matter of fairness. (Or fairness may be shaped more than we realize by our sense of communal boundaries.) In

---

[38] I have in mind a theory of fairness such as that developed by Iris Young in *Justice and the Politics of Difference* (Princeton, N.J.: Princeton University Press, 1990).

[39] For an excellent discussion of these cases, see Martha Minow, *Making All the Difference* (Ithaca, N.Y.: Cornell University Press, 1990).

the case of race riots, we generally agree that someone should alleviate the harm but disagree about who should do so. Should middle-class citizens of Baltimore be expected to worry about the plight of the un-employed in South Central Los Angeles? Should the unemployed in South Central Los Angeles be expected to worry about the rise in the cost of college tuition that middle-class Baltimore citizens now face? Should the Hasidim of Crown Heights be expected to fight against the racist treatment of blacks in their neighborhood? Should the blacks of Crown Heights be expected to fight against the anti-Semitism that members of the Hasidic community face in their neighborhood? What if the neighborhood happens to be the same in both cases?

In the end, if we want to understand moral responsibility and argue profitably about it, we will have to consider questions concerning communal membership and the expectations that we impose on others. Likewise, in answering these questions, we will have to take much more seriously the extent to which moral values, and concepts such as moral responsibility, evolve out of and govern social and political practices that are themselves grounded in relations of both power and moral convention. Moral inquiry about responsibility can be enhanced by reconstructing the concept of moral responsibility historically and as part of our practical judgments. It also can be deepened by bringing the virtues of moral philosophy—its conceptual rigor and focus on principle—together with the worldly and theoretical knowledge that historians, sociologists, and political theorists have to contribute to the study of ethics and public affairs.

4

Moral confidence: Three cheers for naturalized ethics

OWEN FLANAGAN

The question I address is this: how do the human sciences, generally, and moral psychology, in particular, matter to moral philosophy? The question assumes that they do matter to each other since it asks *how* not *whether*. This assumption will be challenged by those who believe in "Kant's Dogma," the doctrine that normative ethics and what Kant called "philosophical anthropology" should not be mixed.

The chapter indicates some of the reasons for rejecting Kant's dogma and shows some of the gains that can be had by ignoring the prohibition of mixing the descriptive and normative. The discussion ranges over much terrain. I try to keep it centered by continually returning to one example: *moral confidence*. Confidence is a psychological attitude, and moral confidence is one kind of confidence. I claim that often the most sensible attitude to have toward one's overall moral conception, one's moral aims, acts, aspirations, motives, and reasons, is an attitude of unconfident confidence. This is a normative claim, but the argument for it involves deploying and interweaving resources from philosophy and the human sciences. Furthermore, the normative claim is a claim about what sort of psychological attitude we ought to adopt. There is, I think, no way to characterize the discussion or the claim as purely normative or purely psychological.

The chapter has three parts. The first part is a narrative, partly autobiographical, about what, as a Roman Catholic and as a budding professional philosopher, I learned or was taught about the nature of morality. The second part addresses what we can learn from realistic, empirical psychological work. The final part shows the importance of a more general sort of reflection, a blend of cultural criticism, philosophical psychology, and social theory.

A VERY SHORT HISTORY OF ETHICS

The Catechism was good. It had questions and it had answers. Answers you could memorize. Answers you could believe in. But its appeal waned for many of us Roman Catholic kids when puberty hit. Disenchantment with the transcendental, the Trinity, and transubstantiation, as well as with a neat and tidy moral universe, had its benefits and its costs. On the one hand, it felt good to be over certain superstitions. On the other hand, since I had little understanding of how morality was possible without theological foundations, I felt as if I was pulling the rug out from underneath myself.

In college I discovered philosophy and with it the prospect of an alternative to God's morality. Philosophy seemed extremely irreverent to me—openly antireligious, if one read Hume and Nietzsche; secularist, if one read Plato, Aristotle, Mill, even Kant. But at the same time that philosophy seemed irreverent, it was morally serious. Irreverence combined with moral seriousness had tremendous appeal.

Reading Dostoevsky and Nietzsche showed me a way around moral nihilism. It may be that God is dead, and it may be that if there is no God, then everything is allowed. But from the fact that everything is allowed, it does not follow that everything is equally acceptable, let alone decent or good. Some action is "allowed," in my sense of the term if, in fact, it can be done—if it is not logically or physically impossible— and there are no theological grounds for declaring the action wrong. Being allowed is not equivalent to being acceptable because there might be some other basis than theology for finding an allowable action unacceptable, wrong, or indecent. The action might, for example, harm an individual's own character or harm other people, even if there is no "God's-eye-point-of view" from which it is deemed wrong. Moral seriousness was not, I came to see, incompatible with a secular, even an antireligious, metaphysics and epistemology. Furthermore, Mill and Kant, devoted as they were to the project of grounding morality in reason, afforded me the possibility that nonreligious moral foundations were conceivable.

The project of the Enlightenment, the project exemplified by Mill and Kant and dedicated to discovering the right foundational moral principle, resonated more than a little with, what I suspected, was a rather typical impulse for a former Roman Catholic. Like the Catechism, the

Enlightenment project, would, if it succeeded, provide grounds for moral confidence, but this time *without* God. The Enlightenment motto might, I thought, be put this way: what is moral is rational and what is rational is moral (or, at least, not immoral). Religion was out of the equation altogether.

I went to graduate school in 1971 and had my short-lived hopes for the success of the project of the Enlightenment dashed. I read A. J. Ayer's *Language, Truth, and Logic* in a first-year metaphysics course and was impressed by his argument that normative ethics, despite Enlightenment pretenses, was not a rational enterprise—at least not in the relevant sense of "rational."[1] In the hands of the positivists for whom Ayer spoke, the project of providing a rational foundation for ethics was misguided. Moral judgments are just (disguised) emotional responses, and so the argument went, make no rational or cognitive claims.

Ethical discourse—why people say normative things—was ripe for analysis, but it was analysis to be done by linguistic philosophy, psychology, sociology, and the rest of the human sciences. Causal, interpretive, and deconstructive analyses made sense, but the pure philosophical project of grounding morality in reason did not.

According to the emotivists, when people speak of what someone (or some group) ought to do, they are doing something akin to rooting for their home team and trying to influence the other fans to cheer along, or to get the guy at bat to get a clutch hit. Rooting for your home team is normally okay, and it is easy to explain why one does so. But the explanation will hardly appeal to rational causes. Rooting for a sports team is a parochial practice par excellence. The practice is reasonable, not rational. Still, the world works out okay given rooting practices, and little harm is done by sports fans (soccer aside). The causes of fanhood are radically contingent in a way most people understand: "I was born in Boston and I love the Red Sox. Of course, if I were a New Yorker, I would hate the Red Sox."

It would be misleading if I were to give the impression that emotivism implied moral nihilism or a disregard for human welfare or ethical lassitude, as if one can no more dispute ethical beliefs and practices than one can (certain) tastes or rooting practices. Emotivists were well aware that great harm could be done by people with vicious ideas, es-

[1] A. J. Ayer, *Language, Truth, and Logic*, 2d ed. (New York: Dover, 1948).

pecially people with power. Indeed, the positivists' project of demarcation—the project of finding a criterion to distinguish science from
pseudoscience—was in part motivated by the horror of Nazi doctrines
of Aryan superiority. Emotivism was one result of this morally serious
project. The emotivists thought that unreflective rooting for one's ethnic
group or nation-state was as nonrational as all other kinds of unreflective rooting, but much more harmful. Furthermore, certain things
judged good or bad are so judged for sound, defensible reasons. Sometimes one can say *why* a certain kind of action is good or bad, right or
wrong, where the reason goes beyond the merely parochial. Or, as is often the case with rooting in sports, one can accept the parochiality but
point out that as a matter of empirical fact, rooting for the home team
produces little harm and much good (for example, feelings of community solidarity). Similarly, on the moral side, one can sensibly claim that
killing is (usually) wrong because it thwarts a normal, basic desire that
all persons have. A society that did not make "thou shall not kill" a basic commandment would produce a citizenry that had difficulties with
social coordination and psychological health. Similarly, lying is (usually) bad because it undermines social coordination, something rational
persons—for example, persons operating according to a principle of enlightened self-interest—should favor. Other sorts of evils involve
measurable harms perpetrated by people who claim justification from
science but whose claims are in fact pseudoscientific (for example, proponents of Aryan superiority).

This room for making reasoned judgments about value and worth
within an emotivist framework is often underestimated. One cause for
this underestimation lurks in taking too literally and too far the analogy
I have been pushing between rooting in sports and favoring a certain
ethical code. If I am a fan of both the Red Sox and of Judeo-Christian
morality, there is, I think, a legitimate prima facie presumption that my
fanhood in both cases is largely based on certain contingent causes that
in themselves do not, indeed could not, rationalize my loyalties.
However, once I am a fan of a particular baseball team, there are questions open to rational discussion: Does the team have strong pitching?
Is the team well coached? And so on. The same thing goes for the ethical
case. I favor Judeo-Christian morality in the first instance, one might
say, simply because of the way I was raised. But once that is conceded,
one can ask of each and every aspect of the moral code: Is it a
good idea? Does it make sense? What is the rationale behind a partic-

ular moral recommendation or prohibition? Once one sees the burden as that of providing reasons for the moral code one favors, of giving reasons for the emotional attitudes one has, the prospect arises that while certain aspects of the code can be rationalized, others cannot. Emotivism allowed for the prospect that any moral code might receive a mixed verdict. And so it seemed with the moral code I had learned as a youngster.

I was deeply attracted to this emotivist view, as deeply attracted as I was to the Enlightenment project to which it served as counterpoint. Having grown up Catholic, I was easy prey for the view that nuns and priests—and sometimes even my parents—were often thoughtless cheerleaders for a strange and mean-spirited form of life. In addition, by the early 1970s it did seem that moral rhetoric was impotent, at least as far as ending the Vietnam War went.

The emotivist view also helped me answer a question I had kept hush-hush about during the under-the-desk air raid drills in grammar school in the late 1950s and early 1960s. Why were we so sure of our form of life that we would consider annihilating the Soviets and they us? Communism even sounded economically just—"golden rulish" to me. Until the Cuban missile crisis, when I lost respect for politicians and grown-ups generally, I was sure that I was missing something really important. The cold war, hot as it was at times, seemed to me even as a youngster to be too ethnocentric to make sense, let alone to carry moral weight. Perhaps rooting in sports is explicable and benign, but rooting for nations or one's own group, despite being explicable in pretty much the same way, seemed vicious.

As I have said, moral nihilism held no appeal. Just as I had read Nietzsche in a way that avoided nihilism—God is dead, everything is allowed, but not everything is equally worthy or noble or good—so I had read the emotivists in a similar way—morality may consist of expressions of feelings, but certain feelings are better suited than others to certain situations.

The difference between Enlightenment foundationalism, on the one hand, and the Nietzschean and emotivist views, on the other, was that the first promised a formula, a general-purpose algorithm to guide all moral thought and action, while the second offered no such security blanket. One ought to be morally serious, but there were no algorithms to guide one to the right answers.

I do not want to claim that my philosophical education was typical.

But I also do not think it was atypical. At Boston University where I received my Ph.D., we read Alasdair MacIntyre's *A Short History of Ethics* to pass our ethics qualifying exam.[2] MacIntyre was on the faculty, and his own historicism and critique of the Enlightenment project promoted among me and my peers an attitude that steered most of us away from doing ethics. MacIntyre historicized emotivism as well as the Enlightenment. Roughly speaking, emotivism was for him a response to, or an analysis of, the ubiquitous and interminable moral disagreements that color our time; emotivism happens when there is no agreement about basics. This was only mildly consoling. MacIntyre's brilliant analyses left me, like many of my peers, not knowing which way was up.

Within the philosophical profession at that time, the early to mid-1970s, historicizing every ethical tradition was tantamount to showing that morals were relative and that the project of making ethics a pure and systematic science (as Kant hoped) was not in the cards. MacIntyre saw the possibility of nonfoundationalist, historicist, morally serious ethics. But few philosophers then shared his vision. To put matters simply, it was standard to believe that either the foundationalist project of the Enlightenment would succeed, or we would be left at worst with moral relativism, skepticism, and nihilism, and at best with something like the morally serious attitude of Nietzsche and sophisticated emotivism, which would lead to nothing systematic and thus nothing distinctively philosophical in normative ethics. If there was no prospect for a timeless ethical conception, then there was nothing in particular for *professional* ethicists to do. This was, I think, part of MacIntyre's message. But it took a while for the message and its meaning to sink in. I do not mean to suggest that MacIntyre did not think that there was lots of work to be done in ethics. It was just that if the project of *professional* ethicists was conceived along Enlightenment lines, as the project of finding *the* correct moral theory, *the* right general-purpose algorithm that could govern moral thought and action across all places and times, then professional ethicists—those trained up with Enlightenment aspirations—were committed to a project that was just not going to succeed.

Within academic philosophy John Rawls's 1971 book, *A Theory of Justice*, marked the articulation of nonemotivist political theory.[3] Rawls

---

[2] Alasdair MacIntyre, *A Short History of Ethics* (New York: Macmillan, 1966).
[3] John Rawls, *A Theory of Justice* (Cambridge, Mass.: Harvard University Press, 1971).

provided a persuasive argument that certain ethical and political claims can be rationally vindicated. Initially, the theory of justice looked like a major success for the project of the Enlightenment even if only in the domain of justice. Yet more recently Rawls himself has made clear that his project does not succeed, nor is it intended to succeed, in the way the project of the Enlightenment was supposed to, that is, foundationally. Rawls provides no culturally universal theory of justice. Rather, he offers a reconstruction of the foundations and rationale for the principles already accepted in the abstract by citizens of liberal democracies such as Sweden and the United States—a sort of *local knowledge*.

Rawls's concession that his theory of justice is a rational reconstruction of the implicit views held in the abstract in certain developed Western democracies is to concede MacIntyre's main point about the cultural relativity of moral and political conceptions. Although Rawls admires liberalism and MacIntyre does not, neither of them believes that the historically specific rationale for a particular moral or political conception poses the slightest obstacle to reasoned debate about the merits of that particular conception.

One might take the history of moral and political philosophy after Rawls as an effort to conceive of the ethical enterprise as situated somewhere between the Enlightenment (that is, rationalist) and emotivist poles. In the work of Alasdair MacIntyre, Bernard Williams, and Richard Rorty, one sees allergies to Enlightenment theories that claim to provide objective ground for some single moral theory *and* one notes a rejection of a simple emotivism, of the view that we cannot speak rationally about our moral and political commitments.[4]

---

[4] Alasdair C. MacIntyre, *After Virtue: A Study in Moral Theory* (Notre Dame: University of Notre Dame Press, 1981); Bernard Williams, *Ethics and the Limits of Philosophy* (Cambridge, Mass.: Harvard University Press, 1985); Richard Rorty, *Contingency, Irony, and Solidarity* (Cambridge: Cambridge University Press, 1989). And in the work of philosophers such as Allan Gibbard and Simon Blackburn, one sees a defense of *expressivism* and *quasirealism*. Their views lie somewhere between the Enlightenment idea that ethical statements are cognitive in every respect or that they are cognitive in no respects *and* the view that the universe contains moral properties in the way it contains atoms or that it contains no moral properties. See Allan Gibbard, *Wise Choices, Apt Feelings* (Cambridge, Mass.: Harvard University Press, 1990); and Simon Blackburn, *Spreading the Word: Groundings in the Philosophy of Language* (Oxford: Clarendon Press, 1984). Moral statements have descriptive-expressive-emotive-imperatival properties (as did my "The cat is on the mat" when you were stepping on her tail!) and there are patterns in the world that our moral judgments are aimed at detecting, but these patterns are complex—not as simple as the patterns expressed in statements like "Trees exist," but no more odd than statements like "Learning to read and write is good" or than "Picasso's *Guernica* is better than any of my paintings." Some value judgments are

Despite these developments in moral philosophy, Kant's dogma, the dogma that ethics should be purely rational, a priori, non-theological—hardly budged. Kant's personal position was in tension with his dogmatic expectation that a nontheological foundation to morality could be discovered. Despite his commitment to the project of the Enlightenment, Kant believed in God, the God of pietistic Lutheranism. And he believed that God was the ultimate source of morality. Kant's key insight was that disagreement about theological details could be circumvented so long as God had given human beings a faculty of pure practical reason with which to discover the right moral principle—and indeed God had. Kantian morality was secular without being naturalistic.

Indeed, as I said at the start, thanks (or no thanks) to Kant, the dominant conception of the intellectual division of labor continues to make a sharp distinction between moral philosophy and moral psychology. Moral philosophy is in the business of saying what ought to be, what is really right and wrong, good and evil, what the proper moral principles and rules are, what counts as genuine moral motivation, and what types of persons count as genuinely good. Most importantly, the job of moral philosophy is to provide philosophical justification for its shoulds and oughts, for its principles and its rules.

Moral psychology, what Kant called the "empirical side of morals," might tell us what people think ought to be done, what they believe is right or wrong, what they think makes a good person, and so on. But all the psychological facts taken together, including those that are widely and strongly believed, could never justify any of these views. Mottoes abound to express the basic idea: one cannot make inferences from "is" to "ought"; one cannot derive values from facts. The empirical tells us what is the case; the normative tells us what ought to be the case.

In *The Groundwork to the Metaphysics of Morals*, Kant writes that a "worse service cannot be rendered morality than that an attempt be made to derive it from examples."[5] Trying to derive ethical principles "from the disgusting mishmash" of psychological, sociological, or anthropological observations, from the insights about human nature that abound "in the chit-chat of daily life" and that delight "the multitude" and upon which "the empty headed regale themselves," is not the right

---

"apt," to use Gibbard's word, and can be conversationally vindicated; other value judgments are not apt and have little to be said in their favor.

[5] Immanuel Kant, *The Groundwork to the Metaphysics of Morals*, trans. H. J. Paton (New York: Harper and Row, 1964).

way to do moral philosophy. What then is the right way? According to Kant, we need "a completely isolated metaphysics of morals," a pure ethics unmixed with the empirical study of human nature.[6] Once moral philosophy has derived the principles that ought to govern the wills of all rational beings, then and only then should we seek "the extremely rare merit of a truly philosophical popularity."[7]

EMPIRICAL PSYCHOLOGY

To my generation of philosophers, worries about the alleged naturalistic fallacies (attempting to derive "ought from is" and attempting to define "good") helped increase the impression that Kant's dogma expressed some deep and timeless truth. In fact, Kant's dogma articulates no long-standing philosophical consensus. Indeed, the sharp separation of ethics from reflection on human nature is not respected by the great moralists from Plato and Aristotle to Hume and Smith.[8] Nonetheless, the sharp separation of the normative from the empirical has dominated philosophical thought since Kant. Furthermore, one can see the appeal of Kant's dogma. Just as grounding morals in God would warrant moral confidence, so would grounding it in a (God-given) faculty of pure practical reason. But looking for the right moral principles in the practices and conventions of real historical people seems arbitrary and insubstantial.

Enter Lawrence Kohlberg. There was, Kohlberg claimed in several papers published in the 1970s, a way to get from "is" to "ought," a way to commit the naturalistic fallacy and get away with it. Kohlberg claimed to have discovered *empirically* the "highest stage" of moral development. Furthermore, by happy coincidence, the highest stage coincided with Kant's categorical imperative, Rawls's theory of justice, and Jesus's golden rule.[9]

Kohlberg, who was involved during and after the Second World War with delivering Jews to Palestine, was no naïf about conventional mo-

---

[6] Ibid., 408–10.
[7] Ibid., 409.
[8] Alasdair MacIntyre, "How Moral Agents Became Ghosts: Or, Why the History of Ethics Diverged from that of the Philosophy of Mind," *Synthese* 53 (1982): 295–312.
[9] Lawrence Kohlberg, *Essays on Moral Development: The Philosophy of Moral Development: Moral Stages and the Idea of Justice* (San Francisco: Harper and Row, 1981); and *Essays on Moral Development: The Psychology of Moral Development: The Nature and Validity of Moral Stages* (San Francisco: Harper and Row, 1984).

rality. Like many thinkers of his generation, Kohlberg was in some measure motivated by these questions: How was the Holocaust possible?
How could seemingly decent people come to think and behave in such
horrid ways? The Holocaust seemed to prove that there was, just as
Kant had said, no credible way to take ordinary ways of moral thinking,
distill their essence, and claim to have discovered what is right and good.

Still, Kohlberg thought, there was a way of being a Kantian without
accepting Kant's dogma. Here Plato held the key. When Plato's teacher
Socrates plays gadfly, it is conventional morality, the thoughtless morality of the multitude, that is his target. The Sophists take conventional
morality *as* morality. But Plato through the voice of Socrates rejects the
equation of the conventional with the moral and suggests instead that
the morally good be viewed in terms of the insights of only a few, the
philosopher kings. The few, who have seen the good, have reason to
be confident and stand their ground against the moral views of the
multitude.

It is a virtue of Kohlberg's attempt to draw normative ethics and
moral psychology back together that he does not take statistical normativity as the measure of appropriate or ideal ethical norms. Had he
done so, then the "conventional" stages in his six-stage scheme (stages
3 and 4), by virtue of being most common, would be set out as normative ideals. But this is not the case. Kohlberg elaborated a six-stage
scheme of moral development with "postconventional" morality (stages
5 and 6) as the ideal.

In broad strokes Kohlberg's stage theory runs as follows. Stage one
is a stage of naive moral realism. Rules are objectively authoritative, and
one abides by them because it is in one's self-interest to do so. Stage two
involves a shift in perspective: moral rules are ways groups of individuals
collectively get ahead and live in an orderly manner without conflict. It
is in one's interest as a member of a group to abide by moral rules.
Whereas punishment for rule breaking has greatest saliency at stage one,
stage two reasoners start to see some of the merits in moral rule conformity. Beyond these two stages, there are four more. Stage three involves local conventionalism, doing what one's family, neighborhood,
and group expect. Stage four has a wider social-contract orientation:
what is right and good is what society at large has determined is right
and good and what will maintain order, social welfare, and the like.

Kohlberg designated the first two stages, preconventional, and stages
three and four as conventional. Stages five and six are postconventional

in the following straightforward respect. At stage five one is a utilitarian willing to violate convention for the greater good. At stage six one is also willing to violate convention, but one abides by the categorical imperative rather than the principle of utility. The sorts of conventions one will violate at this stage are ones that show disrespect for persons (for example, racist practices). At stage five one might favor the death penalty because of belief in its deterrent effects, whereas at stage six respect for persons as ends will lead one to oppose the death penalty. (I use the example because the death penalty is one of the few substantive examples Kohlberg gives of where stage six reasoning leads.)

Kohlberg was well aware that the order of psychological development did not establish the normative order. Still, certain psychological discoveries and convergences matter to ethics. For example, the fact that most people get stuck at stages three and four explains why conventional morality is dominant. However, since stages five and six are found, even if rarely, across all cultures, they are always available. And because they are judged better than the alternatives by those who have been there (allegedly people always prefer the highest stage they have reached), they are worthy of aspiration. Kohlberg offered empirical data to suggest that the highest moral reasoners are implicit Kantians, not utilitarians; they deliberate deontologically rather than consequentially. They are completely impartial and go behind a veil of ignorance for each and every moral decision (something not even Rawls recommended). The question of who one is, or how one is situated in relation to the others involved in some moral episode, is disregarded.

Despite the continued dominance of stage theory among moral educators, the theory itself is coming undone.[10] There are several reasons for this. First, moral stage theory does not allow regression, but evidence for regression abounds. People reason and act in self-serving ways. This

---

[10] In most schools of education in North America, as well as in psychology departments, Kohlberg's theory, usually supplemented by discussion of Carol Gilligan's critique, continues to dominate what is taught under the rubric of "moral psychology." There are two main reasons for this. First, Kohlberg suggested many credible strategies for getting children and teenagers to talk about real-life moral problems. (Most of these strategies can be retained even if his overall stage theory is rejected.) Second, North Americans have long seen a need for moral education in public schools but no way to engage in such education without violating the separation of church and state. Kohlberg's theory promoted the main insights of the favored liberal version of Judeo-Christian morality. Kohlberg often mentions the convergence of his highest stage, the stage depicted in the writings of Kant and Rawls, with thinking in accordance with the golden rule—without in any way bringing religion as such into the picture.

is true even when they have previously judged hypothetical situations in impersonal terms and predicted that they would act according to those impersonal judgments in real life. Second, under pressure from his colleague and collaborator Carol Gilligan, Kohlberg conceded in the early 1980s that his theory was, at best, a theory of "justice reasoning," and this is a concession that the theory is incomplete.[11]

What sort of confidence should a highest-stage-justice reasoner have once incompleteness is conceded? Perhaps, one should feel extremely confident when one is reasoning about matters of justice, but maybe not. One may be excellent at identifying what is demanded from an impartial point of view on a problem of justice, but real situations present issues not only of justice, but of love, friendship, mercy, and so on.

To make matters worse, Kohlberg's research team revised its scoring manual to get rid of the evidence of regressors. This theoretically motivated revision resulted in the elimination of *all* confirmed cases of stage-six reasoners. This is troubling because it is a premise of the argument for the moral superiority of stage six that people at that stage prefer it to all the others. But if no one is at stage six, there can be no such evidence. With regard to the problem of moral confidence, one consequence of there being no confirmed cases of stage-six reasoners is that no one ought to be confident that he or she reasons at this highest stage, even on narrow problems of justice. This is simply because there is no evidence that any individual on earth reasons at that level.

Fortunately, there is other work in empirical psychology, primarily in social and personality psychology that is important to ethics even though it does not call itself "moral psychology." This work improves on moral stage theory in offering a more realistic assessment of moral activity. According to moral stage theory, moral personality involves a holistic, general-purpose, domain nonspecific style of moral thinking. Moral thinking is done from the perspective of a unified stage, a holistic mini-moral philosophy, as it were. The alternative model conceives of moral personality as involving the complex interpenetration of special-purpose and domain-specific habits of thought, action, and feeling. "Character" or "personality" is a complex structure of what John Dewey described as interpenetrating habits. In normal cases, not all aspects of character are equally well developed. We expect people to be morally consistent,

[11] Carol Gilligan, *In a Different Voice: Psychological Theory and Women's Development* (Cambridge, Mass.: Harvard University Press, 1982).

and thus express surprise when the champion of social justice turns out to be an adulterer. But evidence for moral modularity abounds and cannot be swept under the rug because it violates certain philosophical hopes.[12] The traits that interpenetrate and constitute a character are situation sensitive to a high degree, and the degree to which they interact are individually and culturally specific. Thus, the conception of a virtue as a disposition that steels a person against all temptation or that leads to right action come-what-may is a philosopher's fantasy. There are *no* situation-insensitive traits. None.

Still, personality is composed of global and impenetrable character traits. A person either is courageous or she is not, and if she is, she will be courageous across situations that call for courage, and if she is not, she will be cowardly across these same situations. But the assumptions of trait globality and impenetrability are mistaken.

The evidence for this claim comes from a wide variety of works, but the initial source is the volumes of studies in the nature of character conducted by Hugh Hartshorne and M. A. May in the late 1920s.[13] They found that although there is consistency in self-attribution of moral traits over time, the consistency between self-attribution and behavior is not great (only about 0.3). Hartshorne and May found that most children are dishonest to a moderate degree, and that scrupulous honesty in one context, such as a testing situation, failed to predict behavior in a different context, such as a stealing situation. Subsequent studies have regularly confirmed that consistency persists over time on cognitive measures of intelligence, as well as on self-description along trait dimensions, but not on behavior.

Attribution theory is the area of psychology that studies trait ascription, and it sheds light on the matters under discussion. Three tendencies are relevant to understanding the "logic" of ordinary moral judgment. First, the *Fundamental Attribution Error* (FAE) is the tendency to overestimate the impact of dispositional factors and to underestimate situational ones: "Marie lied to me and said she had no money to lend. She is so *dishonest*." FAE is overridden when there is strong motivation to

---

[12] Owen Flanagan, *Varieties of Moral Personality: Ethics and Psychological Realism* (Cambridge, Mass.: Harvard University Press, 1991).

[13] Hugh Hartshorne and M. A. May, *Studies in the Nature of Character*: vol. 1, *Studies in Deceit* (New York: Macmillan, 1928); vol. 2, *Studies in Self-Control* (New York: Macmillan, 1929); vol. 3, *Studies in the Organization of Character* (New York: Macmillan, 1930).

do so. If Marie is my sister or my true love, then I will speak this way about the very same episode: "Marie said she had no money to lend you because she knows that *you* would use it to buy drugs. In fact, it is true that she has *no money* to lend *you*."

Actor-Observer Divergence (AOD) is the tendency of observers to attribute actions of others to standing dispositions in them, even when in their own case they attribute such actions to situational variables. For example, if one sees someone volunteer to do a job, one will be likely to impute some general trait—the person is generally charitable, generous, or benevolent. In our own case, however, we will cite the specific aspects of the task that are motivationally salient—"I am doing fundraising because it will help the school my kids go to."

The *Self-Serving Bias* (SSB) is what its name implies: when it serves our interests we are more than happy to impute deep-seated and situationally invulnerable traits to ourselves and to dismiss our foibles as owing to external factors. "I am a faithful person. Oh, my infidelity? Well, that was exceptional. They served strong liquor and a Lolita-type caught me off guard."

These tendencies are powerful in ordinary life and lead many philosophers and psychologists to overestimate the power of personality, character, and cognition, and the globality and impenetrability of traits, and to underestimate the power of situations to lead even an apparently stable and resilient character to do surprising things.

Hannah Arendt wrote that "in certain circumstances the most ordinary decent person can become a criminal."[14] The circumstances she had in mind were the structures of everyday life during the Nazi era. T. W. Adorno and his colleagues attempted to find out what sorts of persons are most likely to fall prey to such circumstances.[15] Research using the F-scale (F for fascism) indicated that the following attitudes hang together: conventionalism; a submissive, uncritical attitude toward in-group ideals; punitive and aggressive attitudes toward violation of conventional norms; opposition to the imaginative, subjective, and tender minded; a tendency to think in rigid and stereotyped ways; preoccupation with power and hierarchy; an exaggerated concern with sex and a rigid conception of sex roles; and idealization of one's parents and

---

[14] Hannah Arendt, *Eichmann in Jerusalem: A Report on the Banality of Evil* (New York: Viking, 1963), 253.

[15] T. W. Adorno et al., *The Authoritarian Personality* (New York: Harper and Row, 1950).

oneself (prejudiced persons have more consistently favorable impressions of themselves than do unprejudiced persons). Despite various methodological problems, these results have been generally confirmed.

Work such as this focuses on character types, but the crucial point is that an authoritarian personality will not cause any *major* moral problems until certain circumstances or situations arise. Authoritarian personalities are like nuclear weapons or hand grenades: they are harmless until certain activating conditions occur. What sorts of situations will do the trick? What pulls the pin on an authoritarian personality? Stanley Milgram's studies yielded insight on this matter.[16] He showed that one did not need to plant otherwise decent people in a whole socioeconomic environment gone off the deep end—as was the case in the Nazi era— to get them to act badly. An isolated psychological experiment of the right kind could easily bring about this result.

Milgram studied more than 1,000 subjects during a three-year period (1960–63) until his studies were deemed unethical. Subjects aged twenty to fifty and of various socioeconomic and educational backgrounds were paid to participate in an experiment allegedly designed to examine the effects of punishment on learning. Subjects agreed to administer an electric shock to a person who, by previous arrangement with the psychologist in charge, was to answer only one in four questions accurately. The shock generator consisted of a panel with thirty levers, marked to indicate increasing voltage. Subjects were instructed to move up the voltage ladder thus delivering (they had reason to believe) a more painful shock after each error. Engraved on the panel at various intervals were labels indicating slight shock, moderate, strong, very strong, intense, extreme intensity, danger, and severe shock. The last two levers were simply marked XXX. If during the experiment subjects expressed concern about the welfare of the learner—and virtually all did—the psychologist in charge said, "Please go on." "The experiment requires you to continue." "It is essential that you continue." "You agreed to participate; you must go on."

Across a variety of similar protocols, 65 percent of the subjects went all the way to the top, even though the learner was feigning extreme pain and distress long before they had reached this point. These studies were replicated in a half dozen countries with the same degree of com-

---

[16] Stanley Milgram, *Obedience to Authority: An Experimental View* (New York: Harper and Row, 1974).

pliance and with no gender differences. Furthermore, and perhaps most surprisingly, there were no significant differences on standard personality measures between the maximally obedient subjects and the maximally rebellious subjects.[17]

In the standard Milgram experiment, it is one against one: the experimenter versus the subject. (The confederate makes it two against one, but this is not known by the subject.) If the number of subjects increases, so does the probability of rebellion. In Milgram-like experiments involving groups, rebellion in the face of morally problematic demands is much more likely.[18] In particular, if members of a group are asked to do something morally problematic and are able to share their worries, and if these worries are shared and confirmed, the individuals and group will gain courage and will refuse to do what is found morally objectionable. There is, as they say, strength in numbers. The difficulty is that it is the degree of consensus within the group that matters most; the actual moral quality of the consensus is less important. If the other members of the group tell the worrier that all is well, that she should go along, fulfill her agreement to participate in the study, and so on, then conformism will be more likely.

The experiments discussed so far involve situational variables that one might think of as inherently normative. By this I mean that we are social animals, and we take into account what others think, say, and do, including what they think we should do, when we are trying to decide what to do. The opinions of others deserve at least prima facie respect in one's private moral deliberation. So perhaps moral pressures are a uniquely powerful if ultimately unsurprising source of influence.

This is a plausible notion. But other important experiments show that prima facie non-normative variables—the mundane influences of everyday life—can dramatically affect decency in behavior. For example, in a delightfully mischievous experiment, J. M. Darley and C. D. Batson used as subjects seminarians who were randomly assigned to prepare a short talk on either the parable of the Good Samaritan or the issue of job opportunities for seminary graduates.[19] After organizing their talks

[17] A. C. Elms and Stanley Milgram, "Personality Characteristics Associated with Obedience and Defiance toward Authoritative Command," *Journal of Experimental Research in Personality* 1 (1966): 282–9.

[18] William A. Gamson, Bruce Fireman, and Steven Rytina, *Encounters with Unjust Authority* (Homewood, Ill.: Dorsey, 1982).

[19] J. M. Darley and C. D. Batson, "From Jerusalem to Jericho: A Study of Situational and

in a designated room, the seminarians were sent off to give their speeches. Half of the students in each group were told that they were running late and should hurry to the delivery site. The experimenters planted a student en route who was slumped over in apparent distress, and they then counted the number of seminarians who stopped to help. Not many did. Did stopping to help correspond to the content of the talk they were about to give? Not at all. The only variable of any significance was whether the seminarian was in a rush. The less the subjects were rushed, the more likely they were to help.

Several other tendencies displayed by characters-in-situations bear on realistic thinking about moral life—for example, "In-Group, Out-Group Bias." It is possible to create all the characteristics of ethnocentrism by assigning strangers to groups that are then put into competition. In fact, disdain for the out-group will occur, even in very young children, when the members of the other group are unknown, never seen, and there is no actual competition.[20] It has been suggested that this tendency is related to gaining and maintaining self-esteem and self-confidence. A strong sense of self requires a contrastive case, some other who is not as worthy of esteem, respect, and admiration.

Studies of moral heroes, such as those who resisted the ethical abominations of the Holocaust, again provide results that are surprising for the naively hopeful. Ethical decency usually marks such heroes, but so do characteristics such as adventurousness, strong identification with a morally good parent, and a sense of being socially marginal.[21]

One might think that the "In-Group-Out Group" results, as well as the studies of altruism, are sad if true. But we are animals, not angels, and perfect moral design is not one of the things evolution cares

Dispositional Variables in Helping Behavior," *Journal of Personality and Social Psychology* 27 (1973): 100–8.

[20] Muzafer Sherif et al., *Intergroup Conflict and Cooperation: The Robbers Cave Experiment* (Norman: University of Oklahoma Book Exchange, 1961); Henri Tajfel and J. C Turner, "An Integrative Theory of Social Conflict," in *The Social Psychology of Intergroup Relations*, ed. William G. Austin and Stephen Worchel (Monterey, Calif.: Brooks/Cole, 1979); and Henri Tajfel, *Human Groups and Social Categories* (Cambridge: Cambridge University Press, 1981).

[21] Perry London, "The Rescuers: Motivational Hypotheses about Christians Who Saved Jews from the Nazis," in *Altruism and Helping Behavior*, ed. J. R. Macaulay and L. Berkowitz (New York: Academic Press, 1970); Samuel P. Oliner and Pearl M. Oliner, *The Altruistic Personality: Rescuers of Jews in Nazi Europe* (New York: Free Press, 1988); and Necamah Tec, *When Light Pierced the Darkness: Christian Rescue of Jews in Nazi-Occupied Poland* (Oxford: Oxford University Press, 1986).

about. Human beings have all sorts of countermoral tendencies. But knowledge is power, and knowing where our faults lie, when they are likely to show themselves, allows for greater self-knowledge and for a kind of watchfulness. This empirical research also teaches, it seems to me, that we ought to beware of overconfidence in ourselves. The reason is simple: the research shows that we have tendencies to be overconfident, self-serving, bull-headed, and so on, when we ought not to be. One way to keep such tendencies in check is to beware of over-confidence.

Kant's dogma rests on the assumption that a faculty of pure Reason exists in which and with which we can discover the ideal moral princi-ple—the categorical imperative. No contemporary psychological theory, however, holds that such a faculty exists. This is wise of psychology. But if there is no such faculty, then there is nothing to be found by it or in it.

How then are moral principles and our standards of good character arrived at? One favored source is convention. What is right and good is what consensus says is right and good. This idea is a nonstarter for reasons Socrates, Plato, Kant, and Kohlberg, among many, have tried to explain. Conventional morality shows itself, again and again, to be mor-ally repugnant: anti-Semitic, racist, sexist, homophobic, xenophobic—you name it.

We seem to need higher, more angelic, moral sources. Nonetheless, if there is no faculty of pure practical Reason in which our ethical ideals are to be discovered, then the alternative is empirical, if not conven-tional. The only place to look for moral values is in human life, in the world. Naturalistic methods in ethics require that we attend to empirical psychology. But psychology alone is not enough. Ethical reflection, even empirical ethical reflection, must avail itself of the insights of history, literature, anthropology, sociology, evolutionary biology, indeed all the human sciences, in the difficult task of developing a moral vision and finding a place for the moral in human life.[22]

---

[22] The history of moral philosophy is full of empirical claims that can be tested (but not only by psychology), and the truth or falsity of these claims matters to our moral standards and expectations, to our moral educational practices, and to our ways of assigning responsibility. Here are examples of the empirical claims I have in mind: he who knows the good does it; if one has one virtue one has them all; morality breaks down in a roughly linear fashion with the breakdown of visible social constraints; hu-mans are naturally selfish; humans are naturally altruistic.

PHILOSOPHICAL PSYCHOLOGY

I turn therefore from empirical moral psychology to a more traditional form of philosophical reflection—a form that involves not experiments in the usual sense, but close attention to the actual lives we live, the worlds we inhabit, the virtues and vices, strengths and weaknesses we display. Thus far I have indicated some ways that empirical moral psychology matters to moral philosophy. In this final section I want to show how moral philosophy, philosophical psychology, and cultural criticism matter to moral psychology—how, that is, philosophical reflection in the broadest sense can illuminate the nature of persons, moral agency, and moral life.

From here on I will focus even more resolutely on the issue of moral confidence, the thread I have until now been weaving in and out of the discussion. I will try to describe a type I will call a "confident unconfident" or an "unconfident confident," and suggest some of the ways one gains and maintains confidence in one's moral attitudes, commitments, and actions, while at the same time being a self-conscious fallibilist, and in that way being unconfident.

There are several kinds of confidence. First, there is *self-confidence simpliciter*, or not so simpliciter, which is a state we ascribe to those who exude evidence of the state, as when we say of someone that he is extremely or even supremely self-confident. This can be a general character trait ascription or it can be ascribed to the self-in-a-domain. So we might say of the world's fastest sprinter that he is supremely confident whenever he races—but not say the same about his feelings or demeanor in interpersonal contexts. And of course, the world's fastest sprinter may not be confident in the domain in which he most deserves to be, and it is not clear what this says about him or whether it matters. When we say of some individual that she is supremely self-confident, domain-be-damned, it is not usually a compliment, despite the recognition that this may well be a useful trait for getting ahead in life.

Second, there is confidence *about* the choices one has made or is in the process of making, confidence about one's projects, aims, commitments, relationships, about the direction of one's life. I will call this *project-confidence*. When confidence extends to traits that are central to one's character, to the way one is, the kind of personality one displays, I call this *character-confidence*.

People can be confident about their projects without having even
thought about whether they have the sort of character that might sensibly choose such a project and carry through on it. It seems to me
especially important when contemplating projects whose costs are high
and whose future shape is unclear, that one think about the kind of
person one is. If a certain project, a new open-ended project, makes
sense, it can only be because the person behind the project does. So self-
confidence with respect to one's character and personal capacities is often what brings whatever confidence can be brought to choices in which
the outcomes are obscure. Some risks are worth taking. But when the
future is unclear, and it may be worse than the present (this possibility
always exists), it helps to trust, if not blindly, in oneself. Confidence,
esteem, and respect are great goods, but untempered by self-knowledge
they may lead to a narcissistic void.

Finally, there is confidence about matters unconnected to self, about
who will win the race, about how talented a certain student is, and so on.
This is *confidence about external states of affairs*. Making such judgments
presupposes self-confidence in one's capacity to judge. But when we speak
of confidence in such matters, our interest is focused on the *content* of the
confident judgment, not on qualities of the agent. Furthermore, no significant inferences can be made on the basis of such judgments about self-
confidence or project-confidence, or character-confidence.

The first thing I am inclined to say with conviction is that project-
confidence and character-confidence are more important to us than
self-confidence simpliciter. And I have already said that when it comes
to major changes in projects, character-confidence is important—if for
no other reason than to assure oneself that one is not mad. These types
of confidence often do not coexist in the same person, and all three can
be unwarranted. Self-confidence is a good if warranted, but it is more
of a characterological accessory, nice to have if one can, but much less
important to the meaning of life than project-confidence or the real confidence that one's traits will serve one well in the daunting project of
making a good life. Of course, a person who is confident about the
projects she is pursuing has reason to respect herself. Whether she does,
of course, is a different matter. It should be clear from the discussion so
far that although I think confidence is a good, it is a relative one, and
it needs to be tempered by some other traits—including humility, second
guessing, and content-evaluation.

Pol Pot, the Khmer Rouge leader, was confident. But he was evil. For all I know, Pol Pot may have had both character and project-confidence, which would mean that even these are not remotely sufficient for decency. I suspect this is the case. Others have the right and the good on their side—possibly they are even decent personally—but they are unconfident. Oppressed individuals or groups often suffer from sheepishness, excessive underconfidence, and self-undermining behaviors. Think of the struggles of the civil rights and women's rights movements in America and the behavior of those oppressed by apartheid in South Africa. These are cases where confidence is and was warranted but was not always achieved. The relative success of such movements should not lead us to forget such phenomena as identification with the oppressor or even the more mundane forms of self-effacement that occur when one thinks one might not be doing so well because one is not really worthy.

As governor of Alabama, George Wallace was once very confident about racially segregationist views he now regrets. It is hard to know whether Wallace suffered culturally contagious blindsight that caused him not to see one side of the field of play and to be overconfident about the goodness of certain policies, or whether he was a racist who worked at his racism. (He was surely the former but possibly not the latter.) Perhaps Wallace was something other than confident. Maybe he was running scared and, in fact, lacked confidence in his views—a case of reaction formation. My own amateurish view is that Wallace did not think about his character, although he thought obsessively about how he appeared and even about integrity. (Integrity, Rawls rightly says, is a virtue of form, not substance.) Character is more than this—more of what? I am not sure how to put it (in fact I don't know). If Wallace's story is as he says, if he has learned to abhor racism, he is still a sorry emblem of horrible social forces, but possibly less culpable because he had reasons, bad as they were, confidently to believe the intra- and interpersonally ruinous things that he once did.

Oliver North of Iran-Contra fame has self-confidence simpliciter as well as character- and project-confidence. So what went wrong? He has bad values as well as bad, or at least incomplete, ways of assessing his character, and problematic ways of assessing his actions. North was and is overconfident across the board. These in my opinion are the worst kinds of people. His case feeds a suspicion that self-confidence domain-be-damned is really dangerous.

Robert McNamara, former U.S. secretary of defense, claims not *ever* to have been confident about what we used to call "McNamara's war." McNamara was not confident, or so he says, about the possibilities of American military victory in Vietnam, the normative justification of the war, or the horrors of South East Asian communism.

Whereas Wallace was once confident about means and ends and now claims to have been wrong—to have had grounds at the time to be unconfident about both, grounds that he did not or could not see— McNamara now reports that he was unconfident about means and ends at the time. Both cases remind us of the difficulties with first-person authority. I prefer that McNamara's case be one of hindsight rather than blindsight for there is more blood on his hands if he knew but did not say. Still, he did worry about his character, and for McNamara his character-confidence depended on doing his job, and his job involved accepting a certain place in the chain of command—a place that involved being silent at key points. Thinking about real-life cases such as these can be helpful, but they point up the fact that there are no formal algorithms for thinking about one's character and projects, no way to guarantee that one gets things right.

In understanding better the character of the "confident unconfident" I am sketching, it will help to consider two general attitudes toward self that dominate recent philosophical discussion: that of the strong evaluator and that of the ironist. This is not because these are the only options or even my favorite options—although I find both deeply attractive—but because much can be said in their favor. I have always wondered about combining seemingly contradictory attitudes—playing "attitude tennis" with oneself. Integration may be an overrated virtue if it entails a single method for self-reflection and self-scrutiny.

Charles Taylor argues that the capacity for strong evaluation is a necessary feature of persons. He writes that "the capacity for strong evaluation is essential to our notion of the human subject. . . . Without it an agent would lack a kind of depth we consider essential to humanity."[23] This argument originates with Harry Frankfurt. For Frankfurt, "someone has a desire of the second order either when he wants simply to have a certain desire or when he wants a certain desire to be

---

[23] Charles Taylor, "What Is Human Agency?" in Charles Taylor, *Philosophy and the Human Sciences: Philosophical Papers*, vol. 2 (Cambridge: Cambridge University Press, 1985), 28.

his will."[24] When a person constructs or acts upon second-order volitions, she has satisfied the conditions "essential to being a person."[25]
The typical case is one in which if I have a desire to have a certain
desire, it is because I am trying to affect or adjust my motivational tendencies. Suppose I have a desire to go drinking with my pals, but wish
that I did not have this desire. I want not to want to go drinking with
my pals because I want to have the strength of will to prevent me from
going drinking with them, or to prevent me from going drinking, period.
The aim of the game is to develop one's character in such a way that
one's reflective second-order volitions win out when it comes to action.
When second-order volitions are impotent in the face of first-order volitions, we think of ourselves as suffering weakness of will, of yielding
to temptation.

Taylor's conception of weak and strong evaluation develops Frankfurt's argument in the following way. A weak evaluator satisfies two
conditions. First, the weak evaluator has a set, possibly an ever-changing
set, of first-order desires. Second, the weak evaluator evaluates his desires in terms of quantitative saliencies. The lion faced with two equally
easy kills—an elk and a giraffe—will calculate which is tastier. Lions
also perhaps schedule desires in certain sequences: now it is time to eat,
now to drink, now to sleep.

The strong evaluator differs from the weak evaluator in that she is
concerned with the quality of her desires, her commitments, and her
plans. Indeed, she is concerned with the quality of her character, her
reason, and her will. It is distinctive of persons that they are, or at least
can be, strong evaluators. The lion, being a weak evaluator, takes her
desires for granted. A person who is a strong evaluator understands that
desires can be evaluated in terms of their value, their worth. She does
so with the aim of creating a character that is not merely self-governing,
but self-governing in light of the highest standards, or at least high
standards.

What sort of qualities matter to the strong evaluator? The strong
evaluator is concerned that her desires, commitments, plans, and character satisfy high ethical or spiritual standards. She evaluates her desires,

---

[24] Harry G. Frankfurt, "Freedom of the Will and the Concept of a Person," in *The Importance of What We Care About—Philosophical Essays* (Cambridge: Cambridge University Press, 1988), 16.
[25] Ibid.

commitments, plans, and character in terms of categories such as "nobility" and "worth." What makes her evaluation strong is that she engages systematically in moral inspection.

Furthermore, strong evaluation involves depth. The lion being a weak evaluator evaluates along a single vertical dimension. For the lion faced with the choice of eating the elk or the giraffe, the tastiest alternative is chosen. The person who is a strong evaluator evaluates competing desires vertically and horizontally. Faced with the lion's choice, the hungry strong evaluator may seek a third option, neither elk nor giraffe. The strong evaluator might consider, for example, the question of the moral status of nonhuman animals. Perhaps she will eat mushrooms instead. In assessing situations in this way, the strong evaluator moves to a level beneath and behind the field of play to considerations and principles that recast the field.

Strong evaluation is distinguished from weak evaluation not because it involves second-order desires, nor because it involves qualitative assessment at the second level, nor because it involves assessment from the perspective of long-standing life plans, nor even because it involves depth. Gustav Mahler had depth. Oscar Schindler had very limited depth. Andy Warhol, Edvard Munch, Pablo Picasso, George Eliot, and Virginia Woolf had depth, and so did Janis Joplin. I will let you put them on the right list: strong or weak evaluators? Taylor is onto something, but his universalist and essentialist claims are odd. We are not all strong evaluators. It is not part of the nature of personhood that one often, let alone always, engages in strong evaluation.

The strong evaluator assesses his or her motives, desires, projects, and plans in terms of normative categories that are centered on the ethical. The strong evaluator is *moralistic*—possibly, but not necessarily, decent or good. Pol Pot was a strong evaluator, so perhaps were Hitler and Mussolini. Bill Clinton perhaps is not, but Jimmy Carter was and is.

It is curious that Charles Taylor, the greatest defender of strong evaluation as a sort of confidence-securing technique, ends up experiencing moral vertigo at the end of his *Sources of the Self*.[26] He writes that high moral standards need "strong sources," and he worries that none are available. Commitment to human rights, and the protection of the environment, to justice and benevolence, to truth, to gay rights, opposition to racism and sexism, and so on, can pass strong evaluation if we stick

---

[26] Charles Taylor, *Sources of the Self* (Cambridge, Mass.: Harvard University Press, 1989).

to the requirement that credible judgments of worth can be made. What they cannot pass are skeptical challenges. Judgments of nobility and worth do not take one to self-evident foundations.

Taylor ends *Sources* hoping that God, the God of Christianity, can do the rest. This is odd, and one could treat it as an aberration, for strong evaluation need not be a foundationalist attitude. But then again Taylor's own fall is telling, for it encourages a suspicion I have: strong evaluation may be a good attitude to adopt sometimes, but it does not contain a principle telling us when reflection has gone deep enough. Is the strong evaluator allowed to stop self-scrutiny because she is getting mental cramps having passed from things that can be said with some assurance to things that are mixed up and unclear? If not, the place Taylor ends up is inevitable. The strong evaluative attitude certainly seems like a good thing in many respects. It involves evaluative serious-ness. But interpreted one way the attitude is too demanding. It engenders moral self-indulgence and offers no hope of ending up in a state of reflective security.

The second attitude that interests me is that of the "ironist." One virtue of "ironism" is that it provides a rationale for quitting the Sisy-phean job of requiring everything to pass strong evaluative muster. Rich-ard Rorty defines a "final vocabulary" as the "set of words" we use to "justify" our actions, beliefs, and lives. He then characterizes an "iro-nist" as someone who fulfills three conditions: "(1) She has radical and continuing doubts about the final vocabulary she currently uses, because she has been impressed by other vocabularies, vocabularies taken as final by people or books she has encountered; (2) she realizes that argument phrased in her current vocabulary can neither underwrite nor dissolve these doubts; (3) insofar as she philosophizes about her situation, she does not think that her vocabulary is closer to reality than others, that it is in touch with a power not herself." The main point is that a final vocabulary is not the one that "puts all doubt to rest."[27]

The ironist relishes and is amused by contingency, including the con-tingency of her character, aspirations, and projects. She is not confident that her final vocabulary has things right. Indeed, she is confident that it does not. She is too much of a historicist to think otherwise. She is a confident unconfident. I like her. Why? Because she is a realist, and

[27] Richard Rorty, *Contingency, Irony, and Solidarity* (Cambridge: Cambridge University Press, 1989), 73, 75.

realism is a form of authenticity, and authenticity seems to turn out—
on the strong evaluation story, as well as all others—to be good, better
at any rate than the alternative.

Bernard Williams, more than anyone else, has pushed the idea that
reflection can undermine confidence. If I am right so far, we can see how
commitment to strong evaluation can do so. Ironism, however, is not so
much a confidence-undermining attitude as it is an attitude adopted by
individuals already convinced of their contingency. They are convinced
as well of the fact that the ways they think things through, distinguish
the ethical from the rest of life, are so much contrivance—possibly wise,
useful, and well-motivated contrivance but contrivance nonetheless, and
something that may well be found laughable in another time and place.

Some doubt that an ironist could be serious and comic at the same
time. I do not see why not. An ironist seems like a natural to occupy
this space I admire—the space of the "confident unconfident." But it is
worth arguing about. Do so if you wish. The ironist is reflective, she is
a virtuoso of playing mirrors off against herself, of saying "right . . . but
then again." Or, "I am going ahead in this way, there's more to be said,
and some of that more will undermine my present confidence in going
ahead in this way, but there is not world enough and time. So here I
stand."

Before I proceed further, I want to spend a moment on the apparent
contradiction between teaching stable values to the young and passing
on to them the destabilizing attitudes of reflection and ironism that I
have been recommending. There are issues of hypocrisy and paternalism
at stake, and there are issues about learning things on one's own—joining the secret society when and if one is ready—and about when it is,
as the psychologists say, "developmentally appropriate" to learn certain
things. Here are two passages that pose the problem I am worried about
pretty clearly.

Richard Rorty writes:

Even if I am right in thinking that a liberal culture whose public rhetoric is
nominalist and historicist is both possible and desirable, I cannot go on to claim
that there could or ought to be a culture whose public rhetoric is *ironist*. I cannot
imagine a culture which socialized its youth in such a way as to make them
continually dubious about their own process of socialization. Irony seems inherently a private matter.[28]

---

[28] Ibid., 87.

In a similar vein Bernard Williams writes: "To be confident in trying to make sure that future generations shared our values, we would need, it seems to me, not only to be confident in those values—which, if we can achieve it, is a good thing to be—but also convinced that they were objective, which is a misguided thing to be. If we do not have this conviction, then we have reason to stand back from affecting the future, as we have reason to stand back from judging the past. We should not try to seal determinate values into future society." But Williams believes there are also "some positive steps" to take. We will want to transmit our ideals of reflectiveness and free inquiry. And "to our immediate successors, our children at least, we have reason to try to transmit more: it is a mark of our having ethical values that we aim to reproduce them. But this does not affect very determinately what remoter generations will hold."[29]

I think Williams has it more right than Rorty. The ironist who keeps his ironism private reminds one of Nietzsche's peacock who hides his true colors and calls them his pride. I do not see why one cannot convey—quite publicly, and to young people—that contingency, historicism, and the like properly yield reason for avoiding overconfidence. To be sure, there probably are developmental reasons not to teach relativistic, second-guessing, and ironic attitudes to the very young. But I see no reason not to want to make one's children reflective, historicist, anti-essentialist, fallibilist, ironist, relativist, and morally serious all at once.

It seems to me that the overconfidence of adults in their values promotes pompous self-righteousness that is passed on to the young in the form of intolerance, disrespect, and moralistic posturing. What overconfident adults also pass on to their children is resourcelessness, an incapacity to make a decent self and worthwhile life amidst the unexpected contingencies that are bound to come one's way. Adults fail to convey to the young that grown-ups have trouble finding their way. Knowing that we do and then seeing that we go on, sometimes with assurance, sometimes in fear and trembling, willing to bear costs, but always in hope of finding greater good and meaning, seems a good lesson. There will be times when things come apart, times when the center cannot hold. We will be better equipped to maintain self-respect if we have not been deluded into thinking that in the normal course of life,

[29] Bernard Williams, *Ethics and the Limits of Philosophy* (Cambridge, Mass.: Harvard University Press, 1985), 173.

things go smoothly, that those who made the right choices operate with complete confidence.

The Grand Inquisitor lies to his charges in the *Brothers Karamazov* to keep them happy and protect them from the horrible truth that there is no God. Dostoevsky, like Nietzsche, thought that most people cannot bear the truth, cannot bear to see how life goes, how dangerous it is, and how vulnerable one is as the creator of a meaningful life. But I see Dostoevsky and Nietzsche as underestimating persons. If what they say is true, it is a truth that is nevertheless historically conditioned. We could get used to the news. The ironist, it seems to me, is in a good position to see and accept this. The ironist understands that he or she would not be the way he or she is, and would not suffer certain benefits and costs associated with his or her identity, had life not situated him or her in a certain way. For the ironist, seeing that *who* he is is as much a matter of cosmic contingency as *that* he is at all—that he is something rather than nothing—undermines excessive seriousness in self-regard and self-righteousness. It might lead to a healthy acceptance that there are certain things about one's being that are absolutely quirky and contingent and that are best accepted with a wry smile.

Nonetheless, a strong evaluative attitude has much to be said in its favor. One reason for caution in adopting this attitude, however, is that engaging in strong evaluation, subjecting one's traits to strong moral scrutiny, can undermine identity. On the other hand, strong evaluation, assuming one finds a way to put on the evaluative brakes, can help secure self-respect if one's character can pass strong moral inspection. But it can result in loss of self-confidence, character-confidence, and project-confidence if things do not measure up to the high standards a strong evaluator sets, and if one cannot muster the ability to change.

Where does all this leave us? Here is the lesson I am inclined to draw. Think hard about your character and your projects when faced with moral challenges. This will make you as confident as you can be under important, meaning-constituting circumstances. You may not get to be all *that* confident. Still, if you have done this much honest labor, you may have grounds for self-respect.

We are animals who care about value and worth. We are creatures who make complex plans and projects, and develop complex relations with others. Reflection on how to move ahead, to accrue meaning in carrying out our projects and relations, is a daunting task. Risks abound. Some of the stakes are moral ones. The best way to engage ourselves in honest and profitable reflection about the worth of our projects, aims, commitments, and principles is by gaining understanding of our natures—as a kind of animal, *homo sapiens*, and as socially constructed and situated beings, living in times and places that make unique and special demands on us as human beings in general, and as particular individuals. Understanding ourselves and our situations requires realistic reflection using all possible sources of knowledge. There is no credible way to do moral philosophy without making it impure, without, that is, utilizing all the information and insight one can gather from the human sciences, from art, literature, and cultural criticism. Finding our way is hard enough. It would be foolish to make it harder still by requiring adherence to Kant's dogma and looking for moral truth in Pure Reason, and as far from the madding crowd as we can get. This is one thing I think we can be pretty confident about.

5

Fighting (over) words: Speech, power, and the
moral imagination in American history

JANE KAMENSKY

There is no getting away from it: historians traffic in morals. Reconsti-
tuting past worlds—insofar as that is possible—amounts to only part of
what we actually do for a living. For the past, in and of itself, is not
history. Where the past is chaos, history is neat. Where the past lacks
sense and order, history is coherent and linear. Where the past has no
organic boundaries (chronological, geographical, social, cultural), history demarcates eras, nations, classes, and shifting mentalités. Mediating
between the past as lived and history as written, the historian acts as
gatherer and evaluator of evidence, diviner of causes and effects, pro-
nouncer of truths, weaver of stories.[1]

Because her job involves weighing competing claims and assigning
significance, the historian's task is, by necessity, a moral one. The past
merely exists; history makes it *mean* in the present. No one, as cultural
theorist Tzvetan Todorov has recently written, "is content merely to
know the color of Henry IV's horse." When, who, and what are not
enough; we crave to know *why, what for, and who cares*.[2] In their efforts to answer these questions of significance, of meaning, all historians

For their suggestions on earlier versions of this chapter, I would like to thank Richard
Fox, Thomas Haskell, Nancy Cott, Cathy Corman, John Demos, Paul Forman, Martha
Gardner, Jenny Pulsipher, Chris Sterba, Brook Thomas, and all the participants at the May
1995 Woodrow Wilson Center workshop on Moral Inquiry. I have drawn on their wisdom
for much of what differs in the revised version. All errors of fact, judgment, and moral
imagining remain, of course, completely my own.
[1] On the distinction between history as story and history as mere "chronicle," see William
  J. Cronon, "A Place for Stories: Nature, History, and Narrative," *Journal of American
  History* 78 (March 1992): 1347–76.
[2] Tzvetan Todorov, *The Morals of History*, trans. Alyson Waters (Minneapolis: University
  of Minnesota Press, 1995), 90. A narrow focus on facts for their own sake reduces
  history to what David Fischer has called "the antiquarian fallacy"; see David Hackett

from Herodotus to Hayden White have practiced a form of moral inquiry whether they would admit it or not. Seen in this light, the present state of our practice represents no departure. There is no wholesale revival of moral inquiry under way precisely because it never really disappeared.

Which is not to say that there is nothing new under the sun. If the core moral purpose of history has remained more or less constant for the last few millennia, the ways historians have chosen to inhabit their role as arbiters of past meanings have not. The twentieth century alone has witnessed sweeping redefinitions of history's mission. Debate over what might be called the politics of historical scholarship has been especially fierce since the 1960s, when scholars, influenced by the New Left's drive for social justice and human equality, pressed Clio into service for their cause. In so doing, they broadened the purview of "legitimate" inquiry, ensuring that an ever broader array of historical actors—women, members of racial and ethnic minorities, laborers, peasants, children, even animals—would have their own, clearly articulated stories. Building on the work of their Progressive forebears, New Left historians and their descendants advanced a notion of historical scholarship that was not only *inherently* moral, but *explicitly* so. To use the contemporary vernacular, scholars beginning in the tumultuous decade of the 1960s "outed" the moral underpinnings of historical reasoning to a degree that was previously unimaginable.[3]

What changed in the 1960s—probably forever and, I believe, much

Fischer, *Historians' Fallacies: Toward a Logic of Historical Thought* (New York: Harper and Row, 1970), 140–2.

[3] On the long history of the place of morality in historians' definitions of themselves and their enterprise, see Peter Novick, *That Noble Dream: The 'Objectivity Question' and the American Historical Profession* (New York: Cambridge University Press, 1988); and Joyce Appleby, Lynn Hunt, and Margaret Jacobs, *Telling the Truth about History* (New York: Norton, 1994). The search throughout the twentieth century for a middle ground between rigidly "objectivist" and "relativist" positions is explored in James T. Kloppenberg, "Objectivity and Historicism: A Century of American Historical Writing," *American Historical Review* 94 (October 1989): 1011–30, esp. 1017–8; and William H. McNeill, "Mythistory, or Truth, Myth, History, and Historians," *American Historical Review* 91 (February 1986): 3–10. See also Norma Haan et al., eds., *Social Science as Moral Inquiry* (New York: Columbia University Press, 1983), esp. 1–18. In some respects, the angst today's historians bring to this dilemma—a *problematique* reformulated in the new languages of postmodernism and poststructuralism—adds up to a classic case of old wine in new bottles. For a previous generation's gloss on the debate, see John Higham, "Beyond Consensus: The Historian as Moral Critic" (reprinted in *Writing American History: Essays on Modern Scholarship*, Bloomington, Ind.: Indiana University Press, 1970), 138–56.

for the better—was less the moral underpinnings of the historian's enterprise than the language that enacts and describes it. Scholars writing
in the past thirty or so years may talk about racial, social, and gender
equality, but we are still doing more or less what we have always done:
culling the leavings (usually, though not always, written) of yesterday in
order to tell stories that make sense today. Yet if this shift in moral
vocabularies is as much rhetorical as it is substantive, it is nonetheless
hotly contested. As the so-called culture wars of the post-Reagan era
demonstrate with particular force, Americans take their history very seriously indeed. Screeds denouncing the invasion of Clio's empyrean by
a motley and disrespectful crew of Marxists, postmodernists, feminists,
pacifists, atheists, gay rights activists, multiculturalists, and assorted
other "-ists" appear, it often seems, almost daily.[4] In what has become
an increasingly angry debate about the politics of some history, the underlying moral purpose of *all* history is being forgotten.

The tone of the current debate is most unfortunate for several reasons.
First, it represents a needless distraction from the great mass of im
portant work that remains to be done on both the scholarly front and
in the fight for social justice. But more than that, the depiction of
a Manichean struggle between the old history and the new is regrettable because it is fundamentally false. In caricaturing two types of history—the staid, traditional, "factual" sort and the funky, postmodern,
fast-and-loose-with-the-truth variety—the current debate erases abiding
similarities between the two. Whether a given author speaks for Tradition Militant or Postmodernism Unchained, the metamessage of much
of the best current historical writing is the same: history has something
to teach us. The past sheds light on the present, and vice versa. The two
exist, at least insofar as we can apprehend them, in dialogue with each
other.

Gertrude Himmelfarb, a distinguished historian of nineteenth-century
England and one of the most vocal contributors to the conservative po-

---

[4] The debate among scholars is well represented, on the right, by Gertrude Himmelfarb,
On Looking into the Abyss: Untimely Thoughts on Society and Culture (New York:
Knopf, 1994); and Himmelfarb, "Some Reflections on the New History," *American
Historical Review* 94 (June 1989): 661–70. For the postmodernists' side of the story,
see David Harlan, "Intellectual History and the Return of Literature," *American
Historical Review* 94 (June 1989): 581–609. A middle ground is sought by Appleby et
al., *Telling the Truth about History.*

litical scene, says as much in a recent book exploring Victorian solutions to the problem of poverty. The English past, she says, offers lessons for the American present. A healthy dose of Thomas Carlyle's bootstraps reasoning might restore moral order to the blighted cities of the late-twentieth-century United States.[5] If, in the right-wing version, history is supposed to prod the poor from their welfare-dependent complacency, left-leaning scholars make Clio a kinder, gentler liberator. By restoring once silenced voices to the chorus of witnesses to the ages, liberal historians seek a more inclusive version of both past and present. Such an "intellectual stance," Joyce Appleby, Lynn Hunt, and Margaret Jacobs argue, "will promote an ever more democratic society." Much like the supposedly politics-free history advanced by Himmelfarb and other conservatives, the "new" history championed by Appleby and Co. casts its practitioners in the "role of the social critic . . . pointing their research toward moral lessons." This does not imply, as Appleby and her coauthors make clear, that "new" historians take a mechanically "instrumentalist" view of the past, using history "to inflate reputations, deny past cruelties, dispense comfort, and rationalize actions." It means, instead, that we need to recognize the role history plays in the ethical contests of individuals and nations. Paraphrasing Milan Kundera, Appleby, Hunt, and Jacobs leave us with a lofty moral vision: history becomes part of "the struggle of people against power . . . the struggle of memory against forgetting."[6] Could Himmelfarb disagree?

Despite their opposing goals, then, both liberal and conservative ideologues imbue the archival scroungings of historians with moral purpose. History is about significance, both camps say. A usable past—with facts cut to fit a given fashion—may be despised; but so, too, is a *useless* past. Our stories should be, must be, *useful*. On this, if on little else, most historians working in the field today seem to agree. This is the shared conviction, for example, conveyed by the responses of more than

---

[5] Gertrude Himmelfarb, *The De-Moralization of Society: From Victorian Virtues to Modern Values* (New York: Knopf, 1995); see also Himmelfarb, "Queen Victoria Was Right," *USA Today*, 13 March 1995, A15; "The Victorians Get a Bad Rap," *New York Times*, 1 January 1995, A15; and "Re-Moralizing America," *Wall Street Journal*, 7 February 1995, A22. For evidence that politicians took up Himmelfarb's historical call to arms, see Katharine Q. Seelye, "Gingrich Looks to Victorian Age to Cure Today's Social Failings," *New York Times*, 14 March 1995, A19; and Michiko Kakutani, "If Gingrich Only Knew about Victoria's Secret," *New York Times*, 19 March 1995, E5.

[6] Appleby et al., *Telling the Truth about History*, 4, 154, 156, 270.

1,000 professional historians in the United States and elsewhere to a
survey on "The Practice of American History" distributed in June 1993
by the Organization of American Historians. As the compiler of the
survey data summarized, respondents "seemed to derive their greatest
satisfaction from *using the past to make personal connections with the
present.*"[7] Surely this quest for meaning, for connection, is moral inquiry
at its most elemental.

Consensus, then, on one score, at least: historians are in the business
not only of uncovering truth but also of making sense, making meaning,
making morals. Yet we have, as the veritable chasm between Himmelfarb and Appleby suggests, radically different notions of how best to go
about this business. In the remainder of this chapter, I want to sketch
out three routes to significance in contemporary historical scholarship
and then locate my own work within these various traditions. The first
as well as the newest of these modes of practice engages the morality of
history at the level of epistemology, making historians both more present
and more problematic as actors in their own stories. The second form
of inquiry, at once more overtly political and more traditional, explores
the early stirrings of current moral dilemmas. Finally, a third strand
displaces questions of morality from historians to the historical actors
they study by mapping the moral domains of past actors. Despite their
many differences, all of these approaches share the conviction that the
past can be—indeed, must be—brought to bear upon the present. History, the authors of the following works tell us, shows us who we were.
But more than that, it offers glimpses of who we are and, just maybe,
of who we ought to be.

Life in the history business isn't easy these days. Like the proverbial wolf
at the door, the epistemological crises that have shaken the confidence
of other breeds of humanists in recent decades have at last made their
way to our intellectual homes. To many among us, this is a grim realization. Tethered as we are to the real traces of a real past, historians
make famously bad epistemologists. We tend to be a resolutely, even
defiantly, unselfconscious lot. Literary scholars and anthropologists have
long anguished over the role they play in their own scholarly productions. But historians, for the most part, have, in David Harlan's words,

---

[7] David Thelen, "The Practice of American History," *Journal of American History: A
Special Issue* 81 (December 1994): 941, 947, 946; emphasis mine.

"avert[ed] their eyes" as if such issues were "something one should avoid as a matter of intellectual hygiene."[8] Yet it seems, increasingly, that there is no place left for us to hide. Old questions about the nature of the evidence available to us, the possibility of arriving at a universal truth, and the role our own politics plays in our work have metastasized into new and larger doubts about how we write, what we study, and why—about the very essence of who we are.

These are the sorts of meta-historical dilemmas confronted by several recent works that place historians at the center of the dialogue between past and present. It is a brand of moral inquiry that probes the ethics of the relationship between storyteller and story, author and audience, content and form. To what extent ought historians to conceal themselves from their readers, and to what extent *can* we? How can we acknowledge our own role in shaping a given text without betraying our commitment to truth? And what kind of *voice* best suits such tales? Can we meaningfully address the world of Thomas Pynchon in the language of Jane Austen, or must we find some new way of speaking our piece?[9]

Finding such a voice is one of the signal achievements of Robert A. Rosenstone's beautifully written and under-read *Mirror in the Shrine: American Encounters in Meiji Japan*. In an essay that is difficult to relegate to a traditional historical subfield (Is it nineteenth-century American cultural history? Modern Japanese history? The history of imperialism? None of the above?), Rosenstone gropes tentatively and self-consciously toward a textual form that will "move beyond the 'realistic'

---

[8] Harlan, "Intellectual History and the Return of Literature," 583. On historians' lack of awareness of their own philosophical commitments, see Thomas L. Haskell, "The Curious Persistence of Rights Talk in the 'Age of Interpretation,' " *Journal of American History* 74 (December 1987): 984–1012, esp. 985; McNeill, "Mythistory, or Truth, Myth, History, and Historians," 8; Novick, *That Noble Dream*, 15; and Kloppenberg, "Objectivity and Historicism," 1016. On epistemological uncertainty in other disciplines, see, for example, Clifford Geertz's recent memoir, where he quips that the first entry in the index of many a current anthropology text is "anthropology, crisis of." Geertz, *After the Fact: Two Countries, Four Decades, One Anthropologist* (Cambridge, Mass.: Harvard University Press, 1995), 97–8. (It is the ninth entry in Geertz's index, and one of the longest; ibid., 196.)
[9] The current debate on the so-called new narrative history received its opening salvo in Lawrence Stone, "The Revival of Narrative: Reflections on a New Old History," *Past and Present* 85 (November 1979): 3–24. The theoretical debate over narrativity is well summarized in James West Davidson, "The New Narrative History: How New? How Narrative?" *Reviews in American History* 12 (September 1984): 322–34; Nancy F. Partner, "Making up Lost Time: Writing on the Writing of History," *Speculum* 61 (January 1986): 90–117; and in the many works of Hayden White, especially *The Content of the Form: Narrative Discourse and Historical Representation* (Baltimore: Johns Hopkins University Press, 1987).

nineteenth-century novel as a paradigm for the historian's 'art.' " Grabbing freely from the contemporary novelist's bag of tricks—perspecti-
valism, fractured chronology, self-reflexivity, cinematic montage—he
fashions a work which, he concedes, will "seem odd to some academic
historians." It is, he tells us, less a history of United States–Japan relations than "a book about the search for continuities between then and
now"—between "the personal and the historical. The history and the
historian."[10]

Rosenstone makes clear, moreover, that his experiment in form is an
ethical statement as well as a stylistic one: a formulation of the only kind
of intellectual integrity he can imagine amidst the swirling winds of postmodernist doubt. Only by making himself a prominent character in the
story, Rosenstone implies, can he write in a way that is both subjective
(as all history must be) and true (as it always strives to be).

Like many narrators in modern fiction, Rosenstone makes clear that
he is a somewhat unreliable guide to the past with which he seeks to
connect. At times, it seems, he doesn't quite know what he's doing.
Refusing to speak as a disembodied expert, Rosenstone places himself
down in the mire with the rest of us. He searches out truth in dusty
documents and comes up empty-handed. He looks for heroes and finds
rather ordinary men: figures whom he labels "unreflective," even "dis-
appointing." What's more, he frequently calls our attention to their—
and his—feet of clay. In the broadest sense, Rosenstone yearns for the
past but remains trapped in the present; it is no accident that every one
of the book's 275 pages is written, breathlessly, in the present tense.

In this and other formal ways, Rosenstone tells us repeatedly: *Mirror
in the Shrine* is not the past, but a book. His book. Only one of many
possible books, necessarily partial and fallible. He shows us this by forcing us to share his scholarly process, revealing the puppeteer behind the
curtain. The confidence and coherence of the worldview of his nineteenth-century subjects yield before the clouded vision of the twentieth-
century historian. What is left at the end, therefore, is not only a vivid
(if impressionistic) picture of this particular slice of history, but also a

[10]   Robert A. Rosenstone, *Mirror in the Shrine: American Encounters in Meiji Japan* (Cam-
       bridge, Mass.: Harvard University Press, 1988), xi, xii, 272. Brook Thomas has pointed
       out to me that many of these narrative techniques, which seem so utterly postmodern
       to historians, were the *sine qua non* of the modernist movement in fiction and may, in
       fact, predate it; Daniel Defoe and Laurence Sterne, after all, were playing with form in
       the eighteenth century.

palpable sense of unfulfilled desire—of the poignancy of our doomed longing to enter the past "rather than remaining a spectator" who peers "through that ancient, supple, but ultimately distant camera we know as words."[11]

Know thyself and show thyself might well be the first commandment of the kind of historical enterprise sketched by Rosenstone and expanded upon in important recent works by Simon Schama and John Demos. It is a way of exploring the past that takes the epistemological turmoil of the present as a starting point, telling stories about the possibility of telling one true story. It is moral inquiry in the sense that it is deeply concerned with the historian's role in society—with the politics of unflinching honesty in an age characterized by what Schama calls "dead certainties."[12] But it is a form of inquiry that engages that role chiefly at the level of narrative style. This means that it is also, as some critics have charged, a way of exploring history that places the scholar ahead of his subject, making the historian's quixotic search for the past more of a main event than the past itself.[13] Thus, if these experiments in storytelling represent a meaningful response to the moral quandaries of the late twentieth century—and I believe they do—the answer they offer is, necessarily, an incomplete one.

A second type of scholarship takes the present as a starting point for a decidedly different type of investigation: one that traces the historical roots of contemporary moral quandaries. There is, to be sure, nothing particularly novel about this sort of moral inquiry. In the early part of this century, Charles Beard and his Progressive colleagues looked to the era of the American Revolution to discover the roots of rapacious individualism. Scholars in the 1960s and 1970s were particularly concerned with the historical origins of racism, a political hot button in their day, as in ours. Two of the contemporary social issues that claim pride of place in much current scholarship are matters of sexual identity

---

[11] Rosenstone, *Mirror in the Shrine*, 272, 96.
[12] Simon Schama, *Dead Certainties (Unwarranted Speculations)* (New York: Knopf, 1991); and John Demos, *The Unredeemed Captive: A Family Story from Early America* (New York: Knopf, 1994). For other recent works that explore the obligations of historians to invent forms that disclose their own manipulations of evidence, see Elinor Langer, *Josephine Herbst* (1983; reprint, Boston: Northeastern University Press, 1993); Janet Malcolm, *The Silent Woman: Sylvia Plath and Ted Hughes* (New York: Knopf, 1994); and James Goodman, *Stories of Scottsboro* (New York: Pantheon, 1994).
[13] See, for example, Gordon S. Wood, "Novel History," *New York Review of Books* 38 (27 June 1991): 12–6; and Himmelfarb, "Some Reflections on the New History," esp. 666–8.

and fears for the fate of the environment. In both cases, authors have shown, documenting the struggles of people in remote times and places can lend nuance as well as ammunition to the battles of the present.

Does exploring aspects of the past that coincide with matters of urgent present-day concern cheapen or deepen historical writing? The late John Boswell, a medieval historian whose opus focused on the nexus of sexuality and social tolerance, strove mightily to ensure the latter. His final book, *Same-Sex Unions in Premodern Europe*, has become one of the most hotly debated works of scholarship in recent memory, prompting feature articles in *People* and the *New Yorker*, an appearance on ABC TV's "Day One," and a starring role in Garry Trudeau's *Doonesbury*, as well as the usual flurry of scholarly reviews.[14] The tenor of public reaction (not to say outcry) provoked by the book suggests that Boswell had his finger on the moral pulse of the United States in 1994—a curious achievement for one whose research interests began in classical antiquity and stopped just short of the fourteenth century. Just how Boswell chose to play his role as contemporary cultural critic makes it, as Alice might say, even curiouser. For *Same-Sex Unions* is a deeply, even ostentatiously, learned work. The book that some reviewers portrayed as the polemic of a stark raving queer announces itself as something altogether different: the archival gleanings of a milquetoast medievalist who is as shocked as the next guy to discover the (possible) contemporary implications of his work.[15]

Same-Sex Unions claims to be a user-friendly book, replete with instructions to the general reader. Yet despite Boswell's customarily lucid prose, I doubt that *any* general reader would feel at home in such a rarefied atmosphere.[16] The work explicates texts written in German, Spanish, French, Italian, Latin, Greek, Hebrew, early and modern Russian, Old Church Slavonic, several Scandinavian languages, Syriac, Armenian, Arabic, and Akkadian. Untranslated Greek, Latin, and Hebrew

[14] John Boswell, *Same-Sex Unions in Premodern Europe* (New York: Villard Books, 1994). See, for example, Bill Hewitt and Anne Longley, "Gay Rites," *People*, 27 June 1994, 57–8; "Beyond Stonewall: Gay Struggles, 25 Years On," *The New Yorker*, 20 June 1994, 35–6; and *Doonesbury*, syndicated nationally, 8–10 June 1994.
[15] A content analysis of reviews of Boswell's book would likely reveal "tendentious" as the most frequently used adjective of the work's detractors. See, for example, Brent D. Shaw, "A Groom of One's Own?" *The New Republic*, 18 and 25 July 1994, 33–41; and Kenneth L. Woodward, "Do You Paul, Take Ralph . . . ?" *Newsweek*, 20 June 1994, 76–7.
[16] I suspect further that the *Brief History of Time* topos is at work here: that far more layfolk have bought the book than have or will read it.

appear frequently in the text as well as in the notes. And what notes they are! Boswell's good old-fashioned stick-to-itiveness comes through in literally hundreds of footnotes—over 1,100 in just eight short chapters by my rough count. Indeed, he paints himself as such an i-dotting, t-crossing egghead that he must attribute a reference to the phrase "sea of love" ("From a No. 1 American song of 1959, 'Sea of Love,' recorded by Lou Phillips"). Lest the reader finish the book unpersuaded of the sheer brilliance of its author, Boswell appends over 100 pages of documents, including original language versions of a score of medieval rites of union.[17]

I am admittedly a nonspecialist here and can scarcely answer the vultures who have circled Boswell's book, carping over the fine points of translation. What I can say without hesitation is that the *Same-Sex Unions* I have read is a very different book than the one I have read about. It is a work far more stunning in its rhetorical cautiousness than in nearly any other respect. Sure, Boswell tells us in the preface that he has experienced "the deaths of many close friends from AIDS." This has made him sad and angry—and with good reason; his own death from that hated plague was only months away when the book appeared. But the text itself bears the imprint of privilege and prestige (the mantle of the Harvard-trained, duly tenured Yale professor) far more deeply than it does that of the activist. "Speculation has been kept to a minimum," Boswell assures the reader at the outset; the personal, no matter how compelling, will not intrude upon the scholarly. Rosenstone would doubtless find such a choice regrettable. But Boswell is insistent: the meaning of his findings lies in the past, not the present. "[W]hatever significance the ceremony might (or might not) have for persons living at this juncture of history," he writes, "its greatest importance lies . . . in its role in European history. *It is not the province of the historian to direct the actions of future human beings, but only to reflect accurately on those of the past.*"[18]

Where Boswell sees the activist's role as distinct from that of the historian, Donald Worster looks to merge the two. Long recognized as the Old Testament prophet of American environmental history, Worster has made a career out of deploring the material depredations of the present and looking for guidance, even solace, in the past. In a collection

---

[17] Boswell, *Same-Sex Unions*, xix, note 1; xxx; 191–2.
[18] Ibid., ix, xxvii, 37, 191, emphasis added. See also 280–2.

of essays entitled *The Wealth of Nature*, he argues forcefully for the historian's role as moral arbiter. History, Worster tells us, "ought to be more than knowledge chasing its own tail."

> [Our stories should] have a few *ideas* to offer the public, and those ideas ought to have a little conviction in them as well as reason and evidence. The historian should let people know what he cares about and encourage them to care about it too. He should not hide all day in the archives . . . but now and then try to take part in the great public issues that animate our times.

In short, we should not only practice what we preach; we must also preach about what we wish others to practice. Instead of leading our readers "off into deserts of relativism and leaving them stranded there with no map," we should, Worster says, be unafraid to tell them which direction to take.[19]

This is precisely what Worster sets out to do in his essays, with varying degrees of success. His model in the endeavor is not William Cronon or Richard White (two of the cooler heads in a branch of history that has never shied away from contemporary politics) but rather Aldo Leopold, the nature writer and wildlife biologist whose *Sand County Almanac* (1949) was a clarion call to the modern environmental movement. In Worster's (and Leopold's) analysis, the twin threats to the fate of the earth are private property and capitalism. The solution Worster offers is simple enough: off with their heads. We "must live in a country in which most of the land is held under some form of communal ownership or control," he insists. In order "to move forward . . . we will surely have to make a few more changes in the way Americans own and use property": minor tinkering that might include "a revised Constitution" privileging land-use rights over fee simple ownership. We *must* (a favorite word of Worster's) do so not only because of what history shows us, but also because of a deeper and more sustaining sense of beauty and ugliness, good and evil. In these days of anti-essentialism and social-constructionism, Worster waxes poetic about the "intrinsic value" of the natural world. In his vision, ethics and aesthetics, history and poetry, art and science serve the same purpose: to remind us of "the intrinsic worth of all beings, the beauty and wonder of the cosmos."[20]

---

[19] Donald Worster, *The Wealth of Nature: Environmental History and the Ecological Imagination* (New York: Oxford University Press, 1993), vii, viii-ix; emphasis added.

[20] Worster, *Wealth of Nature*, 110–1, 155, 219. Compare with the notion of "truth-adequation" sketched in Todorov, *The Morals of History*, 87–125.

For Worster, history is a heady business indeed. And yet for all its rhetorical fire, *The Wealth of Nature* appears to have left but faint impressions on popular consciousness. Aside from brief, glowing reviews in *Sierra* and *Garbage*, response to Worster's passionate declaration has been confined largely to scholarly journals, where the reviews tended to be tepid and bland. Sure, Roy Porter called him a Luddite in the *New Republic* and suggested that scholars ought to be "self-critical as well as evangelical." But, on the whole, the response to Worster's assault is marked by a kind of in-group solidarity. He may be a Luddite, reviewers effectively concede, but at least he's our Luddite.[21]

There is a paradox at work here. Looking at the receptions of Boswell's and Worster's recent forays into this second strain of moral inquiry, we might well conclude that the stridency of public and scholarly reaction is inversely proportional to the author's own decibel level.[22] After all, Boswell does not tell his readers to become gay, marry their same-sex partners, and live happily ever. Worster, in contrast, *does* all but insist that we deed our homes to the government and take up communal living under a new Constitution. Why is his sermonizing less provocative than Boswell's expressed reluctance to preach? Perhaps Worster fails to earn serious rebuttal; maybe nobody feels compelled to drag out the heavy critical artillery against a wild-eyed lone gunman taking pot shots at capitalism. It may also be, as Boswell argues repeatedly, that the specter of (homo)sexuality terrifies us more than any other contemporary social "threat," including radical environmentalism.[23] While these explanations may partly account for the fact that Worster's book made ripples whereas Boswell's made waves, I suspect that another dynamic is at work. We seem to like our historians to act at least a little scholarly, even a touch dour. When moral inquiry blurs into passionate moralizing, the academy prefers to ignore it rather than to engage it.

However different Boswell's and Worster's approaches to the past, and however disparate the reactions they provoked from readers, their

---

[21] See Bob Schildgen, "Reviews: *The Wealth of Nature*," *Sierra* 78 (November 1993): 104; Hannah Holmes, "Resources," *Garbage* 5 (September 1993): 56; Roy Porter, "Field of Dreams," *The New Republic*, 5 July 1993, 33–6, esp. 35. Reviews in scholarly journals include those by Roderick Nash, *American Historical Review* 99 (April 1994): 632–3; and Richard White, "Back to Nature," *Reviews in American History* 22 (March 1994): 1–6.

[22] I am reminded of an old television commercial in which a seductive woman hawking perfume mouthed, "If you want to capture someone's attention, *whisper*."

[23] See Boswell, *Same-Sex Unions*, 101, 161, 187, 191.

piece of the moral inquiry pie is a relatively small and specialized one; few historical topics resonate as compellingly or as obviously in the present as either sexual identity or environmental calamity. In contrast, a third way of drawing meaning from history has almost universal potential. Instead of asking how people living in the past thought and felt about what interests us today, this third form of moral inquiry asks: What interested *them*? How was the good life defined in other places and at other times? What did it mean to act morally in, say, nineteenth-century Bali, or thirteenth-century France, or eighteenth-century New England? This is the central question posed by scholars dedicated to plumbing what Clifford Geertz has called "the social history of the moral imagination."[24] Unlike Boswell's or Worster's timely works, theirs is a kind of storytelling that speaks to our own dilemmas in only the most roundabout way. But despite this seeming indirection, it speaks to us with considerable force—perhaps more forcefully than Worster's impassioned exhortation.

There is no shortage of examples of this third kind of moral inquiry. Historians of many stripes—scholars of ideas and party politics, as well as those who study folkways and popular culture—have long worked to recover the now vanished belief systems of people in the past. Since the 1960s historians of early modern Europe, in particular, have raised the reconstruction of common people's "mentalités" to the status of art.[25] In my own field of early American history it would be possible to sketch a similarly august genealogy, stretching back beyond Bernard Bailyn and Edmund Morgan to include the work of Perry Miller and perhaps even that of Francis Parkman. Today, to my mind, it is the work of Laurel Thatcher Ulrich that best exemplifies this tradition.

Ulrich, a historian whose research interests center on women's lives and gendered patterns of work in the New England colonies, labors in

---

[24] Clifford Geertz, "Found in the Translation: On the Social History of the Moral Imagination," in *Local Knowledge: Further Essays in Interpretive Anthropology* (New York: Basic Books, 1983), 36–54; see also Lionel Trilling, "Why We Read Jane Austen," in *The Last Decade: Essays and Reviews, 1965–75*, ed. Diana Trilling (New York: Harcourt, Brace, Jovanovich, 1979), 204–25.

[25] See, for example, Emmanuel Le Roy Ladurie, *Montaillou: The Promised Land of Error*, trans. Barbara Bray (New York: George Braziller, 1978); Carlo Ginzburg, *The Cheese and the Worms: The Cosmos of a Sixteenth-Century Miller*, trans. John and Anne Tedeschi (New York: Penguin Books, 1980); Natalie Zemon Davis, *Society and Culture in Early Modern France* (Stanford, Calif.: Stanford University Press, 1975); and Robert F. Darnton, *The Great Cat Massacre and Other Episodes in French Cultural History* (New York: Basic Books, 1984).

a field that has proved curiously resistant to nuanced moral inquiry. Since, as she tells us in *Good Wives*, the proper New England matron "earned the dignity of anonymity," colonial women left scant evidence of their lives to posterity.[26] Faced with this paucity of sources, historians have taken a variety of shortcuts. Many have ignored women's presence altogether, writing the history of the "New England Mind" as if belief systems had no gender. Others, taking ministers' prescriptions for women's roles as gospel, have indicted Puritan culture for its misogyny and offered only pity to the women who lived within (and helped to create) that culture, thus reducing them to mere ciphers.[27]

Ulrich, in contrast, struggles painstakingly to reconstruct both the social and moral domains of these actors who left behind such faint impressions of their own consciousness. *A Midwife's Tale*, her Pulitzer Prize–winning account of the life of a female healer in eighteenth-century Maine, is a shining example. A quieter heroine than Worster's environmentally correct native Americans or even Boswell's marrying medieval brethren, Ulrich's Martha Ballard champions nothing that speaks directly to modern social agendas. Neither a protofeminist nor a cloying model of Victorian womanhood, Ballard is something altogether more complicated: a consort, helpmate, mother, farmer, and cloth-producer who also delivered some 816 babies between 1785 and 1812. Drawn to a subject whose day-to-day roles positively elude modern labels (was she a homemaker? a medical professional? an agricultural laborer?), Ulrich replaces twentieth-century categories with eighteenth-century ones: the multiple facets of Martha Ballard's own ways of ordering the world. Recovering Ballard's consciousness is no mean feat. Although she, unlike most early American women, faithfully kept a diary over a period of decades, the entries are almost comically terse: "I have been pulling flax." "I have been at home. Pikt green peas in our garden." And so on.[28]

---

[26] Laurel Thatcher Ulrich, *Good Wives: Image and Reality in the Lives of Women in Northern New England, 1650–1750* (New York: Knopf, 1982), 3. On the reticent sources divulging the lives of early American women, see also Ulrich, "Of Pens and Needles: Sources in Early American Women's History," *Journal of American History* 77 (June 1990): 200–7.

[27] See, for example, Lyle Koehler, *A Search for Power: The "Weaker" Sex in Seventeenth-Century New England* (Urbana, Ill.: University of Illinois Press, 1980).

[28] Laurel Thatcher Ulrich, *A Midwife's Tale: The Life of Martha Ballard, Based on Her Diary 1785–1812* (New York: Knopf, 1990), 36, 103. Each chapter opens with a several page transcription from Ballard's diary, all of which are similarly unforthcoming.

In Ulrich's hands, this careful record of the most mundane daily doings becomes testimony to a whole way of *being*. As she points out, "the exhaustive, repetitive dailiness" of the Ballard diary is, in many ways, the point of the story. Ballard's world emerges as one in which the ever-renewing play of seasons mattered more than the accumulation of property or personal accomplishments. It was also a place in time where the warp and weft of connections that knitted people together took primacy over the unique expression of discrete selves. Fittingly, textile metaphors figure heavily in Ulrich's work, just as textile production did in the lives of the women she studies. Their lives, she tells us, played out in intricate patterns that wove together work and home, male and female, personal and communal. Rather than cleaving the world into separate men's and women's "spheres," women like Martha Ballard located themselves within a "social web" of relations. In the end, the portrait Ulrich limns is one in which the quiet dignity of Martha Ballard's work and her ethos of mutual support possess more dramatic power than the great events of the day, events that included the American Revolution and its contentious aftermath in Maine.[29] It is a narrative, in other words, in which Ballard's own vision of the world claims absolute pride of place. It is a way of being almost completely divorced from our own, and that very remoteness is the source of the book's moral force.

Taken together, the different ways in which Rosenstone, Boswell, Worster, and Ulrich approach the present through the past show that there is more than one way for historians to skin a moral dilemma. Each of these works confronts the essential paradox of doing history: How do we step out of our time and place and find meaning for ourselves at the same time? How do we keep the time-boundedness of historical inquiry intact while looking for messages and meanings that transcend the particular? How, in short, can we craft pasts that are neither reductively usable nor morally useless? Rosenstone, Boswell, Worster, and Ulrich offer a variety of challenging and often contradictory answers. One might be tempted to dismiss such multiplicity as a fad—to call it another casualty of the postmodern condition. This would be a mistake. There is more than intellectual fashion underlying the contradictions among these authors' moral stances. The complexity of the historiographical landscape today testifies to the very real difficulties of creating a mean-

[29] Ibid., 9, 75–80, 254–5, 27, 30, 32, 316.

ingful dialogue among an ever-receding past, a terribly uncertain present, and an increasingly obscure future.

Where does my current research, an exploration of the politics of speaking in seventeenth-century New England, fit into all this? In the postmodern spirit of self-disclosure, I will come clean and tell you that it has been difficult for me to locate my work within these three competing and overlapping approaches to moral inquiry in history. Experimental narrative voices, for example, seem to suit some scholarly projects better than others; I still haven't found one that sits well with mine. At any rate, novelistic liberties seem to come most naturally to (or perhaps appear least unseemly in) the long-tenured.[30] Advocacy, too, has limited appeal, especially when the subjects of one's scholarly passion are famous chiefly for funny hats, buckled shoes, and a much-maligned intolerant streak. On the face of it, at least, the Puritans seem to serve as anti-models for today's wants and needs. Easy enough for Donald Worster to look up at historical skies teeming with long-vanished passenger pigeons and tell us to recycle our garbage. What sort of lesson for the living could I possibly draw from the experiences of speech offenders like Salem's John Porter who, in 1661, set off an international incident by calling his father "shittabed?"

Indeed, of the three approaches I have outlined above, only the third offers an even approximate fit. For my project, in essence, is about deep and thoroughgoing human difference. The inhabitants of early New England fashioned a view of the world that was, as Perry Miller demonstrated back in the 1930s, profoundly, even irretrievably different from our own.[31] This remoteness manifests itself with particular force in their dealings with the spoken word. The beliefs and actions of New England Puritans inverted nearly everything we now believe about speech. They did not, for example, recognize an easy distinction between words and things. As folklorist Robert St. George has pointed out, "speech seemed inherently more mysterious, dangerous, and 'real' " to premodern Eng-

---

[30] Indeed, to my knowledge, James Goodman is the only novice who has plunged so boldly into the so-called "new narrative" history, which tends to be the province of senior scholars who have already paid their professional "dues" by publishing more conventional monographs.

[31] Perry Miller, *The New England Mind: The Seventeenth Century* (Cambridge, Mass.: Harvard University Press, 1939); and Miller, *The New England Mind: From Colony to Province* (Cambridge, Mass.: Harvard University Press, 1953).

lishmen and women than it does to us today.[32] It is no accident that
writers of the day who took up the issue of speech—and many did—often
depicted the tongue as a protagonist in its own right: an actor who alter-
nately shored up and tore down civil society. English preachers well knew
that the spoken word, a divine gift separating humans from the lower orders, could also consume like a raging fire, nip like a "sneaking little cur,"
or burst its banks like "a torrent, which must and will flow."[33]

Ordinary men and women had every reason to agree with elite taste-
makers. Loose talk, they knew, had the power to make and unmake even
the most eminent of men. Even more palpably, their own painful experiences with the malevolent tongues of neighborhood "witches" taught
them the awesome power of words left unchecked. When witches cursed,
babies and animals dropped dead. Inanimate objects moved at will. Luck
ran out. The literal power of words as curses is a special case. But the general point would have been well taken by any seventeenth-century vil-
lager: saying was a form of doing. This was especially true, it seemed,
when the sayer in question was female. It is no coincidence that women,
who were thought to be especially prone to the sins of the tongue, constituted more than 80 percent of New England's suspected witches.[34]

[32] Robert B. St. George, " 'Heated' Speech and Literacy in Seventeenth-Century New England," in *Seventeenth-Century New England: A Conference Held by the Colonial Society of Massachusetts*, ed. David D. Hall and David Grayson Allen (Boston: Colonial
Society of Massachusetts, 1984), 275–322, esp. 277–8.

[33] See, for example, George Webbe, *The Arraignment of an Unruly Tongue* (London,
1619); Richard Allestree, *The Government of the Tongue*, 4th ed. (Oxford, 1675);
"J. W.," *The Baseness and Perniciousness of the Sin of Slandering and Backbiting* (Boston: John Boyles, 1769); and Joseph Butler, "Upon the Government of the Tongue"
(1729), in *The Works of Joseph Butler*, 2 vols., comp. Samuel Halifax (London: Scott
and Webster, 1834), II: 55. Further detail on the English prescriptive literature is found
in Jane Kamensky, *Governing the Tongue: The Politics of Speaking in Early New England* (New York: Oxford University Press, 1997), chap. 1.

[34] On witchcraft as speech see Kamensky, *Governing the Tongue*, chap. 6; Jeanne Favret-
Saada, *Deadly Words: Witchcraft in the Bocage*, trans. Catherine Cullen (New York:
Cambridge University Press, 1980); and Keith Thomas, *Religion and the Decline of
Magic* (New York: Scribner's, 1971), 61, 182–3, 436–7, 502–9. On the canon of female
scolding, see David Underdown, "The Taming of the Scold: The Enforcement of Patri-
archal Authority in Early Modern England," in *Order and Disorder in Early Modern
England*, ed. Anthony Fletcher and John Stevens (Cambridge: Cambridge University
Press, 1985), 116–36; Lynda E. Boose, "Scolding Brides and Bridling Scolds: Taming
the Woman's Unruly Member," *Shakespeare Quarterly* 42 (Summer 1991): 185, 189,
195, 203; and the tract literature excerpted in Katherine Usher Henderson and Barbara
F. McManus, *Half Humankind: Contexts and Texts of the Controversy about Women
in England, 1540–1640* (Urbana, Ill.: University of Illinois Press, 1985). The proportion
of suspected witches who were women appears in Carol F. Karlsen, *The Devil in the
Shape of a Woman: Witchcraft in Colonial New England* (New York: Norton, 1987),
47–51.

It is worth emphasizing that seventeenth-century English speakers attributed this fearful power not to language production in general but to speech—its verbal form—in particular. This, too, is a radical challenge to our own way of ordering the world. Not only do we subordinate words to deeds. We also tend to privilege writing over speaking. Speaking is primitive; writing, evolved. Speaking is what children do; writing is for grown-ups. Speaking is for low, unmediated, unreasoned thoughts; writing is for sober reflection and high culture. None of these things would have seemed axiomatic to early modern folks. Speech, they believed, could be rude: a veritable symbol of barbarism. But it was never merely trivial.[35] Which is not to say that seventeenth-century New Englanders weren't literate; by the standards of their own day they were highly lettered, particularly the men.[36] Even so, speaking was, in many respects, a more essential form of communication than writing or printing. Indeed, in the context of village life, "publishing" one's thoughts verbally—a frequent early modern locution—might spread the word faster and more widely than firing off a pamphlet or nailing one's dissenting opinions to the meetinghouse door.[37]

In many respects, such a diminished distance between words and things, between speaking and writing, is generic to face-to-face communities. Virtually anywhere one might have looked in premodern Europe and, indeed, in many nonindustrial societies even today, the small scale of daily life makes words matter.[38] Still, Puritan New England is a

[35] On the association of orality with barbarism and literacy with civility, see Anthony Pagden, *The Fall of Natural Man: The American Indian and the Origins of Comparative Ethnology* (New York: Cambridge University Press, 1982), 129–30, 183–90; Edward Gordon Gray, "Indian Language in Anglo-American Thought, 1550–1820" (Ph.D. diss., Brown University, 1996), chap. 1; Stephen Greenblatt, *Marvelous Possessions: The Wonder of the New World* (Chicago: University of Chicago Press, 1991), 88, see also 10–2; and Greenblatt, "Learning to Curse: Aspects of Linguistic Colonialism in the Sixteenth Century," in *First Images of America*, 2 vols., ed. Fredi Chiapelli, Michael J. B. Allen, and Robert L. Benson (Berkeley: University of California Press, 1976), II: 561–80.

[36] On literacy and its meanings in New England culture, see St. George, " 'Heated' Speech"; David D. Hall, *Worlds of Wonder, Days of Judgment: Popular Religious Belief in Early New England* (New York: Knopf, 1989), 21–70; and Kenneth Lockridge, *Literacy in Colonial New England: An Enquiry into the Social Context of Literacy in the Early Modern West* (New York: Norton, 1974).

[37] See Richard D. Brown, *Knowledge Is Power: The Diffusion of Information in Early America, 1700–1865* (New York: Oxford University Press, 1989); and Kamensky, *Governing the Tongue*, chaps. 1, 4.

[38] For a review of some of the countless anthropological works on small societies, see Mary Beth Norton, "Gender and Defamation in Seventeenth-Century Maryland," *William and Mary Quarterly*, 3d series, 44 (January 1987): 5, note 4.

special case. There, ideology and circumstance combined to give speech
deeper and broader meanings than it has claimed in any other place in
time I can think of.

The contributions of Puritan theology in this regard are easy to spot.
In their religious ideals as well as in their social and spatial arrangements, early New Englanders were not just people of words but, more
pointedly, people of the Word. An overly literal rendering of John Calvin's translation of the Gospel of John emphasizes the primacy of voice
at the dawn of the world: "In the beginning was Speech, and Speech
was with God; and Speech was God."[39] Scripture, for Calvin's English
descendants, was not mere text; it was a form of speech—the instrument
through which God "opens his own most hallowed lips."[40] Thus, it is
only logical that, from the late sixteenth century on, Puritan spirituality
was an affair of the mouth and the ear. In a culture that banished most
other forms of ritual (religious plays and paintings, sacred calendars and
festivals), reading, intoning, and hearing scripture were the central acts
of meaning.[41] The Puritan emphasis on the sermon and on prayer held
out new possibilities for speaking both to and of God, for ministers and
layfolk alike. Reformers exhorted ordinary men and women to address
God directly and condemned the priestly intermediaries whose specious
mumbo-jumbo came between common people's voices and God's ears.
For preachers, belief in the absolute primacy of the (spoken) Word of
God also translated into heightened respect for their own voices.

This redefinition of religious order provoked drastic reactions from
orthodox clergymen. That the Puritan reconception of the sacred was
rooted in new kinds of speaking was perhaps the only point of consensus

---

[39] "*Au commencement estoit la Parole, et la Parole estoit avec Dieu; et icelle Parole estoit
Dieu.*" John 1:1 as explicated in Jean Calvin, *Évangile selon Saint Jean*, vol. 2 of M.
Reveillard, ed., *Commentaires de Jean Calvin sur le Noveau Testament* (Aix-en-
Provence: Editions Kerygma, 1967), 12–5; see also Sandra Marie Gustafson, "Perform-
ing the Word: American Oratory, 1630–1860" (Ph.D. diss., University of California at
Berkeley, 1993), 93.

[40] John T. McNeill, ed., *Calvin: Institutes of the Christian Religion*, 2 vols., trans. Ford
Lewis Battles (Philadelphia: Westminster Press, 1960), I: 75, 70, 81.

[41] Hall, *Worlds of Wonder*, chap. 4 passim, esp. 167. On the primacy of the sermon over
visual aspects of Puritan worship, see also Patrick Collinson, *The Birthpangs of Prot-
estant England: Religious and Cultural Change in the Sixteenth and Seventeenth Cen-
turies* (New York: St. Martin's Press, 1988), 94–126; Collinson, *From Iconoclasm to
Iconophobia: The Cultural Impact of the Second English Reformation* (Reading,
England: University of Reading, 1986), 8–25; and Harry S. Stout, *The New England
Soul: Preaching and Religious Culture in Colonial New England* (New York: Oxford
University Press, 1986), 3, 19.

between the dissenters and their opponents. Both sides agreed, in effect,
that you could *hear* a Puritan coming. To a significant degree, the en-
suing decades of contention between Puritan reformers and Anglican
traditionalists can be construed as an extended battle over speech. The
dissenters strove to train inspiring clerics who would be *"known by
voice*, learning and doctrine" rather than "cap, gowne, and tippet." Par-
ish clergy, who had degenerated into "bare readers," must be replaced
by those capable of "preaching of the worde purely."[42] Outraged defenders of the Church of England turned the tables, accusing the "Puritans" (at first, an epithet hurled by the sect's detractors) of being
"murmurers, complayners, mockers" who went about their work by
"rayling, libelling, and lying."[43] And these accusations, in turn, made
the reformers take up the struggle for the right to complain.

All of which suggests that Puritan ideology argued for allowing the
tongue—that doer of both vile and noble deeds—a freer rein than it was
otherwise granted in early modern England. And to be sure, where scripture was concerned, Puritans preached a new directness, extolling the
necessity of encountering God's Word without barriers. Yet their legacy
is considerably more complicated. For neither Puritan theologians nor
their followers actually *lived* in the Word; they lived in the world—in
social as well as sacred space and time. Along with their less zealous
neighbors, they inhabited a landscape of overlapping authorities and
dependencies. In the more mundane landscape of meetinghouse, neighborhood, and household, the license Puritan thinkers granted the tongue
was often problematic. Their pleas for "freeing" speech, therefore,
tended to be halting and partial ones.

True, John Milton, out on the radical fringe of the movement for
religious reform, did suggest that the only solution to all this wrangling
over speech was more speech. *But only up to a point.* Indeed, one of
the reasons Milton advocated relaxing restrictions on printing and
preaching was to keep *verbal* "publishing" in check. As he wrote in the
Areopagitica, widely (and wrongly) considered a direct precursor to

[42] [John Field and Thomas Wilcox], *An admonition to the parliament* (1572), in *Puritan
Manifestoes: A Study of the Origin of the Puritan Revolt*, ed. W. H. Frere and C. E.
Douglas (London: Church Historical Society, 1954), 11, 9; emphasis added. On English
Puritanism, see Patrick Collinson, *The Elizabethan Puritan Movement* (1967; reprint,
London: Methuen, 1982).
[43] Richard Bancroft, *Dayngerovs positions and proceedings, published and practiced
within this Iland of Brytaine, under pretence of Reformation, and for the Presbiteriall
Discipline* (1593; reprint, New York: Da Capo Press, 1972), 2–3; see also 14–5, 20–2.

modern notions of free expression, spreading one's opinion "privily from
house to house" was surely "more dangerous" than doing so "openly
by writing." Some words, Milton demurred, must always and necessarily
"be extirpate." The speech of dissenters should be encouraged—unless
they were Catholics.[44] The tongues of layfolk should proceed unim-
peded—unless their words threatened to drown out the authority of
godly ministers. And wives should address God directly, without fear or
fetters—so long as they kept silent before their husbands. In other
words, Puritanism (or Puritanisms, for there were nearly as many theologies as there were theologians among the Elizabethan dissenters) were
at odds with themselves where speech was concerned.

This would have been difficult enough to resolve if Puritan ideology
had been tested in a controlled environment that held constant everything else in English culture. But, of course, it was not tested under those
conditions—at least not by those whose beliefs led them out of England
in the first decades of the seventeenth century. The fact of being colonials
at the far Western edge of a metropolitan culture further complicated
the ways in which speech ramified in early New England. In the Puritans'
"New World," old markers of status and power carried diminished importance. Where land was abundant, vast holdings meant less than they
had in East Anglia. Where the institutions of authority (government,
schools, parishes, and trading empires) were in their infancy, men would
have to find new means by which to articulate their places in the world.
Here, social control would have to be manifested in different ways and
measured in different terms. And here, too, lived different peoples to
define oneself against. Native cultures offered the English powerful coun-
terexamples of ways in which social order and verbal order might be
arranged.[45]

[44] John Milton, *Areopagitica: A Speech of Mr. John Milton for the Liberty of Unlicensed Printing*, ed. Richard C. Jebb (1644; reprint, Cambridge: Cambridge University Press, 1918), 47, 60. On contemporary misinterpretations of Milton, see Stanley Fish, *There's No Such Thing as Free Speech . . . and It's a Good Thing, Too* (New York: Oxford University Press, 1994), esp. 103.

[45] For English reactions to native social and gender orders, see James Axtell, ed., *The Indian Peoples of Eastern America: A Documentary History of the Sexes* (New York: Oxford University Press, 1981). English observers from William Bradford to Mary Rowlandson were also obsessed with the speech of America's "Indians." See, for example, Roger Williams, *A Key into the Language of America* (1643; facsimile reprinted Menston, England: The Scolar Press, 1971), 9–10, 54–6, 61; Edward Winslow, *Good News from New England* (1624), in *Chronicles of the Pilgrim Fathers*, ed. Alexander Young (New York: Dutton, 1910), esp. 276–301, 328, 351; and William Wood, *New England's Prospect* (1634), ed. Alden T. Vaughan (Amherst: University of Massa-

And so it was that white New Englanders of all stripes—clerical and civil leaders, ordinary men and women—came to invest a great deal of energy in what they called "governing the tongue." It was a project with two closely intertwined goals: fostering what preachers called "Christian-like conversation," and containing the damage inflicted by "heated" speech of various sorts. If the tongue had the tendency to be "every man's best or worst" in equal measures, governing the tongue meant steering a middle course and ensuring that most people adhered to it most of the time.[46] In essence, regulating speech in early New England was about establishing and policing social boundaries in a world where few boundaries of any sort—of any sort Europeans recognized, that is— had yet been built.

There were many ways of going about this difficult task. A rich vocabulary of words and gestures—the facial expressions and spoken rebukes that warned a speaker when she crossed the line dividing the decorous from the profane—was doubtless the most important safeguard of "Christian-like conversation." But such everyday remedies for mis-speaking vanished as soon as they were applied. In contrast, the mechanisms that remain visible more than three centuries after the fact tend be of a rather clumsy, official sort. We can "overhear" negotiations about right speaking only at points where, for one reason or another, they entered the written record.

Fortunately for historians, New Englanders' widely shared preoccupation with verbal governance meant that talk became a matter of record far more frequently than we might suppose. Speech is one of the many aspects of personal deportment that in other places and times falls within the (unofficial) spheres of manners and customs, but that was a matter of public policy in New England. Simply put: wrongful speech was not just a breach of etiquette; it was an affront to God and to civil society, a matter for church discipline and a breach of secular law. Of course we, too, insist that certain kinds of speech, in some circumstances, be

chusetts Press, 1977), esp. 101–14. This issue is discussed at greater length in Kamensky, *Governing the Tongue*, chap. 2; and Gray, "Indian Languages," chap. 2.

[46] Thomas Adams, "The Taming of the Tongue," in *The Works of Thomas Adams*, 3 vols., ed. Joseph Angus (1629; reprint, Edinburgh: James Nichol, 1862), 11, 12. For exhortations to "Christian-like conversation," see William Hubbard, *The Benefit of a Well-Ordered Conversation* (Boston: S. Green, 1684). In seventeenth-century parlance, conversation referred to both a way of life and more literally to spoken exchange; see Charles Hambrick-Stowe, *The Practice of Piety: Puritan Devotional Disciplines in Seventeenth-Century New England* (Chapel Hill: University of North Carolina Press, 1982), 200–2, 278.

deemed illegal: slander and libel (narrowly defined), and words that
threaten to incite imminent violence still constitute breaches of our official boundaries. But it is a gross understatement to say that those
boundaries were much more closely drawn in the seventeenth century.
In addition to the usual suspects—slander, libel, and sedition—speech
acts prosecuted in the Massachusetts courts between 1630 and 1692
included affronting, calumniating, contemning, fawning, flattering, nick-
naming, provoking, quarreling, railing, reproaching, reviling, scolding,
scoffing, slighting, swearing, taunting, threatening, and dozens more.[47]
There were more serious verbal offenses as well. Blasphemy, for example, was a capital crime in Massachusetts and New Haven. And malign
words were among the chief symptoms used to diagnose the presence of
two other offenses punishable by death: witchcraft (often made manifest
by a variety of verbal missteps), and filial rebellion ("cursing or smiting"
one's parents). In these ways New England was a place where the scrip-
tural precept that "by a man's words he may lose his life" became law.[48]

This does not mean that early Massachusetts was a police state where
every thought was squelched by overzealous authorities. In fact, some
legal scholars have made much of the fact that New England men possessed much wider latitude to speak in civic forums than did their English counterparts. Provided they did so "in convenient time, due order,
and *respective manner*," the freemen of Massachusetts Bay were granted
"*full freedome*" to voice "any advise, vote, verdict, or sentence in any
Court, Counsell, or Civill Assembly."[49] New England was a place where
local leaders and their subjects were forever negotiating the proper bal-

[47] See St. George, " 'Heated' Speech," 318–9. On evolving definitions of slander and libel
in the colonial period see Norton, "Gender and Defamation"; Norman L. Rosenberg,
Protecting the Best Men: An Interpretive History of the Law of Libel (Chapel Hill:
University of North Carolina Press, 1986); and Cornelia Dayton, *Women before the
Bar: Gender, Law, and Society in Connecticut, 1639–1789* (Chapel Hill: University of
North Carolina Press, 1995), esp. chap. 6. A good seventeenth-century English defini-
tion is found in John March, *Actions for Slaunder, Or, a Methodicall Collection under
Certain Grounds and Heads, of What Words are Actionable in the LAW, and What
Not?* (London, 1647).
[48] New Haven's courts explicitly cited this biblical grounding. See Charles J. Hoadly, ed.,
Records of the Colony and Plantation of New Haven, 1638–1649 (Hartford: Case,
Lockwood, 1857), I: 293. For laws regulating speech in Massachusetts, see William H.
Whitmore, ed., *The Colonial Laws of Massachusetts, Reprinted from the Edition of
1660, With the supplements to 1672, Containing also the body of Liberties of 1641*
(Boston: Rockwell and Churchill, 1889), 55, 128–9, 143, 148.
[49] *Body of Liberties*, 35, 45, 49; emphasis mine. On the comparison to English custom,
see George Lee Haskins, *Law and Authority in Early Massachusetts: A Study in Tradition and Design* (New York: Macmillan, 1960), esp. 130, 196–7.

ance between these two poles of "full freedome" and Christian-like deference and respect.

Gender was an important ingredient of this ordered freedom, and these negotiations had wildly different outcomes for men and women. For men, the boundaries of right speaking—boundaries constructed through an ongoing dialogue between law and custom, prescription and reality—can best be imagined as a barrier constructed of widely spaced planks. Christian-like conversation was a set of precepts that good men could easily transgress, thus stepping through to the outside of the fence. But such breaches were usually temporary; men did not often find themselves irrevocably on the wrong side of right speaking. Even the most heinous offenders could set things in order by demonstrating, publicly, a renewed capacity for decorous speech. The ritual of public apology, the favored remedy for male speech offenders who insulted authority, was simultaneously self-abnegating and self-aggrandizing: a performance after which repentant male mis-speakers found themselves again on the right side of a loosely constructed boundary. For women the barrier more closely resembled a well-built stockade fence. Getting *out* was a simple matter, for the gatekeepers who policed a neighborhood's verbal borderlands were only too happy to pronounce female speech transgressive. Allotted a narrower range in which their words could roam freely, women were deemed to be evil speakers more readily than men. But once so named, the price of readmission to the community could be steep—sometimes impossibly so. Anne Hutchinson, Ann Hibbens, and numerous other women whom New England communities exiled, one way or another, for their words learned this lesson the hard way.[50]

On the afternoon of June 18, 1681, Cotton Mather—an earnest young man who would soon become New England's leading theologian—retired to his prayer closet to reflect upon the *"Kindnesses of God"* toward him. Chief among these, Mather thought, was his own *voice*—the instrument through which he would command throngs of prayerful followers. And thus he cried out with customary seriousness, "How *Miraculous* a Thing is the *Freedom of Speech*."[51] It goes almost without saying: Mather was extolling a very different kind of freedom than most of us would recognize. In the most literal sense, it was a

---

[50] This paragraph collapses extensive research on the respective crimes and punishments of male and female mis-speakers. See Kamensky, *Governing the Tongue*, chaps. 4–6.
[51] Worthington Chauncey Ford, ed., *Diary of Cotton Mather*, 2 vols. (1912; reprint, New York: Frederick Ungar Publishing, 1957), I: 2–3, 19–20; emphasis original.

somatic freedom—the lifting of a debilitating stutter that had plagued
him throughout his youth. But even in a broader symbolic sense, this
was no modern liberty. Mather's "freedom of speech" was the freedom
for those whose rightful province it was to speak (read: mostly whites,
mostly men), to speak when and where they ought (read: primarily in
private for women, sometimes in wider circles for men), in decorous and
respectful tones (read: like penitents before their ministers), in ways that
pleased both Man (read: men like Mather) and God. By any other definition, Mather would have been the first to insist, speech simply could
not be free. Everything around him proved the contrary. The wrong
word, from the wrong mouth, in the wrong place, at the wrong time
was very costly indeed.

Skip just over a century. It is 1789. Cotton Mather has been dead for
more than sixty years, and much of his world has gone with him. The
North American seaboard is a denser, busier, vastly more complex place.
The colonies are no longer colonies. The Puritan church is no longer established in Massachusetts or anyplace else. The king has become a president. And freedom of speech—our phrase if not quite our understanding
of it—is suddenly the supreme law of the land. The right to unfettered ut-
terance (printed as well as verbal, as the publishing economy of the late
eighteenth century demands) has somehow become a defining element of
American nationhood. The belief that the articulation of such a right and
its gradual expansion over the course of the nineteenth and twentieth centuries were good things has long been an article of faith in the West. From
here forward, my plot seems to be: onward and upward, out of the darkness and into the light. Great oaks from little acorns grow.[52] And so one
moral meaning my little piece of history might claim is that of a caution-
ary tale. The headline reads: *Puritan Pundits Show Dangers of Repression—Don't Let This Happen to You.*

Or maybe not. Fast forward again, two centuries this time. It is 1992,

---

[52] The history of speech in the United States, to the extent that it has been written at all,
remains a quintessentially Whiggish history. Two works illustrate this point. Leonard
W. Levy's *Emergence of a Free Press* (revised ed. of *Legacy of Suppression: Freedom
of Speech and Press in Early American History*, New York: Oxford University Press,
1985) portrays the glorious history of verbal participation in modern American life
chiefly through a stark contrast with the "bad old days" before the American Revolution. Larry Eldridge, whose recent monograph is framed as an explicit challenge to
Levy's paradigm, succeeds only in pushing this vaunted evolution back farther in time.
The "bad old days," he argues, were really getting much better by 1660 or so. See
Larry D. Eldridge, *A Distant Heritage: The Growth of Free Speech in Early America*
(New York: New York University Press, 1994).

exactly 300 years after the Salem witch trials, and a cartoon appears in the *New Yorker* poking fun at a strange, seemingly modern predicament. In the quickly sketched scene, a stern father warns a tearful son: "Sticks and stones may break your bones, but hate speech is actionable."[53] The gag (in my overdetermined reading, at least) is very much about the profound gap between then and now. Until recently, the cartoonist implies, we felt secure in the knowledge that (as the rhyme implicitly continues) "names can never hurt us." To the extent that we imputed any power to speech, we imputed only power for good. As legal scholar Mary Ellen Gale puts it, liberals eagerly cloaked themselves in the First Amendment, believing that if only "everyone . . . could think, write, speak, and listen without fear of governmental repression, we could sing, dance, laugh, and persuade our way to the promised land." Gale, along with most activists for civil rights and civil liberties in the 1950s and 1960s, assumed that malign speech was no longer capable of causing harm. "Well," she concedes, "we were wrong."[54]

Gale is one of a number of prominent thinkers who today are seeking new ways to balance the First Amendment's guarantees of expressive liberty with the Fourteenth Amendment's promise of substantive equality. The call to reexamine the meanings and consequences of free speech comes primarily from two fronts. One powerful challenge is mounted by feminists who believe that in recent decades the First Amendment has too frequently been caught in bed with pornographers. A second group is made up primarily of scholars, especially critical race theorists, concerned about the chilling effect of so-called hate speech on college campuses across the United States. Together, these critics of prevailing understandings of words and their social impact are reviving modes of thinking that the Puritans would certainly have recognized. This is not necessarily such a bad thing. While the charge of neo-Puritanism is an insult currently fashionable in "postfeminist" circles, I would not be surprised if Cotton Mather had something to teach us yet.[55]

---

[53] *The New Yorker*, 7 December 1992, 96. For another example of much merrymaking over the notion that speech can harm, see James Barron, "Up against the Wall in a No-Curse Zone," *New York Times*, 16 October 1994, section 4, 2.

[54] Mary Ellen Gale, "First Amendment But . . . On Curbing Racial Speech," *The Responsive Community: Rights and Responsibilities* 1 (Winter 1990–91): 48.

[55] On the charge that modern feminism is "Puritanical," see "Political Correctness and the Assault on Individuality," *The Heritage Lectures* (Heritage Foundation Reports), 29 January 1993; and John Irving, "Pornography and the New Puritans," *New York Times Book Review*, 29 March 1992, esp. 25–6.

At the core of both the antipornography and the anti-hate speech challenges to what these theorists like to call "First Amendment absolutism" is a redefinition of the relationship between words and things. Modern First Amendment jurisprudence—indeed, the text of the amendment itself—assumes a radical dichotomy between saying and doing. Just imagine, as Stanley Fish suggests, a society governed by a Bill of Rights that declared, "Congress shall make no law abridging freedom of *action*."[56] What's more, defenders of the First Amendment status quo concede that some words count as deeds even under the most libertarian interpretations of Constitutional doctrine. Were this not the case, jurist Frederick Schauer points out, virtually all of our "contract law, most of antitrust law, and much of criminal law" would have to be summarily scrapped.[57]

Of course, the Puritans went much farther and so, too, would antipornography feminists and critical race theorists. Words, they argue, are pathogens of a sort; they frequently describe the plague of hate speech as an "epidemic" or an "outbreak."[58] Like bacteria set loose in the public water supply, loose words poison the health of society, causing harm that the state has an interest in controlling. The reality of hate speech, Mari J. Matsuda writes, "explodes the notions that there are clear lines between words and deeds." Whether screamed or scrawled, expressions of racial hatred cause "real harm to real people." "We are not safe when these violent words are among us," she argues.[59]

Others concur, making clear that the wounds inflicted by hateful speech are more than imagined slights. Charles Lawrence, co-author

---

[56] Fish, *There's No Such Thing as Free Speech*, 105, emphasis added.

[57] Schauer quoted in Mari J. Matsuda, "Public Response to Racist Speech: Considering the Victim's Story," in Matsuda et al., *Words That Wound: Critical Race Theory, Assaultive Speech, and the First Amendment* (Boulder, Colo.: Westview, 1993), 35.

[58] See Matsuda et al., *Words That Wound*, 1, 83. For seventeenth-century discourse that compares words to wounds, see "A Report of the Trial of Mrs. Anne Hutchinson before the Church in Boston" (March 1638), in *The Antinomian Controversy, 1636–1638: A Documentary History*, David D. Hall (Durham, N.C.: Duke University Press, 1990), 373; Morris Palmer Tilley, *A Dictionary of Proverbs in England in the Sixteenth and Seventeenth Centuries* (Ann Arbor: University of Michigan Press, 1950), 618, entries S646–9; and *Watson v. Webster*, Salem, 1681, in Archie N. Frost, comp., *Verbatim Transcript of the File Papers of the Essex County Quarterly Courts, 1636–1692*, 75 vols. (typescript on deposit at the Essex Institute, Salem, Mass.; microfilm copy at Sterling Memorial Library, Yale University), 37: 101–2, 101–3.

[59] Matsuda, "Public Response to Racist Speech," 23, 50, 38.

with Matsuda of the definitive statement by critical race theorists on the problem of words, calls hate speech "assaultive . . . a verbal slap in the face." Drawing on anecdotal evidence from his own family as well as the findings of research psychologists, Lawrence evokes a world of hurt that many of us will remember from the schoolyard. Verbal assaults, he writes, can "produce physical symptoms that temporarily disable the victim," leaving "pain and scars . . . no less enduring because the injury had not been physical."[60] A recent advertising campaign by Planned Parenthood in response to escalating violence at abortion clinics puts it still more starkly: "WORDS KILL. Words are like bullets—they can be used to kill."[61] Taking their cues from ordinary language philosopher J. L. Austin among others, those active in the movement to stamp out hate speech and the campaign to criminalize pornography decry the neat separation of our mental world into "speech" on one side and "action" on the other. As Catharine MacKinnon recently noted, "speech acts" and "acts speak."[62] No seventeenth-century victim of a witch's discontented muttering would disagree.

Critical race theorists and antipornography feminists also seek to call attention to the relationship between speech and power. Words create, enact, and reinforce the structures of authority, these thinkers argue. Thus, one of the central tasks of critical race theory is to reexamine "the relationships between naming and reality, knowledge and power."[63] By making the expressive rights of individuals absolutely paramount over the equality interests of groups (African-Americans, gays, women, Latinos, and so on), free speech liberals unwittingly abet the silencing of minorities. Instead of a free marketplace of words and ideas, critics of the First Amendment status quo see "a rigged game": a world of "masters and slaves" in which "there can be no truly free speech."[64] Where Lawrence finds a world of black and white, MacKinnon sees a landscape

---

[60] Charles R. Lawrence III, "If He Hollers, Let Him Go: Regulating Racist Speech on Campus," in Matsuda et al., *Words That Wound*, 68, 72–3. See also Richard Delgado, "Words That Wound: A Tort Action for Racial Insults, Epithets, and Name-Calling," *Harvard Civil Rights–Civil Liberties Law Review* 17 (Spring 1982): 135–43. (Delgado's article is also reprinted in the eponymous *Words That Wound* by Matsuda et al.)
[61] Advertisement printed nationally. See *New York Times*, 5 January 1995, A17.
[62] Catharine A. MacKinnon, *Only Words* (Cambridge, Mass.: Harvard University Press, 1993), 30–1, 48.
[63] Matsuda et al., *Words That Wound*, 5.
[64] Lawrence, "If He Hollers, Let Him Go," 87.

of pornographers and victims, men and women. In her universe, too, "some people get a lot more speech than others." What's more, she points out, "the less speech you have, the more speech of those who have it keeps you unequal."[65]

On this point, the Puritan exemplar is more problematic. Early New Englanders would surely have understood the argument MacKinnon and Lawrence outline—which is more than I can say for many of their liberal critics. Still, Mather and his ilk would have made ambivalent champions for MacKinnon and crew. Although they recognized that speech constructs power relations, the Puritans advocated diametrically opposite goals from those of the First Amendment's postliberal critics. Cotton Mather and his coreligionists favored neither expressive liberty nor substantive equality—not in the ways we define these concepts today. In a world where, in John Winthrop's words, "at all times some must be rich[,] some poore, some highe and eminent in power and dignitie; others meane and in subjection," power was generally assumed to devolve upon those worthy of it.[66] From the Puritan perspective, unchecked speech was dangerous chiefly because it could damage those who had (rightly) come out on top of a steeply vertical social order. True, the notion that speech enacted a world of masters and slaves would have seemed reasonable to early New Englanders; everyone knew that speech was either the ally or the enemy of those in power. But we also must recognize that, at least until the end of the seventeenth century, nobody *objected* to a world of masters and slaves.

Now, of course, the words are on the Other's tongue. In our contemporary debates about speech and power, it is typically those without power who are leading the challenge against unfettered expression and those with power who defend the more libertarian interpretation of the First Amendment. It is the historically voiceless who are claiming the ability to speak—and the right to dictate what historically vocal groups can and cannot say. As Toni Morrison commented in a recent interview, the "definers" or dominant groups have always monopolized "the power to name." Now "the defined are . . . taking that power away from

---

[65] MacKinnon, *Only Words*, 72; see also 31–3.
[66] I am referring here to social equality; the place of spiritual equality in Puritan thought is a more complicated matter. The quote is from John Winthrop's famous shipboard lecture, "A Modell of Christian Charity" (1630), in *The Puritans: A Sourcebook of their Writings*, 2 vols., ed. Perry Miller (New York: Harper and Row, 1963), I: 195.

them."[67] In this battle the Puritans would more likely have been enemies than allies.

This is precisely the argument advanced by the most nuanced and compelling rebuttals of the critical race theorists' claims. In a persuasive, well-argued essay, Henry Louis Gates Jr. credits much of what the First Amendment challengers have to say while finding the overall thrust of their argument fundamentally wrong-headed. His objection is not so much philosophical as practical. True, Gates concedes (following Stanley Fish's lead), First Amendment absolutism is a legal fiction—"a paradigm instance of invented tradition." To be sure, university communities and the society at large have witnessed an explosive increase in verbal and other threats against the inclusion of racial, ethnic, and sexual minorities. Moreover, who could dispute the notion that power (to speak) begets power (to rule)? But tactics, Gates insists, are the key. If words construct power, why would those without voices look to those in power to determine who can say what to whom, when, and in what circumstances? "You don't go to the teacher to complain about the school bully unless you know that the teacher is on your side," he argues. And, as the numerous instances in which restricted "speech codes" of one kind or another have been used as cudgels against those who designed them make clear, "teacher" is often on one side today and on another tomorrow.[68]

There is another reason, Gates insists, that moving from a recognition of the relationship between speech and power to the regulation of that relationship is wide of the mark. The effort, he claims, is a costly distraction. For if words indeed shape our social order, they are neither the sole nor the most powerful instrument to do so. The First Amendment "antis," he says, risk "missing the civic forest for the legal trees." Words may shore up racism and sexism, but they do not equal racism and sexism. Gates fears for a world in which

the pendulum has swung from the absurd position that words don't matter to the equally absurd position that *only* words matter. . . . Yes, speech is a species

[67] Claudia Dreifus, "Chloe Wofford Talks about Toni Morrison," *New York Times Magazine*, 11 September 1994, 74.
[68] Henry Louis Gates Jr., "War of Words: Critical Race Theory and the First Amendment," in *Speaking of Race, Speaking of Sex: Hate Speech, Civil Rights, and Civil Liberties*, ed. Gates et al. (New York: New York University Press, 1994), 21–2, 42. The ironic use of MacKinnon's and Dworkin's antipornography thought to censor their own work is chronicled in Jeffrey Toobin, "X-Rated: Annals of Law," *The New Yorker*, 3 October 1994, 70–8.

of action. Yes, there are some acts that only speech can perform. But there are some acts that speech alone cannot accomplish. You cannot heal the sick by pronouncing them well.[69]

In many of these particulars, Cotton Mather would doubtless have begged to differ. But that is as it should be; his world was not ours. And it is the inescapable—and, in some sense, desirable—gulf that separates us from him and his cohort that limits the efficacy of his example. The thoughts and deeds and words of New England Puritans are (to me at least) fascinating. They may even be illuminating. Theirs is, in this regard, a *useful* past. The Puritan example reminds us to listen carefully to the dense counterpoint of voices that make up our communities of discourse, to pay close attention to who is trying to silence others, who is resisting those demands, and why. It does not convey a sense that the postmodern present is either better or worse than the premodern past. Rather, it reminds us that neither moment in our history is quite so transparent as it sometimes seems.

Yet the Puritan example does not constitute a *usable* past. The example is not, and cannot be, instructive or pragmatic. It does not suggest a program of action, nor does it even help us evaluate those programs that other sources propose. Popular paeans to the need to avoid repeating past mistakes aside, attending to the cultural history of speaking in early New England will not do much to solve the problems of the present—at least not in any direct sense. In the end the lesson it best teaches us is Martha Ballard's lesson: some of the most taken-for-granted elements of our everyday world were not always arranged in the ways they are now. In its own small way this is a profound lesson. For it promises, as Natalie Davis once put it, that "things don't have to be the way they are now." History—careful history—teaches us that the world "could be different, that it was different, that there are alternatives," that it can be different again.[70]

Being reminded of the irreducible differentness of other places and other times is, to my mind at least, an intellectually satisfying lesson. But is it a morally sufficient one? Does confronting the fallibility, the contingency, the very evanescence of our own ways of being, doing,

[69] Gates, "War of Words," 48, 54.
[70] Henry Abelove et al., ed., "Interview with Natalie Zemon Davis," *Visions of History* (New York: Pantheon, 1983), 99–122, quote from 114–5.

having, and knowing do anything to answer the craving for meaning that has become a staple of contemporary American life? Instead of posing ever more unanswerable questions, should historians be in the business of producing answers—answers we can believe in?[71] The year 1995, more than any other in my lifetime, witnessed considerable public debate on precisely this point. In a season punctuated by what the *Nation* cleverly dubbed "the fiftieth anniversary of almost everything"—from the bombing of Hiroshima, to the liberation of Auschwitz, to the death of Franklin Delano Roosevelt—ordinary Americans have reflected with new energy upon the meanings and purposes of our national history.[72]

This wrangling over what history ought to teach us provides a necessary context for analyzing the concurrent debate over the ways we should teach history. The flap over the release, in the fall of 1994, of the *National Standards for United States History* funded by the National Endowment for the Humanities, masquerades as a battle about the content of a particular version of the history of the United States. "Counting how many times different subjects are mentioned," Lynne Cheney tells us, "yields telling results." The score is in: Ku Klux Klan, 17; J. P. Morgan, 0. What more need be said?[73] However effectively such punditry plays on the talk-show circuit, this critique-by-arithmetic is a smokescreen; much more is really at stake than the ratio of George Washingtons to Sojourner Truths. At a deeper level the debate over the *Standards* is a debate about the process of learning history.[74] It is a struggle over how historians should go about translating their findings for the people who are arguably their most important audience: schoolchildren.

---

[71] See, for example, Owen Flanagan's chapter on moral confidence in this volume.

[72] *The Nation*, special issue celebrating "1945 at Fifty," 260 (15 May 1995); see also "Viewpoints Forum: Public History and Disney's America," *Perspectives: The American Historical Association Newsletter* 33 (March 1995), 1, 3–11; and Karen J. Winkler, "Who Owns History?" *Chronicle of Higher Education*, 20 January 1995, A11, A18.

[73] Lynne V. Cheney, "The End of History," *Wall Street Journal*, 20 October 1994, A22.

[74] The mere titles assigned by the *Journal* editorial staff to responses to Cheney's column are instructive. See "The History Thieves," *Wall Street Journal*, 8 November 1994, A23; and "Senate Rescues History," *Wall Street Journal*, 19 January 1995, A18. See also the contrary views expressed in Arnita A. Jones, "Our Stake in the History Standards," *Chronicle of Higher Education*, 6 January 1995, B1ff.; Diane Ravitch, "Revise, but Don't Abandon, the History Standards," *Chronicle of Higher Education*, 17 February 1995, A52; "History According to Whom," *New York Times*, 19 November 1994, A23; Gary Nash, "A History of All the People Isn't PC," *Wall Street Journal*, 21 November 1994, A17; and Joyce Appleby, "Standards Criticisms Nonsense on Stilts," *Wall Street Journal*, 6 December 1994, A29.

Does the moral calculus of doing history change when the readers in question are citizens-in-training? Just how much irony and contingency can ten-year-olds stand? The virulence of the current wave of debate to the contrary, these are not new questions. The claim that history classes should be concerned with "teaching patriotism" and instilling pride in "American heroes and American ideals" long predates Cheney and other opponents of the *Standards*. These particular sentiments were voiced, for instance, by the president of the Board of Education of Muncie, Indiana, in the early 1920s at the peak of fear about the impact of immigration. At that time it was widely accepted that history lessons were civics lessons, inculcating children with the beliefs of their community: that the "white race is the best race on earth" and that the "United States is unquestionably the best country in the world," for example.[75] As if to prove William Faulkner's maxim that the past isn't dead or even past, the school board governing the classrooms of Lake County, Florida, recently decided to reenlist history as the ideological field agent of patriotism. Trying to recapture the nationalistic zeal of the early twentieth century amidst a new and rising tide of immigration, the Board mandated that every course in the system teach "that American culture, values and political institutions are inherently 'superior to other foreign or historic cultures.' " Pat Hart, the Board's chair and the drafter of the policy, put it starkly: "we are the best of the best."[76] Lynne Cheney is slicker than Pat Hart; her rhetoric is neither hokey nor jingoistic. But for her, too, history is about making citizens for the future by making (she would doubtless say *finding*) heroes from the past. A more acceptable version of the *Standards*, Cheney says, would be one that "regularly manages *a tone of affirmation*," in part by emphasizing "individual greatness." "We are *a better people* than the National Standards indicate," she proclaims, "and our children deserve to know it."[77]

This argument is predicated upon the notion that some competing version of history (an ill-defined "multiculturalism" in Lake County's case, and the *Standards* themselves in Cheney's) teaches that Americans are *worse* people than we thought and, by inference, that some other nation is or was *better*. And indeed this is precisely how many critics

---

[75] Robert S. Lynd and Helen Merrell Lynd, *Middletown: A Study in Modern American Culture* (New York: Harcourt Brace, 1929), 198, 200.

[76] Larry Rohter, "Battle over Patriotism Curriculum," *New York Times*, 15 May 1994, A22.

[77] Cheney, "The End of History," emphasis added.

have portrayed the *Standards*. The *Standards*, one letter writer infers from Cheney's editorial, are nothing but "a cynical ploy to indoctrinate children with [historians'] own hatred of America."[78] Instead of revering George Washington and capitalism, these poor deluded kids, left to stand "naked and defenseless" before the America-bashing membership of the Organization of American Historians, will apparently be taught to love a rag-tag bunch of Africans and Indians, from Mansa Musa's court in the ancient kingdom of Mali to the Aztec agriculturists of Mesoamerica.[79]

I will be the first to admit that the silliness quotient of the *Standards* is just high enough to fuel the conservative bonfire. Anyone who has studied Iroquois torture rituals, for example, may suspect that students asked "to analyze how the Mohawk, Oneida, Onondaga, Cayuga, and Seneca united to solve conflicts peaceably" will solve only half of a puzzle. Similarly, a question about whether "Native American societies [were] 'primitive,' as the first Europeans to encounter them believed, or had . . . developed complex patterns of social organization, trading networks, and political culture" is not really a question at all.[80] But these much ballyhooed excesses (and there are, on the whole, few of them) are not the real culprit. The graver threat, I suspect, is the mode of thinking the *Standards* encourage.

Gary Nash and his coauthors of the *Standards* share with Cheney and her fellow critics an appreciation of the necessity of historical knowledge to an informed and active citizenry. In a "democratic society," the authors of the *Standards* argue, "*knowledge of history is the precondition of political intelligence*. . . . [W]ithout historical knowledge and inquiry, we cannot achieve the informed, discriminating citizenship essential to effective participation in the democratic processes of governance."[81] Where the two camps (and they are all but armed camps; this debate has proved exceptionally nasty) part company is in their respective definitions of what constitutes historical knowledge.

For Nash, historical knowledge is a set of facts *and* the processes

---

[78] Kim Weisman letter, "The History Thieves," *Wall Street Journal*, 8 November 1994, A23. All the letters in this group make clear in their texts that none of the respondents to Cheney has read the *Standards*.

[79] "Naked and defenseless" from Balint Vazsonyi letter, "The History Thieves." Questions about Mansa Musa et al. are examples from the *Standards* singled out by Cheney, "The End of History."

[80] Nash et al., *National Standards for United States History*, 41, 44.

[81] Ibid., 1, emphasis in original.

through which historians discover and deploy those facts. The *Standards* stress what the authors call "active learning," which amounts to both memorizing and utilizing bits of information about the past. Historical thinking, they argue, is more than "the passive absorption of facts, dates, names, and places." Students are encouraged to master these specifics, but also to "*go beyond the facts presented* . . . and examine the historical record for themselves." The *Standards* ask students to think about the points of view that underlie historical arguments, including those perspectives or voices an "author . . . chose to omit." Instead of merely absorbing, they are encouraged to "differentiate between historical facts and historical interpretations," to "consider multiple perspectives," and to "hold interpretations of history as tentative." They are warned to "avoid 'present-mindedness' by not judging the past solely in terms of the norms and values of today." In addition, they are asked to eschew the "related trap" of "lineality and inevitability": thinking that events have unfolded logically, orderly, and as they had to. For the authors of the *Standards*, the real enemy is neither Western Civilization nor its champions—those much-maligned Dead White Males. The real danger is intellectual passivity. To make a cardboard civics lesson out of the many dimensions of the lived past is to suggest, they write, that "individual action count[s] for nothing. No attitude is more likely to feed civic apathy, cynicism, and resignation." Instead, students should recognize both that history is always "value laden," and that some history is better than others. Students who master "the complex skills of principled thinking and moral reasoning" can make their own critical judgments.[82]

For Cheney, historical knowledge is a set of facts, the building blocks of the "lessons" she would like to see taught. Being creative, thinking imaginatively, and what Nash calls "go[ing] beyond the facts presented" to get at underlying meanings, have no place in her definition. For her and for other critics on the right, such an approach signals the beginning of a precipitous and irreversible descent into relativism. Balint Vazsonyi, a supporter of Cheney's arguments, claims, for example, that the *Standards*, like Nazi and Bolshevik "official" histories, teach "that facts do not exist, that history is always arbitrary," and thus that "solid ground can be replaced by anyone's brand of quicksand. Soon, no one knows which [way] is up and those in control can reinvent everything as they

[82] Ibid., 7, 17, 19, 26, 31.

go."[83] Telling schoolchildren that they inhabit a world of irony and contingency, Vazsonyi seems to argue, would be unthinkable. The ground on which we stand is either solid or nonexistent; there is nothing in between. If historians fail to at least strike a pose of utter moral confidence, the consequences are dire; the *Standards* lead students into a world of chaos, degeneracy, even fascism.

Few who have read the *Standards* are likely to agree with Vazsonyi's hysterical claim that they represent "an amensia-inducing drug"—a potent chemical weapon deployed in "a war" on "America's soul." But this panicked letter writer is surely right on one score. The ground upon which historians construct their intellectual houses seems considerably shakier today than it did even half a century ago. This is so, not because we are a particularly obnoxious subspecies of that unsavory breed, intellectuals, but rather because we share the moral universe of the late twentieth century. In the wake of the fiftieth anniversaries that forced us again to stare into the abysses of Auschwitz and Hiroshima, it should be clear that there isn't much moral bedrock left in the world. Instead, there is a whole lot of shifting terrain, and we are all trying to build upon it together. Much as we might like to transport ourselves back to the Enlightenment—to a moment in time when the careful application of human reason seemed to guarantee an orderly world—it is impossible for us to do so. We cannot simply wish away three centuries of moral knowledge, however hideous much of it has been.

This seems to me a fine lesson to teach our children—and ourselves. For one thing, to do anything less would be a form of lying. And what could be more profoundly at odds with the historical enterprise than deliberate deception? Yet if we are to acknowledge that we face a cold and frightening universe, we need not embrace a nihilistic one. Questioning our foundations does not mean trading bedrock for quicksand. Indeed, to assume, as Cheney and her set do, that a world of dead certainties is a world in which all speculations are equally plausible, is to defy common sense. Just because historical knowledge, like all knowledge, is culturally constructed doesn't make it useless, and doesn't mean we can't tell finer efforts from lesser ones. With his characteristic gift for metaphor, Clifford Geertz puts it this way: a chair, too, "is culturally (historically, socially . . .) constructed . . . yet you can sit in it, it can be

---

[83] Vazsonyi letter, "The History Thieves." For a more sophisticated version of this reasoning, see Gertrude Himmelfarb, "Some Reflections on the New History," 666.

well made or ill, and it cannot, at least in the present state of the art, be made out of water or . . . thought into existence."[84] An awful lot of territory, as Thomas Haskell points out, lies between Platonic absolutism and Nietzschian relativism. In this capacious middle ground there is plenty of room for histories that are contingent, fallible, moral, and true—all at the same time.[85]

And so I would say: Dr. Cheney, take heart! Professor Himmelfarb, stop averting your eyes! The present is not as bleak nor the past as rosy as you think. The distance between then and now remains unbreachably vast, but historians are still struggling to fashion meaningful paths from present to past and back again. The routes may be tortuous: maps in need of perpetual redrafting. It is doubtful that any among us will be able to plot a roadway that leads us on a course straight and narrow from an unproblematic past to a coherent and singular national future. But there is still, I think, some glory left in the attempt. And there are still, I am sure, reliable standards for judging our (tentative, imperfect) successes along the way.

[84] Geertz, *After the Fact*, 62.
[85] Haskell, "Curious Persistence of Rights Talk," esp. 986, 990–1, 1002–4. See also Kloppenberg, "Objectivity and Historicism," 1018.

6

"Of the standard of moral taste": Literary criticism as moral inquiry

WAYNE C. BOOTH

The very phrase "moral inquiry" is for some literary critics an oxymoron. Moral indictment? Of course you can have that. Moral celebration? Perhaps. But inquiry? The word implies the chance of arriving at established, unquestioned conclusions. About morality, some still claim, there can be no such conclusions—and thus no inquiry about them.

Meanwhile, moral indictments seem increasingly fashionable. The accusers show no doubt whatever that certain works of art are corrupting public morality. The National Endowment for the Arts is attacked for sponsoring "immoral" artists like Robert Mapplethorpe. Schools are attacked for assigning "wicked" works like *Huckleberry Finn, Catcher in the Rye*, and *To Kill a Mockingbird*. TV and movie producers are attacked for celebrating violence that may be imitated. Authors and publishers are attacked for producing books ranging from the violence of Bret Ellis's *American Psycho* to the obscenities of Philip Roth's *Sabbath's Theater*. Record companies are attacked for producing gangsta rap and hard rock. Legislators, national and local, work on laws to protect us from being harmed by bad art.

These attacks naturally produce a flood of defenses. Some say that to fuss about the moral effects of art risks slashing the First Amendment.[1] Some argue—especially those who hope to profit from violent exploitation—that there is no scientific evidence for the harmful effects of their

---

[1] The American Civil Liberties Union (to which I belong) often goes too far in opposing *all* objections to any public expression. But as Cass Sunstein argues, there are almost no full "free-speech absolutists" who would accept no limits whatever on public "speech," however defined. He shows how we have committed absurd extensions of the "free speech" defense. See his *Democracy and the Problem of Free Speech* (New York: Free Press, 1993), 56, 121–4.

product.[2] Others make the more challenging case that to attack artistic works on moral grounds is to destroy our most precious possession: the "aesthetic" domain, which is not just different from everyday morality but in effect higher. As Wendy Steiner says in the conclusion to her recent *The Scandal of Pleasure*: "Art occupies a different moral space from that presented in identity politics." For her, since art is obviously "virtual," not "real," it should not be subjected to the kind of moral criticism we offer when everyday events offend us.[3]

Throughout this controversy nearly everyone concedes, and all imply, that no matter what we do about the moral powers of art, those powers are real. Even the most ardent opponents of censorship do not deny that many art works can harm some who "take them in." And even the most ardent would-be censors imply by their every gesture that certain other works, in contrast, are not just morally defensible, not just beneficial, but essential to any full human life. This claim is clearest when we narrow our attention as I do here from all art to stories, then broaden it to include not just the highbrow stuff we call literature (novels, plays, poems, operas), and not just serious biographies and autobiographies, but gossip, talk shows, soap operas, TV and movie documentaries, and on to the stories and narrative songs we heard in childhood.[4]

Whenever I ask adults who have been ardent readers whether they can think of any one work that changed their lives in a significant way, not just in childhood, almost all of them offer at least one clear example. Sometimes they stress regret ("How I wish I had not stumbled upon Jack Kerouac's *On the Road* when I was sixteen"); more often they express deep gratitude ("Reading Tolstoy's *Resurrection* in my forties transformed my attitude toward religion; I had been an atheist and after reading—thank God!—I was not.") And when the question is generalized—"Do you think that a large share of your moral education was performed by stories, from infancy on?"—most answer "yes." They agree that when we really engage with the characters we meet and the moral choices those charac-

---

[2] On May 31, 1995, then-Senator Bob Dole's televised attack on violent movies prompted an amazing outburst of angry responses, pro and con, including visibly self-serving attempts at rebuttal by Hollywood producers. See *New York Times*, 2 June 1995, 1, 10.

[3] Wendy Steiner, *The Scandal of Pleasure: Art in an Age of Fundamentalism* (Chicago: University of Chicago Press, 1995), 211.

[4] I'm sure that most readers can match memories like that of my weeping as my mother sang the sad, sad story of a lonely orphan boy. The song began: " 'Twas a party for the little ones / And everyone was there" and ended with the refrain, "If I only had a home, sweet home, someone to call my own; like all the other boys and girls. . . ."

ters face, moral changes occur in us, for good or ill. In short, no one who has thought about it for five minutes can deny that we are at least partially constructed, in our most fundamental moral character, by the stories we have heard, or read, or viewed, or acted out in amateur theatricals: the stories we have really *listened* to.[5] (From here on I'll use the language of "listening" to include all "taking in" of stories in any medium.)

Most of the world's successful moral teachers have also taken this generalization for granted, resorting in their homilies to story rather than straight prose exhortation. The authors of the Bible chose mainly to be storytellers, *narrators* rather than mere exhorters. They did not just lay down bare codes, like a list of ten flat commandments. No, they told stories, like the one about a troubled abandoned-child-hero who, as leader of his liberated people, almost botches the job of obtaining some divine rules printed on a tablet, and about a people who largely botch the job of receiving and abiding by them. They did not just print out the sermons of a savior; they placed the sermons into a story, and they surrounded them with other stories, especially the one about how He himself grappled with questions about His status as savior, and about how He told scores of radically ambiguous parables that force His listeners into moral thought. They did not *say* that for God to be incarnated as a man entails irresolvable paradoxes; they *told a story* about how the God/man at the moment of supreme moral testing is ridden with doubt and cries out, as any of us would have done, "My God, my God, why hast thou forsaken me?" Those authors "knew," perhaps without knowing what they knew, that serious stories *educate morally*— and they do so more powerfully than do story-free sermons.

In sum, the great tellers and most of us listeners have known in our bones that stories, whether fictional or historical, in prose or in verse, whether told by mothers to infants or by rabbis and priests to the elderly and dying, whether labelled as sacred or profane or as teaching good morality or bad—*stories* are our major moral teachers. Some stories teach only a particular moral perspective, one that can be captured with a moral tag, as in some of Aesop's fables and the simpler biblical tales. Many of them teach a morality that you and I would reject. But all of them teach, and thus in a sense are open to moral inquiry, even when they do not seem to invite it.

---

[5] See, for developments of this claim, the works by Robert Coles, Bruno Bettelheim, and Marina Warner in the appendix to this chapter.

I could spend the rest of this essay summarizing a long history of arguments for this generalization—arguments a bit "soft" judged by some research standards, but to me convincing. Instead I must simply take it as assumed and move to more controversial issues. Even if "everyone" is right in assuming that stories teach morality, good or bad, can literary criticism inquire responsibly into the differences between the good and bad of that teaching without corrupting or destroying the domain defended by Steiner: the world of purified artistic pleasure, the genuinely "artistic," the "aesthetic"? Most of us believe that if we are to have criticism of the "right kind," it should reinforce the "right kinds" of moral effects and protect listeners from the "wrong kinds," without denigrating the glories of *art*. But to say that raises, in threatening form, the two questions central here: Who are the judges who earn the right to determine which are the right kinds? And just how should such judges practice their inquiry before passing judgment?

Few modern critics or philosophers have faced these twin questions with full attention. Even those who aggressively assert their moral judgments rarely discuss how we decide that one critic—for the fun of it, let's call him Booth—is more credible than some opponent. Yet obviously if I proclaim, "That work is morally disgusting," or "That work is morally inspiriting," I imply that I am more qualified to pass such judgments than is my opponent, because I know how to inquire about them. My claim here is that if we paid more attention to the two key questions, battles over opposing judgments might end in impasse less often.

CONTROVERSY ABOUT MORAL CRITICISM: A POTTED HISTORY

Is genuine moral inquiry possible, or even pertinent, in appraising literary quality? The history of answers to this question in Western culture could be reductively summarized as a pendulum swing from "yes" to "no" to "yes" again.

Epoch I (about two-and-a-half millennia)

Before modernism of various kinds broke into our scene, almost every critic agreed that the moral worth of stories must be addressed with rational inquiry and that some inquirers do the job better than others.

If one had asked Plato or Sir Philip Sidney or Samuel Johnson or Samuel Taylor Coleridge or Matthew Arnold whether the critic's job included questions about literature's moral worth, they would have scorned the questioner, even if they disagreed in their particular judgments. Every responsible critic, they assumed, must ask about the moral value of any work addressed. Such critics conflated, as I do here, narrow notions of "moral codes" with broad questions of total ethical effect: transformations of character, of self, of soul, of *ethos*. Is this work good for its listeners? Does experiencing it build their character in the right way? Is it morally educational or *mis*educational? Is this author using artistic power to heal or harm? Is this story potentially a true friend?

The more theoretically minded critics went further and faced an even more troublesome question: Is this work's moral quality an essential element in our judgment, not just of its moral value, but of its artistic worth? And again they answered with a firm "yes." As one cliché put it from classical times on, the goal of *good* art is to "delight *and* instruct"; it should be useful as well as pleasing (*utile et dulce*). The subtler critics went further to show just how all art instructs *as* it pleases; it instructs *through* its pleasures—for good *or* ill. The highly "human" moral seductions that make us love art works are the powers that demand our critical appraisal. Rhetorically minded critics like Horace were aware that different audiences respond to different qualities, and they put the pairing of instruction and pleasure in either/or terms: good literature must *either* teach *or* delight: *aut prodesse aut delectare*. But Horace made it clear in the *Ars Poetica* that he preferred the kind of poetry that does both simultaneously.

Epoch II (not much more than half a century)

From the last years of the nineteenth century to the 1960s, more and more critics reversed the field to answer "no": moral rightness or wrongness has little or nothing to do with literary or aesthetic worth, and debate about the moral worth of any artistic work consequently leads nowhere. In *The Company We Keep*, arguing for a return to "yes," I traced briefly this swing from "yes" to "no" and suggested possible causes for the widespread rejection of morally centered artistic criticism: the immense difficulties the moral critic faces in the seemingly irresolvable contradictions among critics; the philosophical fashion, starting in the eighteenth century, of assuming an unbridgeable chasm between the

world of fact and the world of value, the world of "is" and the world
of "ought";[6] the obvious incoherence and carelessness and dogmatism
that too many moral critics exhibited; the decline of confidence in the
demonstrative powers of any rhetoric that offered—as is always true of
moral criticism—no scientific proof; the decline of religious faith, "religion" having been seen as the best or only source of moral standards;
and so on.

Possibly the most powerful cause for the rejection of moral criticism
of art was the new passion (growing out of the eighteenth-century invention of "the aesthetic") for placing art or poetry in the special domain
celebrated by Steiner, the higher world of pure or artistic pleasure: a
world exempt from the chaotic problems of a lower world. To impose
moral judgments on what we meet in this utterly different world, as we
embrace art for the sake of the embrace, was said to be not just difficult,
nor just dangerous: it was irrelevant to true quality, and it should be
ruled out of all serious criticism. Indeed, genuine literary art, often given
the elevating label "poetry," is in this view somehow above all ordinary
beliefs and practices. As Archibald MacLeish's much quoted poem "Ars
Poetica" put it, "A poem should not mean but be." W. H. Auden's aph-
orism "Poetry makes nothing happen" became a slogan for many.[7]

---

[6] On the subject of how philosophical fashions, like the oversimplified reliance on separation of fact and value, resist rational disproof and persist even after being thoroughly
refuted, see Hilary Putnam's cogent chapter, "Fact and Value," in *Reason, Truth, and
History* (Cambridge: Cambridge University Press, 1981), 127–49. As long ago as 1974
I had listed, in *Modern Dogma and the Rhetoric of Assent* (Chicago: University of
Chicago Press, 1974), more than two score refutations of the fact-value split—all of
them by "philosophers" and many of them carefully reasoned. Those scores are by now
raised to hundreds. See also Bernard Williams in *Ethics and the Limits of Philosophy*
(Cambridge, Mass.: Harvard University Press, 1985), esp. chap. 5 and *Morality* (Cambridge: Cambridge University Press, 1972). Or, for a neglected earlier turn on the question, see A. E. Taylor's "Actuality and Value," chap. 2 of *The Faith of a Moralist*
(London: Macmillan, 1930). For any "absolutist" about the distinction, every claim to
engage in real inquiry, not just in this chapter but in this entire book, will be dismissed
out of hand.

[7] They tended to ignore just how passionately Auden could argue for the moral and ethical
"happenings" that good literature *must* achieve.
    "Poetry," he wrote, "can do a hundred and one things, delight, sadden, disturb,
amuse, instruct—it may express every possible shade of emotion, and describe every
conceivable kind of event, but there is only one thing that all poetry *must* do; it must
praise all it can for being and for happening." See W. H. Auden, "Making, Knowing
and Judging," *The Dyer's Hand* (London: Faber and Faber, 1962), 60. Readers who are
not aware of the intense rejection of morality-centered criticism by most prominent
critics by midcentury should have a look at the controversy over the Bollingen Prize
awarded to Ezra Pound in 1949. See Noel Stock, *Ezra Pound: Perspectives* (Chicago:
University of Chicago Press, 1965), esp. the essay by Allen Tate, "Ezra Pound and the
Bollingen Prize" (1959).

Thus art, craft, beauty, skill, or fine style were put on one side of a great divide and all practical intentions and effect on "life" relegated to the other side. When appraising even the most morally questionable works—Louis-Ferdinand Céline's *Journey to the End of the Night*, say— one should attend only to the question of whether the style was beautiful, or at least brilliant or original.[8]

Epoch III (still far short of a half century)

Then, starting in the late sixties, critics of various shapes and shades began to say "yes" again. Indeed, the past three decades have produced an avalanche of moral arguments, one that has felt depressing or overwhelming to many traditionalists. It has been astonishing even to me, a critic who had thought he was fighting a losing battle in defense of moral concerns.[9] Following the lead of the few holdouts through Epoch II— for example, the Marxists, F. R. Leavis, Lionel Trilling, R. P. Blackmur—critics began once again to insist that stories provide, in Kenneth Burke's phrase, both good and bad "equipment for living."[10] Often these post-New-Critic newer critics aggressively attacked the "aestheticizing" or "formalizing" or "objectivizing" that had come to dominate Epoch II. Not only in literary criticism but in every artistic field, critics reopened questions about how stories change listeners and cultures. They thus began to reunite themselves—consciously or unconsciously—with the grand tradition of Plato and Sidney and Arnold.

It is not surprising that this reopening of ultimate "value" questions

---

[8] Many of the art-for-art's-sakers were, like Oscar Wilde, actually passionate moralists, preaching a new set of standards. See Booth, *The Company We Keep*, 11–2. But many of their followers lost that point, talking as if moral reasoning about anything was a thing of the past.

[9] Much of what I have to say here may seem not only obvious but repetitive to those who have read my earlier related work. In addition to *The Company We Keep*, see *The Rhetoric of Fiction*, 2d ed. (Chicago: University of Chicago Press, 1983), chap. 13; "Why Ethical Criticism Fell on Hard Times," *Ethics* 98 (January 1988), 278–93; "Ethics and Criticism," *The New Princeton Encyclopedia of Poetry and Poetics* (Princeton, N.J.: Princeton University Press, 1993); "On Relocating Ethical Criticism," in *Explanation and Value in the Arts*, ed. Salim Kemal and Ivan Gaskell (Cambridge: Cambridge University Press, 1993); "Are We Blessed or Cursed by Our Life with *The Turn of the Screw*?" in *The Turn of the Screw*, teaching edition, ed. Peter G. Beidler (Boston: Bedford Books of St. Martin's Press, 1994); "The Ethics of Forms: Taking Flight with the Wings of the Dove," in *Understanding Narrative*, ed. James Phelan and Peter J. Rabinowitz (Columbus: Ohio State University Press, 1994).

[10] Kenneth Burke, *The Philosophy of Literary Form: Studies in Symbolic Action*, 3d ed. (Baton Rouge: Louisiana State University Press, 1973).

has felt threatening, not only to those who still rely on the hard-and-fast fact-value distinction, but also to those who fear an influx of the wrong values, or at least of values that cannot be debated in rational inquiry. It has seemed to many not an opening at all but a *closing*: a destructive avalanche of irrationality that threatens to close off rational discourse and turn everything into "politics."[11]

This opening, which can hardly be called a single movement because there is so much disagreement among its partisans, is by no means confined to those who emphasize as I do words like "moral" or "ethical." Anyone who looks closely at the work of various "postmodern" critics will discover that many are pursuing questions about the ultimate effects that stories have upon our lives. Whether their overt label is feminism or Marxism or new historicism or deconstruction or cultural critique or gay studies or race studies or postcolonial discourse, they astonishingly agree—though often so far beneath the surface that careless readers miss it—that stories have moral importance. Discussing that importance matters, not just because stories are beautiful, or fun, or good time-killers, but because they make a difference to our *ethos*—who we are, how we behave to others, and what our culture becomes. The new critics are asking, in short, precisely the same kind of questions that the would-be censors of media violence are asking—or at least should be asking. That many in this multiple movement fail to proceed with a scholarly care that deserves the word "inquiry" is lamentable, but it does not affect the plain historical fact of the opening, the return to "yes."[12]

Nevertheless, though I personally embrace many of the questions producing this avalanche, I find that too many of the answers, like too many

---

[11] The avalanche of new moral criticism has been matched by an avalanche of refutations and even angry attacks. Since they can be found "everywhere," I resist any brief listing.

[12] This postsixties avalanche is too huge for adequate footnoting. In the appendix I list, with some annotation, a crude selection that includes mainly those works that actually use the words "moral" or "ethical" in their titles. If you doubt my claim about the avalanche, go to your library's computer and call up not just "morality and literature" or "ethics and literature" but such pairings as "religion and literature," "Christianity and literature," "Judaism and literature," or "literature and culture." The most careful critique of the ideological excesses and careless distortions of literary works exhibited by too many in the "avalanche" has been a series of essays by the Shakespearean scholar Richard Levin. The angry responses of those he has criticized (to me almost always justly) demonstrate both the complexity and importance of the issues raised by "moral inquiry," especially when extended as broadly as I have done here. See, for example, Levin's "The New and the Old Historicizing of Shakespeare," in *The Historical and Political Turn in Literary Studies*, ed. Winfried Fluck (Tübingen: Gunter Narr Verlag, 1995).

of the moral judgments offered by critics in Epoch I and almost all of the recent indictments of popular sex and violence, are arrived at with too little attention to my two central questions: how does one distinguish competent from incompetent judges, and how can even the most competent listener exercise *inquiry* about moral distinctions, not just between individual stories but among *kinds* of stories. These distinctions are acceptable and useful to others—"replicable," if you will—but clearly not in the scientific sense. Perhaps "followable" or "rationally discussable" should be our term for the standards we are pursuing.

A COMPETENT CRITIC OR A BUMBLER OR A FRAUD? HOW DO YOU DISTINGUISH?

Even those who say "no" to our earlier questions assume in their daily practice a real difference between those critics whom they should listen to and those who don't deserve their attention. Each critic implies that "I, the judge, am obviously more competent than those I disagree with." But few critics, ancient or modern, postmodernist or anti-postmodernist, have risked pursuing openly the personal defects that can handicap the critic, as David Hume does in the essay I shall borrow from here, his classic defense of literary judgment, "Of the Standard of Taste."[13]

Hume's main point is implicit in all that I have said so far: our need is not for rival lists of stories—books, movies, videos—to be condemned or celebrated, regardless of context, or for statistical counts of this or that kind of sex or violence, but for *listeners* who are qualified to converse effectively about moral qualities. We need a critical culture: a nation of experienced listeners who practice moral inquiry with at least as much competence as is exercised by a devoted football fan when judging a coach or quarterback. We have many such critical cultures supporting the most popular sports. We have versions of such cultures in those music lovers and amateurs who judge classical music performances or the originality of the latest hard rock disk. But we do not have a comparable culture pursuing *informed* moral inquiry about our heavily storied lives.[14] What we have instead is blind warfare among defenders of

---

[13] David Hume, "Of the Standard of Taste," in *Essays and Treatises on Several Subjects, Containing Essays, Moral, Political, Literary*, 2 vols. (Oxford: Oxford University Press, 1963), 231–58. The essay, first published in 1742, has been reprinted hundreds of times. Until quite recently it appeared in almost every anthology of literary criticism.

[14] It could be argued, perhaps even proved statistically, that people in America these days

this or that canon or anticanon or this or that new opening or return to old values. Too many warriors claim that conflicts about such matters cannot be rationally debated or that "the enemy" is hopelessly irrational and should not be allowed into the conversation. Too often the appraisers have not even tested their claims by listening to the stories they judge, let alone the rival critical approaches.[15]

As I move to Hume's standards, I must stress that to argue that some judgments are better than others is not to argue that *my* judgments are better than *yours*, or that any one group—a collection of professional literary or movie critics, say—is ipso facto more entitled to a hearing than any other group. What is important is to recognize that inquiry about moral quality is quite different from mere reporting of personal experience or emotional response. Moral judgments for or against a story are finally claims about qualities *in the judged works*, and they are thus always implicated in a potentially arrogant claim by the judge:

> I have the qualities required for discerning such and such qualities in a work, and therefore what may look like my merely personal reaction is more than that, even though it includes my feelings and convictions. Though not objective in the sense "independent of all human preferences," it is not merely subjective either. Even though not "replicable" by every conceivable listener, it is sufficiently "followable" to command attention from any listener who will attend to the work as closely and responsibly as I have done.

The very possibility of such a claim has been attacked by one group of participants in the avalanche, extremists in the so-called reader-response movement. Though I share the view that all serious responses, however contradictory, should be taken into account, the claim of some that all judgments are equally valid is absurd. It is true that in some teaching situations something like this egalitarianism can make sense; a good teacher will be careful not to knock down an outlandish reading

---

spend a larger proportion of their time with stories, both obviously fictional and purportedly "real," than has been true in any other culture. Consider their access to TV, radio, movies, gossip, newspapers (including the tabloids inventing "real" stories), audiotapes, rap records, bestselling mysteries, Ann Landers and the flood of anecdote-filled therapy books. We may long for a culture in which people sat around the fire in the evenings and told "real" stories or read Dickens to one another. But more Americans live more hours in *that* story world than would have been found in any older culture.

15 Dole, in his outburst about violence and sex in movies, praised and blamed works that he later admitted he had never experienced. More scandalous, in my view, are the "trained" academics who discourse about novels or works of criticism without reading more than the fragments that happen to offend.

if in doing so the student will lose the love of story.[16] But when we are appraising a response, we obviously must determine whether the appraiser has "taken in" what is there to be taken in. Has she really listened, or instead been taken in by only a fragment, perhaps even a misinterpreted one? There is nothing elitist in this point; just as inexperienced listeners can extract a scene from its context, often reversing the implied author's intended moral judgments, so "sophisticated literary critics" can fail to take in a story because their critical biases blind them. With their attention on their quest for conceptual confirmations, the proffered story simply floats past them unheard. In short, a justified ethical judgment depends, as Hume well knew, on a transaction between the ethical quality of the work and the ethical powers and attention of the listener.[17]

The maiming of critical judgment comes in many shapes and shades. No listener, not even Hume or the proud critic you encounter here, is totally unmaimed: alert to all possible misreadings and the resulting misjudgments. We all discover, on later readings, just how much we have missed or distorted earlier—whether last year or decades ago. That is one reason for attending to alien criticism—it teaches us about our oversights. Some listeners, even among the "literate," are in effect incompetent—though it will always sound arrogant for any critic to say so. The most obvious examples are misinterpreters of irony. Every teacher of ironic works discovers highly intelligent students who miss the cues. My own favorite was a reading of Jonathan Swift's *A Modest Proposal* by a brilliant fourth-year economics major: totally missing the ironies, he attacked Swift for his faulty statistics about the likely profit from selling children as food![18]

---

[16] One of the most prominent of the "responsers" once argued that even if a student suggested that Faulkner's "A Rose for Emily" was about Eskimos, the teacher must take it seriously. For me it would depend on what the "absurd" reading meant for the student offering it.

[17] The rhetorical notion of reading as a transaction between reader and author has been around for a long time—starting with the ancient rhetoricians. In this century it was dramatized most tellingly by the much neglected but groundbreaking work of Louise Rosenblatt. See *Literature as Exploration* (1938; 5th ed., New York: Modern Language Association, 1995) and *The Reader the Text the Poem: The Transactional Theory of the Literary Work* (Carbondale: Southern Illinois University Press, 1978). Rosenblatt avoids the relativistic notions of some reader-response critics: both readers and texts have powers that must be respected.

[18] In *A Rhetoric of Irony* (Chicago: University of Chicago Press, 1974), I report on a large number of such cases, including the claim by ironic columnists like Mike Royko and

You may or may not rule out such nonlisteners from your conversations, depending on your patience and the time of day. Indeed, as in all other moral matters, the question of just which contestants deserve most attention will always be answered diversely—and seldom openly. David Hume's characteristically bold and risky essay is thus of great importance to us, as we face the avalanche of controversial moral claims. Hume's subject is not exactly ours. The "taste" in judges for which he seeks a standard is not "moral taste" but the capacity to discern genuine beauty: artistic or aesthetic worth. His quest is, however, precisely to the point here. The qualities essential to the critic of beauty are indispensable in any appraiser of narrative morality.

Hume first faces the powerful arguments against the very possibility of his quest: the claims that judgments of artistic worth are necessarily no more than subjective opinions and that in consequence all aesthetic judgments can be considered relative only to the judge's subjectivity or culture.[19] As I quote his summary, I shall insert moral terms to achieve my "translation."

There is a species of philosophy, which . . . represents the impossibility of ever attaining any standard of taste [or moral judgment]. The difference, it is said, is very wide between judgment and sentiment [merely personal moral revulsion or celebration]. All sentiment is right; because sentiment has a reference to nothing beyond itself, and is always real, wherever a man is conscious of it. But all determinations of the understanding are not right; because they have a reference to something beyond themselves, to wit, real matter of fact, and are not always conformable to that standard. Among a thousand different opinions which different men may entertain of the same [scientific or factual] subject, there is one, and but one, that is just and true; and the only difficulty is to fix and ascertain it. On the contrary, a thousand different sentiments [or moral responses], excited by the same object, are all right: Because no sentiment [or moral response] represents what is really in the object. It only marks a certain conformity or relation between the object and the organs or faculties of the [individual judge's] mind. . . . One person may even perceive deformity [or vicious immorality], where another is sensible of beauty [or moral enlightenment]; and every individual ought to acquiesce in his own sentiment, without pretending to regulate those of others.[20]

Art Buchwald that they never write an ironic column without having many "straight" readers respond angrily in defense of the very positions the columnists were advocating.

[19] One fashionable version of this relativism, "all values are contingent," is advocated by Barbara Herrnstein Smith in *Contingencies of Value: Alternative Perspectives for Critical Theory* (Cambridge: Cambridge University Press, 1988).

[20] I am quoting from volume I of Hume's *Essays and Treatises*, 256–7. Since in most

Hume's way of refuting such taste relativism is to turn to what he calls the "common sense" observation that some judgments simply carry, for all of us, more weight than others; nobody actually *practices* aesthetic or moral relativism. We all assume that the experience of qualified judges, over time, leads to conclusions that should be honored even by those whose initial responses differ.

The same Homer, who pleased at Athens and Rome two thousand years ago, is still admired at Paris and at London [and, as this modern critic happens to know, still admired after another 250 years in some quarters of Peoria, Illinois, and Phoenix, Arizona, and Richmond, Indiana, and Moscow and Flavigny, France]. All the changes of climate, government, religion, and language, have not been able to obscure his glory. Authority or prejudice may give a temporary vogue to a bad poet or orator; but his reputation will never be durable or general. (para. 11, p. 269)

To face this argument with full honesty, I must admit that one of Hume's examples of "durable" quality, the "obvious" superiority of Joseph Addison to John Bunyan, has led some to reject his case; after all, far more people since his time have read and loved *Pilgrim's Progress* than all of Addison's works put together. Has not Bunyan stood the test of experience over time better than Addison? And doesn't that contradiction of Hume's judgment further demonstrate the case that all literary values are "contingent," relative?

Without giving up his attack on complete relativism, Hume might well have joined me by answering with one version of critical pluralism. His downgrading of Bunyan sprang from his own limited experience and lack of sympathy for a given kind of religious allegory. Within its kind, Bunyan's work has proved its excellence to all readers who like that given kind and are experienced in it. That in itself does not deny Addison's greatness, if not superiority, according to Hume's standards. As a reader and admirer of both authors, I would surely choose Addison over Bunyan if I were given the "desert island" test: which author would you choose to take with you if you knew you would have nothing else to read? On the other hand, if I were choosing which author should be read to me on my death bed, would not Bunyan win? He would certainly win over a lot of other allegorists *of his kind*—thus demonstrating

editions the original paragraphing is maintained, I shall cite paragraph numbers; the present quotation is found in paragraph seven.

Hume's case, from another angle, that differences of quality are real, however elusive.

If we rephrase Hume's question not as "Which judges are indisputably right?" but as "Which judges have earned at least a modicum of right to join in inquiry about the moral quality of a given story?" we can conduct a direct translation of the five criteria he next offers as his answer to the aesthetic relativists. In borrowing his discriminations, I shall again add moral language where needed.

As we consider Hume's list, it will be useful to conduct a thought experiment, one based on actual critical debates I have witnessed lately. Imagine that you and a friend have just seen the much praised and debated movie *Pulp Fiction* or just read the almost as much praised and debated novel *The Information* by Martin Amis, and you find yourselves in radical disagreement. One is shouting "A bad work, however clever, because it's immoral! It celebrates violence, and discounts its consequences." The other is shouting back, "It's a wonderful work; it raises moral questions brilliantly and irresistibly." What questions would you want to put to each other, if you could be totally frank, about your different levels of qualification for judgment? What precise kinds of expertise or training would either of you want to claim in order not to feel at least partially disqualified? (Obviously we should add after each of the five following requirements, the qualifier "other things being equal." None of Hume's standards can operate in isolation from all the others.)

First, Hume turns to "*delicacy* of [moral] imagination, which is requisite to convey a sensibility of . . . finer emotions" (para. 14, p. 261). Some people simply lack either the genetic structure or the kind of cultural experience that allows for sensitive response to moral issues. For example, is a serial killer fully qualified to enter a discussion of the moral quality of *Dr. Jekyll and Mr. Hyde* or *In Cold Blood*? We have the right to ask—though perhaps under our breath: "Are you the kind of person who can attend to the moral nuances of *any* tale? Is it in your very nature to care about moral qualities and distinctions of any kind? Are you able to conceive of a real difference between a moral and an immoral act?"

In other words, if you happen to know that your companion is a sadist who has loved to engage in violent torture from childhood on, you know that he is not qualified to judge whether the killings in *Pulp*

Fiction or the series of vicious attempted maimings by the "hero" of *The Information* call for moral indictment.[21]

It is not enough, of course, just to be someone who *feels* revulsion when a revolting act is portrayed. "Delicacy" of "sensibility" requires attention to the subtle and innumerable clues that every story offers about its actual moral quality. Clever narrators often plan quite subtle acts of indelicacy, early in a tale, as foreshadowing more brutal offenses to come; they assume listeners who catch the tellers' judgments. They may even praise a villain ironically, expecting the listener to catch the irony.

The second quality is more obvious, or at least easier to defend: what Hume calls "practice." If either disputant has never seen any movie before, or read any novel, or has never seen or read movies or novels of these generic kinds, the burden of proof lies heavily on him or her. To paraphrase an example used by Samuel Johnson, if someone calls a building "lofty," and I learn that he has never before seen any building taller than two stories, I have every reason to question the value judgment.

Under "practice" Hume also rightly includes the requirement of repeated encounters with the same work (para. 18, p. 264). If one disputant has seen the movie or read the novel three times, and perhaps even taught it to a class, and the other has seen or read it once quickly, obviously the "practicer" is the one who deserves more attention; there can still be dialogue, but the novice should acknowledge the status of novice. I happen to want to indict both *Pulp Fiction* and *The Information* as morally questionable. (Are you surprised?) But I have not even seen the movie (I now confess)—I have only heard descriptions of its violence and of audience's giggles when the blood spatters. What's more, I have many experienced young friends who have seen it several times and claim that I am wrong in avoiding it. How could I ever possibly claim equal authority in any discussion? On the other hand, I have read *The Information* with some care, and I can thus face any champion of the work and claim something like equal rights in the conversation.[22]

---

[21] Unless of course you yourself are a masochist, in which case you both are disqualified. Sorry.

[22] This doesn't mean that I have any confidence about where I'll come out. And what about Amis's own contributions outside a given work? Can he be the final authority? I don't know how Amis thinks about the morality of what seems to me his deeply nihilistic and potentially destructive novel. But having just read his morally rich encomium of Jane Austen's moral effects (*New Yorker*, 8 January 1996, 31–5), I'm flooded with doubts about my moral indictment of his novel. The "author" who praises Austen

Most of us, especially if we have lived more than a couple of decades, know the shocking reversals of judgments produced by "practice." Novels that in our early years we thought elevating and noble now seem callow and even morally destructive. Operas we were bored or repulsed by when we were eighteen now inspire us. And we all find many occasions on which we are the novices and someone else is the real practitioner.

For Hume, "practice," if it is to qualify anyone fully, includes a closely related third qualification, "comparison." A critic "who has had opportunities of seeing, and examining and weighing several performances, admired in different ages and nations, can alone rate the [moral] merits of a work . . . and assign its proper rank among the productions of genius" (para. 20, pp. 265–6). If my friend has seen a variety of contemporary movies that include (and perhaps condemn) violence, and I have not, my friend's opinion deserves closer attention than my own.

Hume's fourth criterion is perhaps the most crucial: "prejudice." A listener must "preserve his mind from *all* prejudice," allowing "*nothing* to enter into his consideration but the very object, which is submitted to his examination" (my emphasis). Important as this point is, Hume obviously carries it too far with words like "all" and "nothing." As Louise Rosenblatt and other reader-response critics have insisted, no one manages that degree of freedom from prejudgments: without preconceptions, prejudices—without the frame of mind produced by earlier experience—we could not engage fully with any story (see note 17). At the same time Hume is surely right in saying that "prejudice is most destructive of sound judgment, and perverts all operations of the intellectual faculties" (para. 21, p. 267). If my friend reads *The Information* and says "You know, I detest all British authors, and it's lovely to see them brutalized by Amis's British-novelist-hero," I must question his judgment of the book. But this is where comparison of the standards themselves enters. If another friend has read the novel thrice and says, "Look, dummy, the author with his gift for comedy constantly criticizes the brutalizing," I must listen to her.

Hume concludes with "good sense," which amounts to sound reasoning capacity: critics who are unable to reason clearly will obviously

---

in this way could not have written the novel as I read it. Did I simply miss the author's implied moral clues?

be unable to appraise the reasonings that fill all powerful narrative. (And—a point only slightly less important—their arguments for and against other critics will be faulty.) Hume writes, "The persons, introduced in tragedy and epic poetry, must be represented as reasoning and thinking, and concluding and acting, suitable to their characters and circumstances; and without judgment [sound reasoning] a poet [and thus the moral critic] can never hope to succeed" (para. 22, p. 268).

In other words, if you are to judge the moral choices made by reasoning characters—and the main characters in both works I am using as examples do a lot of reasoning—how can you claim competence unless you can think at least as clearly as the clearest of the portrayed characters or (more important) as the implied author who has created those characters?

For Hume to bring the capacity for sound reasoning into his case is significant not just to our quest for trustworthy moral inquirers but to the history of all reasoning about values. Hume is often thought of as one of the founders of the sharp and unbridgeable fact-value, is-ought distinction: you can reason to hard, genuine conclusions only about fact, never about values (see footnote 6). But in practice, whenever Hume turns to writing history or to real-life problems like "Is there a standard of taste?" he becomes a brilliant exemplar of sound practical reasoning about values.[23] Radically skeptical about all hard and certain proof, even in so-called scientific matters, and especially skeptical about decisive demonstration of moral and religious conclusions, he nevertheless always distinguishes those who make their practical or rhetorical claims carelessly from those who use a rational discourse to pursue common ground.

Implicit in at least the last three of Hume's five standards is one that all five depend on, if critics are not to sit proudly alone, stroking their egos. I refer not just to delicacy, not just to comparison of works, not just to practice, not just to the struggle to cast aside prejudices, not just to sound reasoning, but to conversation with other critics. Trustworthy moral judgments about stories can *never* be arrived at through a private

---

[23] A term more accurate here than "practical" might be "rhetorical" in the classical sense—a sense standard in Hume's time. But modern connotations would make it seem pejorative. For Hume's wonderfully moving and carefully reasoned discussion of how the thinker is to live after proving, as he believes, that "reason" has nothing to say about it, see his conclusion to Book One, "Conclusion of this Book," *A Treatise of Human Nature*, 2 vols. (London, 1738).

investigation by any lone individual, however brilliant. Such judgments simply cannot be demonstrated by any form of rigorous deductive or inductive reasoning pursuable in private. Too many efforts at moral judgment imply syllogistic deduction from absolute premises: "Any work with the word 'fuck' in it is immoral; *Catcher in the Rye* uses the word. Therefore it is immoral." Instead, effective moral critics always employ a form of "-duction" that is not "in-" or "de-" but *co*duction: they *listen* not only to stories but to their friends' responses to stories, and they change their minds steadily as they listen. As Hume talks about the authority of the traditional judgments that we inherit from centuries of "friends" who have praised Homer and the other greats, he is implying, without ever stating, that coduction is essential to good criticism.

Considering all these requirements in any critic deserving full attention,[24] Hume is forced as I am to conclude that "few are qualified to give judgment on any work of art, or establish their own sentiment as the standard of beauty [or morality]." Indeed I would go beyond the word "few"; no one person, not even myself on the rare morning when I'm feeling in charge, is qualified. Only communicating coductors are. With that bit of tightening I expand Hume's own summary:

(1) The organs of internal sensation [and moral discernment] are seldom so perfect as to allow . . . full play [to moral principles], and to produce a feeling correspondent to those principles. They either labour under some defect, or are vitiated by some disorder. . . .
(2) Where he [the critic] is not aided by practice, his verdict is attended with confusion and hesitation.
(3) Where no comparison has been employed, the most frivolous beauties [moral virtues], such as rather merit the name of defects, are the objects of his admiration.
(4) Where he lies under the influence of prejudice, all his natural [moral] sentiments are perverted.
(5) Where good sense is wanting, he is not qualified to discern the beauties [or moral issues] of design and reasoning, which are the highest and most excellent.
[(6) When no coduction has occurred, the critic risks absurdly private, prejudicial judgments.]

Under some one or other of these imperfections, the generality of men labour; and hence a true judge is observed, even during the most advanced [and morally sensitive] ages, to be so rare a character: Strong [moral] sense united to delicate [moral] feelings, improved by practice, perfected by comparison, and cleared of all prejudice [through coduction pursued with other critics], can alone entitle

---

[24] In practice, I would add one more: the critic's hidden motives other than the pursuit of critical truth. I turn to this point in my conclusion.

critics to this valuable character; and the *joint* verdict of such, wherever they are to be found, is the true standard of taste and beauty [and moral quality]. (para. 22, p. 269; emphasis mine)

Hume rightly goes on to concede once more that differences of cultural background and differences of personal experience will affect all of these criteria. "At twenty, Ovid may be the favourite author; Horace at forty; and perhaps Tacitus at fifty. . . . We chuse our favourite author as we do our friend, from a conformity of humours and dispositions" (para. 29, p. 272). As we today might put it, "where we come from" makes a great difference. "It is plainly an error in a critic, to confine his approbation to one species or style of writing, and condemn all the rest. But it is almost impossible not to feel a predilection for that which suits our particular turn and disposition. Such preferences are innocent and unavoidable . . ." (para. 30, p. 273).

But these differences, he concludes, do not undermine his standards. Nor do they lead to the claim that there is only one right moral reading of any story. Though there can be many wrong judgments, we must always make room for different perspectives.[25] Dangerous as it may be in our own time to make this claim, we should not make *much* room for critics who do not meet Hume's standards. And whether you who have kept with Hume and me this far are inclined to celebrate or condemn the avalanche of moral criticism in Epoch III, I hope you will join me in a lament: too many who hail it, like too many who curse it, exhibit the faults Hume describes. Opening almost any literary journal these days, left, right, or center, one finds at most a smattering of the critical virtues Hume celebrates.

GOOD KINDS, BAD KINDS: WHAT'S THE DIFFERENCE?

Hume concludes his essay with a few judgments that he considers self-evident. Since he simply asserts them without argument, he offers no help to the moral inquirer who decides to go beyond particular evalu-

---

[25] In this conclusion Hume at last moves openly into our territory by risking some moral judgments against specific works. He freely reveals strong convictions about how certain moral beliefs will mar fictions and ought to be judged negatively by the kind of critic he has set up as model. I do wish that he had employed a few paragraphs of serious argument about such conclusions. As they stand they sound like the exercise of prejudice.

ations, asking not just "Is work X more praiseworthy than work Y?"—
that is difficult enough—but "Are there good reasons to grant moral
superiority to some kinds of stories? The question is not: Are some kinds
of stories more beneficial for all readers in all circumstances? Obviously,
no story will be either harmful or beneficial to every conceivable listener—a point that was forgotten by my ninth-grade English teacher
who almost destroyed my budding passion for reading by imposing *Silas
Marner* on us and teaching it as if it were little more than a moral tract.
What may heal one listener may drive another to suicide. Our question
here is whether some kinds of story are more *likely* to be harmful or
beneficial to listeners?

We are dealing at best, then, in probabilities that are beyond strictly
scientific study. Even the rare critic who might meet Hume's high standards (if there is such a person), must depend on rhetorical resources
that will not carry "hard" proof.

As a first step we should reject the widespread notion that to prove
immoral quality you must be able to prove harmful effects on behavior.
It may well be impossible to prove scientifically that any story or kind
of story has been the cause of any specific action. *Post hoc* never establishes *propter hoc*, especially when the connections between the listening
world and the action world are as tenuous as they usually are. The
presumed fact that the suicide rate in Europe went up after young men
read Goethe's *The Sorrows of Werther* proves nothing, even though to
most of us it may seem likely that Goethe's sympathetic portrayal of his
hero would produce imitators.

Those who oppose laws against violent drama often talk as if we must
wait for statistical studies of how many murders are caused by the violence before we have any right to exert public critical pressure. Sometimes they cite a statistical decline in the number of portrayed murders
as evidence that things are getting better. That's nonsense. No matter
how strong our conviction that stories get imitated, we should not let
our inability to offer proof for that conviction silence our criticism. Our
questions should not be in the form, "Was Johnnie led by this story to
commit misdeed Y?" but rather, "Was the life Johnnie spent while 'taking it in' enhanced or corrupted or just plain wasted?" "What kind of
life was he living, during the two or eight or twenty hours spent listening?" Put another way: "What kind of person was implied as the ideal
listener to this story, whether or not it included portrayals of viciousness
or violence?"

I can now deal with only two of the many differences of kind that could be explored in answering such questions, still using gratuitous violence as my most obvious test case. First, there is a crucial contrast between stories that in themselves engage in overt or strongly implied moral judgment or inquiry about the acts they portray and those that leave the inquiry entirely up to the listener. If we are concerned about the quality of the life lived during the listening, then we must attend to the ways in which what Hume calls our "delicacy," our moral sensitivity, is heightened or lowered by the author's strokes.

From this perspective, no story can be judged bad or good just because it does or does not portray a given violent act or expression. It all depends on where and how the detail is placed within the whole story. Everyone agrees, for example, that to beat or kill the innocent or to commit rape are evil acts, and almost everyone agrees that evil is likely to be furthered by any story that celebrates such acts. Yet we all know that many of the stories we admire most, including the classical epics and dramas and the Bible, are full of such acts. Modern movie makers and authors of pulp fiction did not invent the joys of witnessing the rape of the Sabine women, or the slaughter of untold numbers of Philistines, or the delicious horror of seeing an enemy's severed head brought in on a platter, or the gruesome vision of a totally innocent God/man nailed to a cross, sweating blood as a bystander pokes a spear in his ribs. Go read again your favorite fairy tale in the Grimm or pre-Grimm version and prepare for a blood bath. Most of us not only enjoy but admire many stories old and new that dwell on scenes of horrifying cruelty. Most of us have also reveled in bloody dénouements and then, on reflection, felt some shame. Either the tellers exploited us by failing to provide any helpful moral placement, any set of clues about where to stand as we listen; or we missed the clues and simply wallowed in the blood and guts.

The best tellers make such mistakes unlikely for any fully engaged listener. Franz Kafka's story "The Penal Colony," for example, is one of the most physically sickening of "modernist" stories, yet in my view it is one of the most admirable. Should it be condemned because the anonymous victim is tortured to death, slowly, brutally, as it were before our eyes? Or—perhaps the most striking example of all—should the New Testament be bowdlerized to protect our children from learning the sadistic pleasures of contemplating a crucifixion?

When we look behind the general attacks on violent portrayals, we find that hardly anyone is naive enough to object to all violent stories. Rather, most of us give at least tacit approval to violence against those we think deserve it.[26] Consequently, criticism should pay more attention to the difference between those stories that provide reasons or explanations or moral clues and those that simply exploit our natural pleasure—I'm afraid that it *is* natural—in witnessing pain.

The stories we rightly celebrate by listening to them again and again, generation after generation, *place* and *judge* their violent portrayals: the best of the fairy tales, "The Penal Colony," the story of Cain and Abel, Christ's passion, the *Iliad, War and Peace. . . .* The stories we rightly question are those that present the evil in a way that leaves listeners utterly unaided in their judgment. They provide nothing like a moral *placement*—a street address in the moral world, a location within the intricate and often contradictory range of human virtues and vices in which we all live.[27]

Authorial placement can come in many forms, only one of them—often the weakest—in direct moral tags. The conviction of modernists that the best authors maintain distance or "objectivity," that they "show" rather than "tell," led some critics to reject all direct commentary, especially if it had a moral tone. It is true that much of the traditional moral guidance that they objected to had been puerile. But when we ask for moral placement we do not say that all moral placements are of equal value: "Sunday schoolish" sentimental placements of good guys and gals triumphing over the wicked won't make for a good story.[28]

I could explore examples of many a modern novel or movie that admirably and unobjectionably judge their vividly portrayed violence.[29]

---

[26] The best recent account I have seen dealing with revenge-violence in the "real" world is Sister Helen Prejean's *Dead Man Walking: An Eyewitness Account of the Death Penalty in the United States* (New York: Random House, 1993). I attempt to deal with the problems raised by righteous killing of demonized victims, especially in religious literature, in "Story as Spiritual Quest," *Christianity and Literature* (Winter 1996), 163–90.

[27] The notion that many genuine virtues or "truths" are contradictory and thus "incommensurable" with other genuine virtues has been attacked by some as destructively relativistic. See Putnam, *Reason, Truth and History*, 113–9 and Williams, *Morality*, 88–97. And it has been defended by others who join him in rejecting relativism. Isaiah Berlin in several books makes the case that values can be both real and contradictory.

[28] Yet for Sunday school purposes, which are not to be sneezed at, they will still be morally superior to some children's books that these days make harmful and dangerous behavior look unqualifiedly "cool"—and radically imitable. I'm thinking, for example, of some of Roald Dahl's clever enticements in works like *Charlie and the Chocolate Factory* (1964), made into the even more questionable movie *Willie Wonka and the Chocolate Factory* (1974).

[29] An outstanding example is Austin Wright's *Tony and Susan* (New York: Baskerville

But since premodern works are usually a bit clearer in their placements, I choose as my prime example *King Lear*, a play that offers some undebatable moral judgments while at the same time leading us into one of the most complex moral experiences in the history of drama. Putting the complexities to one side for the moment, consider the play's long list of unambiguous moral judgments that no serious critic could ever question.

One of the most obvious of these is the gruesome scene when Cornwall grinds out Gloucester's eyes with his boot. He does this on stage and *one at a time*, with Cornwall pronouncing, after he kills a servant for saying that Gloucester still has one eye left to witness the viciousness, "Lest it see more, prevent it. Out, vile jelly! Where is thy lustre now?" (Act III, Scene vii, 1. 84). Shakespeare could have told the same story much more briefly: both eyes at once with Cornwall saying something like, "This'll show you," or "Take that, and that." But he chose to stretch out the violence as far as possible.

Few modern spectacular effects are more gruesome than that. We can be sure that any production in our time will exploit the physical grindings, including blood and "jelly" visibly dripping. Would that make it immoral? Those critics of the media who simply tot up the number of violent acts per week would have to say that this scene should either be cut entirely or sent to the wings to be told less vividly, as the Greek tragedians would have done. Yet to cut such a scene would be to deprive us of a crucial moment in the moral experience of the play. As handled by Shakespeare, the scene is implacably judged, *placed* as unforgivable, monstrous, an act that no viewer should ever condone (regardless of visceral, or even pathological, thrills). Those critics who have followed Keats in praising Shakespeare as a chameleon poet—neutral, impersonal, objective, shifting from morality to morality—have ignored how hard he often works, as he does here, to ensure that we not only condemn vicious acts but feel in our guts just why we should. He could not be less neutral than he is here.

His moves throughout the play are worth tracing, if only because such

---

Publishers, 1983), a gut-wrenching page-turner that implicates the reader in strong moral judgments from beginning to end: one emerges having been not just thrilled and torn but educated about the meaning of violence itself. Many a violent movie, like Sam Peckinpah's *The Wild Bunch*, gives any attentive spectator a clear sense of the director's strong disapproval of what goes on. There is often an ironic contrast, of course, between the expressed disapproval and the actual exploitation: crime does not pay—except when portrayed enticingly.

moves are so often missing from modern works whose authors claim, when criticized, that they strongly condemn the violence they portray. First, in the scene itself Cornwall's courageous servant sees the outrage coming and protests: "Hold your hand, my lord! . . . better service have I never done you / Than now to bid you hold" (Act III, Scene vii, 1. 75). In effect that is Shakespeare speaking, the implied author as moralist. Cornwall slays him for interrupting the cruelty. Second, we are forced, by the structure of events before the scene, to be on Gloucester's side in the encounter. Third, the play punishes Cornwall with defeat and death: Shakespeare does not let him get away with it. Fourth, and perhaps most important emotionally, we are taken vividly and distressfully through scenes dwelling on the miserable consequences of the cruelty, as the sympathetic Gloucester suffers from the blinding, driven to an attempted suicide.

Thus the moral judgment is not simply tacked on, like the last-minute deaths or imprisonments in those crime thrillers that used to conclude with a voice intoning, "Crime Does Not Pay." In *King Lear*, it is not only that crime does not pay, though that is something; this crime is fiercely condemned, condemned not with moral platitudes but with wrenching dramatic rendering. Even if it "paid"—even if, say, Cornwall became king—we would still know that it was, in Shakespeare's eyes, an unforgivable act.[30]

We have in this scene, then, a revolting act that in its very portrayal insists on our revulsion and on the terrible consequences of evil actions. How different this is from much of the violence that fills many of our books and screens. Too many of them portray no internal protests; no morally credited "servant" comes forward to say, in effect, "I'd rather die than allow you to perpetrate that act." What's more, we are not led to care for the victims; we experience no emotional consequences of the violence except perhaps physical nausea—and even that is diminished decade by decade as we see more and more vivid awfulness. Indeed, we are often led, by technical maneuver, to sympathize most strongly with the perpetrator.

Thus too many tellers imply, even when they feel quite moral as they tell their tales, that there are no real values according to which any act

---

[30] Or we would know that as implied dramatist he wants us to see it as unforgivable; as I suggest in my conclusion, tellers can and do create works that imply authors far better, on this or that scale, than their everyday selves.

could be considered really immoral. The overt values are reduced to something like what the narrator says to the reader at the end of *The Information*, with no hint of distance between the authoritative voice and Amis's own.

> Your watch knows exactly what time is doing to you: *tsk, tsk*, it says, every second of every day. . . . Beware the aged critic with his hair of winebar sawdust. Beware the nun and the witchy buckles of her shoes. Beware the man at the callbox, with the suitcase: this man is you. The planesaw whines, whining for its planesaw mummy. And then there is the information, which is nothing, and comes at night.[31]

This brings us to the second distinction, between stories that provide flat, unquestioning placement and stories that take us beyond strengthened moral convictions to moral inquiry. After all, a story by Aesop, with its little moral tag at the end, does place the action in the moral world. But all motive for inquiry about such a tale must come from the listener, not the tale. Inquiry results only from questioning, and questioning results not from comfortable reassurance about previous placements but from conflicts among rival placements. It is true that clear placement that shocks listeners can in itself lead to inquiry of a kind: any listener whose values conflict with the placement is forced into debate with the values of the story. Even Amis forces me to think, once again, about nihilism, about the ways in which current mores encourage nihilistic thought, and about how nihilism might be responded to, either in narrative or plain argument. Indeed, many writers and critics in our time have proclaimed that to shatter moral complacency in this way is the supreme task of literature.[32] To provide what I am calling placement would for them be to undermine the moral effectiveness of the negative challenge.

---

[31] This ending seems to me utterly, deliberately empty, but, as I noted earlier, I may have missed moral clues.

[32] For a brilliant celebration of the role of "shattering," see Walter A. Davis, *Get the Guests: Psychoanalysis, Modern American Drama, and the Audience* (Madison: University of Wisconsin Press, 1994). His critique of the traditional view that tragedy's gift is catharsis is especially challenging. He argues that genuinely powerful tragedy does not purge our pity and fear but probes our deepest consciousness so that we can "enter the Crypt, know the power death-work and soul-murder have in the constitution and regulation of the psyche, and begin to seek out the possibility of the dialectic that could attempt their reversal . . . brought face to face with the existential imperative which drama inserts directly into the deepest places of our psyche" (263). That case resembles, in ways that might surprise Davis himself, my claim that the best moral effect is not just placement but inquiry.

But wherever we come out on that issue, it seems clear that neither flat moral placement nor plain negative challenge is sufficient to produce lasting and productive moral inquiry. Flat placement, with labels like "wicked" and "virtuous," though they may assist naive readers, can easily kill all serious thought about moral questions. What would be the effect on us if every action in *King Lear* were as clearly placed in the moral spectrum as is the blinding of Gloucester? Well, it is true that we would have to call the play "moral," in the sense of reinforcing our abhorrence of gratuitous brutality. But we could hardly claim that Shakespeare had educated us in the demands and skills of moral inquiry.

On the one hand, then, we have short "moral" folktales with or without overt tags, or the scene with Gloucester's eyes, with its internal un-equivocal judgments, or a fiction that shocks us with decisive implied negatives. On the other, we have stories that engage us in moral inquiry. A full treatment of the difference would require another long essay. But one inescapable point is this: a great moral educator like *King Lear* not only places many acts as clearly, undeniably wrong, and others, such as Edgar's self-denying loyalty to Gloucester, as unquestionably admirable; it also places such clarities into contexts that force listeners into conflicts that provoke inquiry. No one can really listen to the whole story and rest in simple comfortable clarity about how the portrayed world joins or violates the world that the listener inhabits. Immensely troubling moral issues face the attentive listener at almost every moment. Just how should a foolish (and foolishly mean) old father be treated? What is the meaning of an action that ends with so much grief and so many equiv-ocations? (As is well known, performances in the eighteenth-century re-vised the ending so that Cordelia and Lear do not die: they are happily united.) How much should we blame Lear for his disaster? Just how immoral is his treatment of Cordelia? Is there a difference in the level of wickedness of Goneril, Regan, Cornwall, and Edmund? Just how much deception is justified, as the "good" minor characters try to aid the sufferers?

Turning to even larger questions: How should one respond to the prevalence of violence in the world of the play? *Are* we "like flies to the Gods," who "kill us for their sport"? Just how *should* a king, sane or mad, deal with the fact of widespread poverty and suffering? We may leave a fine performance of this play feeling in some sense purged, as Aristotle says great tragedy leaves us, but we are not purged of all moral confusion or questioning. Rather, we are steeped in the task of interrelating, comparing, contrasting rival moral judgments: we are caught up in moral inquiry.

When stories neither place values nor throw placements into productive conflict, they throw the would-be moral critic back upon Hume's first chancey criterion: the claim to "delicacy," a preexisting capacity to make the right judgments. She is left saying, "Though this work gives me little help in figuring out where the author stands, that doesn't matter because I am one of those rare creatures who can distinguish moral and immoral acts."

CONCLUSION: AUTHORS AS "PURIFIED" FRIENDS

Throughout I have been implying that one key question should always be, "What kind of person, what kind of critical listener am I asked to be while I dwell 'here'—while I join, in my listening, the world offered by this tale?" Nothing could be more crucial for us or our children than the quality of our lives as we listen to stories: that is who we *are* during the hours of listening, regardless of what happens next hour or next day.

But to repeat that point underlines the tricky task that is implied in all of my questions: determining just what are the moral qualities of any specific storyteller, as implied in all of the details of his or her seemingly friendly gesture. To tell a story, and especially to publish one, is to offer a gift that the giver presumably admires. Whoever the flesh-and-blood teller (or, in the case of performed plays and movies, tellers) may be, the creator I listen to here has chosen to offer me these actions, these qualities, these placements or lack of placements, these stylistic nuances, these images, this implicit or explicit ethical "code" or "world of values," this "ordering of loves."[33]

We meet here at the end, then, a final sharp difference of kinds, among the creators themselves implied in the stories they offer. In one pile, I suspect larger than in any previous era, we listen to tellers who think only or primarily of what will capture us as listeners—of what will sell the "product." The creators are not asking, "Is this story an act of friendship?" or "Is this implied portrait of my own character one I

---

[33] I borrow this phrase from a wonderfully inquiring current novel, *The Good Husband* by Gail Godwin (New York: Ballantine Books, 1994). A central character, on her deathbed, makes the claim that the key task in life is "ordering one's loves," determining not just which loves we care about but which loves we ought to care about most.

really admire?" The only question for too many is "What will the audience buy?"

In a much smaller pile we still meet, thank God, creators who, while not pretending to be above the desire to capture as many listeners as possible, care mainly about telling the best story they can tell. And the word "best" for them goes beyond the mere "craft of grabbing" to include moral questions of the kind I have been raising. Some few even testify to asking explicitly, "Will this do any good in the world?" As James Baldwin once put it, "You write in order to change the world, knowing perfectly well that you probably can't, but also knowing that literature is indispensable to the world. . . . The world changes according to the way people see it, and if you alter, even by a millimeter, the way . . . people look at reality, then you can change it."[34] Others seem to ask not so much whether the work will improve the world as whether it will present the listener with an experience worth having. Or they may ask, "Would I want to listen to this one if it were told by someone else?" The creators we consider great are usually those who have worked hard, often through extensive revisions, to improve or purify the self-portrait implicit in any creative act. They thus create an implied self superior to the everyday creature whose frequently abominable or stupid actions we learn about in later biographies.

The way in which writing a story washes away at least some of the author's weaknesses was dramatized for me by Saul Bellow years ago, after he had told me he was spending four hours a day revising *Herzog*. "What are you really up to," I asked, "during those four hours?" "Well," he said (as I remember it), "it's just sitting at that desk cutting out those parts of myself that I don't like."[35]

The cheering truth is that we still have a small but impressive chorus of fine creators, inquirers who labor passionately to become, during the act of creation, more morally perceptive than they could ever manage to be after they leave the desk. Although some in the first heap simply cook up a false implied portrait—whatever current culture demands— those of the second kind perform, in the very act of telling a story, an

---

[34] James Baldwin, interview by Mel Watkins, *New York Times Book Review* (23 September 1979), 3.

[35] I have been told, by a student of his manuscripts, that the published novel was extracted, as it were, from roughly 5,000 manuscript pages! The Bellow we meet in those extracted pages is a much improved version over the one we would meet if some enemy searched the 5,000 pages for the 300 or so worst ones.

act of moral inquiry. Winnowing out day by day everything that violates their own best insights, they finally present an imagined persona far superior to what their spouses or lovers usually meet at the breakfast table. Consequently, those "selves" are often much more morally perceptive than you and I can ever hope to be—except in the hours we spend with them.

The effort to appraise the value of such heightened offerings resembles closely our choices (in our nonliterary lives) of friends and enemies. The final ethical judgment of any narrative offering is perhaps best thought of as employing the metaphor of friendship—friendship with friends superior to any we ever meet in the "real" world. Does this gift seem to me, I ask, now that I have lived with it intimately, like the gift of a friend? Or is it more like that of a con artist, or even a recruiter for gang membership? Perhaps this seeming gift is, in fact, a packet of poisons—the "gift" of an enemy?

You and I will always reveal some differences about which of these friends are worth recommending to our everyday friends. But if we work at freeing ourselves of the critical handicaps Hume describes, and engage in coduction rather than individual pontification, the astonishing revival of moral inquiry of the past three decades may prove to be not a destructive avalanche, but rather—

Alas, there is no adequate metaphor for my dream of a critical world full of tellers and listeners engaged in genuine moral inquiry.

APPENDIX: A SELECTION OF MORAL AND ETHICAL
CRITICISM SINCE 1970

In *The Company We Keep* (1988), my bibliography listed hundreds of modern authors who, along with their ancestors, seem to me to be genuinely pursuing moral criticism of literature. Here I select some of the more representative of those and add a few more recent publications. The notes to Adam Newton's *Narrative Ethics* provide a rich introduction to the many recent books aggressively pressing into the moral scene.

I have listed almost none that primarily address debates about theory, though they would be pertinent to some parts of this chapter. To get on the list here a critic must engage at least some of the time with the specific moral power of individual stories or kinds of story.

Needless to say, I know many books that are higher in quality than some listed here but that do not quite belong on such a list. Moral (or ethical) criticism is not the only legitimate game in town. (I provide a few handy—and perhaps partly misleading—labels for some titles, the presence or theoretical location of which may seem puzzling.)

If anyone listed feels offended, I know not what to do. To the many who will rightly be surprised to find themselves missing, I can only say: write to me and complain.

Altieri, Charles. *Act and Quality: A Theory of Literary Meaning and Humanistic Understanding*. Amherst: University of Massachusetts Press, 1981.

Barbour, John D. *Tragedy as a Critique of Virtue: The Novel and Ethical Reflection*. Chico, Calif.: Scholars Press, 1984.

Berthoff, Warner. *Literature and the Continuances of Virtue*. Princeton, N.J.: Princeton University Press, 1986.

Bettelheim, Bruno. *The Uses of Enchantment*. New York: Random House, 1976. (Fairy tales; children's literature.)

Booth, Alison, ed. *Famous Last Words: Changes in Gender and Narrative Closure*. Charlottesville: University Press of Virginia, 1993. (Feminism with a structural formal emphasis.)

Booth, Wayne C. *The Company We Keep: An Ethics of Fiction*. Berkeley: University of California Press, 1988.

Cairns, Douglas L. *Aidos: The Psychology and Ethics of Honour and Shame in Ancient Greek Literature*. Oxford: Clarendon Press, 1993.

Cavell, Stanley. *The Claim of Reason*. Oxford: Oxford University Press, 1979.

———. *Pursuits of Happiness: The Hollywood Comedy of Remarriage*. Cambridge, Mass: Harvard University Press, 1981. (Cinematic transformations—and exploitations—of cultural roots.)

Clausen, Christopher. *The Moral Imagination: Essays on Literature and Ethics*. Iowa City: University of Iowa Press, 1986.

Coles, Robert. *The Call of Stories: Teaching and the Moral Imagination*. Boston: Houghton Mifflin, 1989. (Therapeutic uses of story.)

Davis, Walter A. *Get the Guests: Psychoanalysis, Modern American Drama, and the Audience*. Madison: University of Wisconsin Press, 1994. (Psychoanalysis and Philosophy.)

Eagleton, Terry. *Criticism and Ideology: A Study in Marxist Literary Theory*. New York: Schoken Books, 1985.

Gardner, John. *On Moral Fiction*. New York: Basic Books, 1978.

Gates, Henry Louis Jr., ed. *Loose Canons: Notes on the Culture Wars*. New York: Oxford University Press, 1992. (The problems of racism placed in a larger context.)

Greenblatt, Stephen. *Renaissance Self-Fashioning: From More to Shakespeare*. Chicago: University of Chicago Press, 1980. (Labeled a "new historicist," the author might better be labeled a "moralist of cultures.")

Johannesen, Richard L. *Ethics in Human Communication*. 2d ed. Prospect Heights, Ill.: Waveland Press, 1983. (Public rhetoric, advertising, "everyday" communication.)

Harpham, Geoffrey Galt. *Getting It Right: Language, Literature, and Ethics.* Chicago: University of Chicago Press, 1992.

Henberg, Marvin. *Retribution: Evil for Evil in Ethics, Law, and Literature.* Philadelphia: Temple University Press, 1990.

Johnson, Barbara. *The Critical Difference: Essays in the Contemporary Rhetoric of Reading.* Baltimore: Johns Hopkins University Press, 1981. (Deconstructionist, with strong ethical commitments.)

Kane, Sean. *Spenser's Moral Allegory.* Toronto: University of Toronto Press, 1989.

Kort, Wesley A. *Moral Fiber: Character and Belief in Recent American Fiction.* Philadelphia: Fortress Press, 1982.

Lanser, Sniader Susan. *The Narrative Act: Point of View in Prose Fiction.* Princeton, N.J.: Princeton University Press, 1981. (Feminism matched with structural interests.)

Marshall, David. *The Surprising Effects of Sympathy: Marivaux, Diderot, Rousseau, and Mary Shelley.* Chicago: University of Chicago Press, 1988.

Massey, Irving. *Find You the Virtue: Ethics, Image, and Desire in Literature.* Fairfax, Va.: George Mason University Press, 1987.

McGann, Jerome J. *Social Values and Poetic Acts: The Historical Judgment of Literary Work.* Cambridge, Mass.: Harvard University Press, 1988. (Poems as social acts.)

Miller, J. Hillis. *The Ethics of Reading: Kant, de Man, Eliot, Trollope, James, and Benjamin.* Oxford: Blackwell, 1991. (Deconstructionist, celebrating the ethical importance of all careful reading.)

Morson, Saul. *Narrative and Freedom: The Shadows of Time.* New Haven: Yale University Press, 1994.

New Literary History. The special issue *Literature and/as Moral Philosophy* 15 (Autumn 1983).

Newton, Adam Zachary. *Narrative Ethics.* Cambridge, Mass.: Harvard University Press, 1995.

Nouvet, Claire, ed. *Literature and the Ethical Question.* Special issue of *Yale French Studies* 79 (1991).

Nussbaum, Martha. *Love's Knowledge: Essays on Philosophy and Literature.* Berkeley: University of California Press, 1991. (Moral readings of individual works, especially Henry James's *The Golden Bowl.*)

Packard, Vance. *The People Shapers.* Boston: Little, Brown, 1977. (Popular culture.)

Palmer, Frank. *Literature and Moral Understanding: A Philosophical Essay on Ethics, Aesthetics, Education, and Culture.* Oxford: Clarendon Press, 1992.

Parker, David. *Ethics, Theory, and the Novel.* New York: Cambridge University Press, 1994.

Phelan, James. *Reading People, Reading Plots: Character, Progression, and the Interpretation of Narrative.* Chicago: University of Chicago Press, 1989.

Rabinowitz, Peter J. *Before Reading: Narrative Conventions and the Politics of Interpretation.* Ithaca, N.Y.: Cornell University Press, 1987.

Rosenblatt, Louise M. *The Reader the Text the Poem: The Transactional Theory of the Literary Work.* Carbondale: Southern Illinois University Press, 1978.

Schwarz, Daniel R. *The Humanistic Heritage: Critical Theories of the English*

Novel from James to Hillis Miller. Philadelphia: University of Pennsylvania Press, 1986.

Scott, Nathan. *The Poetry of Civic Virtue.* Minneapolis, Minn.: Augsburg/Fortress Press, 1976. (Broadly "religious" criticism.)

Sharp, Ronald A. *Friendship and Literature: Spirit and Form.* Durham, N.C.: Duke University Press, 1986.

Siebers, Tobin. *The Ethics of Criticism.* Ithaca, N.Y.: Cornell University Press, 1988.

Springer, Mary Doyle. *A Rhetoric of Literary Character: Some Women of Henry James.* Chicago: University of Chicago Press, 1978.

Trotter, David. *The Making of the Reader: Language and Subjectivity in Modern American, English and Irish Poetry.* London: Macmillan, 1984. (Poetry as "story.")

Warner, Marina. *From the Beast to the Blonde: On Fairy Tales and Their Tellers.* New York: Farrar, Straus and Giroux, 1995.

White, James Boyd. *"This Book of Starres": Learning to Read George Herbert.* Ann Arbor: University of Michigan Press, 1994. (Ethical effects of religious poetry.)

Williams, Raymond. *Marxism and Literature.* Oxford: Oxford University Press, 1977.

Yamagata, Naoko. *Homeric Morality.* Leiden (Netherlands) and New York: E. J. Brill, 1993.

7

The moral force field of Haitian Vodou

KAREN McCARTHY BROWN

In 1980, nearly a decade after I started conducting field research in Haiti, I had an experience that caused me to question how I positioned myself as a scholar in relation to this complicated culture. I had had dinner with friends in a small town just outside Port-au-Prince, and four or five of us were lingering in the yard, gathered in a semicircle of straight-backed wooden chairs around the charcoal brazier on which our food had been cooked. Darkness fell quickly, and before long the embers from our fire provided the only light in the yard of the *lakou*, a cluster of modest dwellings around a central open space. Traditionally, a *lakou* is occupied by an extended family, but here, on the fringe of Haiti's capital and largest city, a disparate group of renters occupied the one- and two-room houses.

Without warning, the door of one of the small houses was thrown open, and a shaft of light cut across the yard, carrying with it the sounds of a heated argument—screams, accusations, the dreadful thud of fists on flesh. Moments later a tangle of human bodies rolled out the door. Members of our group were instantly mobilized—albeit chaotically. Everyone was shouting orders at someone else. By the time the couple had been pulled apart, the man was holding a fistful of the woman's hair, and she had a patch of oozing, red skin on the back of her head. Only later did I realize that my voice had been one of the loudest. I had been shouting: "Make him stop!" "Make him stop!"

In general, when I am in Haiti I am more patient with people and situations than I am in the United States, more willing to suspend judgment, more open to the attractions of difference. This attitude has been urged on me by my basic socialization (an emphasis in my childhood on the good manners expected from a guest) and by professional training

181

(a strong emphasis on the "otherness" of the other that pervaded anthropology when I was doing graduate work in the 1970s). In Haiti, when confronted with anything as dramatic as this incident, my first response would usually be to question whether I understood what was happening, but there were no such questions in my mind that night. Without an instant's pause for reflection, I felt I knew what was happening: domestic violence. I also knew it was wrong and needed to be stopped.

My initial certitude about what was happening in this incident came in large part from my feminism, a central force in my intellectual and moral-political development. Like most academic feminists in the United States, I have read a fair amount about domestic violence, and I have worked its alarming U.S. statistical profile into my understanding of gender dynamics. Yet in relation to that evening in Haiti, I eventually concluded that the lens of U.S. feminism had simultaneously revealed and concealed the nature of the incident. At a distance from the episode I was somewhat less sanguine about the startling rapidity of my judgment. My feminist sensibilities had delivered a quick diagnosis of the situation, but the uncomplicated singularity of that diagnosis deflected my attention from important differences between the interpretive matrices for domestic violence in Haiti and in the United States.

It is not my purpose here to analyze those differences, but I will suggest one direction such analysis might take. Gender categories are the primary analytic tools for U.S. feminists, and they generally take precedence over economic and political categories, as well as those of race. But it is not as easy for women in Haiti to create an analytical separation between gender dynamics and, to take the strongest example, economic ones. For poor Haitian women, that is to say for the great majority of Haitian women, decisions about relationships with men have to be considered in terms of potential economic gains and losses. Since survival is always, at some level, an issue in relationships between poor men and women in Haiti, any analytic system that suppresses the connections between gender dynamics and economics, or even makes the second subservient to the first, will not serve the needs of Haitian women.

My lightning diagnosis that applied what I knew of domestic violence in the United States to what I was witnessing in Haiti, if unexamined, might have led me to some unjustifiable second-order conclusions. I might have concluded that, by choosing to stay in this relationship, the

woman was deluding herself, or that she lacked self-confidence.[1] More
to the point, I might have assumed that she would be better off out of
the relationship.[2] I could have reached any of these conclusions, when
in fact none need be true. I may simply have been looking at a woman
with few options in life, none of them good.

The story of my 1980 brush with domestic violence in Haiti leads
neither to a definitive description of the episode nor to final moral judgments about it, but it has begun to take on the coloring of an anthropological parable. This is a story situated at anthropology's crossroads,
at the place where awareness of profound differences between cultures
intersects with a gut-level conviction that we share a common humanity
that makes it possible to reach understandings and even make moral
judgments across culture boundaries. The history of the academic discipline of anthropology can be charted using these two positions as
coordinates.

CULTURE, MORALITY, AND ANTHROPOLOGY

When anthropology was a young social science, it was preoccupied with
the question of the psychic unity of humankind. Were so-called primi-
tives essentially different from civilized Europeans, or was there a shared
humanness that underlay all of the apparent differences? When anthropologists reached consensus that we share a common humanity, it was
one of the great moral and intellectual achievements of all time. It laid
to rest the last ghosts of arguments such as the theological one that
appeared intermittently throughout the period of trans-Atlantic slavery,
the argument that blacks did not have souls and therefore could be en-
slaved with impunity.

Beginning with Franz Boas, a figure who dominated anthropology in

---

[1] Haitian culture is as misogynist as that of the United States, yet in my experience Haitian
women do not internalize the regnant hatred and fear of women to the same extent that
U.S. white feminists seem to do. In other words, Haitian culture, at least that of the
impoverished 80 percent, seems not to routinely set women at war with themselves, their
bodies, their sexuality, and their agency. There are surely many reasons for this. Perhaps
one is that the forces that hold poor Haitian women down—the tender pride of poor
men, the jealousy of neighbors, the corruptions of the local marketplace, the demonic
perversions of Haitian politicians, the exploitive nature of U.S. and European development schemes—are more tangible than those that oppress economically advantaged
women in the United States.

[2] In many instances North American feminists assume social support for battered women
(shelters, restraining orders, welfare) without noting how culture-specific this is and how
much it is a product of economic privilege.

the United States during the first half of the twentieth century, the field became more and more focused on the internal integrity of individual cultures, as well as on their mutual untranslatability. In the early days of the discipline, scholars, relying heavily on secondary sources, built grand theories about human nature and culture, but after Boas anthropologists were required to have extensive field experience of their own. Largely as a result of this, they became more and more cautious in making generalizations across cultures or comparisons between them.

These tendencies eventually fed into a theory of cultural relativism. The attitudes behind cultural relativism originated in broadly based intellectual and cultural trends, but they received theoretical articulation in the field of anthropology. Like the doctrine of the psychic unity of humankind, the theory of cultural relativism has been a major player in significant, long-term moral debates that have extended well beyond the academy. Cultural relativism was evoked as a positive value in the Great Society politics of the 1960s and more recently attacked as the major intellectual pollutant of the second half of the twentieth century by right-wing theoretician Dinesh D'Souza in his controversial book *The End of Racism*.[3]

Other sorts of moral issues arising from the practice of anthropology are more specific in their focus. These include anthropologists working for government agencies, such as the United States Agency for International Development, getting involved in politics in their fieldwork locations and representing subjects in their writings in ways that perpetuate colonial power structures.[4] Yet none of these issues can claim the wide moral play of the general theories of human sameness and difference, most succinctly articulated by anthropologists, that have shaped entire chapters of human intellectual history.

The challenge of anthropology in the contemporary world is that it

---

[3] Dinesh D'Souza, *The End of Racism: Principles for a Multiracial Society* (New York: Free Press, 1995).

[4] Early anthropology rose in concert with imperialism and colonialism, and it is still most active in postcolonial parts of the world. After the 1986 publication of James Clifford and George Marcus's collection of essays, *Writing Culture* (Berkeley and Los Angeles: University of California Press, 1986), the challenge of postmodernism for the academic field of anthropology seemed starkly apparent. Many felt that it was no longer possible to write ethnography with integrity. Ethnographies were seen as fictions spun by the empowered about the disempowered, ultimately revealing more about the mind of the author than about the culture of those subjected to study. The deconstruction of anthropologists' narratives, research methods, and social and political roles has now been going on for almost a decade.

is no longer a simple matter of choosing sides in these old debates. Anthropologists now can deny neither the ultimate psychic unity of humankind nor the radical nature of cultural relativism. One reason for this is that issues of human sameness and difference are no longer intellectual positions. More than ever before, they have become daily social realities. The jolt of cultural pluralism has moved from the experiential field of the intrepid traveler on the "other side" of the globe, to the center of major cities sprinkled throughout the world. Acts of cultural translation and other sorts of boundary crossing are routine, daily events in practically every contemporary city, and general cultural hybridization is increasingly the ethos of large urban centers everywhere.[5] At the same time the depth of differences is also impossible to deny; it is one of the most frequent sources of friction in contemporary urban environments. The challenge facing anthropologists today is not to construct theories about sameness and difference, but to observe and record this ongoing, dynamic encounter of the world's peoples.

Contemporary anthropologists live with and work with both the sameness and the differences among human beings. In his remarkably wise essay "Found in Translation: On the Social History of the Moral Imagination," Clifford Geertz suggested one way this can be done with intelligence—and even a bit of grace.

The truth of the doctrine of cultural (or historical—it is the same thing) relativism is that we can never apprehend another people's or another period's imagination neatly, as though it were our own. The falsity of it is that we can therefore never genuinely apprehend it at all. We can apprehend it well enough, at least as well as we apprehend anything else not properly ours; but we do so not by looking *behind* the interfering glosses that connect us to it but *through* them.[6]

---

[5] See Renato Rosaldo, *Culture and Truth: The Remaking of Social Analysis* (Boston: Beacon Press, 1989). Rosaldo uses the image of the borderland to deconstruct the notion of self-contained, mutually incomprehensible "cultures." In a border area such as that between the United States and Mexico, cultures routinely mix and interact. Many people belong to more than one ethnic group, and all are shaped by more than one so-called culture. But Rosaldo takes the point further. The borderlands, he says, are found in the center of every contemporary country. Every city of any size is a place of culture mixing. On Rosaldo's terms, the concept of culture is desentimentalized and actual cultures become less uniform, less fixed, less precious, and less fragile than they appear to be in much anthropological writing. This is all to the good, since it assists anthropologists in doing work that accurately reflects the complex interconnectedness of the contemporary world.

[6] Clifford Geertz, "Found in Translation: On the Social History of the Moral Imagination," in *Local Knowledge: Further Essays in Interpretive Anthropology* (New York: Basic Books, 1983), 44.

Geertz, following Lionel Trilling, named the challenge well when he referred, not to the need to possess the right values, but to the need to
nurture moral imagination.[7]

In addition to studies of urban cultural crossroads, the contemporary
field of anthropology would benefit from more investigations of the internal dynamics of moral life in non-Western cultures. From the early
days of the discipline, anthropologists have raised moral questions in
relation to the peoples they have worked with. There is, for example, a
long history of anthropologists engaging in social and political activism
on behalf of "their people." Some few ethnographers also have noted
and commented on moral issues internal to the cultures they have studied. Yet what anthropology has not produced is a significant collection
of rigorous, dense ethnographies that give sustained attention to morality as a key component of culture. It seems an appropriate time to call
for attention to this project.

There are other, more practical reasons to urge this direction on the
field of anthropology at the present time. The dynamics of the hermeneu-
tical circle dictate that learning about the "other" occasions learning
about the self. Moral discourse in the United States and in much of Europe
is currently rigid and polarized. At this point in history, at the end of the
cold war, Westerners could do worse than draw on the sizable pool of cul-
tural-moral resources latent in the field of anthropology. The point is certainly not to adopt other peoples' values, but rather to learn about our
own through recognition and appreciation of other groups' methods for
generating values, for articulating them, for putting them into social play,
and, finally, for passing them on to subsequent generations. The following
study of moral dynamism in Vodou is intended as an illustration of the insights and questions that emerge from sustained attention to the cultural
vehicles that shape, carry, and pass on values within Haiti.

MORALITY AND HAITIAN VODOU

In the fall of 1994, Mama Lola, a Vodou priestess living in Brooklyn,
produced a *mare djòl*, a charm called "shut the mouth," for one of her
clients.[8] Inside a terra cotta pot, roughly the size of a bulging milk bottle,

---

[7] Ibid., 40.
[8] *Mare djòl* translates literally as tie the lips; the same type of charm can also be called a
mare bouch, tie the mouth.

she put *sabilye* leaves (to foster forgetting), salt (a prophylactic), molasses (a sweetener), the name of an electronics company on Long Island, and the name of a female employee of that company. She completely covered the pot with a white cloth ("you tie the mouth with a white cloth") and then wrapped yard after yard of white cotton string around the pot until it came to resemble a small, fat mummy. Having produced a wide loop with the last few feet of string, she suspended the *mare djòl* from a heating pipe that crossed the ceiling of her small basement altar room. Whenever she thought of it in the course of a day's work, she would reach up and set the charm swinging.

My intention is to use the *mare djòl* as a road into Vodou morality. In the process of evoking a religious context and then focusing on the operation of values within that context, I will quote Mama Lola and refer often to her style of practicing Vodou. I have worked with Mama Lola since 1978, and it is largely to her that I am indebted for what I know of the intricacies and intimacies of Haitian Vodou, the religion of the great majority of Haitian people.[9]

A web of relationships

Mama Lola's *mare djòl* was created for a man having trouble with his supervisor at the electronics plant where he worked. The supervisor was jealous of him because he attracted favorable attention from those higher up in the firm. So, she gossiped about Mama Lola's client in ways that damaged his reputation and, he feared, threatened his job. Healing work (one-on-one treatment sessions for problems of health, family, job, love, and money) is the most time-consuming part of the work of a *manbo*, Vodou priestess, or a *oungan*, Vodou priest. And yet it is more than metaphoric speech to claim that all Vodou, even elaborate public ceremonies, is about healing. All healing orchestrated by Vodou priests and priestesses concerns the healing of relationships.

Mama Lola practices the "science of the concrete" in her healing

[9] Vodou—spelled according to the phonetic orthography of Haitian Creole most widely used in Haiti today—usually combined with Roman Catholicism, is the religion of 85 percent of the Haitian population. Since participation in Vodou is not a matter of formal membership, but of practice that can include anything from an occasional consultation with a priest to structuring one's entire life around obligations to the spirits, others put the figure closer to 100 percent.

work; she objectifies complex relational situations.[10] She turns them into objects in the physical world and then changes them, in this instance, by introducing more desirable ingredients into the social-emotional mix. Into the red clay pot containing the names of the supervisor and the electronics firm, Lola put *sabilye* leaves to make the supervisor and those she influenced forget the entire affair. Salt and molasses were also added; the first as a cleanser and the second as a sweetener of the office atmosphere.

There were several distinct African religious traditions practiced among the people who made up Haiti's slave population. Haitian Vodou originated as the blending of these traditions with a number of eighteenth-century European spiritualities represented in the French colonial population. Of the latter, Catholicism was by far the most important influence, although by no means the only one. Freemasonry, for example, has also left a significant mark on Haitian Vodou. Despite the bouquet of detectable influences in Vodou, it remains at the core an African religion displaced to and transformed by the Caribbean.[11] The assumptions about the nature of personhood in Vodou make this judgment clear.

In the Vodou view of things, human beings are not only defined by the web of relationships that surrounds them; it is more accurate to say that they are created out of those relations. This relational web has both temporal and spacial dimensions. It connects persons to living family members of all ages, as well as to ancestors, and through ancestors, to the many *lwa*, Vodou spirits.

On the plane of the living, the dense relational web may be stretched by the creation of honorary "mothers" and "fathers," "aunts" and "uncles," and innumerable ad hoc "sisters," "brothers," and "cousins." These are persons who, through social influence, relative wealth, exceptional wisdom, or the goodness of their hearts, have come to play the role of a family member. When considering this somewhat cumbersome fictive family, it is good to remember that Haiti is one of the poorest countries in the world. Adding members beyond blood kin to one's

---

[10] Claude Levi-Strauss, "The Science of the Concrete," in *The Savage Mind* (Chicago: University of Chicago Press, 1966).

[11] In my classes I have often compared Vodou to an amoeba. When confronted with a foreign substance the Vodou amoeba does not recoil and cry "heresy"; instead it sends out its pseudopods, surrounds the new spirituality, absorbs it, and turns it into fuel for the maintenance of *its own system*.

exchange network provides extra strength in the social safety net, something that is important to impoverished Haitians.

Ideally, all relations within the web are reciprocal. It is easiest to grasp this point in relation to the living family where reciprocity entails not only the respect and service the young are expected to give their elders as a matter of course, but also the shelter, food, and general care due to children from those same elders. From this perspective, biology is not sufficient to establish the parenthood of the parent; acting like a father or mother is. Theoretically, a Haitian who neglects the responsibilities of the parental role, or abuses the power that comes along with it, can be shamed into compliance by a respectful speech in which the offender is frequently referred to as "father" or "mother."[12]

There are other ways in which the Vodou ethos reinforces the ties and responsibilities among the living. For example, Vodou underwrites the influence of children and of the poor, the least powerful of society's creatures. It designates both as exceptional sources of blessing and of luck. For example, to ensure the continued good fortune of the family, every family with the means to do it is expected to host a *manje pov*, a ritual feeding of the poor. The *manje pov*, which ideally should be held every few years, begins with a highly stylized feeding of the spirit children, the *mawasa* or divine twins. This special pre-meal is presented to the stand-ins for the *mawasa*, the children of the poor people who have been invited to the patron's temple or home for the feast. Being both children and poor, this is a group doubly empowered to dispense blessings. When everyone has eaten, the poor—children and adults—wash their hands in an infusion of basil leaves and wipe them on the clothing of the patron of the feast, thus passing on their blessings to their host.

Like the poor, the ancestors are both dependent and powerful. Mama Lola recently remarked: "When you die you have more power than when you alive. When somebody die he can help his children." Yet she has also told me more than once that *vivan-yo*, the living, do not envy the

---

[12] Consider this event in a different sort of fictive kin relationship. In 1986, just after Jean-Claude Duvalier abdicated the presidency of Haiti and left the country, Haitians were wary about how the United States, which had long backed the Duvalier family, would respond to the power vacuum. During that time, a hardscrabble farmer in northern Haiti was quoted in the *New York Times* as saying something like: "Uncle Sam is a good uncle and we know he will help us." The reporter mistook this for evidence of Haitian affection for the United States. A Haitian hearing this line would have known that whatever else was being communicated, this was also a pointed suggestion that the United States ought to refrain from being abusive in its relations with the small island republic of Haiti.

condition of the dead. In Vodou the dead do not go to heaven; instead they descend to the bottom of the water, a place of chill and dampness. Furthermore, after a year or more has passed, it is up to the living to rehabilitate the souls of the dead, or at least those that had important spiritual connections during their lives. The *rele mò nan dlo*, calling the dead from the waters, is a lengthy and expensive Vodou ceremony without which these ancestors can do nothing more constructive than harass their descendants. This ceremony warms the dead, raises them up from the water (they emerge complaining of cold and hunger), feeds them, and finally installs them in consecrated *govi*, pots, on Vodou altars.[13] Periodic feeding is necessary after the ancestral spirits have taken their place on the family altars. Without attention from the living, the ancestors could not continue to work for the living by warding off danger, countering malevolence, giving advice, and enhancing luck.

The *lwa*, spirits who were brought to Haiti from Africa, are central to the religion of Vodou, and they are not to be confused with the ancestors, or with God. God is called Bondye by those who serve the Vodou spirits, and it is Bondye who created and sustains the world. But as Mama Lola frequently observes: "He is too busy." A person cannot plead with Bondye or demand from him; if it is determined that a disease "comes from God," the Vodou healer can do nothing about it. The *lwa* are different. The *lwa* enjoy the song and dance performed for them. They need the food prepared for them, the candles that are lighted for them, and the libations that are poured.

Some *lwa* are like intimate family members who can be coaxed and cajoled. Others are fiercer. But if the one who serves the spirits knows how to treat the fierce *lwa*, they too will deliver healing, luck, and even money. Sometimes the *lwa* can even be told what to do. The living occasionally explode in anger at the spirits and threaten to cut off the flow of gifts and honors if they do not come through with the desired help. (Haitian Vodou is a religion that values self-confidence more than humility.) *Lwa* interact with the living mainly through possession-trance, during which they take over the body and voice of an adept in order to

---

[13] At the *rele mò nan dlo*, calling the dead from the water, the spirits of the dead seem to speak from the water-filled jugs in which the spirits are housed and later carried back to the family altars. This same type of possession, involving throwing the voice, can be used subsequently when the spirits are called after the *govi* have been installed on the altars.

sing and dance with the faithful, as well as give them advice and, when necessary, chastisement. Interaction with the *lwa* by means of possession-trance is frequent, powerful, intimate, and central to Vodou.

The living, the dead, and the spirits are all caught up in this dense relational web, and furthermore, it is not always easy to mark the boundaries among the three important groups. Just as the line between persons and their spirits is blurred during possession, so the dividing line between spirits and ancestors can sometimes appear less than distinct. One example demonstrates both of these types of boundary blurring equally well. People speak of Mama Lola's major spirit as "Lola's Ogou," and when she dies the family member who takes over her altar, and therefore her spiritual obligations, may well be possessed by a spirit identified as "Lola's Ogou." Such an occurrence would be both a return of the ancestor and a visit from the spirit. Also, both spirit and ancestor would manifest by possessing the body of the living family member.

The intermingling and overlapping of the living and the dead, the human and the divine, is beautifully captured in a song often sung at the opening of Vodou ceremonies. It begins:

> Anonse o zanj nan dlo,
> Bak odsu miwa. . . .

> Alert the angels down in the water,
> Back beneath the mirror. . . .

Vodou's Ginen, or Africa, is the watery home of the spirits, who also are called "angels," and of the dead as well. Ginen lies under the sea, "back beneath the mirror." With sparse language this song evokes the image of devotees gazing into the calm, mirroring surface of the sea, a boundary that separates them from Africa, and seeing there faces composed from transparent layers: their own reflections in the mirror; beneath their reflections, the faces of the ancestors; and, deeper still, those of the spirits themselves.

When Mama Lola made the *mare djòl*, she sought to clear blockage in the relational network that sustains her client—most immediately, a constriction in the relationship between him and his supervisor at the place where he worked. (Note that the problem was not conceptualized as an essential flaw in either one of the persons involved; it was located in the space between them.) Yet the blockage in that relationship was indicative of other, more serious, blockages. It was understood that for Mama Lola's client to have a problem of this sort there must be parallel problems in his relationship with the spirits. If all had been well with them, they would have prevented his problem with the supervisor from developing in the first place. Because of this two-tier diagnosis, treatment for the problem proceeded on two levels as well. Mama Lola told her client what to do in his own home, on a daily basis, that would feed and strengthen his spiritual protectors. Then, turning to the more im-mediate symptom of the problem, Mama Lola made the *mare djòl* to "tie up the mouth" of the gossiping supervisor. Several months later, when her client told Mama Lola that his supervisor had been promoted and, at the same time, transferred to another branch of the company outside New York, both he and Mama Lola pronounced the healing work successful.

The spirits in and around the head

It is generally assumed in Vodou circles that the character of a person is largely composed of the various spiritual influences playing in and around that person, including but not limited to spirits inherited within the family.[14] Each person has one spirit called the *mèt tèt*, master of the head, and this spirit is thought of as residing in the head of the person, as well as being a free-moving spirit in the larger social world. ("The spirit is a wind," Mama Lola is fond of saying.)

The Vodou system of identifying each person's *mèt tèt* amounts to a method for personality typing, and this system is of great significance for understanding the moral force field of Haitian Vodou. For example, one whose *mèt tèt* is Ogou, the warrior spirit, can be expected to have a life larded with issues of justice and power. Since each Vodou spirit is not so much a moral exemplar as a moral catalyst, both the constructive and destructive dimensions of the spirit's particular domains are likely to surface in the life of the person served by that spirit. Again, consider Ogou. He is connected to the soldier-liberators of Haiti's slave popula-

---

[14] For a creative essay on the spiritual diversity within the self, see Jim Wafer, *The Taste of Blood: Spirit Possession in Brazilian Candomble* (Philadelphia: University of Penn-sylvania Press, 1991).

tion, Toussaint L'Ouverture and Jean-Jacques Dessalines, but there are other manifestations of Ogou as well, ones that mirror him back to the devotee as braggart, drunkard, and liar.

Ogou's possession-performances act out a wide range of possible outcomes from the aggressive use of power. For example, military power can liberate, but it can also betray, and even become self-destructive.[15] Ogou thus preserves, in highly condensed form, the lessons of Haitian history, a history that includes not only the single successful slave revolution in the history of trans-Atlantic slavery, but also brutal dictators drawn from the Haitian population, as well as two occupations by the U.S. armed forces. In all layers of this dense history, themes of pride and liberation are interwoven with those of shame, anger, betrayal, and self-destruction. By extension, Ogou also explores the many kinds of metaphoric "war" a person is faced with in a place like New York City, home of the largest Haitian diaspora community. At the same time the various personae of this warrior spirit present an almost clinical analysis of the beneficial uses of anger and aggression, as well as their attendant pathologies.[16]

Vodou is a system able to configure considerable nuance and complexity in the character of individual persons because of its recognition of secondary spirit influences. The dominance of the *mèt tèt* over a person's character and consciousness is significantly modulated by the counterweights of a small number of other spirits (usually two or three) also said to "love" that person. These coteries of personal *lwa* vary from one individual to another and cause the Vodou community to have some-

---

[15] The following passage is from Karen McCarthy Brown, *Mama Lola: A Vodou Priestess in Brooklyn* (Berkeley and Los Angeles: University of California Press, 1991), 94–5. It describes a ceremony in 1979 during which Mama Lola was "ridden" by Ogou.

> Ogou's possession-performance began with a series of familiar gestures. Taking his ritual sword in hand and slicing the air in broad aggressive strokes, Ogou first attacked an invisible enemy. Then he took more controlled, menacing jabs at those members of [Mama Lola's] . . . Vodou family standing nearest him. Finally, in a gesture full of bravado that also hinted at self-wounding, Ogou turned the sword on himself. Lodging the point in one hip, he bent the rapierlike blade into an arc. Ogou performs his dance with the sword at nearly every public occasion on which he makes an appearance. Its elegant gestures are to body language what proverbs are to spoken language, a condensation point for complex truths: power liberates, power betrays, power turns on those who wield it.

[16] For further discussion of Ogou and his relation to the lessons of Haitian history as well as to contemporary struggles in Haiti and in the New York diaspora community, see Karen McCarthy Brown, "Systematic Remembering, Systematic Forgetting: Ogou in Haiti," in *Africa's Ogun: Old World and New*, ed. Sandra T. Barnes (Bloomington: Indiana University Press, 1989), 65–89; and Brown, *Mama Lola*, 94–139.

what different behavioral expectations of persons who "serve," that is observe ritual obligation to, different configurations of *lwa*.

For example, Mama Lola serves two of the Ezili sisters, Freda and Dantò, in addition to Ogou. Ezili Freda is a spirit of wealth, beauty, and sexuality whose destructiveness emerges as self-involvement and an insatiable hunger for attention and affection. Dantò is stronger, more effective, and also potentially more destructive. She is the woman who bears children, something Freda cannot do, and the mother who raises them on her own, as most poor women in Haiti do. Ezili Dantò's ability to endure in the midst of great hardship is paramount in her character. Equally pronounced is her willingness to defend her children at all costs, but, when her anger-driven persistence skids off track and runs amuck, she can quickly transform into the kind of mother who might well attack her own children.[17]

Ogou energy is individualistic; it takes risks and has adventures. The character traits Mama Lola shares with Ogou are those that pushed her to take the risk of leaving Haiti and trying life in the United States. Yet, were it not for almost equally strong Dantò energy, Mama Lola would not be who she is, the mother of four and the head of a lively multi-generational Brooklyn household. Similarly, without a visible though subtle Freda presence, Mama Lola would be less of a playful vamp than I know her to be, and she probably would not be taking on a new "boyfriend" as she approaches her sixty-third birthday.

The matrix of spiritual energies within a single individual provides important moral flexibility for the one who serves the Vodou spirits. Consider the issue of abortion. As a Catholic, Mama Lola feels that abortion is wrong. As one who serves Ezili Dantò, the quintessential mother, she is also opposed to abortion. Nevertheless, she tells two quite different stories about the spirits' influence in relation to this issue in her own life. In one story Ezili Dantò came in a dream and told Lola to stop trying to abort a pregnancy. Even though Lola had been deserted by the father of the child and, at the time, was so poor she had to struggle to feed the two children she already had, she bowed to the wishes of Dantò.

---

[17] Ezili Freda and Ezili Dantò, like Ogou, reflect part of the Haitian social terrain. They also map the complex psychodynamics of women's sexuality and childbearing. Freda, with her pale skin and love of luxury, mirrors the women of the Haitian elite who set the standards for female beauty in Haiti. Dantò, almost always identified as exceptionally black, makes visible the lives of the majority of poor women who raise children without the help of a man. See Brown, *Mama Lola*, 220–57, for a more detailed discussion of the Ezili in Haitian Vodou.

Her third child was born. Some years later, while in a stable relationship with a man, she became pregnant again. Both Lola and her partner wanted the child but, not long after discovering her condition, Lola got word that she had been granted a visa to immigrate to the United States. If the pregnancy had been discovered, she would have lost the visa. So Ogou, the adventurer and risktaker, gave support to Lola's decision to have an abortion in order to take advantage of what might have been her only chance to escape Haiti.[18]

Wande Abimbola, a Nigerian Ogun priest and an internationally known scholar, once described the central moral energy of traditional Yoruba religion as helping people "ride their horses in the direction they are going."[19] In other words, he described a religion that recognizes that people are different from one another, with different talents, different strengths and weaknesses. Living a good life will then mean different things for different people. Thus knowledge of self becomes a prerequisite for knowing how to live a good life, a life of responsibility to the community. The Vodou attitude toward persons is similar.

The Yoruba and the Haitian religious traditions are historically related. Both traditions have elaborate divinatory systems designed to diagnose character, as well as to assess the particular problems in people's lives. What each person who serves the Vodou spirits learns through this divination process is the pattern of spirit influences peculiar to them. Once this is known and a Vodou adept has been given the tools to consult and feed these personal spirits, that person has also garnered some leverage in the moral world and has done so by gaining self-knowledge. The adept can lean into her strengths and anticipate where life's problems are likely to arise.

Along with this dynamic view of personhood, one constituted from several distinct spirit energies, comes considerable appreciation for diversity within the individual. In Vodou communities there is no high premium placed on maintaining a smooth facade or on behaving consistently. In a related way, there is also a high tolerance for diversity within the community at large. For example, in the context of a quite homophobic larger society, gay men and lesbian women are welcomed into the Vodou temples. While this is generally true in all Vodou temples, there are some temples that specifically cater to Haiti's gay population.

---

[18] For a lengthier discussion of this material, see Brown, *Mama Lola*, 241ff.
[19] Wande Abimbola, unpublished talk given at the Liederkranz Club in Manhattan, 1981.

Balanse

"Why did you hang the *mare djòl* from the ceiling in your altar room?"
I asked Mama Lola. "So I could *balanse*. . . . You know, make it go like
that," she replied, swishing her hand from side to side. The word *balanse*
in Haitian Creole is one of those words that is used in everyday discourse
but takes on added meaning in a Vodou context. In ordinary speech a
person might reply, in response to a question about what she is doing
that evening, "I am balancing between going to see a movie and staying
home." In other words, she is undecided and is weighing her options.
The image conjured up is that of a pair of scales, a mechanism on which
one thing is weighed against another. Such a pair of scales, called a
balans, is in fact a central image in Vodou iconography, just as it is in
American jurisprudence. But in the Vodou temple the scales do not sig-
nify the quest for evening scores, balancing punishment against crime,
and achieving equilibrium. On the contrary, in Vodou settings the *balans*
(the scale) signals a quest for dynamism, movement, energy.

A set of scales signals the process by which the static can be reani-
mated. For example, when certain objects are taken off a Vodou altar,
they cannot be introduced into the ritual action until someone has swung
them from side to side, or has turned themselves around and around
while holding the objects in their hands or on their heads. To move thus
with a ritual object is to *balanse*. But there are other layers to the word
as well.

The well-known Haitian painter André Pierre once used the word
balanse in a way that was both shocking and revealing. When I stopped
by to visit one day, I referred to the recent death of someone we had
both known. The grizzled old painter, who is something of a trickster,
gave a loud laugh, slapped his thigh, and hooted: "Bawon Samdi te rive
la. Ah! Li te balanse kay sa." (Bawon Samdi came there. Oh! He bal-
anced that house.)

Bawon Samdi is the head of the Gede, the spirits of death. So André
Pierre seemed to be saying that death arrived and set the house reeling.
That seemed true enough. The troubling part was his laughter. It suggested that, despite the pain, this confrontation with death might be the
source of new life energy for the family of the man who died. The Gede
are the perfect ones to deliver such a hard, contradictory message. The
domain over which the Gede preside comprises sexuality, fertility, and

social satire, as well as death. The Gede are irrepressible tricksters. They often wear dark glasses with one lens missing. One Vodou priest told me this was because they can see into the lands of the living and the dead simultaneously. He also suggested that this was the source of their humor.

The shared use of the verb *balanse* in the Vodou ritual context and in André Pierre's story puts the innocuous swinging of a sacred object on the same spectrum of signification with treating the living to a sudden terrifying look into the face of death. What these two actions have in common is that they both use conflict or contradiction to *chofe*, heat things up or raise energy. In general, the Vodou ethos is one that accepts conflict, works with it, and ultimately orchestrates it to produce something life enhancing. In European and American culture we typically fear that our instinctive energies will get out of hand; in Haiti the fear is that life energy will diminish and go out, like a candle.

The practitioners of Vodou have never been able to kid themselves about death and suffering. They do not have either the power or the resources to sustain the kinds of fictions about mortality and pain (e.g. cosmetics, plastic surgery, the mortuary arts) that are commonplace among wealthier peoples. The sickness and death of a family member is still a hands-on experience in most parts of Haiti. Since they cannot directly distance suffering, those who serve the Vodou spirits laugh in its face.

They call on Gede for the transformation of death into humor. This alchemical moment is captured for me in a familiar, oft-repeated scene. Bawon Samdi has possessed someone; the person's immobile body lies stiff on the temple floor beneath a white sheet. Suddenly a crude bit of sexual slang slips from the mouth of the ritual corpse, moments before the figure throws off his sheet, jumps up, and grinds his hips lasciviously. Bawon has gone; one of the trickster Gede has taken his place. This is the way Vodou deals with the very human fear of death and of suffering. There is no attempt at theological rationalization. A popular Haitian proverb, one often accompanied by a shrug of the shoulders, says it all: *"Moun fèt pou mouri."* (People are born to die.) The following comments, necessarily broad and suggestive, are intended to hint at what the practitioners of such a religion might bring to a dialogue on morality with North Americans in the late twentieth century.

THE MORAL STYLE OF NORTH AMERICA
FROM THE VANTAGE POINT OF HAITI

The moral orientation of Haitian Vodou rests on the assumption of complex, substantive interconnections among people, as well as among people, their ancestors, their spirits, and God. Yet the same moral system also places a premium on self-knowledge and values self-confidence over humility. Those who enter the Vodou system find out that they must know themselves, and what they are made of, before they can learn how to live with others with integrity. Vodou thus presents a provocative alternative to traditional North American individualism.

Vodou is centrally concerned with healing. Vodou healers address problems of love, family, job, and money, as well as problems of health. As a result they inevitably deal with issues of morality. Yet there is no essential good or evil in the Vodou worldview. The closest thing in the Vodou system is the primary contrast between what is "tied," "chained," or "bound," and that which is "open" and "free flowing." Vodou healing is directed at the relations between parties, and the main method of healing is to untie, or unblock, relationships so that reciprocity between persons, and among persons, ancestors, and spirits can flow freely in all directions. Of course, untying one person may mean tying up another, as Mama Lola tied the mouth of her client's supervisor at the Long Island electronics plant. The point here is that there is no utopian drive in Vodou. Those who serve the spirits accept that as human beings we live in an imperfect world, one in which we can never have perfectly clean hands. So, if securing one person's freedom means temporarily tying up another, it may not represent a perfect solution, but it will nevertheless have to be done. Haitian Vodou thus represents a viewpoint instructively different from the polarities of "right" and "wrong" that often structure discussions of morality in popular U.S. media.

Vodou morality is dynamic, and values cannot be reduced to a set of universal and timeless principles. Yet Vodou morality has stable ways of being and acting at its core and cannot justifiably be called either radically relativist or radically contextual. Furthermore, in its focus on self-knowledge and self-respect, it adds a particular emphasis to a discussion of moral education that is largely missing in North America.

In the Haitian Vodou moral system, survival is a moral goal.[20] Honesty about the nature of human life is a moral requirement. A comparison between popular American morality and Haitian morality, or the morality of any people for whom survival has been a basic issue, could help us North Americans gain perspective on our moral claims. Living in a nation as powerful as the United States in the late twentieth century, while knowing what we do about global economic, ecological, and political interconnections, leaves many of us with a sense of guilt about things we cannot control. Some North Americans appear to be developing a brittle moral fanaticism in an effort to reassert control over their moral well-being.

In a country as privileged as the United States of America, people have trouble accepting the limitations of the human condition. We want to think that moral responsibility extends only to those areas of life over which we have control and furthermore, we think we should be able to keep ourselves morally pure. Sadly, we tend to articulate awareness of our inevitable failures at perfection in metaphors of dirt, rot, and disease. These notions work against the basic self-respect that systems such as Vodou assume are integral to living a moral life. Haitian Vodou offers us the intriguing possibility of thinking about morality in quite a different way, one that keeps such metaphors at bay.

By locating problems in the relations between people, rather than in individuals themselves, and by understanding goodness as a temporary achievement in the midst of life's movement—much as a ballet dancer temporarily achieves beauty—Haitian traditional culture places itself in what could be a productive tension with pervasive moods and motivations in American culture. Vodou offers the intriguing suggestion that moral progress might well be understood as the refinement of a talent called "moral style" or "moral imagination," rather than as increasingly consistent adherence to rules or laws.

Vodou morality is a collection of attitudes and practices that encourages the acceptance of conflict and suffering; the celebration of plurality, both in the group and within the person; and the search for the good through whatever preserves life and enhances life energy. In Vodou, as in many other religious systems, life energy and sexual energy tend to flow together. The Vodou spirit Gede is a prime example of that ten-

---

[20] On this issue see Katie Geneva Cannon, *Black Womanist Ethics* (Atlanta: Scholars Press, 1988).

dency. The suspicion of sexuality that has long characterized European and American Christian culture can easily flow over into a repression of general life energy. The disembodied character of much of white Euro-American culture is striking. As adults, we do so little dancing, and it scarcely occurs to us that this has anything to do with the frequently brittle character of public moral discourse.

In sum, those of us in the United States who are interested in the revival of moral inquiry ought to consider taking Haitian Vodou on as a conversation partner—not to become like it, something we could never do anyway, but to see ourselves from a different angle in relation to it.[21] The challenge of the postmodern age is centrally about hegemonic power or, more precisely, the loss of it. Haitians would be good conversation partners for North Americans precisely because they have never had the money, the power, or the weapons to be tempted to think that they possessed universal truths or that they could speak with authority for the rest of the world. Haitians have lots of experience, however, living in a troubled relationship with the United States, where such assumptions have been routine. Haiti, a country that has long been the target of the most stubborn of U.S. racist projections,[22] might be a *very* interesting interlocutor for the conscience of the United States. The records, oral and written, of United States–Haiti interaction span more than two centuries, starting during the period of trans-Atlantic slavery and running continuously through the end of the cold war. As such, they provide a rich resource for exploring the parameters of moral vision. As Haiti has come increasingly under the sway of U.S. popular culture and political economy during the last century, all of the learning has tended to flow in one direction—from the United States toward Haiti. The time may be right to test what can flow in the other direction.

[21] Much of what is attractive about Vodou morality could not be replicated in the United States. Eighty percent of the Haitian population lives on the land, in small communities where everyone knows everyone else. This circumstance reinforces tolerance for behavioral diversity within each person and among people in general. Such small agricultural communities also foster the strong spirit of cooperation, even communitarianism, that is at the heart of Vodou. Yet, at the same time, rural life where people depend so much on one another also inevitably feeds the more dysfunctional aspects of Vodou, for example, the tendency of the group to accuse talented or wealthy individuals of sorcery.
[22] See Robert Lawless, *Haiti's Bad Press* (Rochester, Vt.: Schenkman Books, 1992).

8

Snakes alive: Resituating the moral in the study of religion

ROBERT A. ORSI

At the end of a compelling account of his two-year sojourn among snake-handling Christians in southern Appalachia, Dennis Covington, a Georgia-based reporter for the *New York Times*, describes the night he realized that he could not join the handlers, whom he had come to love and respect, in their faith. I want to borrow this instance of one man's discovery of radical religious otherness—a discovery that led him to turn away in sorrow and disappointment from his friends—as an opening onto the question of what a renewed emphasis on moral inquiry might mean for the academic study of religion.

The discipline of Religious Studies has always been organized around a distinct and identifiable set of moral values and judgments, most often implicit and commonly evident more in convention than in precept. Disciplinary theorizing about religion has proceeded in accordance with these embedded moral assumptions, even when Religious Studies insisted most vehemently on its "scientific" status.[1] The usually unacknowledged centrality of these values in the working life of the discipline has limited the range of human practices, needs, and responses that count as "religion"—excluding, for example, experiences of the power of holding poisonous snakes against one's face or brandishing them in righteous anger against one's foes. A revival of moral inquiry in Reli-

This chapter is affectionately dedicated to Karen Brown and David Haberman, two masters of the erotics of Religious Studies who are also good friends of mine and conversation partners. I have learned a great deal about the study of religion from both of them. I also have benefited from Richard Fox's careful reading of and commentary on successive drafts of this chapter.

[1] The distinction here between precept and convention in the way moral orientations have informed the study of religion is borrowed from Eric J. Sharpe, *Comparative Religion: A History* (1975; reprint, LaSalle, Ill.: Open Court, 1986), 311.

gious Studies should not be simply an explicit embrace of the old implicit values and judgments: to reauthorize the embedded normative cultural core of the discipline at a moment when the field has an opportunity to break free of it would be a regrettable failure of nerve. Before we practitioners of Religious Studies can introduce moral questions into our approach to other people's religious worlds, we must first excavate our hidden moral history. Otherwise, all that a revival of moral inquiry will be is the discovery, as if we had come upon something new, of our unacknowledged assumptions and prejudices as moral concerns.

SNAKES AND THE NATURE OF GOD

Dennis Covington first entered the culture of snake handlers on assignment from the *Times* to cover the trial of a minister accused of attempting to kill his wife by forcing her to put her hand in a crate of poisonous snakes.[2] Drawn by a religious idiom that fused domains others considered irreconcilable—heaven and earth, spirit and snake, vulnerability and control—and that generated experiences of tremendous visceral power, Covington stayed on. He came to see snake handling as a way for poor, displaced people in a ravaged land to contend with and surmount (at least once in a while, with the snakes in their hands) the violence and danger that bore down on them in their everyday lives. His account is never reductive nor does he stay aloof from the people he writes about. He smells the "sweet savor" of the Holy Spirit moving in the room when the snakes are taken out of their boxes—a smell like "warm bread and apples," discernible, he says, just beneath the smell of reptile—and finally he takes up serpents, too. Until the last night of his years with snake-handlers, Covington offers a good model for an engaged, interpersonal, participatory religious study.

But on this last evening, at the Church of the Lord Jesus Christ in Kingston, Georgia, Covington watches in horror as his photographer, a young woman well known by then to the handlers, is verbally assaulted—by a minister Covington had considered his spiritual father—

---

[2] Dennis Covington, *Salvation on Sand Mountain: Snake Handling and Redemption in Southern Appalachia* (Reading, Mass.: Addison-Wesley, 1995). For a much more existentially challenging account of this culture, see David L. Kimbrough, *Taking Up Serpents: Snake Handlers of Eastern Kentucky* (Chapel Hill and London: University of North Carolina Press, 1995).

for her usurpation of man's scripturally mandated role (as the community understood this). Covington rises to witness against this denial of spiritual equality to women, but he is silenced by his mentor. Then another preacher, a legendary figure named Punkin Brown who was known among other things for wiping his sweat away with rattlesnakes, reached into the serpent box, pulled out a "big yellow-phase timber rattler and slung it across his shoulder like a rope." As he does so, Punkin Brown makes a sound that Covington records as "haaagh," an explosive, angry grunt; and as he bears down into his nasty, woman-hating sermon, the preacher uses this sound to set the cadence of his attack and to underscore his rage. Covington makes sure we hear this: "haaagh" appears ten times on one page—and it is thus—haaagh!—that he reestablishes the border between himself and the handlers that he had up until then so courageously been tearing down.

Covington signals and solidifies his new position vis-à-vis the handlers with a change in rhetoric. Before this evening in Kingston, he had seen an eerie, otherworldly beauty in the moans and movements of the handlers; in particular, his descriptions of female handlers, sobbing and trembling as they drew bundles of snakes close to themselves in religious "ecstasy," are charged with a fierce, unacknowledged erotic intensity. But now he gives us Punkin Brown, a vile, primitive force, "strutting" about the sanctuary with the big snake across his shoulders, his body contorted, his face flushed with blood and hate. The evangelist brushes his lips with the serpent and wipes his face with it, and always there is the brutal "haaagh," like "steam escaping from an *underground* vent."[3] Punkin Brown has become a nightmare figure, a subterranean creature, a snake himself.

Covington believes that he was saved at the last minute from descending into such strangeness himself. He tells us he was all set to give up his work, stock his car trunk with snakes, and make his way across the land as an itinerant, snake-handling evangelist. But the "haaagh!" brought him to his senses and restored his world to him. This appears to be the existential impulse behind the abrupt change in voice: to shield himself from otherness, to impose closure on a dangerous two-year experience that threatened in the end to penetrate the boundaries of his own subjectivity. The description of Punkin Brown—or rather, the construction of "Punkin Brown"—is a barrier enacted in rhetoric against

---

[3] Covington, *Salvation on Sand Mountain*, 234 (my emphasis).

the compulsive attraction of otherness. "Punkin Brown" makes the world safe again for Covington and his readers. Protected now against this alien other—who would ever confuse the author or oneself with this wild creature, one's own fantasies, rages, needs and hopes with his?—Covington can find Punkin Brown ridiculous, "grotesque and funny looking, with his shirttail out and a big rattlesnake draped over his shoulder."[4] Alterity first secures the identity of the observer as safely separate from the other, and then establishes the observer's superiority.

But Covington makes still another move. At stake that night in Georgia, he maintains on the closing page of the book (so that the handlers will never have the opportunity to say anything further for themselves), was not simply the role of women in the church. Nor was it the rightness of taking up serpents, even though this is how Punkin Brown understood the conflict: if the Bible is wrong about women, the preacher believed, then it is wrong about the Christian's invulnerability from poisonous snakes too, so that we who take up such serpents will die. Rather, according to Covington, at issue that night in Georgia was "the nature of God."[5] Punkin Brown's god, Covington reassures himself and his readers, is not, cannot be, my, our, god. This is the final, and most damning, step in the rendering of Punkin Brown as radical other: he has been cast out of the shared domain of the sacred.

What has happened here? How could a writer who managed to bring the alien world of snake handlers so close end by repositioning them at the margins of culture? Covington has inscribed an existential circle, taking a long detour to reestablish the prejudices against snake handlers many readers undoubtedly started out with, alongside whatever fascination drew them to the work as well. I want to explore now the process by which the other is silenced and securely returned to otherness and the world of the writer is restored and reauthorized, rather than transformed.

GOOD RELIGION, BAD RELIGION, AND RELIGION AT ITS BEST

It seems to be virtually impossible to study religion without attempting to distinguish between its good and bad expressions, without working

---

[4] Ibid., 235.
[5] Ibid., 239.

to establish both a normative hierarchy of religious idioms (ascending from negative to positive, "primitive" to high, local to universal, infantile to mature, among other value-laden dichotomies familiar to the field) and a methodological justification for it. These resilient impulses take on special significance in light of the well-known inability of the field to agree on what religion is: normative boundary setting fills in the theoretical vacuum. We may not know what religion is, but at least we can say with certainty what bad religion is, or what religion surely is not. Historian of religion Jonathan Z. Smith has rightly observed that of all the distinctions so dear to scholarly practitioners—sacred/profane, natural/supernatural, magic/religion, with books/without books, and so on—the most fundamental and the most tenaciously held is that between "us" and "them," and this has usually been a moral distinction.[6]

To understand the cultural grounds of this moralizing imperative within Religious Studies, we have to look outside it, specifically to the history of American higher education. The academic study of religion in the United States developed within a university culture that, as historian George Marsden has recently argued, has always had to struggle with the conflicting claims of Christian authority (widely accepted in the culture) and secular learning (as this developed over the nineteenth and early twentieth centuries). Christian authority was never singular in the United States, and so whatever compromises were sought in light of this intellectual and cultural tension had to be acceptable within the broader social context of American denominational diversity. The solution to the dilemma from the early Republic until the years after World War II, says Marsden, was "morally uplifting undergraduate teaching" and voluntary, extracurricular religious activities situated at the margins of academic life in order to satisfy the concerns of Christians inside and outside the academy.[7] Ethics in this context stood in for Christianity in American university culture, but ethics defined in a broad, universalist, nondogmatic, nonsectarian, nondenominational way designed to appeal to a broad "Christian" clientele. Liberal Protestantism, in short, or what Marsden acidly calls "pious nonsectarianism," became the official religious culture of the American academy.[8]

[6] Jonathan Z. Smith, *Imagining Religion: From Babylon to Jonestown* (Chicago: University of Chicago Press, 1982), 6.
[7] George M. Marsden, *The Soul of the American University: From Protestant Establishment to Established Nonbelief* (New York: Oxford University Press, 1994), 31, 85.
[8] Ibid., 89.

This was a pragmatic position: the challenge of the educational marketplace in which colleges and universities competed was to attract students from many different denominations, since not even church schools
could survive on enrollments from one source. But the emphasis on
moral learning of a sort that all Protestant Americans could have access
to as the crown of education was also congruent with the understanding
among American educators of the role of the academy in the turbulent,
pluralist democracy the United States was proving itself to be. The rationale for building colleges in the early Republic was explicitly understood to be civilizing the population; "next to religion," as Marsden
frames the Whig position, "education was the best means of taming an
unruly populace and assimilating diverse peoples into a common culture
with shared ideals," an understanding that persisted down to John
Dewey and the Progressives at the start of this century.[9] The nation with
a soul of a counting house would make its universities into Sunday
schools of moral and social values.

This liberal ethical ethos coincided with broader trends in the re-
orientation of academic culture over the nineteenth century, in particular
the insistence on critical research as the mainstay of learning, the pro-
fessionalization of the professoriate, and the secularization of methodology. Already in the postrevolutionary period, academic leaders
influenced by Scottish Common Sense philosophy asserted that science,
morality, and "true religion" were all allied. Marsden points out that
American evangelicals, whose religion did not resemble this "true" one,
at first went along with the notion of a broad intellectual alliance between tradition and modern learning because at the time they were
secure in their own cultural authority. But things would change, particularly as natural science came to pose an increasingly serious threat to
Christian conservatives; and then, Marsden says, "Christian teaching
itself would have to be adjusted to meet the demands of a scientific
age" and subject itself to the requirements and procedures of critical
scholarship.[10]

Many progressive social scientists at the turn of the century, who
played such an important role in shaping the contemporary university
world in the United States, were often children of orthodox Christian
households. They rejected the faith of their families in favor of a scien-

[9] Ibid., 85.
[10] Ibid., 93.

tific approach to social and psychological knowledge that was nevertheless deeply and passionately informed with liberal Protestant values.[11] They replicated, in their own intellectual and emotional journeys, the development of the American academy from Calvinism to liberalism. But while liberal religious concerns informed the scholarship and pedagogy of this group of explicitly post-Christian Christian academics, which Marsden presents as the last generation of such scholars, those concerns had no effect on the fundamental understanding among these men and women of the university as a place of secular, critical, scientific learning. "After a century of resistance from more traditional Christians," Marsden writes, "the dominant educational ideals were defined by a synthesis of Enlightenment ideals and an enlightened Christianity, or religion of humanity." Outside the gates of the academy, meanwhile, increasingly alienated fundamentalist Christians waged a campaign to restore what they understood to be the primary purpose of education at all levels— "to learn the wisdom of the elders," in Marsden's formulation of their position—in direct opposition to modernists who "gave their ultimate intellectual allegiance to the scientific method as the essence of true education."[12] Liberal Protestantism became the essential buffer within the academy against the ever more intransigent (and panicky) fundamentalists outside it.

It was in this intellectual environment that the academic study of religion first appeared in the United States. Certain key issues had already been settled in the wider academic culture, such as the authority of the scientific method and the primacy of critical research. The new discipline would have to meet these standards and comport itself by these rules if it wanted to be a player in the modern academy. Moreover, the distinction between "Christianity," which was amenable to the aims of modern learning, and "sectarianism," which was hostile to them, had by now been embedded in academic culture in its confrontation with fundamentalism. Finally, the entire curriculum was understood by liberal Christian educational leaders to be morally uplifting, oriented to the shaping of human spiritual and moral development. The impact of these

[11] See Murray G. Murphey, "On the Scientific Study of Religion in the United States, 1870–1980," in *Religion and Twentieth-Century American Intellectual Life*, ed. Michael J. Lacey (Washington, D.C., and Cambridge: Woodrow Wilson Center Press and Cambridge University Press, 1989), 136–7; and Robert M. Crunden, *Ministers of Reform: The Progressives' Achievement in American Civilization, 1889–1920* (Urbana and Chicago: University of Illinois Press, 1984).

[12] Marsden, *Soul of the American University*, 177, 329.

converging forces on the nascent academic discipline of Religious Studies can be seen in University of Chicago founder William Rainey Harper's rationale for including the study of religion in the curriculum of a major research university. According to Marsden,

Harper shared with many of his contemporaries enthusiasm about the powers of "scientific study" to settle longstanding human debates in all areas. He accordingly justified the inclusion of the Bible and other distinctly religious subjects in the broadening university curriculum on the grounds that they could now be studied scientifically. There were "laws of religious life" just as there were laws of health and physical life. Yet "men and women of the highest intelligence in matters of life and thought are discovered to be cultivating a religious life far below the plane of their intellectual life." Advances in the scientific study of religion, not only in biblical studies, but notably also in the psychology of religion, now made possible a scientific approach to this part of life as much as any other.[13]

The true religion long established within American university culture would now become the "religion" studied in the academy.

It was inconceivable that religion would be anything but good religion in this social and intellectual setting, "good" meaning anything acceptable in belief or practice to liberal Protestantism. Profoundly influenced by the evolutionary paradigm of the natural sciences, American sociologists, anthropologists, and psychologists of religion asserted that cultures, society, individuals—indeed, planetary civilization itself—developed from lower, primitive forms successively toward higher expressions of the human religious spirit, expressions that inevitably resembled this good religion. American psychologists of religion, for example, heirs and interpreters of Jamesian pragmatism, designated as religion that component of human personality that moved it toward emotional, spiritual, and existential unity and maturity, success and happiness. Such normative terms were presented as analytical categories, and their implicit moral and cultural assumptions went unchallenged; such was the authority of "true" religion in the academy. Likewise, sociologists tended to emphasize religion's socially integrative functions, its role as the pivot of social stability and solidarity, and to relegate to categories other than religion any phenomenon that did not serve this consensual function.

Of course, Americans outside the academy knew well that religions often did not function this way. American culture has been extraordi-

---

[13] Ibid., 243.

narily rich in religious movements that promoted divisiveness not integration, insisted on authority or emotion rather than reason, resorted to violence, shame, and degradation in pursuing their spiritual ends, and crafted subjectivities of a sort far beyond what was tolerable in the precincts of the academy. Indeed, it was partially the cultural elite's recognition and fear of such popular religious fecundity that led to the insistence on teaching liberal ethics and true religion in the academy, to inoculate the young against the contagion of American religious imaginings. Perhaps this is why religious practitioners often do not recognize what passes for "religion" within religious studies.

Legal scholar Stephen L. Carter expresses the normative academic position in his recently published and widely celebrated account of religion in American public life, *The Culture of Disbelief*. Carter bluntly asserts that "religion at its best" resonates with the values most Americans hold dear and that this religion-at-its-best "tends to be a positive not a negative force in people's lives." Thus is practiced the familiar art of distinguishing true religion from everything else.[14] The point here is not simply that this normative account of "true religion" excludes from the study of religion ugly, violent, or troublesome matters (although it certainly does this). Rather the entire notion of religion has been carefully demarcated to preserve it from ambivalence and ambiguity, from anything not in accordance with certain sanctioned notions of self and society. Religion is gridded along a graph of diametric opposites—in Carter's terms, "positive" rather than "negative," which may be taken as a summary of all the other dichotomies I have mentioned. The possibility that religion can transgress these various normative dualities, that it does its cultural, psychological, and political work precisely by disregarding boundaries between one self and another, or between past, present, and future, or between the natural and the supernatural, is disallowed. True religion is epistemologically and ethically singular; it is rational, respectful of persons, noncoercive, mature, nonanthropomorphic in its higher forms, mystical (as opposed to ritualistic), agreeable to democracy, monotheistic (no angels, saints, demons, ancestors), a reality of mind and spirit not body and matter. It is concerned with ideal essences not actual things. Thus all the complex dynamism of religion is stripped away, its boundary-blurring and border-crossing pro-

---

[14] Stephen L. Carter, *The Culture of Disbelief: How American Law and Politics Trivialize Religious Devotion* (New York: Basic Books, 1993), 268, 270.

pensities eliminated. Not surprisingly, there is only one methodology and one epistemology for studying this "religion," critical, analytical, and "objective" (as opposed to "subjective," existentially engaged, or participatory).

In this way the discipline reflects the religious politics of the United States as well as the distinct history of the academy: the embedded, hidden others against whom the religion in Religious Studies is constituted are the religions on the American landscape that appeared so terrifying and un-American to the guardians of the culture—Mormonism, Catholicism, evangelicalism, Pentecostalism, among others. The discipline was literally constructed by means of the exclusion—in fact and in theory—of these other ways of practicing religion, which were relegated to the world of sects, cults, fundamentalisms, popular piety, ritualism, magic, primitive religion, millennialism, anything but "religion."

The academic study of religion is not an American phenomenon, of course. The notion that religion could be made acceptable to sophisticated and civilized men and women goes back in the modern period at least to Friedrich Schleiermacher, just as Marsden's critique of such religion has its roots in Søren Kierkegaard's contempt for it. American academics who study religion participate in an international community of scholars that is institutionalized in various sorts of academic arrangements, scholarly exchanges, and international symposia. But in this broader context too, liberal notions of religion allied to particular political agendas came to be authoritative.

Eric J. Sharpe points out in his history of the modern development of the discipline that scholars shaped in liberal Christian traditions played important roles in its early formative period and that liberal versions of Christianity acquired a normative status in the work of nineteenth- and early twentieth-century comparativists. Indeed, this Christianity was seen as the *telos* of the evolution of world religions. As the colonial period shuddered to a close, scholars proposed a broadly inclusive, universal religion of man as the goal of both the study and practice of religions. They aspired to gather the world's many different religious traditions into a single, global narrative of the progressive revelation of God.

Given this normative evolutionary orientation in the field, many practitioners began to insist that the academic study of religion itself make a positive contribution to human culture and to the betterment of life on earth, to facilitate relations across cultures and to deepen human tolerance. This social task seemed particularly imperative after World

War II, when many in the discipline held that academic study had a role to play in the reconstruction of Western culture devastated by war and totalitarianism. A hard-core group, comprised mainly of European scholars, held onto an "empiricist" vision of the field (as Sharpe identifies it) and insisted that the emphasis on the moral responsibility of professors of Religious Studies represented the intrusion of theology and normative ethics into the discipline. But these scholars were in the minority. Both in content and method, Religious Studies has long been occupied with "good" religion.

By the time I arrived as an undergraduate at a small New England college with an excellent religion department, this combination of a liberal Protestant understanding of what religion is and a sense of the moral responsibility of the field had become institutionalized in the curriculum. My professors were all educated at Union Theological Seminary in New York, where they learned theology from Paul Tillich and ethics from Reinhold Niebuhr, the two figures whom I thus came to see as the alpha and omega of the study of religion (an unusual conclusion for an Italian American Catholic from the Bronx, but not one that seemed odd at the time). Sharpe points out that "scholars trained in one or the other liberal religious tradition [came] to occupy a prominent position in the newer religious studies enterprise since the early 1970s," a reflection of broader cultural trends in the 1960s, especially the moral animus against the Vietnam War. The discipline is far more varied and complex today, but it is still oriented, as Sam Gill, a prominent scholar, laments, toward "the broadly held essentialist view of religion—that is, that religion is 'the sacred' or 'ultimate concern' and that the attributes of the 'sacred' and 'ultimate concern' are goodness, purity, and unity, or of the center or origin." To study religion from this approach, Gill writes, "means to discern and appreciate these desirable qualities in any culture."[15]

The work of the discipline in constituting itself this way has had grave social consequences far beyond the academy. By inscribing a boundary between good and bad religions at the very foundation of the field, Religious Studies enacts an important cultural discipline. There is no end to human religious creativity; one would have to look to the staggering varieties and complexities of what humans have made of sexuality to

---

[15] Sam Gill, "The Academic Study of Religion," *Journal of the American Academy of Religion* 62 (Winter 1994): 969–70. Gill is here specifically criticizing the way "comparison" is understood in the discipline by some, but he clearly intends his remarks to have broader force.

find another site of such explosive and complicated activity. Yet it has been the impulse of Religious Studies since its inception to impose closure and discipline on religion, to control and contain this complexity. When the Branch Davidian compound was incinerated at Waco, Texas, in April 1993, much was made of the failure of the government and of federal law enforcement officials to recognize the particular religious character of leader David Koresh's movement. It was not as widely noted that the government's failure paralleled the limitations of Religious Studies, which has long offered an authoritative map of religious experience that excluded such a "marginal" group.

It is in this context of the history of Religious Studies and specifically of the centrality of a definition of religion that is essentialist, moralistic, and exclusionary, that we must think about what the current revival of moral inquiry across the disciplines might mean. Any approach to religion that foregrounds ethical issues as these are now embedded in the discipline will only obstruct our understanding of religious idioms, because religion at its root has nothing to do with morality.

Pace Stephen Carter, religion does not make the world better to live in (although some forms of religious practice might); religion does not necessarily conform to the creedal formulations and doctrinal limits developed by cultured and circumspect theologians, church leaders, or ethicists; religion does not unambiguously orient people toward social justice. Particular religious idioms can do all of these things; the religiously motivated civil rights movement is a good example of a social impulse rooted in an evangelical faith and dedicated to a more decent life for men and women. But however much we may love this movement and however much we prefer to teach it (as opposed to, for example, the "cultic" faith of Jonestown or the "magical" beliefs of "popular" religion), this is not the paradigm for religion, nor is it the expression of religion at some idealized best. There is a quality to the religious imagination that blurs distinctions, obliterates boundaries—especially the boundaries we have so long and carefully erected within the discipline— and this can, and often does, contribute to social and domestic violence, not peace. Religion is often enough cruel and dangerous, and the same impulses that result in a special kind of compassion also lead to destruction, often among the same people at the same time. Theories of religion have largely served as a protection against such truths about religion.

It is the challenge of the discipline of Religious Studies not to stop at the border of human practices done in the name of the gods that we scholars find disturbing, dangerous, or even morally repugnant, but rather to enter into the otherness of religious practices in search of an understanding of their human ground. Practitioners must find a way of honoring their own moral and political values, while not masking the common humanity that both researcher and religious adept share—share even with a man like Punkin Brown.

But in attempting such a morally and existentially demanding engagement with the men and women they study, practitioners of Religious Studies will run into a problem. Although the discipline authorizes an implicit account—freighted with moral value—of what religion is, Religious Studies in its quest for legitimacy has also explicitly insisted that scholars adhere to canons of critical and analytical scholarship as defined by the secular academy. In particular, scholars of religion must maintain a critical distance from their subjects, a remove that is understood to be the necessary precondition for analysis and interpretation. (It is not unusual to hear it said for this reason that one cannot study one's own religious tradition.) Scholars of religion are trained to keep their own lives, values, and, above all, religious understandings out of their research; not to do so exposes them to charges of subjectivism, of writing autobiographically, journalistically, or, worst of all, theologically.

Religious Studies acquired its contemporary shape in the American academy after the Second World War in explicit distinction from—and rejection of—seminaries and schools of theology. The severity of the injunction against theology, and more broadly against the moral and religious presence of the scholar in the conduct or presentation of his or her research (other than to articulate the discipline's liberal Protestant moral assumptions), reflects this origin. Theology is the reflection upon the thought and practice of a religious tradition by its adherents; Religious Studies is an outsider's discipline by definition, aspiring to the status of science through a strategy of distance. This paradigm, however, has lately come under attack.

CONTEMPORARY CHRISTIAN CRITIQUES OF RELIGIOUS STUDIES

Among the most severe contemporary critics of Religious Studies are evangelical Christian academics of various denominational affiliations who have felt that the hegemony of the liberal definition of religion and the dominance of liberal approaches to research have precluded full participation by evangelicals in the discipline or in the wider university culture. Evangelical perspectives have survived in the liberal university, according to these critics, only to the extent that evangelicalism denies its own distinctiveness, severs its connections to the believing community, and becomes a branch of cultural studies. Could a Christian scientist, grounded in a particular faith community and certain of the truth of Scripture, conduct her research according to the perspectives of her faith? Would such an alternative be allowed in the academy, which is otherwise so open, by its own account of itself, to the perspectives of the oppressed, marginalized, voiceless? The liberal secular university, in the view of these evangelical critics, is the site of manifold prohibitions masquerading as permissions. Liberalism opens the space for anything to be studied critically so long as the critical perspective brought into play is not religiously particular, and thus theology, a decidedly particularist discipline, has been expunged by academic liberalism.

Religious Studies is an especially egregious expression of this culture since it sets out to study matters of greatest concern to others, usually others who are situated in a distinct religious culture themselves, from a nonconfessional point of view—ostensibly demanding, indeed, the suppression of the researcher's own religious values in the process. Could a Christian scholar of religion frame her classes by what she understood to be the authoritative witness of her church? But how does one assess one's understandings of Christian history or doctrine apart from the guidance of tradition as articulated in a believing community?

Theologian Stanley Hauerwas has written harshly of departments of Religious Studies as being "comprised of people who are willing to study a religion on the condition that it is either dead or that they can teach it in such a way as to kill it. The last thing they would want to acknowledge is that they might actually practice what they teach, because such an acknowledgement might suggest that they are less than objective." Programs in these departments might introduce students to Thomas Aquinas or Karl Barth, but they would never hire such intellectually rigorous but religiously committed intellectuals for their faculties. The discipline is literally founded on the distortion of its own subject, by this account, or worse yet on an act of academic—and personal—bad faith; and it demands the intellectual and religious deformation of scholars who believe as the condition for admission into the guild.[16]

---

[16] Stanley Hauerwas, "Christians in the Hands of Flaccid Secularists: Theology and 'Moral Inquiry' in the Modern University" (paper presented at conference on the Revival of

Christian critics now sense that the moment is right for a challenge to this century-long hegemony. Insurgent groups of younger, conservative Christian theologians, many of them trained and credentialed in departments of Religious Studies at secular universities, have set out to undermine the authority and influence of older, modernist liberal scholars and perspectives in Biblical studies, philosophy of religion, theology, and even religious history. The notion of a nonparticularist study of religion has come to seem almost fusty to some. Ironically or perversely (depending on one's politics), the Christian critique of the liberal, secular university echoes themes of radical young postmodern critics of modernity. As Marsden argues in a polemical "Concluding Unscientific Postscript" to his history of the secularization of learning in American higher education, "the widespread current critiques of scientific objectivity provide a context for reconsidering the near exclusion of religious perspectives from the academic life of American universities of Protestant heritage." Once one admits that "everyone's intellectual inquiry takes place in a framework of communities that shape prior commitments," there is little reason for excluding explicitly religious claims from the teaching and research that take place in the academy.[17] Confessional pedagogy slips into the academic tent through the opening created by postmodernism.

THE POLITICAL CRITIQUE OF RELIGIOUS STUDIES

An alternative account of contemporary university culture posits Christianity in any form, modern or postmodern, as an obstacle for intellectual work, not as an alternative to the frustrations of secularism. Marsden claims that contemporary university culture is anti-Christian, and surely anyone who has spent any time in this world must agree that there is a measure of truth in this charge. Some of this is simply prejudice; some of it is a way for university intellectuals to draw an unmistakable boundary between the culture of learning they value and a surrounding society that they often believe is anti-intellectual because it is Christian. But for some the critique of Christianity is linked with a broader political and epistemological agenda and is meant as a serious

Moral Inquiry in American Scholarship, Woodrow Wilson International Center for Scholars, Washington, D.C., May 15–16, 1995). Cited with permission.
[17] Marsden, *Soul of the American University*, 429–30.

challenge to the hegemony of Western culture, to its ways of knowing and living. Articulated by scholars who have worked in cultures that endured the burden of Christian authority under colonial regimes, this perspective on Christianity is politically charged. Christianity is understood to have been indispensable to Western imperialism, providing its cultural legitimation, moral confidence, and epistemological grounding while spiritually underwriting the military and economic campaigns of the Western powers. Intellectuals, including scholars of religions, crafted the philosophical framework that constituted native populations as other, a key move in the enactment of domination and exploitation; this was the intellectual politics of Orientalism. The representation of native culture as either primitive, proto-Christian, or crypto-Christian was the intellectuals' contribution to imperialism.

The postcolonial world since the 1950s has exposed the cruelty of Western intellectual hegemony, unmasking the practices of domination and exploitation enclosed within the culture of enlightened reason and liberal tolerance. Intellectuals in Asia, Africa, and South America have challenged the canons of Western culture. The task for American university intellectuals now is to rethink American culture from the perspective of the once-dominated other and from alternative and once-oppressed vantage points, a process of decentering and defamiliarizing as the first step to reinterpretation. Western styles of knowledge, which typically give priority to detachment over engagement, to textuality over vocality, to mind over body, are to be exposed to radically different ways of construing and inhabiting reality.

In the context of this broader criticism of Western knowing, the challenge for any revival of moral inquiry among postcolonial scholars of religion would be to become radically aware of their own implicit Western and Christian biases, of the hidden, normative Christianity within the basic methodologies and philosophical orientations of Religious Studies, and then expunge it. Moreover, just as postcolonial intellectual culture calls into question central tenets of Western thought, so a new kind of moral inquiry must be open to construals of the "ethical" profoundly at variance with Christian ideals and formulations.

One example of what this new kind of ethical inquiry would look like is Karen McCarthy Brown's discussion of Haitian Vodou morality in *Mama Lola: A Vodou Priestess in Brooklyn.* Unlike the radically dualist distinction made within Christianity between absolute good and absolute evil, a boundary authorized and presided over by a singular deity, Vodou asserts multiplicity, diversity, and contradiction. Vodou notions of subjectivity understand the self to be multifarious, the site of conflicting energies, capacities, possibilities, without the Christian insistence on consistency in self-presentation. "A moral person, in Vodou," Brown writes, is one who lives "in tune with his or her character, a character defined by the spirits said to love that person." Such moral "flexibility," she adds, "is provided in the midst of moral dilemmas by the support these favorite spirits offer to different and sometimes contradictory values."[18]

Vodou locates fault not inside persons (which by rendering them evil exposes them to harsh proselytism at the least, if not persecution or destruction for their own good, at the worst) but in relationships between persons in the social field. As a healing medium, Vodou seeks to dissolve whatever is holding people in hostile and antagonistic relations. It may be quite extreme in this work of unblocking, heating up the contradictions, conflicts, and inconsistencies within a person or in the social setting—disorientingly, shockingly at times—in order to create a liberating and revealing excitement. In Brown's account, Vodou is the pragmatic idiom by which a poor, politically oppressed, economically marginalized people live their lives with grace, dignity, and compassion in the spaces between the absolutes constituted by intellectuals of more politically powerful and materially comfortable regimes.

Brown and other scholars who have spent personally and intellectually formative years in other cultures call us to juxtapose—playfully and perversely as Vodou does in its healing work—the language of American reality with the realities of those other worlds. They propose to bring the religious and moral vision of the colonized into creative tension with the moral sensibility and religious idioms of the colonizer. The goal is a creole scholarship that draws from the epistemological, aesthetic, religious, and moral idioms of different cultures to decenter and rethink the idioms of the West. Christianity itself—as well as the normative, dualistic, crypto-Christian categories of Religious Studies—looks very different when viewed from Mama Lola's living room.

[18] Karen McCarthy Brown, *Mama Lola: A Vodou Priestess in Brooklyn* (Berkeley and Los Angeles: University of California Press, 1991), 241.

BACK TO THE SNAKES

It may appear that there is little common ground between the evangelical
and the postcolonial critiques of the liberal academic paradigm for
studying religion. But surprisingly and perhaps ironically there are significant convergences. Proponents of both perspectives propose, for
instance, that the universalistic ambitions of Western enlightened rationality give way to local orientations: there is no essential, singular truth,
only situated truths. Both understand the scholar herself to be situated
at a particular cultural location that fundamentally shapes her vision,
and both place passion and commitment at the center of research methodology and pedagogy. Stanley Hauerwas has said that the confessional
teacher "witnesses" in the classroom, makes his or her faith present and
invites students into a dialogue about it, holds it up as a lens for examining and challenging the dominant arrangements of culture. Critical
anthropologists propose a radical critique of Western culture as the appropriate classroom stance. They use the experiences of people in distant
places, their way of construing reality, and their often disastrous encounters with Christianity as the framing device for students' examination of Western religions and their assessment of the claims of Western
reason. Conversion—to Christianity or to other religious idioms—is not
necessarily the explicit goal of either pedagogy, but there is a heightened
existential edge to this kind of teaching compared with the older critical
liberal model. The evangelical and the political critiques challenge the
authority of liberal Protestantism in the discipline and demand that
scholars in the field transgress, in method and in the foci of their work,
the authoritative boundaries of Religious Studies.

I find both critiques compelling and welcome the challenge each
represents to the way we have gone about the study of religion in the
United States. But I am not sure that either one ultimately avoids the
pitfall to which Covington succumbed in reestablishing his barrier
against Punkin Brown. Evangelical and postcolonial scholars themselves rely on the constitution of respective others in doing their
work—the Christian other, in the case of postcolonial critics (for
whom non-Western religions are valued, at least in part, as expressions of not-Christianity), and for evangelicals, either the liberal, secular other or, just as likely, an other made of Christian beliefs and
practices different from those of evangelicals.

The postmodern Christian scholar in the postliberal university would presumably assess Punkin Brown's Christianity from the perspective of a particular theological orientation, a distinct set of Christian beliefs and perspectives, much as Covington himself did in his own criticism of the snake handler. Encountering such a figure would be a ripe moment for "catechesis," the explication of the researcher's own faith through a dialectical interplay between his or her religious world and the religious world of the other. Covington secured the boundary between himself and Punkin Brown by evoking God as his witness, explicitly placing himself in a debate within the Christian community over the "nature of God" (in his words) and the role of women in the church and society. Likewise, the confessional professor might witness to her own faith by affirming that in her reading of Scripture God sanctions the participation of women in religious life; she might say that the God of the handlers is not the God of the New Testament, as Covington did.

I find it even harder to imagine what postcolonial professors would make of Punkin Brown given the resolutely anti-Christian animus of so many of them. His rage against women and his apparent determination to dominate them (religiously and probably otherwise too) disclose what many consider to be the inherent social aggressiveness of Christianity. A cultural critic could help us understand Punkin Brown's impulse to dominate in global and domestic perspectives. He or she might shift the focus of analysis away from the nature of God to the sorts of social conditions that shaped Punkin Brown. But the internal power of the man's religious imagination, his relationship with Jesus crucified, and his deep desire to experience the power of the spirit with the life-threatening snake in his hands might be missed by observers tone deaf to matters of faith and religious practice, especially Christian faith and practice.

Punkin Brown and others like him are just too valuable precisely as *others*, as the unassimilable and intolerable, to be easily surrendered. So long as the point of religious scholarship, even implicitly or unconsciously, is to seal the borders of our own worlds of meaning and morals, whatever these may be, against such others, it will be impossible to relinquish the "Punkin Browns" constituted in the field or the archives. The challenge facing the discipline today, however, is not to find new others, as both the evangelical and postcolonial approaches do, but to get beyond "otherizing" as the basic move of the discipline.

RELIGIOUS STUDIES IN A MOMENT OF TRANSITION

There is another alternative to the liberal paradigm, one that unlike the evangelical or postcolonial options guards more assiduously against the moralistic impulse to construct figures of otherness. This alternative is characterized by a disciplined suspension of the impulse to locate the other (with all her or his discrepant moralities, epistemological orientations, and religious impulses) securely in relation to one's own cosmos. It has no need to fortify the self in relation to the other so constituted. Instead, this alternative destabilizes the authority of one's own world. It is an in-between orientation, located at the intersection of self and other, at the boundary between one's own moral universe and the moral world of the other.

The ground upon which such a researcher stands belongs neither to herself or to the other but has come into being between them, precisely because of the meeting of the two. This is ground that would not have existed apart from the relationship between researcher and her subject. (Covington forgets that Punkin Brown was responding to *him* that night, that the preacher would not have given that sermon had Covington not entered his world.) On this ground, unowned by anyone, each person experiences the taken-for-granted world as vulnerable, decontextualized, realigned. Ideally, after such an exchange, neither party is the same as when it began. Most importantly, such a movement onto the ground between universes of meaning would not permit the kind of closure Covington imposes on Punkin Brown and his world. It requires that the scholar of religion abandon the security offered by the discipline, by its implicit and explicit moral certainty and theoretical apparatuses, and proceed instead by risk, suspension, engagement.

To illustrate what I have in mind here, I want to turn to David Haberman's study of the Ban-Yatra pilgrimage in northern India, *Journey through the Twelve Forests: An Encounter with Krishna*.[19] Like Covington's, this is an intensely personal narrative. It recounts Haberman's deep existential entanglement with the Hindu pilgrims he journeys with through Braj, as the pilgrimage area is called. Haberman never forgets his social location nor the history of Western relations with India. A

---

[19] David L. Haberman, *Journey through the Twelve Forests: An Encounter with Krishna* (New York: Oxford University Press, 1994). I should note that David Haberman is a colleague of mine on the faculty of Indiana University and a friend.

sophisticated theorist of postcolonial culture, he is aware that as a contemporary student of Hinduism he steps into, and attempts to challenge,
a tradition of interpretation with roots in the imperial period.

Braj is dotted with sites central to the narratives about Krishna—the
grove he frolicked in with his consort, Radha, for example, and the
prison cell where he was born. Believers claim that Braj *is* in some sense
the body of god: the landscape is so intimately connected to Krishna
that it is he. The god's body is thus uniquely present to the pilgrims
during their arduous journey through Braj. This trope of physical presence becomes a central device of Haberman's work: early in the journey
Haberman begins to develop awful blisters on his tender feet, and for
the rest of the pilgrimage he must contend with terrible pain and rely
on the assistance of his fellow pilgrims. Just as the god's body is over-
present in Braj, so is the ethnographer's in his experience and account
of the pilgrimage, which as a result becomes a journey through the possibilities and limitations of corporality. On the levels of religious understanding and existential experience, pain is the pathway for Haberman
into the intersection between worlds, the suspensive space where a new
kind of understanding of other religions is possible.

Haberman could see that many of his fellow pilgrims were also in
pain. But this did not prevent them from taking a deep sensual pleasure
at sites commemorating Krishna's own pleasures, an incongruity that
Haberman found confusing at first. How could these weary bodies stumbling into the groves of Krishna's delight experience joy and pleasure,
and how could the anthropologist with his inflamed foot? But as he
enters into this apparent disjuncture of pain and pleasure, deprivation
and sensuality, distress and celebration, Haberman comes to see it as the
dynamic of the pilgrimage. Haberman's confusion, disorientation, and
pain become means of comprehension. He shows us what Covington
might have done differently, at greater personal risk for himself and
cultural disorientation for his readers, that night in Georgia. Covington
might have used the distress and even revulsion occasioned in him by
Punkin Brown's performance as such a pivot of reflection. By suspending
the need to guard himself against whatever fears and revelations Brown's
performance had evoked, Covington could have been led to discover the
common source of both the violence and the beauty of this startling
religious idiom. He might have reflected on the roots of Brown's anger;
he might have explored the intersection between desire and rage, the
sacred and the obscene, and come to grips with his own attraction to

snake handling. Instead, he turns away, and asserts a principled commitment to the spiritual equality of women. This commitment may be laudable in itself, but Covington does not see how invoking it where and when he does amounts to a refusal to engage his real subject.

The key moment in Haberman's account for my purposes—his version of the Punkin Brown encounter—comes when he finds himself standing on bleeding feet in a place called Charan Pahari, the "Mountain of the Foot," where Krishna is said to have left a footprint in a white stone softened by his music. The stone is lovingly, regularly bathed by the god's devout with water and smeared with red powder. Haberman's account of his visit to this spot begins with an acknowledgement of otherness. There is a quality to the site that causes him to step out of his role as pilgrim and admit his place—and confusion—as observer: "Such claims [as that Krishna had stepped on this stone] are naturally met with some doubt on the part of the outsider." He moves still further out in the second half of this sentence: "especially considering the economic benefits gained by the attendants busily collecting money from the pilgrims." A moral distance has opened between him and the caretakers of the shrine. This is the "haaagh" experience: suspicion, detachment, and doubt overwhelm compassion and understanding.[20]

Haberman might have turned away at this moment in disgust at the venality of shrine keepers and the gullibility of the devout, as other visitors to India have done. There are, indeed, good reasons to be suspicious of what goes on at shrines, in India and elsewhere. Shrine priests do not scruple to take advantage of people in considerable emotional need and religious excitement. Moreover, as countless Western critics of popular religion have pointed out wherever they have encountered such human practices, the money spent on feeding, dressing, and adoring the gods in this way might be better spent on peoples' health, clothing, or education. Liberal scholars of religion have been as bemused by immigrant Catholics' devotion to saints as by Hindus in this regard. This could have been the outer boundary of Haberman's journey, the point at which he stopped at otherness and confirmed it, and many readers would have understood his moral concerns.

But he turns back to the experience of the people he is observing and forces himself—and his readers—to recognize that there are many worlds, many different ways of making and inhabiting reality. He writes,

---

[20] Ibid., 168–9.

"upon observing several women bow down and touch their heads to this stone, come up with tears streaming down their faces, and hug each other crying, 'O Sister! O Sister!' I began to think that questions [about the venality of the shrine keepers or the ontological reality of the stone's imprint] . . . were inappropriate." Since "reality is not set for human beings [and] multiple realities or worlds of meaning are available to us," moral judgment is rendered problematic. "Judgments of realities are difficult," Haberman continues, not impossible or unnecessary, "because there is nowhere to stand that is not situated in a particular reality, which by its very nature regards other realities with suspicion."[21] The challenge becomes then to set one's own world, one's own particular reality, now understood as one world among many possible other worlds, in relation to this other reality and to learn how to view the two in relation to each other, moving back and forth between two alternative ways of organizing and experiencing reality. The point is not to make the other world radically and irrevocably other, but to render one's own world other to oneself as prelude to a new understanding of the two worlds in relationship to each other.

Ironically, it is Haberman's constant awareness of his difference that permits him to enter so deeply into the intersection of two worlds; indeed, there would be no intersection without an awareness of difference. Covington portrayed himself initially as having passed over entirely to the culture of snake handling, but that apparent immersion ends up telling us less about either his own or Punkin Brown's world than Haberman's intersectional strategy does about Braj.[22] This is where the pleasure, excitement, and risk of Religious Studies are, its delights as well as its dangers. The space is dangerous because one cannot, after all, simply abandon one's deepest values or tolerate the intolerable, even though something awful and intolerable might make sense in someone else's world; it is delightful because by staying in the space between— indeed, prolonging one's stay there by refusing the initial opportunities for closure—one comes to know something about the other and about oneself through relationship with the other. Haberman identifies this as an erotic methodology, borrowing from French psychoanalytic theorist Jacques Lacan an understanding of desire as that which rejects closure. The erotic orientation to another's religion resists ending the tension

---

[21] Ibid., 169.
[22] I owe the useful phrase "intersectional strategy" to Richard Fox.

provoked by the proximity of two diverse worlds. It is this delight in difference that sets Religious Studies apart from the more conventional orientations of liberal academics, evangelical theologians, and postcolonial critics alike.

Besides imagining himself as a snake-handling minister, there is one other way that Covington attempts to bring the world of the other closer, to himself and to his readers: through an appreciation of the physical beauty of Christian women with snakes in their hands. He invites us to gaze on these women holding snakes and find their spiritual passion beautiful. His account of Aline McGlockin in particular, the wife of one of Covington's closest friends in the community, emphasizes her haunting, lovely appearance in spiritual ecstasy; and again there is a sound. Covington records that Aline cries "akiii, akiii, akiii," as she experiences the spirit's presence, and he finds this unnerving and sexually interesting.

Covington offers us two sounds—"haaagh" and "akiii"—and two choices, the ethical and the aesthetic, one approach through judgment and another through beauty. Haberman offers a third way, neither ethical nor aesthetic. He calls it erotic; living so far from the delights of Krishna's groves, I will call it instead suspensive. Religious Studies is not a moralizing discipline; it exists in the suspension of the ethical, and it steadfastly refuses either to deny or redeem the other. It is a moral discipline, however, in its commitment to examining the variety of human experience and to making contact across boundaries—cultural, psychological, spiritual, existential.

CONCLUSION: A CELEBRATION OF THE POLYTHEISTIC CLASSROOM

The classroom is where many of us perform a significant portion of our daily intellectual work; it is where we invite others to join us in our questions. Our students come to us from many different worlds, bearing many different histories. This is true even in the Bible Belt, where I teach. The world's many cultures are well represented in Midwestern classrooms. Furthermore, "Christian" students bring complex Christianities into the classroom. Many of them—and here I can say *especially* in the Bible Belt—have had truly ruinous experiences in their churches and Christian homes. They are already quite familiar with the power of Christian faith to scar them and, if they have been fortunate, with its powers of liberation and salvation. These students from Bible-reading homes are sick of witnesses and revivals, of experiencing the "truth" as a prescription about the doable, thinkable, or possible. In response, some have put together intricate Christian understandings that draw on neo-paganism, snippets of Asian religions, popular psychology, contemporary science fiction. Others simply will have nothing more to do with religion, finding their way instead to Religious Studies classes in hopes of securing tools to help them reflect critically on their religious experience. Some (the minority in my experience, even here in southern Indiana) are practicing Christians of various sorts. "Christianity" when it is used in the authoritative singular, as if it had secure, discernible boundaries, makes sense only as a symbol for political or cultural mobilization. The social fact of our classrooms, as of American culture, is that there are many, many Christianities.

None of the students in this polytheistic world will be addressed by witnessing to a singular truth, nor will they be awakened by denunciations of their Christianities by postcolonial critics. Having worked hard to undo the tradition of making non-Western cultures "other," these critics have returned to this one only to make it other. Students will not be interested in normative versions of religion that neglect or exclude all the humiliating, destructive, beautiful, mysterious, and terrifying dimensions of it they know from their own experience. It is difficult to see these "Christian" students as agents of Western hegemony, since like Punkin Brown their families have so often been on the receiving end of cultural domination; postcolonial criticism becomes another form of imperial witnessing when it is conducted without a vivid sense of the worlds Americans come from and the varieties of Christianities they have known. Witnessing in any case will always fail as communication in the university, and moral inquiry without communication and conversation is nothing but covert compulsion.

There is no distinct moment of moral inquiry that comes before and exists separately from the communication of one's moral reflections to others. Discernment does not precede rhetoric; talking does not represent the outcome of moral analysis but serves as its necessary vehicle. Moral inquiry proceeds through conversation—which is to say, more broadly, that moral inquirers exist in relationship with each other on a social field comprising cultural traditions, economic and political circumstances, and family patterns. Such inquiry never exists apart from conversations among real, historically situated people, and moral inquiry is always simultaneous with efforts to make its doubts and decisions public. I can imagine that the phrase "moral inquiry" might conjure up for some the image of a person reflecting in solitude upon the grounds for discerning good and bad before he or she goes out into the public to speak about what has been learned, but this is not what I understand by the term. To discuss a particular theory of moral inquiry, therefore, is necessarily not only to examine its explicit notions of moral rhetoric but to grasp that an understanding of morality is not a once-and-for-all acquisition, but an engagement in communication. We narrate what we know and we know by what we narrate.

Since moral reflection is in fact the conversations that constitute it, then the presence of many different histories, memories, experiences— and moral idioms—converging in our classrooms is a unique opportunity for Religious Studies. Moral inquiry in this context proceeds not through the constitution of the other—of "Punkin Brown," or of "Hinduism," or of "cult members" or of "popular" religion. This is the move Religious Studies has been making for the past century. Instead, moral inquiry proceeds through the recognition of the other and a revisioning of one's own story through the lens of the other openly engaged, as Karen Brown does in *Mama Lola* and David Haberman does in *Journey through the Twelve Forests*. It means experiencing one's own world from the disorienting perspective of the other's, and this necessarily entails risk, vulnerability, vertigo; it invites anger and creates distress. Like the discipline itself, the Religious Studies classroom exists in suspension too. Moral understanding in the polytheistic classroom—and in the polytheistic world beyond it—comes only through the multiplicity of stories told and attended to and the new possibilities that emerge in the places between lives and stories.

9

Social science and the moral revival:
Dilemmas and difficulties

ALAN WOLFE

There can be little doubt that a moral revival is taking place in American social science. The notion that a strictly value free social science is both possible and desirable is not as widely shared as it was thirty years ago. Shaken by recent political events, influenced by colleagues in the humanities, and persuaded that good citizenship is a laudatory ideal, an increasingly large number of social scientists are seeking ways to apply their professional training and interests to the larger moral questions facing American society. Social science has rediscovered its moral roots (and, in this way, reforged its links with philosophy). Adam Smith, we are frequently reminded, was a moral philosopher, not just an economist. Immanuel Kant has served as a model for political philosophers such as John Rawls and psychologists such as Lawrence Kohlberg. American pragmatism has been an inspiration for thinkers concerned with communicative action, as well as for those concerned with institutions and organizations.[1]

One of the hardiest of such moral roots, especially for sociologists, is the work of Emile Durkheim.[2] Because sociology studies human be-

---

[1] See Jerry Muller, *Adam Smith in His Time and Ours: Designing the Decent Society* (New York: Free Press, 1993); John Rawls, *A Theory of Justice* (Cambridge, Mass.: Harvard University Press, 1971); and Lawrence Kohlberg, "The Future of Liberalism as the Dominant Ideology of the West," in *Moral Development and Politics*, ed. Richard W. Wilson and Gordon J. Schochet (New York: Praeger, 1980), 55–68. On communicative action, see Jürgen Habermas, *Reason and the Rationalization of Society*, vol. 1 of *The Theory of Communicative Action*, trans. Thomas McCarthy (Boston: Beacon Press, 1984). For an example of a thinker concerned with institutions and organizations, see Philip Selznick, *The Moral Commonwealth: Social Theory and the Promise of Community* (Berkeley and Los Angeles: University of California Press, 1992).

[2] A good overview is Mark S. Cladis, *A Communitarian Defense of Liberalism: Emile*

ings, and because human beings are moral creatures, sociology was, for Durkheim, a moral science. Inspired by Kant, Durkheim believed that truly moral acts were those motivated by disinterest; we engage in moral action when we do something because we ought to do it, and not because it will benefit us or enable us to avoid punishment. But unlike Kant, Durkheim did not believe that the injunction to do the right thing was an abstract and categorical imperative; society was necessary to teach people right from wrong. Societies too weak to impose a sense of duty would be characterized by anomie; their members, as a result, would lack the capacity for altruism that would encourage moral behavior.

The rediscovery of the moral tradition in sociology mirrors these Durkheimian concerns. Just as Durkheim subjected Benthamite utilitarianism to a withering critique, sociologists question the assumption that self-interest rules all conduct.[3] If economists seem determined to find a core of self-interest in even seemingly altruistic acts, sociologists look for signs of altruistic cooperation in seemingly selfish acts.[4]

Sociologists who have studied markets (such as auctions) have highlighted the informal norms and understandings that make them work.[5] Sociologists have also been involved with what has come to be called communitarianism: efforts to balance rights and responsibilities.[6] The underlying notion is classically Durkheimian; the state has to be relied upon to enforce our obligations to each other, but it should not be relied upon too much, for it is too formal and legalistic. People ought to feel a sense of obligation for others; it is insufficient if they just pay taxes and assert their rights. We have paid too much attention to the market and the state and insufficient attention to civil society.[7]

Durkheim and Contemporary Social Theory (Stanford, Calif.: Stanford University Press, 1992).

[3] Beat Bürgenmeier, *Socioeconomics: An Interdisciplinary Approach*, trans. Kevin Cook (Boston: Kluwer Academic, 1992); and Richard Coughlin, *Morality, Rationality and Efficiency: New Perspectives in Socio-Economics* (Armonk, N.Y.: M. E. Sharpe, 1991).

[4] For an overview, see Alan Wolfe, "What Is Altruism?" in *Private Action and the Public Good*, ed. Walter W. Powell and Elisabeth Clemens (New Haven: Yale University Press, forthcoming).

[5] Charles Smith, *Auctions: The Social Construction of Value* (New York: Free Press, 1989).

[6] Amitai Etzioni, *The Moral Dimension: Toward a New Economics* (New York: Free Press, 1988); and Amitai Etzioni, *The Spirit of Community: Rights, Responsibilities, and the Communitarian Agenda* (New York: Crown, 1993).

[7] Alan Wolfe, *Whose Keeper? Social Science and Moral Obligation* (Berkeley and Los Angeles: University of California Press, 1989).

Many sociologists have addressed these themes, none more so than Robert Bellah, the first contemporary sociologist to emphasize the moral side of Durkheim's work.[8] In *Habits of the Heart* and its follow-up volume *The Good Society*, Bellah and his collaborators investigated the degree to which American culture is dominated by an ethos of individualism.[9] Worried that Americans were becoming too preoccupied with the self, they also explored religion and community service as avenues for the expression of more altruistic inclinations. *Habits of the Heart* began a boomlet of moral inquiry in sociology. It certainly influenced my own work.

I have recently interviewed two hundred middle-class Americans (in the suburbs of Boston, Tulsa, San Diego, and Atlanta) about their understandings of moral obligation. My research convinces me that Americans take moral questions very seriously; believing that right and wrong ought to exist, but unsure what is right or wrong in any specific stance, they find that traditional sources of moral teachings, such as organized religion, are not particularly helpful to them, even as they lament their passing. Americans want both freedom and a strong sense of moral obligation and are uncertain how they can be reconciled. This research will appear in my forthcoming publication *One Nation After All*.

The revival of moral inquiry in sociology—as well as in the social sciences more generally—has been anything but consensual. Durkheim may be the inspiration for some writers, but his notion that morality is a social process taught through institutions runs counter to the view of others, inspired primarily by David Hume, who believe that morality is innate in human beings. James Q. Wilson has reached a large audience with his argument that we have a moral sense that requires cultivation by strong families; the mother-infant bond, Wilson suggested, is the foundation of all social relationships that come afterward.[10] Along similar lines, but expressing a very different political sensibility, Robert Wright uses the insights of sociobiology to argue that morality serves the goal of efficient evolutionary adaptation; we

---

[8] Robert N. Bellah, *Emile Durkheim on Morality and Society* (Chicago: University of Chicago Press, 1973).

[9] Robert Bellah et al., *Habits of the Heart* (Berkeley and Los Angeles: University of California Press, 1985); and Robert Bellah et al., *The Good Society* (New York: Knopf, 1991).

[10] James Q. Wilson, *The Moral Sense* (New York: Free Press, 1993). For a critique of some of Wilson's assumptions, see Diane Eyer, *Mother-Infant Bonding: A Scientific Fiction* (New Haven: Yale University Press, 1992).

may sacrifice for others, for example, in order to better enhance the prospects of our offspring.[11]

This revival also has not been politically consensual. Many writers, seeing in moral inquiry a way of challenging the hegemony of capitalist markets, find themselves on the left. Others, equally on the left, worry about possible moral disapprobation of powerless groups and individuals. Some conservatives argue strongly for a return to moral inquiry as the foundation of an ordered society, while others lean toward libertarian and privatistic values. In short, the revival of moral inquiry does not presuppose an intellectual or political consensus; social scientists have become interested in moral questions but from a wide variety of perspectives.

In returning the social sciences to their intellectual origins as a moral science, this movement has broadened the scope of social inquiry beyond professional journals and the pursuit of methodological and theoretical innovations done for their own sake. It has facilitated links between the social sciences and the humanities and, in particular, helped reestablish a connection between social science and philosophy. It has underscored the importance of historical and comparative perspectives in the social sciences, since different societies at different points in time treated moral practices in contrasting ways. This moral revival is not present everywhere; some social science departments, including many at America's leading universities, have been little influenced by it. But for anyone who believes that social science must be a moral science because human beings are inevitably moral creatures, this turn is surely a positive development.

A positive development, however, is not the same as a problem-free development; the moral revival brings with it difficult dilemmas that plague any inquiry into values and the nature of the good society.

OBJECTIONS TO THE MORAL REVIVAL

Objections to moral inquiry have existed as long as moral questions have existed. The four major objections of contemporary social scientists and social theorists can be summarized as follows, although the dividing line between them is not always clear.

---

[11] Robert Wright, *The Moral Animal: Evolutionary Psychology and Everyday Life* (New York: Pantheon Books, 1994).

First, there is the objection from grounds of liberalism. As Ronald Dworkin has taken the lead in arguing, the liberal state should be neutral with respect to moral ends.[12] Precisely because moral issues define our most fundamental values, any effort to ally government with one moral position denies the core beliefs, and hence the very personhood, of individuals who do not share that moral position. Liberalism demands that we confine our agreements to things other than the ends or meaning of life.

Liberals are not pure neutralists; they believe in justice and argue (among themselves) for different ways in which the principle of distributive justice can or should be realized. What worries liberals is the danger that the pursuit of the good through government can become a tool of one party or another in the struggle for power. To avoid this unhappy possibility, social scientists may be better off downplaying the moral aspects of their work.

Second is the objection from grounds of science. Whether or not a value-free social science is possible, the social scientist has a strong obligation not to confuse her moral beliefs with her work as a social scientist. We may have strong feelings about prayer in school, but if we want to understand how participants in controversies over that issue understand their worlds, we have to be simultaneously sympathetic to all sides and skeptical of all sides. A social scientist who becomes too readily identified with either the right or the left can no longer be trusted. Her work will be viewed as ideological, not scientific, and any moral implications it may have will come to be distrusted, precisely because they will be viewed as ideological in inspiration.

The third objection is from the grounds of pluralism. It is often suggested that one of the most important developments in American history took place when Protestantism lost its monopoly on American culture. Our "first" culture war had, miraculously, a successful outcome, based on imperfect moral compromise: Americans would not insist that everyone attend a common school, thereby allowing Catholics and Jews a choice between particular and universal moral values.[13] Now that we face the possibility of a new culture war, we ought to retain this commitment to pluralism, especially with respect to recent immigrants, Af-

[12] Ronald Dworkin, *A Matter of Principle* (Cambridge, Mass.: Harvard University Press, 1985), 33–71, 119–45, 181–204.

[13] Robert T. Handy, *Undermined Establishment: Church-State Relations in America, 1880–1920* (Princeton, N.J.: Princeton University Press, 1991).

rican-Americans, women, and gays. Too great an emphasis on morality interferes with the ability of groups to further their specific identities. (Its emphasis on group claims distinguishes this objection from one grounded in principles of liberal individualism.) We are best off, therefore, resisting the moral turn in social science.

Finally, there is the objection from grounds of enlightenment. The revival of moral inquiry cannot be separated from a revival of interest in religion. But a religious revival could bring with it mythic ways of thinking capable of undermining the Enlightenment tradition of rational skepticism. We ought to be wary of too great an emphasis on morality unless that emphasis is secular—reminding us that morality is, above all, a product of human cognition or experience and guaranteed, not by a supreme being, but by those human constructions called culture and society.

All these objections are serious ones; they raise important issues for which easy answers are unavailable. Because I find much to value in each of them, my response is not the polemical one of trying to demonstrate what is false about them. I will instead pose the following question: if these objections are sound, at least in substantial part, does it follow that the moral revival in the social sciences should be slowed down or even stopped? As will become clear, I do not think it should be. The objections to a moral revival ought to be understood as posing dilemmas, not roadblocks. They raise questions about how, not whether, moral inquiry ought to be conducted. And because they do, they offer the possibility that moral inquiry could be strengthened by taking heed of their implications. By meeting them halfway if they make sense, rather than by dismissing them completely, moral inquiry can strengthen itself.

The objection from liberalism

Because the state exercises a monopoly over the means of violence, one must always be wary of granting it excessive power. Liberal suspicions toward the state are premised particularly on the idea that its powers over matters of conscience ought to be limited. One can, from liberal principles, make an argument for the state's capacity to regulate economic affairs; in order to enhance everyone's chances of maximizing their cognitive potential, government must take steps to redistribute income partially and guarantee a modicum of economic security.[14] But there is no comparable argument for strengthening the state in matters of conscience, except the temporary one that in conditions of anarchy or civil war, restrictions on liberty may be justified in order to protect liberty in the future when those special conditions no longer exist. Since matters of morality always touch on matters of conscience, it follows that the liberal state should stay out of moral affairs as much as possible.

There is one valuable aspect of the liberal call for moral neutrality: a reminder that too much government intervention into questions of what constitutes the good life can turn into a violation of individual rights. Those dangers are illustrated by the 1986 case of *Bowers v. Hardwick*. Upholding Georgia's laws against sodomy, Mr. Justice White refused to find "a fundamental right to engage in homosexual sodomy" in the Constitution or in the Court's earlier recognition of rights that are "implicit in the concept of ordered liberty" (quoting from the 1937 decision *Palko v. Connecticut*). "Proscriptions against that conduct have ancient roots," White continued. Moreover, it is wrong to claim that such proscriptions have no basis "other than the presumed belief of a majority of the electorate in Georgia that homosexual sodomy is immoral and unacceptable" for "the law . . . is constantly based on notions of morality, and if all laws representing essentially moral choices are to be invalidated under the Due Process Clause, the courts will be very busy indeed."[15] For White's critics, including Mr. Justice Blackmun in dissent, the Georgia statute illustrates what happens when the state adopts one point of view in a moral controversy: the rights of individuals are inevitably curtailed, including the right to privacy within the home.

Although liberals are correct to emphasize the dangers that follow when government gives support to one version of the moral life and sanctions others, arguments for moral neutrality nonetheless remain problematic. For one thing, the liberal distinction between the right and the good is not always a clear one. Liberals are strongly committed to rights, but some rights—such as the right of free speech—are closely tied to a moral vision of the good life, one which puts special faith in reason and powers of persuasion.[16]

[14] Stephen Holmes, *Passions and Constraints: On the Theory of Liberal Democracy* (Chicago: University of Chicago Press, 1995).
[15] *Bowers v. Hardwick*, 478 U.S. 186 (1986). See also *Palko v. Connecticut*, 302 U.S. 319 (1937).
[16] See especially Steven Macedo, *Liberal Virtues: Citizenship, Virtue, and Community in*

In this way, state neutrality on moral matters, whatever we think of its desirability, is not always possible. Neutrality favors one side in moral debates, the side of liberal tolerance (and not the side of those, say, who want to see explicit religious teaching in the schools). Furthermore, even if perfect moral neutrality were possible, it is not clear that it would be desirable. The state is not only an administrative apparatus; it is also, as Durkheim emphasized, the symbolic representation of a nation's identity. If that identity is a moral one, the state will have to express a moral position to be true to it. In a world of totalitarian states, the very affirmation of liberal democracy is a moral affirmation.

Communitarian critics of liberalism worry that moral neutrality will produce too "thin" a conception of obligation; without significant agreement about the good life, there can be little shared understanding of what links citizens together. This fear is given credence by one of the most eloquent warnings against state regulation of morality: John Stuart Mill's *On Liberty*.[17] So protective of the rights of conscience is Mill that he goes well beyond an argument for state neutrality in moral matters.

What does it matter, asks Mill, if a right to free thought is abrogated by the state or by the censorious opinion of neighbors or the silent disapproval of others? "Society," he writes, "can and does execute its own mandates; and if it issues wrong mandates instead of right, or any mandates at all in things with which it ought not to meddle, it practices a social tyranny more formidable than many kinds of political oppression, since, though not usually upheld by such extreme penalties, it leaves fewer means of escape, penetrating much more deeply into the details of life, and enslaving the soul itself."[18]

Not only should the state keep out of morality, Mill seems to be claiming, but so should other people. We cannot ask the government to enforce morals, but neither should we ourselves enforce them through our everyday conduct. *On Liberty* is a plea, not only for liberty, but also against morality—if morality is understood as the insistence that individuals regulate their personal conduct for the sake of consensual norms.

Liberal Constitutionalism (Oxford: Clarendon Books, 1990). Also relevant to this point is William Galston, *Liberal Purposes: Goods, Virtues, and Diversity in the Liberal State* (New York: Cambridge University Press, 1991).
[17] John Stuart Mill, *On Liberty* (1859; reprint, Indianapolis: Hackett Publishing Company, 1956).
[18] Ibid., 4.

Certainly, Mill had little love for Christian views of morality: "Christian morality (so called)," he wrote, "has all the characters of a reaction; it is, in great part, a protest against paganism. Its ideal is negative rather than positive; passive rather than active; innocence rather than nobleness; abstinence from evil rather than energetic pursuit of good."[19] Mill finds public discussion morally valuable; little else traditionally associated with morality is.

The debates between liberals and communitarians make one wonder whether it is possible to insist on the need for strong moral narratives about the good life and to be respectful of moral pluralism and liberal individualism. While no answer to such a complex question can be developed here, it is worth stressing one possible line of development: a liberal committed to pluralism and tolerance can object to state interference with questions of the good life, as Mill rightly does, but can also accept, which Mill does not, social intervention and regulation of moral conduct.

As Mill frames the problem, something has to give: all efforts to regulate morality violate liberty; all protections of liberty undercut a common morality. Yet one way moral inquiry can properly ask questions about what we have in common without violating liberal respect for rights is by finding criteria that would justify public concern with private behavior in some cases but not in others.

The very monopoly that the state possesses with respect to violence suggests that while both government and social pressures to induce conformity to moral norms are coercive, they are coercive in very different ways and to very different degrees. No one should underestimate the capacity of groups such as families or small communities to bring about conformity to moral norms; there are certainly cases when their power is more effective than that of government. But the tools available to them for this purpose, especially in a modern society, do not generally involve force but rely on shame, guilt, learning, and other sociological (or social-psychological) processes. Contra Mill, there are two important reasons to prefer these ways of inducing agreement to the sanctions of government. One is positive: they deserve respect as more nuanced methods of enforcing moral obligation than the more utilitarian sanctions associated with criminal justice.

[19] Ibid., 47.

The other is negative: social and psychological ways of obtaining agreement generally abstain from bodily incarceration and torture, which are among the worst methods of obtaining obedience.

There is little question that the pressures of conformity associated with civil society can elevate the parochial over the universal. One well understands the resistance of a cosmopolitan philosopher such as Mill to the "soft" tyranny they can engender. But what makes tyranny soft is that escape from it is possible. So long as what Albert Hirschman calls the exit option is not closed, there is a good reason to value loyalty.[20]

As a liberal wishing to see the state play a minimal role in enforcing common conceptions of the good life, I also require a strong theory of society, one that accords importance to the very pressures toward conformity and "soft" tyranny so worrisome to Mill and others concerned about mass society. Thus, to return to *Bowers,* the fact that one believes the majority opinion wrong does not necessarily mean that one believes homosexual sodomy is right. For one thing, the same neutrality that prohibits the state from declaring homosexual sex immoral would also prevent it from teaching the virtues of homosexual sex. For another, nothing in the principle of neutrality would prevent those who believe in the moral regulation of sexuality to teach their own children (or their own neighbors or parishioners) about their views.[21]

There is an important implication of this argument for the moral revival in the social sciences. Social science itself can be, in authoritarian societies, a direct agent of state power, but in a liberal society the pursuit of social knowledge is a private activity. It is also a social activity, as we know from Charles Peirce and contemporary sociologists of science.[22] In other words, social science takes place in civil society: its home can be found in universities that have a measure of autonomy from government; the rules that structure its practices are determined by peer group cooperation; violations of its tenets do not generally result in jail sentences but in ostracism or shame. In writing or researching about morality, social scientists want to shape the way people think about morality, but they have no direct enforcement powers. They cannot rely

[20] Albert Hirschman, *Exit, Voice, and Loyalty: Responses to Decline in Firms, Organizations, and States* (Cambridge, Mass.: Harvard University Press, 1970).
[21] Nothing I have said in this paragraph should be taken as evidence of my own personal views on *Bowers* v. *Hardwick.*
[22] Julius Buchler, ed., *Philosophical Writings of Peirce* (New York: Dover, 1955); and Bruno Latour, *Science in Action: How to Follow Scientists and Engineers through Society* (Cambridge, Mass.: Harvard University Press, 1987).

on violent sanctions if their advice is ignored; persuasion, research, and rhetoric are their tools.

There is thus little danger that moral inquiry by social scientists will violate the rights of individuals. When the Supreme Court ruled on Georgia's sodomy law, its opinion had consequences. When I write about *Bowers*, the consequences of my opinions are minimal and indirect. Even when a work of social science reaches a large audience, as *The Bell Curve* did, and even when its policy implications are disturbing to many, there is no reason to suppress such an inquiry on the grounds that it can have harmful moral consequences.[23] The only time the moral revival in social science could interfere with the principle of liberal state neutrality is when a social scientist works directly for government and finds support for his ideas among those who exercise government authority. This happens; criminology is one such arena, defense policy another. But with those exceptions, it is possible to meet the objection to morality from liberal neutrality more than half way and still have significant room for moral inquiry in the social sciences.

The objection from science

Even if moral inquiry is held to be necessary and important, one could still object that social science is the wrong place to pursue it. In the years after World War II, social science accepted a radical distinction between "is" and "ought" statements. Under the terms of that distinction, facts were facts and values values. The task of the social scientist was to describe the world and (it is hoped) make predictions about it. In some versions of the fact-value distinction, the social scientist was permitted to take positions on the issues of the day, but only after making clear that her expertise as a scientist played no particular role in forming those opinions. Social scientists should, it was generally believed, stay clear of moral controversies precisely because they were moral and controversial.

There have been many criticisms of the fact-value distinction in recent years, all of which raise important questions about the possibility of an objective social science. The most radical of such criticisms is associated with postmodernism, which questions, not only the existence of non-contested social facts, but even of physical and natural ones. Yet the

---

[23] Richard Herrnstein and Charles Murray, *The Bell Curve: Intelligence and Class Structure in American Life* (New York: Free Press, 1994).

rejection of the possibility of a neutral stance toward knowledge is not helpful in resolving questions of moral inquiry. In rejecting the possibility of an objective science, most versions of postmodernism also reject the possibility of an objective morality. Moral and ethical questions are let in when such approaches are adopted, but they are given no place to stand. We are given permission to address them but no way of answering them. When the fact-value distinction is enshrined, no one has any special claim for making value judgments. The same conclusion is reached when the fact-value distinction is abolished.

A better approach is taken, in somewhat different ways, by Elizabeth Anderson and Marion Smiley in their chapters in this volume. Behind a considerable amount of ideological and moral disagreement lie unasked questions about the nature of moral inquiry, argues Smiley in her chapter, "Moral Inquiry within the Bounds of Politics: A Question of Victimhood." For example, what responsibility do individuals have for their actions? What constitutes an individual? Are the characteristics of individuality and responsibility common to all human beings? By bringing such questions to the surface, we will not necessarily produce agreement, but we can incorporate into philosophical reflections on the nature of morality or justice real-life examples and everyday circumstances—something that professional philosophers, under the sway of the fact-value distinction, have been reluctant to do.

Anderson's arguments are even more relevant to the way social scientists conduct their scholarship. In "Pragmatism, Science, and Moral Inquiry," she discusses the existence of "thick" evaluative concepts, terms that describe a reality but, in so doing, also pass judgment upon it. The statement "this act is cruel," Anderson writes, enables us "to infer both that the act has a particular factual character and that we have a reason to condemn and discourage it." From a pragmatic perspective, one cannot make a sharp distinction between a descriptive statement and an evaluative one. This is particularly true in the social sciences, where, as she writes, "the subject matter . . . is ourselves." But it would even apply to some of the natural sciences as well, for the systems of classification developed to describe natural phenomena are often motivated by human interests and concerns. If Anderson is correct, the objection to moral inquiry from the perspective of science fails, for moral inquiry would be understood as central to the way the sciences, especially the social sciences, do their work.

Although Anderson helps us see the fact-value distinction in a new way, I am not persuaded that she resolves the political, as opposed to the philosophical, concerns that motivated the distinction in the first place.

Philosophers associated with the call for objectivity, such as Karl Popper, were not only philosophers of science; Popper, in particular, was defending a political commitment to open inquiry.[24] The politics of the fact-value distinction was premised on the notion that an open society must value the possibility of falsification in political, as well as scientific, beliefs. Social scientists, approaching questions with an open mind, ought to be prepared to be surprised by their findings. They ought to be willing to revise their political opinions based upon evidence, not use evidence to support their pre-established political positions. To this day, the notion that social science can surprise us by offering a world other than the one we expected is periodically reaffirmed by works in the field, such as Kristin Luker's well-received book on abortion, which introduced pro-choice feminists to the seriousness of the arguments of those who were pro-life.[25] Especially when moral controversy threatens to tear apart the body politic, there is a need for accounts of the world which, because they are gathered with an open mind, question established ideological and political categories. That need can be undermined only if the social scientist advocates one particular position.

Even if we accept Anderson's argument that "thick" social science concepts contain moral and normative implications, political disagreement will still exist over their extent and meaning. Unlike Anderson, I do not think that describing something as "cruel" tells much about whether such a practice ought to condemned. Many social practices are cruel to animals but serve human purposes. Sometimes we have to be cruel in order to be kind. No doubt flunking one of my students who would otherwise graduate is cruel—as is voting against a colleague for tenure—but if I am true to my vocation, I will do it anyway. Capital punishment is cruel and very unusual, but the Supreme Court still permits it, despite the language of the Constitution, at least in part because not taking the life of a murderer could be considered cruel to the victim's family. Our agreement that a practice is cruel says very little about what our political attitude toward that practice should be.

[24] Karl Popper, *The Open Society and Its Enemies* (Princeton, N.J.: Princeton University Press, 1950).
[25] Kristin Luker, *Abortion and the Politics of Motherhood* (Berkeley and Los Angeles: University of California Press, 1984).

It follows that the social scientist, even when studying a human practice that we would all regard as cruel, such as sexual harassment, pornography, or wife battering, has an obligation to explain what is happening before pointing a finger of condemnation. Even if there is no doubt that an act of wife battering has taken place, there may still be, as Smiley's paper illustrates, disagreement about who constitutes a victim and why.

More likely, the facts of a situation are contested ones. Despite Catherine MacKinnon's strictures, some women seem to like pornography. Many cases of ritualistic child abuse were later found to be without merit.[26] The memories of self-described victims are not always reliable. An ethnographic account of any of these topics that began with the social scientist saying to herself that she was determined to root out cruelty would not be trustworthy. Helpful here is a distinction between objectivity and neutrality.[27] We may not be able to state with objective certainty whether an alleged cruelty took place, but we ought to approach the question in a neutral manner before concluding that it was cruel and to whom.

Given the unreliability of memory, Anderson's plea that we incorporate "testimony" into democratic deliberation strikes me as particularly problematic. We ought to respect our fellow citizens, but that does not mean that we take their stories of suffering as necessarily true or real.

If we suspend our critical judgment and skepticism as they recount their testimonies, we are not respecting them as human beings, for we are failing to engage with them in precisely the kind of moral questioning that Smiley recommends. Both in democratic debate and in social research, the observer needs to listen to people's stories but also to probe and question them. Entering into research with our subjects with the belief that they will deliver testimony is bad advice for the social scientist. (Anderson, to be fair, does not give such advice; her point concerns democratic deliberation.) Prepared to be moved by their accounts of woe, we will never be surprised, and our minds will never change. That is a good reason to avoid subjective identification with those we study, even if objectivity is impossible.

---

[26] Catharine A. MacKinnon, *Only Words* (Cambridge: Cambridge University Press, 1993).
[27] This distinction was made by Thomas Haskell at the conference on "The Revival of Moral Inquiry," Woodrow Wilson Center, Washington, D.C., May 15–16, 1995.

One illustration of the dangers of approaching social science in order to obtain testimony is illustrated by Karen McCarthy Brown (Chapter 7). Brown has been studying Haitian Vodou for over twenty years; her work demonstrates a deep understanding of and sympathy for those who engage in this particular religious practice. Brown also is quite frank about her political and ideological commitments; she writes that in describing the world of her main subject, Mama Lola, she also felt compelled to "do justice to Mama Lola and her world." Brown argues that to present Mama Lola's narrative correctly, it was important to win her trust, and this in turn required close identification with her.

But Brown's understanding of her role as a social scientist does not stop with such identification. Mama Lola comes from a society that has been a frequent target of American military and economic intervention. Brown cannot help but draw comparisons between Haiti and the United States, one an imperialistically inclined superpower, the other an island whose residents are primarily black and poor. These comparisons raise serious questions for me as a reader of Brown's work, however. I know very little about Haiti and even less about Vodou, which is why I am interested in reading Brown's fascinating accounts. But I do know a great deal about America and something about its foreign policy. If I come to distrust Brown's account of that topic—which does strike me as moralistic, oversimplified, and riven with a political ideology that I do not share—how can I come to trust Brown's account of Vodou? In winning Mama Lola's trust, Brown has lost mine.

This example suggests to me that what I have been calling the objection to moral inquiry on behalf of science ought to be taken seriously. This is not because the social sciences are so much like the natural sciences that objectivity is possible. It is rather because the social sciences resemble neither the natural sciences nor the humanities. The social scientist cannot get at an unalterable truth, but the social scientist does have an obligation to try to understand the real world as carefully as she can.

Doing justice to subjects, intervening descriptive accounts with political and ideological ones, and proclaiming that the social scientist has an ethical obligation to denounce cruel practices all interfere with fulfilling that obligation. It is not, in short, because we honor a fact-value distinction that we must want to insure that moral inquiry does not spill over into political advocacy; it is rather because we understand the fragility of truth that we ought to respect neutrality.

Like the objection from grounds of liberalism, the objection to moral revival from the grounds of science contains much of value, but it does not lead to an injunction against research and thinking about morality. Social scientists can, in their role as public intellectuals, speak out personally on the moral issues of the day, but they also must, as social scientists, respect evidence, strive for neutrality, develop methodological sophistication, and do original research. If a revival of moral inquiry leads social scientists to believe that their only obligation is to proclaim their biases and move on, not much will be gained as a result.

The objection from pluralism

American society in recent years has seen an increase in what is commonly called "identity politics"—efforts by groups, usually groups against whom discrimination has been common—to assert their unique attributes as groups. Intellectuals who write on behalf of such movements tend to be critical of liberalism, which they view as responsible for a disproportionate focus on individuals stripped of group identity, but they also share something with liberal individualists: for both, a preoccupation with morality and moral obligation contains potential dangers.[28]

A suspicion of universalism runs through identity politics. Of greater concern to this version of pluralism than the commonality of citizens is what Iris Marion Young calls "the politics of difference." "A democratic cultural pluralism," she writes, "requires a dual system of rights: a general system of rights which are the same for all, and a more specific system of group-conscious policies and rights."[29] Moreover, only those groups who have been oppressed are entitled to group rights; there would be no specific group-conscious policies for white males, for example. The result would be a dual system of moral obligation. We would all be obligated to each other in a minimal way, but we would have special obligations to particular groups over and above those minimal obligations. The danger of a common morality from a pluralistic per-

---

[28] An example of this suspicion of liberalism on behalf of identity politics is Michael Piore, *Beyond Individualism: How Social Demands of the New Interest Groups Constrain American Political and Economic Life* (Cambridge, Mass.: Harvard University Press, 1995).

[29] Iris Marion Young, *Justice and the Politics of Difference* (Princeton, N.J.: Princeton University Press, 1990), 174.

spective is the fear that any attempt to delineate one will give insufficient credit and appreciation to the moral practices and beliefs of minority groups.[30]

The politics of identity has become institutionalized in America through such policies as affirmative action or the attempt to create minority majorities in legislative districts. From a moral perspective, however, the most important policy developments have taken place in education. Not only with respect to the canon taught in humanities departments in American universities, but throughout primary and secondary schools as well, there is a general reluctance to teach common religious and moral points of view, even if one accepts that such things exist, out of a fear that specific groups would object. Although this is a development not confined to any particular political view, it is often found on the left. But Protestant fundamentalists have also objected to common curricula in the schools, if those materials include what they deem to be a version of secular humanism.[31]

Because education has become steeped in moral controversy, moral inquiry in the social sciences is bound to spill over into the larger public debate about a common morality spawned by the rise of identity politics. So deep is the suspicion of moral argument that critics sometimes object, not just to universal moral principles, but to a discussion of any moral principles at all. This is especially the case when social scientists touch on such sensitive matters as welfare, single-parent families, or abortion.

Left-wing and feminist writers are very quick to conclude that any discussion of morality involving relatively powerless people is a thinly disguised effort to control their behavior.[32] Better that we not use loaded terms, and no term is more loaded than "moral."

Despite the often eloquent pleas heard on behalf of identity politics, there are at least three points at which the objection from the grounds of pluralism fails. First, while the dominant tradition in thinking about

[30] Margaret A. Farley, "Feminism and Universal Morality," in *Prospects for a Common Morality*, ed. Gene Outka and John P. Reeder (Princeton, N.J.: Princeton University Press, 1993), 178–81.
[31] Stephen Bates, *Battleground: One Mother's Crusade, the Religious Right, and the Struggle for Control of Our Classrooms* (New York: Poseidon Press, 1993); and Joan Delfattore, *What Johnny Shouldn't Read: Textbook Censorship in America* (New Haven, Conn.: Yale University Press, 1992).
[32] See, for example, the essays in Michael Katz, ed., *The "Underclass" Debate: Views from History* (Princeton, N.J.: Princeton University Press, 1993). This point was also made forcefully by Joan Tronto in her comments on this essay at the Woodrow Wilson Center conference, May 15–16, 1995.

moral obligation in the West has been Kantian, and therefore premised on universal assumptions, there is an alternative tradition quite sympathetic to particular moralities. Carol Gilligan's criticism of Lawrence Kohlberg is the most well known, but there also exists the crosscultural research into moral issues conducted by anthropologist Richard Shweder.[33] Ethically and philosophically, the revival of moral inquiry has not been confined to any one particular approach to morality; it includes writers such as Philip Selznick, who leans toward principles of liberal universalism, and Stanley Hauerwas, who is strongly critical of those same principles (and who, therefore, would likely be more sympathetic, not to identity politics per se, but to the assumptions behind it).[34]

Second, there is no reason to assume that universal moral imperatives undermine the search for identity associated with particular groups. In some cases, national rules will work to suppress the moral practices of particular groups: using a local language in schools, wearing particular religious garments or symbols, or celebrating ethnic holidays. But this suppression takes place in the public realm and involves common public activities; it does not require the suppression of moral particularisms in private, in ethnic neighborhoods, or in the family. Furthermore, the universal regulation of particular moralities can strengthen particularism, either by focusing against a common "enemy" (the cosmopolitan culture) or by simply reminding particular groups of why they prize their particularity in the first place. A national elite, wishing to weaken the ties of particular groups, might be wiser to allow those group ties to flourish, thereby smoothing the process of incorporation of second-generation members of the particular group into the general culture.

Finally, respect for minority moralities does not mean acceptance of minority moralities. Just as the social scientist owes her subjects the respect of questioning their accounts of the world, no group can be treated as an equal so long as others restrain their criticisms of that group's

---

[33] Carol Gilligan, *In a Different Voice: Psychological Theory and Women's Development* (Cambridge, Mass.: Harvard University Press, 1982); and Richard A. Shweder, Manamohan Mahapatra, and Joan C. Miller, "Culture and Moral Development," in *Cultural Psychology: Essays on Comparative Human Development*, ed. James W. Stigler, Richard A. Shweder, and Gilbert Herdt (Cambridge, Mass.: Harvard University Press, 1990), 130–204.

[34] Selznick, *The Moral Commonwealth*; and Stanley Hauerwas, *A Community of Character: Toward a Constructive Christian Ethic* (Notre Dame, Ind.: University of Notre Dame Press, 1981).

practices out of fear of seeming disrespectful to them. If we allow free speech in most situations but regulate hateful speech directed against African-Americans or gays, we are not treating the latter with the respectful equality we extend to groups against whom hate speech is not regulated. If we believe that racial segregation is wrong, even if voluntarily chosen, we fail in our obligations to African-Americans if we accept racial segregation because it is advocated by blacks rather than whites. Paradoxically, pluralism does not exist until all groups are subject to the same common morality. It is perfectly appropriate for one of the tenets of that common morality to include respect for group differences within a common moral framework. Indeed, outside that common moral framework respect for group differences cannot exist. Allowing each group moral autonomy would eventually result in separate societies for each one: there would be no need for Czechs and Slovaks to respect each other's moral differences because they would wind up in separate states.

The suspicion of moral inquiry associated with pluralism serves as a helpful reminder that moral behavior is shaped by membership in particular groups. Individuals are not born morally complete. To develop a sense of obligation, they must be taught a sense of obligation, and among the crucial learning places are those groups that teach loyalty. Developing a sense of solidarity with others who share a particular characteristic, including racial, ethnic, and gender characteristics, is surely a crucial ingredient in learning what it means to live for others as well as oneself. But group identity, which does so much to start the process of learning morality, cannot serve as an excuse to end it. Some object to a revival of interest in moral issues on the grounds that moral talk will eventually become the enemy of oppressed groups striving to fashion their identity. Theirs is a defensive and fearful politics. Moral inquiry is not a threat to group identity but an important step in the process of taking group identity seriously.

The objection from enlightenment

The notion that a revival of interest in morality is taking place in American academic life would have come as quite a surprise to academics earlier in this century. American academic culture has historically been suffused with the stuff of morality. Nearly all American universities began as religious institutions. Operating in loco parentis, they assumed

responsibility for the moral development of their students. Their curricula aimed to teach right and wrong. The capstone course of the
senior year was moral philosophy, though, as Frederick Rudolph says,
"preconceived theological views and evangelistic purposes combined
to deprive the course of anything resembling earnest philosophical
investigation."[35]

The shift from religious to secular institutions took place remarkably
late. My own university, Boston University, began as a Methodist institution. It hired its first non-Methodist minister as president in 1967,
choosing, nonetheless, the president of Methodist Cornell College.[36] A
neighboring institution, Boston College, did not institute even minimal
faculty control over curriculum until the 1950s and did not develop a
lay Board of Trustees until 1968; it still has never had a non-Jesuit
president.[37] But if universities retained their religious ties for a long time,
they lost them thoroughly when they were abandoned. As George Marsden has observed, one of the groups most excluded from modern academic culture is the deeply religious—of all faiths.[38]

Although Marsden resents this situation, he has relatively few allies;
not many argue that America should restore closer links between universities and churches, although the same cannot be said for religious
primary and secondary schools, which are experiencing a revival. Most
American academics hardly think about this issue, but when they do,
they would conclude with near unanimity that secularism and the goals
of the university go together. For that very reason they might be suspicious of a moral revival among academics.

This objection assumes a strong link between the study of morality
and religious interests and motivations. Among those active in the moral
revival in the social sciences, this linkage certainly exists; sociologists of
religion such as Robert Bellah and Robert Wuthhow have been among
the most active advocates of moral inquiry. For this reason alone the
moral revival cannot be separated from a revival of academic interest in
religion. The secularization hypothesis—as societies become more mod-

---

[35] Frederick Rudolph, *The American College and University: A History* (Athens: University of Georgia Press, 1990), 141.
[36] George K. Makechnie, *Seventy Stories about Boston University, 1923–1993* (Boston:
Boston University Press, 1993), 96.
[37] Richard M. Freeland, *Academia's Golden Age: Universities in Massachusetts, 1945–
1970* (New York: Oxford University Press, 1992), 244–7.
[38] George Marsden, *The Soul of the American University: From Protestant Establishment
to Established Nonbelief* (New York: Oxford University Press, 1994).

ern, they also become more secular—no longer seems true in an era of spiritual longing.[39] As a consequence, books dealing with the religious revival are flourishing.[40] The context in which the revival of moral inquiry is taking place is not a completely secular one.

Yet it would be incorrect to identify the moral revival and the religious revival as two sides of the same coin. Politics can yield an interest in morality as decidedly as can religion; Philip Selznick, for one, is certain that his current interests in the topic grow out of his Trotskyite politics as a young man, while my own concerns cannot be separated from the radical politics of the 1960s. James Q. Wilson's work seems inspired both by religious and political convictions. (And it also demonstrates that a political interest in morality can be associated with conservatism as well as liberalism.) Because a substantial part of the moral revival has taken place independently of the religious revival, there is no necessary reason to conclude that academic interest in moral questions will threaten the gains of enlightenment.

The objection to the moral revival on grounds of enlightenment could still prove to be a compelling one, depending upon how the moral revival takes place. Deeply religious thinkers will not be—indeed they cannot be—as tolerant of liberalism as (I have been advocating) moral inquiry should be. Hauerwas, for one, takes his Christianity seriously—so seriously that he believes that Christian ethics is an ethics for Christians, not for everyone.[41] Hauerwas does not think it follows from this assertion that non-Christians can have no access to or understanding of Christian ethics. "Of course non-Christians can understand the argument I develop," he writes. "I just do not expect them to agree with it."

---

[39] David Martin, *A General Theory of Secularization* (New York: Harper and Row, 1978). For a more contemporary debate on the hypothesis, see Steve Bruce, ed., *Religion and Modernization: Sociologists and Historians Debate the Secularization Thesis* (New York: Oxford University Press, 1992).

[40] For examples, see Gene Burns, *The Frontiers of Catholicism* (Berkeley and Los Angeles: University of California Press, 1992); José Casanova, *Public Religion in the Modern World* (Chicago: University of Chicago Press, 1994); Wade Clark Roof, *A Generation of Seekers: The Spiritual Journey of the Babyboom Generation* (San Francisco: Harper, 1993); Mark Juergensmeyer, *The New Cold War? Religious Nationalism Confronts the Secular State* (Berkeley and Los Angeles: University of California Press, 1993); Martin Riesebrot, *Pious Passion: The Emergence of Modern Fundamentalism in the United States and Iran*, trans. Don Reneau (Berkeley and Los Angeles: University of California Press, 1993).

[41] Stanley Hauerwas, "Christians in the Hands of Flaccid Secularists: Theology and 'Moral Inquiry' in the Modern University" (paper delivered at the conference on "The Revival of Moral Inquiry," Woodrow Wilson Center, Washington, D.C., May 15–16, 1995), 11.

One has to admire Hauerwas for his honesty, but it seems to me that his position leaves us with two choices, both of which give credence to those who would object to a moral revival on grounds of enlightenment. Let me call these the weak and the strong case for Christian ethics.

The weak case, which Hauerwas seems to be adopting, holds that Christians should develop a Christian ethics, which leaves all other religions free to develop an ethics for their own believers. The result is religious pluralism, not that dissimilar from the kinds of pluralism associated with identity politics. But if this is the case, then the problems of identity politics carry over into the world of religious belief. Each religion would assume responsibility for its own version of moral truth, but none would assume responsibility for the common morality shared by everyone in the society. The objection to this live-and-let-live arrangement, in other words, comes, not from other religions besides Christianity (who could easily adjust themselves to the situation), but from those who believe that there are universal moral precepts without which a good society cannot exist. The search for a common morality is stopped by default: we simply admit that there is nothing that links us as human beings and develop the particular moralities that give meaning to our specific faiths.

But there is also a stronger case for Christian ethics. America remains a predominantly Christian nation, which suggests that in practice, whatever the theory holds, we can expect that Christian morality would become the universal morality. After all, the United States is also a democracy, and if the majority rules on most things, it can also rule on moral questions—as indeed Christianity did for most of the country's history. In this interpretation of what Christian ethics should be, the problem of a common morality is solved, but at the cost of a failure to appreciate minority faiths. The objection to this solution would come, not from advocates of a common morality, but from non-Christian religions, those who might not care about universals but want to protect particulars. This is the dilemma historically faced by Jews in the United States, one that has been resolved by widespread Jewish support for a secular polity, on the grounds that only such secularism can help Jews find their religious place in a predominantly Christian society.[42]

Hauerwas raises the specter of deeply divisive issues that are never

---

[42] Seymour Martin Lipset and Earl Raab, *Jews and the New American Scene* (Cambridge, Mass.: Harvard University Press, 1995).

confronted so long as no serious discussion of morality takes place. But once moral inquiry is called for, the question of how to balance religious and secular approaches immediately asserts itself. Aware of problems of this sort, some philosophers have tried to address moral questions in ways that are vaguely religious, but broad enough not to exclude anyone: John Dewey's *A Common Faith* is one such example.[43] The dangers of this kind of compromise are obvious: moral rules become watered-down suggestions; obedience is made voluntary; the narratives designed to express a group's highest and most spiritual sentiments are stripped of majesty—all with the result that morality loses its capacity to apply sanctions and therefore loses much of its power. Yet I know of no credible alternative to such an approach, at least none that accepts individual rights and even pluralist claims. However imperfect, quasi-secular approaches to morality offer the best alternative to liberal neutrality's fear of enforced conceptions of the good life and the religious believer's insistence on a particular morality. The question for a secular social scientist contemplating a moral revival is whether it is better to have half a morality than none at all. I believe that it is, but that may be, as they say, a matter of faith.

CONCLUSION

As a liberal (and secular) social scientist, I share three of the four objections to moral inquiry; the only objection that I unreservedly dismiss is the one grounded in identity politics. Given these commitments, perhaps I should be among the critics of this trend rather than among its advocates.

There are clearly those who want the lines I have tried to cross to remain in place: secular humanists persuaded that all moral talk is a cover for the violation of rights and religious moralists certain that too much modernity undermines faith. One is tempted to say: we have had those debates, and they lead nowhere. As I noted above, liberals such as William Galston and Stephen Macedo have argued that the liberal tradition does have moral resources; John Locke certainly knew it had spiritual ones.[44] Religiously inspired moralists such as Robert Bellah

---

[43] John Dewey, *A Common Faith* (New Haven, Conn.: Yale University Press, 1934).
[44] On John Locke's religiosity, see John Dunn, *The Political Thought of John Locke: An Historical Account of the Argument of 'The Two Treatises of Government'* (Cambridge: Cambridge University Press, 1969).

have made clear their commitments to liberal values including freedom and pluralism.[45] These efforts toward a middle position can, on occasion, be intellectually fragile, as in Amitai Etzioni's "Communitarian Manifesto," which tends to shy away from a full exploration of the intellectual tensions between the positions it advocates.[46] Given this fragility, there will always exist temptations to split apart the tenuous, to argue, as Mill tended to do, that liberty and morality can never be satisfactorily reconciled.

Such an outcome would be understandable but regrettable nonetheless. The very tension between liberty and morality (as Mill understood it) leads one to believe that human beings require both. In an odd way there is thus some encouragement that ways will be found to reconcile them. One hopes that among those ways will be efforts by scholars to demonstrate the dependence that liberty has on morality and vice-versa; a substantial part of the moral revival in the social sciences, in my opinion, ought to have that task as its major objective.

Even in the absence of such a development, there is one other reason to believe that we will not return to outright conflict between secular humanists and religious moralists. Whatever the scholars think, most people, I discovered in my research, are torn between their strong sense that morality ought to be strict and their desire to protect what to them are the obvious benefits of modernity. Americans do not like abortion, but they want to protect a limited right to choose. They may believe, some of them, that homosexuality is a sin, but they are not prepared to let those with AIDS die in disgrace. In taking such contradictory, but nonetheless commonsensical attitudes, they understand that strongly principled views on either side of what is called America's culture war probably ought to be distrusted. This would not be a bad position for social scientists interested in the revival of moral inquiry to take as well.

---

[45] This is how I read Bellah et al., *The Good Society*.
[46] This platform is printed in Etzioni, *The Spirit of Community*, 251–67.

10

Religion, morality, and other unmentionables:
The revival of moral discourse in the law

JOAN C. WILLIAMS

People who embrace the revitalization of moral discourse in their own fields often are uneasy about a similar agenda in the law. They might want to revive morality, but they do not want judges dictating it. If judges follow their own particular moral precepts instead of "the law," they fear for the rule of law.

Ironies abound in this debate. One is that courts in the United States involve themselves in political and moral debates much more frequently and openly than do courts in Europe, Britain, or Canada. As Alexis de Tocqueville noted in the 1830s, Americans persistently tend to turn political questions into legal questions.[1] A second irony is that most lawyers are less perturbed by the notion that law is "political" than is the general public: the view that judges are political actors whose decisions reflect their values has been a commonplace among lawyers since the legal realism of the 1920s. Critical legal studies reiterated the law's value-laden character amidst much fanfare in the 1980s, as do outsider-scholars in feminist and critical race theory today.

Many thanks to friends and colleagues who have helped me on this chapter: Greg Alexander, Connie Buchanan, Adrienne Davis, Terry Fisher, Mark Hager, Laura Kalman, Jim Kloppenberg, James May, Martha Minow, Andy Popper, Jamin Raskin, Mitt Regan, Thomas Sargentich, Herman Schwartz, Mark Tushnet, Robert Vaughn. Special thanks to Steve Winter and Robb Westbrook, whose close attention greatly improved the essay.
[1] Alexis de Tocqueville, *Democracy in America*, ed. J. P. Mayer and Max Lerner (New York: Harper and Row, 1966). "The judicial organization of the United States is the hardest thing there for a foreigner to understand. He finds judicial authority invoked in almost every political context, and he naturally concludes that the judge is one of the most important political powers in the United States" (89). American judges are "invested with immense political power" (90). "In practice few laws can long escape the searching analysis of the judge" (92). "The American judge is dragged in spite of himself onto the political field" (93).

The profound influence of nonfoundationalism within the academy makes anxiety about the law's value-laden character particularly acute today. The nonfoundationalist premise that truths reflect social experience rather than a picture of "outside" reality dissolves the traditional distinction between facts and value judgments. It suggests that one's notion of the "relevant facts" is a reflection of one's presuppositions or (value-laden) world view. If normativity is inescapable, then judges do not escape it.

We badly need an explanation of why this fact does not preclude the rule of law. By way of introduction, I discuss my view of law, address the work of Michael Perry (a leading voice for the frank admission of moral discourse into the law), and explore why the prospect of moral discourse in the law seems so unsettling. Then I consider whether open "moralizing" in the law is as frightening as the reactions to it seem to indicate. I describe new understandings of judicial review and the rule of law to explain why moral discourse undermines neither. I next address the spectre of *Bowers v. Hardwick* (1986), in which the U.S. Supreme Court upheld a state sodomy statute on the grounds that—because the law inevitably involves morality—the Court should not second-guess the legislature's embrace of the traditional aversion to homosexuality. The essay concludes by shifting from constitutional law, which is the usual focus of commentators concerned with the relation of law and morality, to property law. Moral discourse is as inescapable in property law as it is in constitutional law. We need to acknowledge this and to admit the full range of views about property into legal analysis, including those that seem "sentimental," "moralistic," or even "religious." Otherwise, property law analysis will be limited to those normative views that present themselves as common sense or science—which effectively limits legal analysis to the vision of property represented by economic liberalism.

THE PREMISE OF INCOMMENSURABILITY

My view of law starts from the premise of *incommensurability*: the inevitability of different perspectives, characterized by different sets of "commonsense" assumptions, different norms of social engagement, and different "truths." Note that incommensurability does not mean that different perspectives are mutually incomprehensible or exclusive. Mutually exclusive viewpoints are opposites within *the same* paradigm, whereas the whole point of incommensurability is to acknowledge the existence of different paradigms. Incommensurable social visions typically will have ever-shifting points of potential translation and convergence. The best we can hope for is a process of mutually respectful social negotiation across incommensurability, leading to shifting alliances that will depend for their success on how well we understand what really matters to groups of people with whom we profoundly disagree.

Judges can help this process by making explicit the normative visions that lead both to their assessments of the relevant facts and to their conclusions of law.[2] This argument leads not to the conclusion that judges should be involved in moral discourse, but that they always have been. The only question is whether to admit it. Does democracy require hypocrisy?

It does not. Judges should make explicit the moral visions that frame their understanding of the relevant facts and legal conclusions as a way of creating a process of negotiation across incommensurability. The alternative is for judges to pretend that they speak from a viewpoint with which "any reasonable person" will agree. This is bound to threaten the courts' legitimacy, as those left out of a court's notion of reasonableness becomes cynical about its claims to objectivity.[3]

I am rejecting the assumption that if judges are not bound by objectivity, they will be relegated to imposing their own subjective opinions. The whole point of the social theory of knowledge is to reject both sides of the objectivity/subjectivity paradigm. The central premise is that knowledge is *social*—neither a mere picture of some external reality or the kind of unsocialized, unfettered subjectivity beloved of the Romantics. Instead, judges should be viewed as inevitably and legitimately "engaged in, rather than separate from, the[ir] communities." Once we see judges in this way, we will recognize that "an idea of reason [cannot be] abstracted from context and generalizable across communities. . . . All knowledge depends on a culturally and historically situated shared world of meaning. Norms cannot be separated from facts; justifications depend on the community in which those statements matter."[4] A prominent

---

[2] See Martha L. Minow, "Judging Inside Out," *University of Colorado Law Review* 61 (1990): 795–801. "[P]artly due to neglect, but also due to the rigidities in prevailing theories, the actual practices and experiences involved in judgment remain largely unexamined . . . by scholars and theorists" (797).

[3] For another argument that the taboo on "ethical argument" leads to cynicism, see Philip Bobbitt, *Constitutional Fate: Theory of the Constitution* (New York: Oxford University Press, 1982), 137.

[4] Martha Minow, "Partial Justice," in *The Fate of Law*, ed. Austin Sarat and Thomas R.

recent example is the O. J. Simpson case, in which African- and European-Americans sharply diverged on their views on whether Simpson should have been convicted. Feminists, critical race scholars, and critical legal scholars have pointed out many other contexts in which notions of what seems reasonable differ across communities.[5]

My views on incommensurability lie within an established tradition that includes feminist jurisprudence, critical race theory, and critical legal studies. But commentators in those traditions tend to say, not that law involves moral discourse, but that it is "political." One of the few legal commentators to argue that law entails moral decisionmaking is Michael Perry.

LAW AND MORAL DECISIONMAKING

Perry's analysis starts with a highly sophisticated reading of nonfoundationalist texts to reach the conclusions that neutrality is an unworkable norm and that all legal interpretation is inevitably normative. He argues that morality, politics, and law are linked: "the legislator's (and the citizen's) moral beliefs, including her religious beliefs about human good, are ultimately determinative of her politics." Constitutional discourse, he concludes, "is simply political-moral discourse in which the operative basic standards of judgment are the fundamental aspirations of the American political tradition . . . signified by the Constitution."[6]

Kearns (Ann Arbor: University of Michigan Press, 1993), 36–45, esp. 37 (characterizing the rule of law) and 39 (judges as part of communities). Perhaps the best treatment of the objectiv/subjective paradigm is Richard J. Bernstein, *Beyond Objectivism and Relativism: Science, Hermeneutics*, and *Praxis* (Philadelphia: University of Pennsylvania Press, 1983).

[5] For a prominent example in feminist theory, see Kathryn Abrams, "Gender Discrimination and the Transformation of Workplace Norms," *Vanderbilt Law Review* 42 (1989): 1183–248 (arguing that women often perceive as sexual harassment what men perceive as flattering attention); in critical race theory, see Charles Lawrence III, "The Ego, the Id, and Equal Protection: Reckoning with Unconscious Racism," *Stanford Law Review* 39 (1987): 317–88 (much of what whites see as harmless, blacks see as racism); in critical legal studies, see Robert Gordon, "Unfreezing Legal Reality: Critical Approaches to Law," *Florida State University Law Review* 15 (Summer 1987): 195–220 (arguing that much of what is commonly understood as common sense is in fact contingent and should be changed). This is not to suggest that individuals belong to only one community. In fact, they may belong to several and feel torn in their loyalties. Feminist critical race scholars have pointed out that African-American women are often in this situation. See Kimberlé Crenshaw, "Whose Story Is It Anyway? Feminist and Antiracist Appropriations of Anita Hill," in *Race-ing Justice, En-gendering Power*, ed. Toni Morrison (New York: Pantheon Books, 1992), 402–40.

[6] Michael Perry, *Morality, Politics and Law* (New York: Oxford University Press, 1988), 103, 156.

At times, Perry's nonfoundationalism leads him to acknowledge the inevitability of disagreement in a pluralistic society characterized by incommensurable world views: "In politics, and therefore in law, moral discourse often runs out before agreement—consensus—is reached, especially in a morally pluralistic society like our own." Perry points out that any consensus we share is to vague ideals such as equality, with little agreement on what our commitment to equality entails. He writes, "Even if moral discourse probably can't go very far in resolving a particular conflict, such discourse is almost surely worth attempting, given the alternatives."[7]

Despite this conclusion, Perry finds it hard to give up the conviction that all reasonable people ultimately will agree if they proceed in good faith. His is a "naturalist" perspective, designed to refute "relativism," which he defines as the view that there can be no moral knowledge. The issue is not whether moral knowledge can exist—clearly people act on moral precepts all the time—but whether we can assume agreement on what morality requires. Despite his conscientious provisos, Perry assumes we can. He notes that, while "truth is framework-relative . . . for a large range of propositions nearly all frameworks coincide." He talks persistently about "common human interests" and concludes that "[t]he facts that human beings are members of a single species, that they have at least some basic interests in common as members of the same species, and that they inhabit the same planetary environment explain why there *are* beliefs common to all human beings." The only ones he mentions are beliefs in space, time and causality, which hardly seem sufficiently robust to anchor a consensus on social ethics in our highly divided society.[8]

In other contexts, Perry turns to process norms: "moral discourse among members of different moral communities, if conducted in good faith and with a gentle, ecumenical openness to the beliefs, experience, and person of the interlocutor who is not a member of one's own community, can be a principal medium through which different moral communities 'meet one another and exchange or modify practices and

---

[7] Ibid., 77, 53, 75.
[8] Ibid., 51 (citing Devine). Another formulation Perry seems to favor is Philippa Foot's assertion that all "need affection, the cooperation of others, a place in a community, and help in trouble," 49. Again, this is a noble sentiment with which most people would agree in the abstract. This does not mean they would agree with what it means in particular cases. Agreement on ideals—on self-description—should not be mistaken for agreement on what those ideals mean in practice.

attitudes.' " What is striking about this second claim is the assumption that (given a gentle process) members of the different moral communities will want to "exchange or modify practices and attitudes"—a heroic assumption for which no evidence whatsoever is offered.[9]

Perry hardly mentions his naturalist perspective when he gets down to cases, but his assumption of consensus is highlighted by his analysis of the 1973 Supreme Court case holding that access to abortion is a constitutional right, *Roe v. Wade*. His argument is that *Roe v. Wade* is wrong because, though judges should be free to engage in moral decisionmaking, they should not be "arrogant." He maintains that the *Roe* Court should have limited itself to constitutionalizing access to abortion in four situations: when the life of the mother is in danger, to protect the health of the mother from "a significant threat of serious damage"; to terminate a pregnancy "that would result in the birth of a genetically defective child whose life would be short and painful"; or previability abortions for pregnancies that result from rape or incest. He recommends such a ruling because "nonoriginalist constitutional adjudication must be moderate. . . . No conversation is likely to be productive if the judiciary assumes an arrogant stance, pontificating rather than listening patiently and patiently searching for common ground."[10]

Despite Perry's earlier acknowledgement of incommensurability, he ignores the basic insight that what seems "reasonable" or "moderate" depends upon one's frame of reference. One can readily see how this position may seem reasonable and moderate from his perspective as a liberal Catholic; it is slightly more liberal than the official position of the Catholic Church.[11] From my own perspective, it does not seem moderate at all, for it allows states to outlaw abortions in the overwhelming majority of cases where women seek them.

Perry cites in support of his position the official positions of the American Medical Association, the American Bar Association, and the American Law Institute. This privileging of the conventional avenues and

---

[9] Ibid., 51. For a discussion of why this seems unlikely, see Joan Williams, "Abortion, Incommensurability and Jurisprudence," *Tulane Law Review* 63 (June 1989): 1651–72. Much of the discussion of abortion in the text tracks my argument in this earlier article.

[10] Perry, *Morality*, 177.

[11] As of the time Perry wrote, the Church sanctioned abortion in a slightly narrower range of cases than Perry recommends. Williams, "Abortion," 1672, note 99.

representatives of power seems to contradict Perry's sensitivity in other contexts to the need not to privilege the views of some as the views of all.[12]

Ultimately, Perry uses a covert consensus argument when what he really means is that *Roe* should have adopted the position that, in his world view, seems the right amount of constitutional protection for abortion. From my quite different social location, his proposed rule gives abortion rights far too little protection. We have reached the point where we return to Perry's insight that, in a morally pluralistic society, "moral discourse often runs out before agreement—consensus—is reached." We must face the fact of disagreement and take account of it in our theory of constitutional adjudication, without privileging one side with value-laden proclamations of what is "arrogant" or "moderate."

The abortion debate dramatizes why moral discourse often runs out before consensus is reached by showing how moral judgments relate to the shape of people's lives. Some people—I am one of them—are convinced that the Constitution's mandate of equality protects a woman's right to abort. But I also see how that "truth" reflects my social position as a class-privileged woman in a highly secular society where a key luxury of the ruling class is satisfying work, where work roles are virtually the only avenue to economic independence and social influence, and where attention typically is focused on social rather than spiritual accomplishments. Consequently, work is a key axis of identity, including my own. I take as a premise that sexuality is another key human entitlement. I am, moreover, a member of a social group that views children as needing tremendous amounts of personal attention—much more time and attention than they were believed to need in my grandmother's generation. And I believe, like most women (but not most men), that I personally should give much of that personal attention. Finally, I live in an economic system that defines the ideal worker as someone who has few daytime responsibilities for child care and can work overtime at short notice—and rigorously marginalizes anyone who cannot live up to this ideal. To these social factors I add the biological fact that, for me, pregnancy is very debilitating.

This is the social context in which access to abortion seems so vi-

---

[12] See, for example, Perry, *Morality*, 77.

tal. If these factors were changed—if I did not believe that child rearing was so time intensive, if workplaces assumed an ideal worker who was also a primary caregiver, if my experience of pregnancy or my views on sexuality were different—I might well feel differently about abortion.

But the world is as it is, and I am who I am. Given both, access to abortion, for me, is an absolute. Yet I can readily see how this conclusion seems foreign, even repulsive, to (a) an idealistic celibate priest who has no incentive to think through what denial of abortion means in the lives of actual women (and whose own spiritual and temporal ambitions might well be furthered by opposition to abortion rights) or (b) a middle-aged Mormon mother of five who believes that her purpose in life is to be a good wife and mother, that sexuality and reproduction were meant to be linked, that sex outside of marriage is wicked, and that the wicked shall be punished.

Neither the priestly nor the Mormon path seems an indefensible way of life. And I can readily see how, from those perspectives, abortion seems unjustifiable. Moreover, I do not foresee a convergence between the Mormon mother and myself unless I decide to change the fundamental premises of my life—or she does. Consensus between us on abortion is simply not in the cards. Our visions of the good life are just too different.

The standard liberal view is that the Supreme Court should adopt my position on abortion because the state should be neutral. But the Court cannot be neutral. The view that abortion deserves constitutional protection is as much premised on a vision of the good life—built around assumptions about the roles of sexuality, work, and a certain kind of child rearing—as is the opposing view. For pro-life advocates, for the priest or the Mormon mother, constitutionalizing abortion rights will not seem neutral at all. Instead, it will seem like selfish baby killing and an endorsement of irresponsible sexuality.[13]

---

[13] The assumption that abortion is baby killing reflects social judgments about women's roles and the traditional invisibility of women's caretaking work. See Reva Siegel, "Reasoning from the Body: A Historical Perspective on Abortion Regulation and Questions of Equal Protection," *Stanford Law Review* 44 (1992): 261–380 (arguing that abortion-restrictive legislation is caste legislation, concerned with compelling women to perform the mothering work traditionally allocated to them). For a study that stresses the different attitudes toward motherhood and sexuality of pro-choice and pro-life advocates, see Kristen Luker, *Abortion and the Politics of Motherhood* (Berkeley: University of California Press, 1984).

ANXIETIES ABOUT THE RULE OF LAW

Judges cannot avoid assumptions about the good life. Neither can they represent a neutral viewpoint, or one everyone will see as moderate. These conclusions awaken four related anxieties: about the rule of law, the need for professionalism, the role of religious language, and the theory of judicial review.[14]

The overriding fear concerns the rule of law. If judges enforce not the law but their own morality, goes the argument, we will lose our government of laws not men. Implicit in this formulation is the assumption that morality is subjective and that law must be based on something firmer than judges' personal, subjective opinions.

A related fear reflects the historical process by which modern professionalism defined itself in opposition to old-fashioned moralizing. Until the Civil War, "the life of the mind in the United States was largely dominated by the concerns and controversies, innovations, and accommodations, of the Protestant clergy."[15] Many colleges and universities were affiliated with particular denominations; theology held sway, and the social sciences were taught within the framework of moral philosophy.

All this changed in the Gilded Age, as the educated gentry shifted

---

[14] H. Jefferson Powell is a leader in acknowledging moral discourse in legal decisionmaking. *The Moral Tradition of American Constitutionalism* (Durham, N.C.: Duke University Press, 1993). Powell brilliantly tracks when courts have seen constitutional lawmaking as independent of moral decisionmaking and when they have not. I question, however, Powell's Alasdair MacIntyre-inspired "crisis" model, which exaggerates the discontinuity between a lost past (with a coherent tradition), and a fallen present (without one). His discussion of "tradition-dependent modes of making public moral decisions" (146) appears to intimate content where little exists. Powell's assertion that the common law methods of "extending recognized legal norms by combination and analogy" (174) ignores the fact that any competent lawyer can create an argument to reach virtually any conclusion using the norms of "combination and analogy." My second major reservation is that Powell does not fully grapple with the implications of his use of religion. His explicitly theological approach offers Christian ethics as a riverbed for channeling America's polity away from its "employment of violence that is increasing wayward, increasingly brutal" (262). This is an intriguing and certainly an original approach, yet the purpose of this "Christian response to the democracy-versus-judicial-review struggle within contemporary constitutionalism" (281) remains unclear. Are Christian judges supposed to effect it in the service of a populace that includes many who have expressly rejected Christianity and others who do not adhere to the liberal formulation of religion Powell advocates? If not, what is its proposed role?

[15] Michael J. Lacey, "Introduction: The Academic Revolution and American Religious Thought," in *Religion and Twentieth-Century American Intellectual Life*, ed. Michael J. Lacey (Washington, D.C., and Cambridge: Woodrow Wilson Center Press and Cambridge University Press, 1989), 2.

from traditional forms of authority based on deference and religion to
new claims of authority based on science. Dorothy Ross has documented
the process by which, in the social sciences, the older moralizing style was
replaced with a new style dominated by the objectivizing language of science. Value judgments were driven underground and structured into systems of putatively objective assumptions. Once this transformation was
complete, open moralizing came to seem old fashioned and out of place in
modern discussions of social problems, both in the "social sciences" and
in Christopher Columbus Langdell's "science of the law."[16]

   This ban on moralizing was reinforced by the banishment of religious
language from public discourse. Traditionally, political issues were
framed in religious language. Examples include debates about independence in the eighteenth century and debates about slavery in the nineteenth century. Even in the twentieth century thinly veiled religious
motivations and language played a major role in Progressivism.[17]

   According to one scholar, this changed in the first half of the twentieth century: "In the late nineteenth century, political morality was secured by the truth of religion. . . . By FDR's era, such a justification of
political virtue was old hat. Instead, there was a new, scientist justification."[18] Mainstream political language became rigorously secular,
with religious language largely relegated to the far right and associated

---

[16] On the shift to a model based on natural science, see Dorothy Ross, *The Origins of
American Social Science* (Cambridge: Cambridge University Press, 1991). On the shift
in the universities from a model based on religion to one based on expertise, see Julie
Reuben, *The Making of the Modern University: Intellectual Transformation and the
Marginalization of Morality* (Chicago: University of Chicago Press, 1996); Thomas Has-
kell, *The Authority of Experts: Studies in History and Theory* (Bloomington: Indiana
University Press, 1984); and William P. LaPiana, *Logic and Experience: The Origin of
Modern American Legal Education* (New York: Oxford University Press, 1994). La-
Piana writes, "Langdell studied and taught law not as a system of principles whose
validity could ultimately be traced to the Creator, but as a logically coherent system of
technical rules, principles that are applicable only to the decision of cases in the courts
and which come from those cases. The case method . . . would give birth . . . to a new
model of legal science" (70).

[17] See Joan D. Hedrick, *Harriet Beecher Stowe: A Life* (New York: Oxford University
Press, 1994); and Robert M. Crunden, *Ministers of Reform: The Progressives' Achievement in American Civilization, 1889–1920* (Champaign: University of Illinois Press,
1982), 24. In *Religion and American Politics: From the Colonial Period to the 1980s*,
ed. Mark A. Noll (New York: Oxford University Press, 1990), see the following chapters: George M. Marsden, "Afterword: Religion, Politics, and the Search for American
Consensus," 380–90, esp. 380; Ruth H. Bloch, "Religion and Ideological Change in the
American Revolution," 45; Daniel Walker Howe, "Religion and Politics in the Ante-
bellum North," 123; Robert P. Swierenga, "Ethnoreligious Political Behavior in the
Mid-Nineteenth Century: Voting, Values, and Cultures," 146–71, esp. 163.

[18] Bruce Kuklick, "Dewey, American Theology, and Scientific Politics," in Lacey, ed.,

with anti-intellectualism. As religion was barred as a language of main-stream politics, normativity came to be seen as subjective and sentimental, in contrast to the masculine rigor of science and facts.[19]

The banishment of religion from politics and professionals' ban on moralizing drove normativity underground. Fears for the rule of law helped keep it there, reinforced by an important shift in the theory of judicial review. The founding fathers did not believe that direct elections were the only procedure suitable for generating a legitimate government—as is evidenced by their stipulation that senators be elected by state legislators. The nineteenth century saw a shift in the accepted theory of representation: political legitimacy came to be identified with direct election.[20] This shift created conceptual problems for judicial review. Once democratic representation was identified with direct elections, judicial review seemed to thwart the will of the people.[21]

These developments crystallized into what one commentator has called the Modern Theory of constitutional law. James B. Thayer adopted its basic assumptions as early as 1893, but the theory is better known today in the version developed by Alexander Bickel. Under the Modern Theory, a key issue in constitutional law is what Bickel called "the countermajoritarian difficulty": how to justify nonelected judges overturning the decisions of popularly elected legislatures.[22] The obvious

---

Religion, 89. For an insightful essay that explores how the insistent secularism of the intellectual elite has isolated it from ordinary people, see Henry F. May, "Religion and American Intellectual History," in Lacey, ed., *Religion,* 12–2.

[19] For considerations of the religious model of virtue, see Elizabeth Mensch and Alan Freeman, *The Politics of Virtue: Is Abortion Debatable?* (Durham, N.C.: Duke University Press, 1993); Joan Williams, "Virtue and Oppression," in *Virtue: Nomos XXXIV,* ed. John W. Chapman and William A. Galston (New York: New York University Press, 1992). When compared with European countries, America ranks as the second most religious country and has the highest ranking for the importance of God in its citizens' lives. Mensch and Freeman, *Politics of Virtue,* 167. Perhaps the best known (if unconscious) proponent of the Romantic view that values are subjective is Robert Bork, "Neutral Principles and Some First Amendment Problems," *Indiana Law Journal* 47 (1971): 1–35. "There is no principled way to prefer any claimed human value to any other" (8).

[20] I am indebted to my collegue Jamin Raskin for this point. Note women and African-Americans continued to be represented by white men with no sense that the principles of democracy were thereby jeopardized.

[21] The distrust of direct elections stemmed from the fear of factions, in particular that a majority faction would tyrannize the minority. James Madison was particularly vocal. The famous expression of this argument is Federalist No. 10., James Madison, *The Federalist Papers,* ed. Jacob E. Cooke (Cleveland: World Publishing Co., 1961), 57. The fear of majority factions was the chief focus on the Federalists' politics, according to Gordon Wood. Gordon S. Wood, *The Creation of the American Republic, 1776–1787* (New York: Norton, 1972), 502.

[22] The term "Modern Theory" is from Powell, *Moral Tradition,* 144–6, 170–2, who also

defense is to assert that judges' decisions involve, not "mere politics" but objective judgments requiring precisely the kind of expertise judges possess. The Modern Theory exerts steady pressure on judges to deny that they are political actors. As a result, as legal historians William W. Fisher III and Laura Kalman have documented, constitutional theory is dominated by an endless stream of neo-objectivisms.[23]

To summarize: in a country famous for the activism of its courts, we have trouble admitting that courts involve themselves in controversial political and moral decisionmaking. Courts consistently get dragged into political controversies; once there, they are under intense pressure to avoid open normativity, particularly that expressed as moral(izing) discourse. This brief introduction suggests why. To defend the existence of moral discourse in the law requires us to change a number of preconceptions about the law. It requires us first to change our understanding of both judicial review and the rule of law.

DOES JUDICIAL REVIEW THREATEN DEMOCRACY?

Normativity only threatens the legitimacy of judicial review if we preserve the assumptions of the Modern Theory of constitutional law. Upon reflection these assumptions are unconvincing. The Modern Theory rests on highly mannered descriptions of courts as antidemocratic and legislatures as the untrammeled voice of the people. In fact, neither courts nor legislatures are unmediated mouthpieces; both have complex relationships to "the people."

The vast literature on the influence of wealth on electoral and legislative processes challenges the assumption that the legislatures are mere transcribers of the people's will; instead, they represent some people more than others. The equally vast literature on public choice portrays "legislation as arbitary and legislators as self-seeking," or, at best, representing particular interest groups rather than the people as a whole.

has an illuminating discussion of Thayer. See also Alexander Bickel, *The Least Dangerous Branch* (New Haven, Conn.: Yale University Press, 1962), 16. See also "One Hundred Years of Judicial Review: The Thayer Centennial Symposium," *Northwestern University Law Review* 88 (1993): 1–468.

23   Laura Kalman, *The Strange Career of Legal Liberation* (New Haven, Conn.: Yale University Press, 1996); William W. Fisher III, "The Development of Modern American Legal Theory and the Judicial Interpretation of the Bill of Rights," in *A Culture of Rights: The Bill of Rights in Philosophy, Politics, and Law, 1791 and 1991,* ed. Michael J. Lacey and Knud Haakonssen (Washington, D.C., and Cambridge: Woodrow Wilson Center Press and Cambridge University Press, 1991), 266–365.

The literature applying game theory to legislatures suggests that, rather than having an exclusive (or any?) focus on reflecting the will of the majority, legislators focus primarily on getting reelected. Even conventional theorists that call upon legislators to exercise critical judgment and leadership call into question the "untrammeled voice" model of legislatures.[24]

Constitutional theorists seeking to defend judicial review sometimes assume they must attack the legitimacy of majoritarian rule or try to prove that courts are indeed majoritarian.[25] Neither is necessary: the real issue is whether two political processes—one legislative, one judicial— serve the country better than one. In place of the traditional description of legislatures who make the laws and judges who apply them, we need to think of courts and legislatures as two differently structured political processes.[26]

William Eskridge and Philip Frickey have begun the important pro-

---

[24] For similar critiques of the premises of judicial review, see Steven L. Winter, "An Upside/Downside View of the Countermajoritarian Difficulty," *Texas Law Review* 69 (1991): 1881–927, esp. 1919–27; Barry Friedman, "Dialogue and Judicial Review," *Michigan Law Review* 91 (1993): 577–682. For a review of the literature on the impact of wealth on elections and an important contribution, see Jamin Raskin and John Bonifax, "Equal Protection and the Wealth Primary," *Yale Law and Policy Review* 11 (1991): 273–332. For a measured assessment of public choice theory, see Daniel A. Farber and Philip P. Frickey, *Law and Public Choice: A Critical Introduction* (Chicago: University of Chicago Press, 1991); quotes are from page 5. There are many versions of the "exercise judgment" model. See "Burke to Sheriffs of Bristol," in *The Philosophy of Edmund Burke*, ed. Louis I. Bredvold and Ralph G. Ross (Ann Arbor: University of Michigan Press, 1960) 98; and Ronald Dworkin, *Law's Empire* (Cambridge, Mass.: Harvard University Press, 1986), 167, 217–9.

[25] For arguments that legislatures are not always majoritarian, see Samuel Kislov, *The Supreme Court and Political Freedom* (New York: Free Press, 1968), 20; William R. Bishin, "Judical Review in Democratic Theory," *Southern California Law Review* 50 (1977): 1099–137. For an analysis that defends courts as majoritarian, see Perry, *Morality*; and Friedman, "Dialogue," 586–615.

[26] Friedman's insightful article offers a thoughtful critique of the Modern Theory, but leaves too many of its assumptions in place, notably the assumption that legitimacy is tied to proof that courts "really" are majoritarian. The fact is that, at times, they are not—and that our constitutional system relies on courts as a counterweight to majoritarian rule. See David Luban, "Justice Holmes and the Metaphysics of Judicial Restraint," *Duke Law Journal* 44 (1994): 449–523, esp. 454–462. Friedman asserts that judges will impose "our values" but then acknowledges that "ours is not one society with one monolithic set of values." See Friedman, "Dialogue," 615. Friedman fails to come to terms with his own statement that the values discussed will be only the "values of some of us." He goes right back to a notion of "society's values." Many contemporary writers acknowledge the social theory of knowledge only to evade the disturbing implications of incommensurability by assuming a consensus on values (or knowledge). I have called this pattern the "culture as consensus" theory. Joan Williams, "Culture as Consensus: Legal History and the Reconstructive Project," *Virginia Law Review* 76 (1990): 713–46.

cess of redescribing the role of courts as political actors with complex relationships to "the people." As Eskridge points out, legal realists and political scientists long ago analyzed judges as political actors.[27] Yet legal realists used their descriptions of judges as political actors chiefly as a way of challenging the legitimacy of their decisions, whereas Eskridge and Frickey do not use their claim that judges are political actors to attack their legitimacy. Instead, they assume that it is appropriate for judges to play a role in the "dynamic" process of negotiation between courts, legislatures, and the executive that determines the "meaning" of a given statute.[28]

We need to replace the Modern Theory of constitutional interpretation with a Dynamic Theory focused on the question of whether a system with four differently structured forums (state and federal courts and state and federal legislatures) provides better opportunities for democratic living than does a system without judicial review.[29] This question frames a very different debate than does the current interminable discussion about judicial activism.

Jane Schacter offers a useful approach for starting this discussion. She argues that we need to "recast the debate about legitimacy in statutory interpretation in terms of substantive theories about democracy that ought to share and drive interpretive rules." She concludes that this debate "would be far more fruitful than remaining mired in futile

[27] William N. Eskridge, "Reneging on History? Playing the Court/Congress/President Civil Rights Game," *California Law Review* 79 (1991): 665, notes 254–5.

[28] A hefty literature exists on the "dynamic" theory of statutory interpretation. For a critique that can also act as a review essay, see Martin H. Redish and Theodore T. Chung, "Democratic Theory and the Legislative Process: Mourning the Death of Originalism in Statutory Interpretation," *Tulane Law Review* 68 (1994): 803–81, esp. note 121 (citing the basic texts in which the theory is developed). The signal that this school has "arrived" came when Eskridge and Frickey wrote the *Harvard Law Review* "Foreword" for the 1993 Supreme Court term. See William N. Eskridge and Philip P. Frickey, "Foreword: Law as Equilibrium," *Harvard Law Review* 108 (1994): 26–69. Cass Sunstein arguably takes a dynamic view according to Jane S. Schacter, "Metademocracy: The Changing Structure of Legitimacy in Statutory Interpretation," *Harvard Law Review* 108 (1995): 593–663. Guido Calibresi, T. Alexander Aleinikoff, and Ronald Dworkin also take such a view according to Redish and Chung, "Democratic Theory," 881, note 13. See Martin Shapiro, "Political Jurisprudence," 52 *Kentucky Law Journal* 294 (1964). He discusses political scientists in the 1930s who argued that constitutional adjudication was a form of politics.

[29] For examples of work where the Dynamic Theory has been applied to constitutional as well as statutory interpretation, see Eskridge and Frickey, "Foreword"; William N. Eskridge, "The Judicial Review Game," *Northwestern University Law Review* 88 (1993): 382–95; and Eskridge, "Civil Rights Game." The Dynamic Theory I suggest here, in effect, combines Eskridge and Frickey's focus on the interactive quality of constitutional interpretation with Schacter's focus on alternative social visions.

pursuit of interpretive 'neutrality.' "[30] She challenges courts to make clear the vision of democracy that informs their interpretations, in the hopes of shifting discussion about judicial legitimacy away from debates about judicial activism toward discussion of alternative models of democracy.

A key strength of Schacter's approach is that she does not link the legitimacy of judicial review with courts' access to some objective truth or consensus. Instead, she demonstrates the existence of a number of incommensurable, and inherently normative, views about democracy, which will be reflected in the exercise of statutory interpretation (and, I would add, judicial review). Schacter argues not only for a new model, but for new norms of legal practice. She argues that judges should be explicit about the normative visions that inform their interpretations, on the grounds that this will improve the quality of exchange among those holding different viewpoints about fundamental issues.[31] To use the metaphor common to many contemporary commentators, the best that we can hope for is a respectful conversation that may help us move toward mutual understanding.[32]

---

[30] Schacter, "Metademocracy," 596.

[31] For an extensive review of the literature on whether judges should be completely candid about their reasons and motivations, see Scott C. Idleman, "A Prudential Theory of Candor," *Texas Law Review* 73 (1995): 1307–417. Note that I am arguing for one kind of candor: judges should make clear the normative social vision that informs their view of the facts, the relevant law, and their legal conclusions. I am not arguing that judges should always tell all: truth-telling, in judging as elsewhere, is limited by the restraints of social role, courtesy, and many other considerations.

[32] The social theory of knowledge leads many theorists to the metaphor of a dialogue or conversation. Richard Rorty is the most influential. Richard Rorty, *Contingency, Irony, and Solidarity* (New York: Cambridge University Press, 1989). Many legal theorists have picked up this imagery. Perhaps the best introduction to this contemporary literature is the critiques of it: Earl M. Maltz, "The Supreme Court and the Quality of Political Dialogue," *Constitutional Commentary* 5 (1988): 375–91; and Steven D. Smith, "In Pursuit of Pragmatism," *Yale Law Journal* 100 (1990): 409–49, esp. 434–7. Smith decries dialogue as "the all-purpose elixir of our time" (435). I have attempted to meet Smith's criticism by suggesting what people should say. For a particularly insightful critique of "dialogism," see Margaret Jane Radin and Frank Michelman, "Pragmatist and Poststructuralist Critical Legal Practice," *University of Pennsylvania Law Review* 139 (1991): 1019–58, esp. 1040–3. Radin and Michelman seem overly worried that dialogue cannot proceed without a total absence of oppression: the history of blacks in the United States and South Africa suggests that oppressed people often communicate very effectively (which is not to say they are not often silenced, particularly in the short term). Radin and Michelman also worry that we cannot communicate absent universal cognitive structures. What we need to achieve mutual understanding are not universals (inside or outside the brain) but a genuine commitment to engage in acts of translation to help us understand people whose assumptions and conclusions are very different from our own.

A NONFOUNDATIONALIST VIEW OF THE RULE OF LAW

Open normativity will improve judicial discourse rather than undermine it; neither would it undermine the rule of law. The rule of law requires judges to be impartial, neutral, and objective, but a closer look at these norms reveals two quite different sorts of concerns.

They first mandate observance of certain procedural rules: no person is above the law; legal (especially criminal) rules should not be retroactive; any person adversely affected by or accused of violating a law has the right to a day in court. Note that these procedural rules do not get us anywhere near a consensus on substantive principles of justice: they set up a few basic ground rules, not a consensus on conclusions. Nonetheless, they are important rules that can be observed even if law openly reflects incommensurable social perspectives.[33] The fact that we as Americans can agree on the undesirability of "telephone justice," on the desirability of prosecuting people only for acts that were illegal when they were performed, and on the need for the accused to have their day in court does not prove that our commitment to keywords like equality signals a consensus about what equal treatment entails. Such keywords mandate a way of talking rather than a consensus on conclusions. Daniel Rodgers writes, "Vying for control of a common vocabulary, stealing each other's terms in hopes of investing them with radically altered meanings, political opponents often left behind an illusion of

[33] I take the "impartial, neutral, objective" formulation from Minow, "Partial Justice," 37; the more detailed description is from Fisher, "Modern American Legal Theory," 285–6. Minow's discussion is important because she changes the traditional encounter between the rule of law and the social theory of knowledge, which typically ends with the social-theory theorist proclaiming the rule of law as an impossible and/or oppressive ideal. For a particularly learned example, see *The Rule of Law: Ideal or Ideology*, ed. Allan C. Hutchinson and Patrick Monahan (Toronto: Carswell, 1987). My notion of the two different types of "objectivity" is developed further in Joan Williams, "Clio Meets Portia: Objectivity in the Courtroom and the Classroom," in *Ethics and Public History: An Anthology*, ed. Theodore J. Karamanski (Malabar, Fla.: Robert E. Krieger Publishing Co., 1990), 45–56. See also Francis Moontz III, "Is the Rule of Law Possible in a Postmodern World?" *Washington Law Review* 68 (1993): 249–305; and Francis J. Moontz III, "Rethinking the Rule of Law: A Demonstration That the Obvious Is Plausible," *Tennessee Law Review* 61 (1993): 69–195. Moontz develops the important point that postmodernism leads to a reformulation of the rule of law, rather than its abandonment. This topic was discussed extensively in the indeterminacy debate of the 1980s and apparently is still going on. See James E. Herget, "Unearthing the Origins of a Radical Idea: The Case of Legal Indeterminacy," *American Journal of Legal History* 39 (1995): 59–70. Moontz's use of Gadamer to resolve this issue is insightful, although his description of exactly how Gadamer's "fusion of horizons" works to resolve the debate is vague and underdeveloped.

consensus."[34] Current debates dramatize instead the widely divergent understandings of our national commitment to equality. What we share is the self-image of a commitment to equality, not a consensus on what that commitment entails in action.[35]

To the extent that impartiality, neutrality, and objectivity refer not to procedural rules but to foundationalist premises, we need to move beyond the traditional encounter between the rule of law and the social theory of knowledge. This encounter typically ends with nonfoundationalist critics proclaiming the rule of law an impossible and/or oppressive ideal. It leaves many wondering if nonfoundationalists see no difference between telephone justice and our honorable tradition of independent courts. Let it be said that I do. But a judiciary independent of the executive is not the same thing as a judiciary capable of making decisions that will seem objective, neutral, and reasonable to everyone. A theoretical framework that insists that judges present their decisions as neutral and objective will not serve to build consensus between the Mormon mother and me. It will only increase the cynicism of whoever loses.

A nonfoundationalist understanding of the rule of law would decouple judicial legitimacy and objectivity, substituting instead a view of judges as inevitably and legitimately "engaged in, rather than separate from, the[ir] communities," to quote Minow's phrase again. Judges can best fulfill their role by acknowledging the linkage between their social location and their interpretations of the keywords of the American tradition.[36] Then those who disagree can give reasons for their disagree-

---

[34] Daniel T. Rodgers, *Contested Truths: Keywords in American Politics since Independence* (New York: Basic Books, 1985), 8. "Telephone justice" is associated with stories that judges in the Soviet Union would phone party officials to see which side they should come down on in a given case. The term keywords comes from Raymond Williams via Daniel Rodgers. Raymond Williams, *Keywords: A Vocabulary of Culture and Society* (New York: Oxford University Press, 1985).

[35] This is not the place for an extended response to the argument that, although we may diverge on visions of the good life, we share principles of justice. I simply refer the reader to Michael Perry's response: "If it is the case (as I believe it is) that a person— a "self"—is partly constituted by her moral convictions, then, in choosing principles of justice, the partisan cannot bracket her membership in her moral community, her particular moral convictions, for that membership. Those convictions are constitutive of her very self." Perry, *Morality*, 72. The assumption that a viable distinction exists between the good life and principles of justice is an integral part of the viewpoint that "we" can agree on principles of justice. Those who reject the first assumption (concerning the existence of principles of justice) typically also reject the second assumption (that a viable distinction exists between the good life and principles of justice).

[36] Margaret Jane Radin, "Reconsidering the Rule of Law," *Boston University Law Review*

ment, instead of descending into cynicism in the face of unconvincing judicial claims to objectivity.

THE SPECTER OF *BOWERS V. HARDWICK*

Another fear awakened by the prospect of open normativity is that it will lead to judicial intrusion into spheres of private decisionmaking, notably sexuality. The case that typically is cited in this context is *Bowers v. Hardwick*, in which the U.S. Supreme Court upheld Georgia's antisodomy statute. The Court cleverly used the nonfoundationalist critique of objectivity to defend the traditionalist moral opprobrium of homosexuality, on the grounds that "the law . . . is constantly based on notions of morality, and if all laws representing essentially moral choices are to be invalidated under the [Constitution], the courts will be very busy indeed."[37]

One reaction to *Hardwick* is to conclude, with Alan Wolfe in his chapter in this volume, that it "illustrates what happens when the state adopts one point of view in a moral controversy: the rights of individuals are inevitably curtailed." Wolfe supports this argument with a defense of the traditional liberal position that the state should be neutral as between visions of the good. As I have indicated, I do not find this convincing. Surely Wolfe would not argue for moral neutrality if the issue were infanticide. Implicit in his argument is the assumption that homosexuality is not a moral abomination and therefore should be embraced within the realm of tolerance. But this is precisely the premise his opponents reject. Wolfe's position on *Hardwick* involves a particular moral vision that views sexuality as a key arena of self-expression and refuses to privilege heterosexuality over homosexuality. The issue is whether we should defend this vision—for I share it, too—with the claim that state neutrality requires it.[38]

I think not, for two reasons. First, the fact that Wolfe's position on *Hardwick* stems from a particular world view is plainly apparent to anyone who does not share it. In sharp contrast to the view that sexuality belongs primarily to the arena of self-expression and self-fulfillment is the view that sexuality should be linked with reproduction in the arena

69 (1989): 781–819, esp. 815–17, develops some similar themes, notably the notion that legislatures and courts play different social roles that are not captured by the traditional descriptions of courts as rule followers and legislatures as rule makers.
[37] *Bowers v. Hardwick*, 478 U.S. 186, 196 (1986).
[38] See also Perry, *Morality*, 66–8.

of reciprocal duties within conventional marriage. I disagree with this view, but I do see—from that perspective—that my views on homosexuality seem to float in a misguided moral universe. The core message of nonfoundationalism is that opposing opinions rest less often on faulty logic than on incommensurable forms of life—in this case about the purpose of sexuality, its relationship to reproduction, the relationship between sex and gender, and much more.

The crucial question is whether we should begin from the premise that most profound disagreements involve, not ignorance or evil, but incommensurability.[39] I think we should. To do otherwise gives an undesirable structure and emotional tone to our continuing social encounters. For, as we all know, it is infuriating to argue with someone who is committed to proving that *his* opinion is neutral and objective truth, while yours is just an ignorant opinion.

We as a society disagree profoundly about homosexuality. If we should allow it—and I believe we should—we need to explain why by reference to some theory about what our commitment to equality means. The real issue is not that forbidding sodomy involves the judiciary in moral decisionmaking, while allowing it does not: both decisions rest on assumptions about the meaning and the goals of life. Just as the courts must either protect access to abortion or abandon it, they must take sides on the question of whether our constitutional commitment to equality requires the free exercise of homosexuality in a society where it is repugnant to some. In neither context will the courts please both myself and the Mormon mother, but at least they can avoid the insult of a transparently false claim that they are acting without preconceptions as to what constitutes the good life.

Note that my reframing of the argument deprives me of the on-off argumentative structure of the "your-argument-is-not-neutral-but-mine-is" mode. It brings us face to face with disagreements over what our shared commitment to equality compels, in a context that acknowledges that decent people might disagree on this and many other moral and political issues. This strikes me as a conversational structure less infuriating to my opponents, and therefore less divisive, than one in which I proclaim the neutrality of my own positional truths.

---

[39] Note that I am not denying that some viewpoints involve evil and/or ignorance. The traditional contemporary example is the Nazis. The only question is whether we should assume that those who do not agree with us are evil like the Nazis or are sincere people who simply see things very differently. I am arguing for the latter as a default model.

Part of the unease in allowing moral discourse into the law stems from anxieties about the rule of law, including those about the legitimacy of judges. The remaining anxieties go not so much to formal doctrines of judicial legitimacy, but to the relationship between moralizing and modern professionalism. Self-respecting professionals do not engage in old-fashioned moralizing. Instead, they use good common sense and rigorously apply existing rules to hard facts. This self-description is readily recognizable as part of the ideology of professionalism that developed within the past century. I will argue that it embeds a way of masking moral discourse rather than avoiding it.

PROPERTY LAW

Thus far I have focused on constitutional law, which is the traditional arena for discussions of morality, religion, politics, and the law. In the remainder of this chapter I switch the focus to property law to examine how key professional norms concerning science, religion, and common sense embed a particular set of normative assumptions and prescriptions about property. I examine the rhetorical devices through which this view of property presents itself as common sense or science, and I argue that it in fact is no less normative than open "moralizing." I also question the traditional boundary between religion and other forms of normative argument.

The accepted formulation of property within the law begins with John Locke. Locke's theory of property, in its original formulation, had moments of open normativity. He ties his initial premise—that all property was originally owned in common—to his Christian beliefs. Locke also ties his famous proviso (which approves private appropriation of property only as long as "enough, and as good" remains for others) to religious precepts.[40]

Locke's religious sensibility rarely is acknowledged by legal commen-

---

[40] The discussion from here to the end of the chapter draws upon Joan Williams, "The Rhetoric of Property," *Iowa Law Review* 83 (1998). John Locke, *Two Treaties on Government*, ed. Peter Laslett (1968; reprint, New York: Cambridge University Press, 1967). God gave the world to mankind in common (304, paragraph 26); all creatures are equal "unless the Lord and Master of them all, should by any manifest Declaration of his Will set one above another" (287, paragraph 4). Discussions of the influence of religion on Locke include John Dunn, *Rethinking Modern Political Theory: Essays, 1979–1983* (Cambridge: Cambridge University Press, 1985); and James T. Kloppenberg, "The Virtues of Liberalism: Christianity, Republicanism, and Ethics in Early American Political Discourse," *Journal of American History* 74 (1987): 9–33.

tators. Instead, they focus on what we may call the nature narrative, which Locke used to explain why property rights (which, in feudal theory, originated from the king) retained their legitimacy even after the king was overthrown.[41] Locke argued that property rights are presocial by projecting them into a mythic past. Property rights began, Locke argued, when men began to inject labor into the common.

> He that is nourished by the Acorns he pickt up under an Oak . . . has certainly appropriated them to himself. . . . I ask then, When did they begin to be his? When he digested? Or when he eat? . . . Or when he pickt them up? . . . And 'tis plain, if the first gather made them not his, nothing else could. That *labour* put a distinction between them and common.[42]

Note how the nature narrative smuggles in the assumption that all property rights reflect the labor of the owner, which (given the laws of inheritance) they do not and never have. The narrative also deflects attention from the current distribution of property rights by intimating (without ever arguing the point directly) that redistribution is unthinkable because the only relevant time for deciding the just distribution of property rights is some mythic moment when current property owners earned their property by the sweat of their brows. The narrative also embeds the assumption that property is inevitably about economics, in contrast to the view (ascendent at the time Locke wrote) that the allocation and design of property rights are inherently political. Most powerfully, the nature narrative intimates that property rights as we know them reflect mere common sense.

These themes are picked up by an influential modern commentator, Carol Rose, in her analysis of Locke: "He pointed out that life depends on property, in a very primitive sense: if one cannot literally *appropriate* those berries and fruits, one will simply die."[43]

The alternative to property is death? Rose captures the way the nature narrative intimates that the existing distribution of property rights is part

---

[41] Paul Lucas, "Essays on the Margin of Blackstone's Commentaries" (unpublished Ph.D. diss., Princeton University, 1963), quoted in Stanley N. Katz, "Thomas Jefferson and the Right to Property in Revolutionary America," *Journal of Law and Economics* 19 (1976), 467–88. "Locke made private property antecedent to government and divorced society from government, thereby allowing for limited revolutions" (469). For an insightful study of the purpose of narrative in property theory, see Carol M. Rose, "Property as Storytelling: Perspectives from Game Theory, Narrative Theory, Feminist Theory," *Yale Journal of Law and Humanities* 2 (1990): 37–57.

[42] Locke, *Two Treatises on Government*, 330.

[43] Rose, "Property as Storytelling," 37–52.

of the structure of the universe: fighting it makes as much sense as fighting human hunger and the inevitability of death. She continues:

And so acquisitiveness, the desire to have property, is "just there" . . . universal and omnipresent; thus one can always predict a human desire to have things for one's self, or as they say more lately, the human propensity to be a self-interested rational utility maximizer. The propensity is just a kind of a fact of life. . . . [E]ighteenth century political economists took it for granted, rejecting as unrealistic the earlier condemnation of acquisitiveness.[44]

Here Rose shows how the nature narrative is commonly linked with Hobbes's war of all against all. She also shows how modern commentators often translate this mixture of Locke and Hobbes into the language of economics. "Indeed, if we do take these preferences for life and acquisition as givens, then economics can make a bid to be a kind of logical science in politics and law," says Rose. This passage traces the modern translation of "common sense" into economic "science."

The last major ingredient of the nature narrative is utilitarianism. . . . [B]y allocating exclusive control of resources to individuals, a property regime winds up by satisfying even more desires, because it mediates conflicts between individuals and encourages everyone to work and trade instead of fighting, thus making possible even a greater satisfaction of desires.[45]

On top of all their other virtues and inevitabilities, property rights make everybody better off. Note that this application of utilitarianism does not include much talk about what constitutes being "better off." Who could possibly object to "the satisfaction of more desires," or, as the economists say more lately, a wealthier society? Note that nothing is said about how the society's wealth will be *distributed*. Many might object to a society in which some people get richer and richer while others get poorer and poorer—although such a society may in the aggregate be a "richer society."

All this is buried in our "common sense" about property, which combines an antiredistributive version of utilitarianism with a version of Locke shorn of religious arguments and heavily influenced by Hobbes.[46]

---

[44] Ibid., 42.

[45] Ibid.

[46] For a formal defense of wealth maximization as a desirable goal, see Richard Posner, "The Ethical and Political Basis of the Efficiency Norm in Common Law Adjudication," *Hofstra Law Review* 8 (1980): 486–507. For critiques of the wealth maximization rationale, see Jules L. Coleman, "Efficiency, Utility, and Wealth Maximization" *Hofstra Law Review* 8 (1980): 509–51. Coleman questions the normative appeal of wealth

The resulting mixture (which I call economic liberalism) presents itself as common sense or science, tying a particular system of property rights into the structure of the universe—into human hunger, desire, and human sweat.

This is not "the truth" about property. It is, instead, a particular theory about the role and proper distribution of property rights. Alternative traditions are disadvantaged to the extent they do not describe themselves as science or common sense. To place these alternative visions of property on an even playing field requires redefining the relationships between common sense, religion, science, and sentimental moralizing.

In the law the only commonly recognized alternative to economic liberalism is the property and personhood theory associated with Margaret Jane Radin.[47] In contrast to economic liberalism, Radin's theory is explicitly normative. In her initial formulation Radin argued that property tied up with people's sense of self *should* be given greater protection than property treated by its owners as merely fungible. She cites Hegel as support for this position. Radin's formulation makes it appear that the only alternative to economic liberalism is an openly normative "theory."[48]

Perhaps not surprisingly, courts rarely use the property and personhood approach. Radin's initial article proposed property and personhood as a basis for awarding tenants substantially more rights in their homes. Courts appear never to have used her theory to redistribute property rights from landlords to tenants. The only context in which Radin's analysis has been extensively cited is in situations involving commodification of the human body, where it does not threaten the current distribution of traditional property rights.[49] In other words, Radin's

maximization from two perspectives: assuming a fundamental social goal of efficiency, (1) whether a principle of wealth maximization serves efficiency any better than does a principle of utility; and (2) whether a principle of wealth maximization is fundamentally preferable to "the full range" of alternative moral theories (526–8). See also Anthony Kronman, "Wealth Maximization as a Normative Principle," *Journal of Legal Studies* 9 (1980): 227–42, 220 (arguing that wealth maximization does not work as social goal in itself or even as an instrumentality to achieve other goals, such as rights or greater social utility); and Ronald Dworkin, "Is Wealth a Value?" *Journal of Legal Studies* 9 (1980): 191–226, 242 (criticizing wealth maximization as both "bad" [immoral] and "incoherent" in that it intensifies the destructive effects of the "natural lottery": "wealth maximization is biased in favor of those who are already well off").

[47] See Margaret Jane Radin, *Reinterpreting Property* (Chicago: University of Chicago Press, 1993).

[48] Radin acknowledges that her property and personhood approach owes as much to Kant as it does to Hegel. See ibid., 7.

[49] See, for example, *Stiver v. Parker*, 975 F.2d 261, 267 n.8 (6th Cir. 1992) (acknowl-

explicitly normative "theory" has not been used by courts to undermine "commonsense" property rights.

Legal commentators on property law commonly consider only three theories of property: Locke, utilitarianism, and property and personhood.[50] The drawbacks of this approach are now apparent. Locke and utilitarianism typically are not used as alternative theories, but as part of the mix in economic liberalism. Personhood theory, presented as the only alternative, is a less resonant and openly moralizing "theory," striving manfully to hold its own against common sense.

This formulation of property theory reflects the dominance of economic liberalism because it erases two other resonant strains of property rhetoric that judges and legislators actually use in deciding property issues. Drawing on intellectual and cultural history, I have argued that these alternatives need to be given their rightful place in the canon of property theory. Before this can be done, we must acknowledge the legitimacy of moral discourse within the law, for both of the two alternative visions use explicitly normative language. One even lapses into religious language, presenting further problems of legitimacy.

One alternative tradition is the republican view of property, which held that the purpose of property was to give men (gender intended) the independence to pursue the common good. Without property, republicans argue, men fell into venality and subservience. "Dependence begets subservience," said Thomas Jefferson, explicitly linking property and power. This linkage is an important difference between republican and liberal visions of property.[51]

In the hands of social critics in the nineteenth century, the republican vision turned into an egalitarian argument that property should be widely distributed so that the maximum number of citizens could attain the virtue and independence that would qualify them for participation

---

edging Radin's work on paid surrogacy arrangements and commodification of children); *Johnson v. Calvert*, 851 P.2d 776, 792 (Cal. 1993) (Kennard, J., dissenting) (surrogacy case citing Radin's work); *In re Baby M*, 537 A.2d 1227, 1249 (N.J. 1988) (citing Radin's "market-inalienability" piece for proposition that upper-class couples will benefit from surrogacy contracts at expense of poor women).

[50] I take this formulation from Margaret Jane Radin, "Time, Possession, and Alienation," *Washington University Law Review* 64 (1986): 739–58. She notes that this is a formulation of liberal property theory, but she does not discuss any alternative to the liberal tradition (739).

[51] Katz, "Thomas Jefferson," 473. The most extended discussion of the republican vision of property in the law reviews is Gregory S. Alexander, "Time and Property in the American Republican Legal Culture," *New York University Law Review* 66 (1991): 273–315.

in civil life. The Homestead Act of 1862 was a clear expression of this view. It distributed land in small parcels sufficient to support the independence of a yeoman and his family. The same vision gave rise to the freed slaves' expectation after the Civil War that they would be given "forty acres and a mule." Access to enough property to deliver independence was assumed to be integral to citizenship. Arguably, the republican egalitarian vision also informed one of the most powerful redistributive strains in the United States: the dream of home ownership.[52]

The anthropologist Constance Perin has documented the continuing linkage of home ownership with good citizenship. Today, she found, the republican ideal is intermixed with the view that citizens' moral character stems from virtuous family life—a view derived from the gender ideology called domesticity. This strain of republicanism-transmuted-into-domesticity underlies the ideology of home ownership, which has "strong sentimental appeal." A 1992 survey by Fannie Mae reinforces Perin's conclusions. It found that home ownership "is a metaphor for *personal* and *family* security. . . . [O]wning one's home is . . . an empowering act, giving people a stake in society and a sense of control over their lives. . . . Put differently, homeownership strengthens the social fabric." Fannie Mae found that Americans are willing to make dramatic sacrifices to own a home, and that it is one of their highest aspirations.[53]

Linkage of home ownership with good citizenship is a commonplace in U.S. politics. The policy of encouraging home ownership is an uncontroversial one. Although often it is honored in the breach, three important facts remain. First, huge subsidies to home owners (notably the Veterans' Administration and Federal Housing Administration programs and mortgage interest deductions) have garnered the kind of unshakable political support that other redistributive programs never attained. Second, American courts have gone out of their way to protect neighborhoods of single-family houses. Third, American courts have been far more willing to enforce covenants against successive buyers than have

---

[52] Curtis Berger and Joan Williams, *Property: Landownership and Use* (New York: Aspen Law and Business, 1997), chap. 1 (discussing egalitarian strain of the republican vision of property, with cites to relevant sources). For a particularly insightful analysis of this strain, see Linda K. Kerber, "Making Republicanism Useful," *Yale Law Journal* 97 (1988): 1633–72, esp. 1664, 1668.

[53] Berger and Williams, *Property*, chap. 1. Constance Perin, *Everything in Its Place: Social Order and Land Use in America* (Princeton, N.J.: Princeton University Press, 1977), 47, 64, 71–2. Fannie Mae, *National Housing Survey* (Washington, D.C.: Fannie Mae, 1992), 2–3.

courts in Britain.[54] U.S. courts' receptivity to zoning also ties in closely with the desire to protect residential neighborhoods in which republicanism's civic virtue has been transmuted into domesticity's private, family virtue. Exclusionary zoning practices arguably reflect the limits of the nineteenth-century republican egalitarian vision, which worked largely for whites but not for African Americans.[55]

Another strain of republicanism stresses, not its egalitarian potential, but the need to design property rights to achieve some common good. The strongest contemporary expression is in cases in which government regulations are challenged as takings of private property. Historian William Novak has documented how nineteenth-century theorists of the "well-regulated society" carried on themes from republicanism, including the convictions that people are inherently social creatures and that "government is instituted for the common good; for the protection of property and prosperity, and the happiness of the people; and not for the profit, honor, or private interest of any man, family, or class of men." Novak notes that regulation was considered a broad mandate in public life: "only through . . . regulation could man's social nature, his tendency to society and the public good, be realized."[56]

In the nineteenth century the notion that private property rights can by limited by regulation to achieve the public good transmuted into the Progressive ideology of regulation in the public interest. This vision underlies the current sweeping regimes of environmental and land-use regulation.[57]

Restoring the republican vision of property destabilizes the "common

---

[54] For example, American but not British courts have extended covenants at law from their original landlord/tenant context to bind successive buyers; American but not British courts enforce affirmative servitudes, such as the obligation to pay homeowners' association fees; American courts even enforce "implied reciprocal servitudes," in which they allow neighbors to restrict land to residential use in situations where no restrictions whatsoever appear in the restricted owner's chain of title. See "Rhetoric of Property," manuscript pages 66–72.

[55] Joan Williams, "Recovering the Full Complexity of Our Traditions: New Developments in Property Theory," *Journal of Legal Education* 46 (1996): 596–608.

[56] See William J. Novak, "Public Economy and the Well-Regulated Market, 1787–1873" (Ph.D. diss., 1991), 22–3; and William J. Novak, "Public Economy and the Well-Ordered Market: Law and Economic Regulation in Nineteenth-Century America," *Law and Social Inquiry* 18 (1993): 1–32. See also William Novak, *The People's Welfare: Law and Regulation in Nineteenth-Century America* (Chapel Hill: University of North Carolina Press, 1996).

[57] For an analysis of the takings cases as a clash between republican and liberal visions of property, see Carol Rose, "Why Takings Law Is Still a Muddle," *Southern California Law Review* 57 (1984): 561–99; and Berger and Williams, *Property*, chap. 9.

sense" of economic liberalism in several ways. First, it contests the commonsense assumption that property rights should be designed to achieve purely economic goals and highlights instead the view that the design and allocation of property rights involve issues of politics. Second, the egalitarian strain places the *distribution* of property rights at the center of property theory, in sharp contrast to the nature narrative's insistence that the only point in time relevant to the allocation of property rights is the mythic moment when current owners earned their property by the sweat of their brows. The mystique of home ownership presents an important rhetorical resource in a tradition that otherwise marginalizes talk of economic entitlements. Finally, the "common good" strain of republican theory presents a rationale for regulation that rejects the "commonsense" assumption that property rights are absolute in favor of a notion of inherently limited property rights.

The other chief alternative to economic liberalism is a strain of liberal property rhetoric that adds a sense of limits to the liberal demand for respect for property rights. This strain recovers Locke's proviso, typically overlooked by commentators working in the tradition of economic liberalism. The proviso, which approves of appropriation of property rights only if "enough and as good" is left for others, is part of a pattern, for Locke consistently saw the liberal pursuit of self-interest as limited by the demands of duty. Locke also viewed those demands within a religious frame: he explicitly linked the proviso with the notion that all souls have equal dignity before the Lord.

An examination of U.S. property cases shows this strain of property theory, which I call the liberal dignity strain, alive and well in contemporary cases. A dramatic example is *State v. Shack*, a well-known case decided by the New Jersey Supreme Court in 1971. Two Great Society social services workers were denied access to migrant farm workers living in "camps" on the employer's farm. The court held that the farmer had to grant access to the farm workers, as follows:

Property rights serve human values. They are recognized to that end and are limited by it. Title to real property cannot include dominion over the destiny of persons the owner permits to come upon the premises. Their well-being must remain the paramount concern of the law. Indeed the law will deny the occupants the power to contract away what is deemed essential to their health, welfare, or dignity.[58]

---

[58] *State v. Shack*, 58 N.J. 297, 303, 277 A.2d 369, 372 (1971).

Stirring rhetoric, but what *are* "human values"? An answer is suggested by the following quote from the opinion:

As one looks back along the historic road traversed by the law of land in England and America, one sees a change from the viewpoint that one may do as he pleases with what he owns, to a position which hesitatingly embodies an element of stewardship. . . . To one seeing history through the glasses of religion, these changes may seem to evidence increasing embodiments of the golden rule. To one thinking in terms of political and economic ideologies, they are likely to be labeled evidences of "social enlightenment," or "creeping socialism" or even "communistic infiltration."[59]

State v. Shack returns to Locke's original assumption that full commodification of property must be limited by the sanctity of individuals. Note that the court does not take the option of translating the religious conceptions into secularized Kantian language of human dignity. Instead, it retains the original religious frame. Then it carefully displaces responsibility for its use of religious language, in two different ways. First, it quotes from a well-known treatise. This sends the message that, "I am not endorsing religion"—a very unconventional move for a court—only doing what courts do all the time, namely quoting Powell on Property. The court also points to secularized "political" versions of the theme it states in religious language.

More explicit use of religious language to set limits on the commodification of property appears in the 1984 West Virginia case of *Harris v. Crowder. Crowder* involves an attempt by a creditor to partition a family home jointly owned by a husband and wife, in order to satisfy a debt owed by the husband (but not the wife). In the opinion Chief Justice Richard Neely refuses to allow the creditor to partition, even though this, in effect, eliminates the creditor's valuable property right:

Under the free enterprise system our economy is regulated through recurring cycles of human suffering. Successful competitors take the market from unsuccessful competitors; new products are born and older products die; plants and even whole industries migrate in response to opportunities to achieve lower costs. . . . In the United States, then, low costs, high productivity, and steady growth are achieved through the unrelenting discipline of competition and its attendant misery. . . . One of the functions of law is to distribute the costs of operating this society in an equitable way: when loss is inevitable, it should fall on the strong and not upon the weak. St. Matthew 25:40.[60]

---

[59] *Id.*
[60] *Harris v. Crowder*, 322 S.E.2d 854, 860 (W. Va. 1984).

Crowder, even more explicitly than *State v. Shack*, endorses posses-
sive individualism, but stresses that pursuit of economic self-interest
must operate only within limits. Although Justice Neely's open use of
Christian rhetoric is idiosyncratic, it highlights an interesting convention:
where values derive from Judeo-Christian religion, they are acceptable
only if they are translated out of religious language into one of the many
secularized re-treads, notably the Kantian language of equal dignity. Michael Perry has argued that "many elements and aspects of a religious
ethic . . . can be presented in public discussion in ways that do not presume assent to them on the specific premises of a faith grounded in
revelation."[61]

This "principle of public accessibility" blurs the distinction between
religious and nonreligious formulations. In the context of judicial decisions, we probably do not want judges using openly religious language,
given that they are officials in a secular society where many people do
not share their religious premises. Yet the blurring of religious and other
forms of normative talk further destabilizes the distinctions designed to
police the lines between common sense, science, religion, and old-
fashioned moralizing. If common sense and science are as normative as
old-fashioned moralizing, and key religious themes are readily translated
into alternative secularized metaphorics, then we need to rethink the
distinctions between common sense and science, on the one hand, and
religion and other forms of normative talk, on the other.[62]

Crowder shows clearly the rhetorical challenges presented by the liberal dignity strain for a judge less willing than Neely to push the enve-
lope of acceptable judicial behavior: both *State v. Shack* and *Harris v.
Crowder* may well seem, to some, "sentimental" or verging on the un-

---

[61] Michael J. Perry, "Toward an Ecumenical Politics," *George Washington Law Review*
60 (1992): 599–619 (quoting from John Coleman, at 603).

[62] My view of religion as merely one metaphoric among others signals quite a different
approach from Michael Perry's. My argument has some similarity to Michael Perry's
argument that the idea of human rights is ineliminably religious. See Michael J. Perry,
"Is the Idea of Human Rights Ineliminably Religious?" *University of Richmond Law
Review* 27 (1993): 1023–981, but my model is closer to the historians' model of the
"interpenetration of religious and secular themes." See Bloch, "Religion," 45, in contrast to Perry, who privileges religious formulations. For a theologian's analysis of how
religious ideas are inherent, though unrecognized, in many contexts today, see Gordon
D. Kaufman, *In the Face of Mystery: A Constructive Ideology* (Cambridge, Mass.:
Harvard University Press, 1993). See also Robert Wuthnow, *Acts of Compassion: Car-
ing for Others and Helping Ourselves* (Princeton, N.J.: Princeton University Press,
1993). Wuthnow argues that many of our ethical norms are thinly secularized formulations of what originally were religious principles.

professional. The Vermont Supreme Court case of *Hilder v. St. Peter* (1984) sketches out a highly effective rhetorical strategy for mobilizing the liberal dignity strain without raising questions about whether this approach to property is really "sentiment" or "religion," not law.

Because the core of the court's argument in *Hilder* is in its description of the facts, I will quote at length:

The facts are uncontested. In October, 1974, plaintiff began occupying an apartment at defendants' 10–12 Church Street apartment building in Rutland with her three children and new-born grandson. Plaintiff orally agreed to pay defendant Stuart St. Peter [rent and a deposit]. . . . Plaintiff has paid all rent due under her tenancy. Because the previous tenants had left behind garbage and items of personal belongings, defendant offered to refund plaintiff's damage deposit if she would clean the apartment herself prior to taking possession. Plaintiff did clean the apartment, but never received her deposit back because the defendant denied ever receiving it. Upon moving into the apartment, plaintiff discovered a broken kitchen window. Defendant promised to repair it, but after waiting a week and fearing that her two-year-old child might cut herself on the shards of glass, plaintiff repaired the window at her own expense. Although defendant promised to provide a front door key, he never did. For a period of time, whenever plaintiff left the apartment, a member of the family would remain behind for security reasons. Eventually, plaintiff purchased and installed a padlock, again at her own expense. After moving in, plaintiff discovered that the bathroom toilet was clogged with paper and feces and would flush only by dumping pails of water into it. Although plaintiff repeatedly complained about the toilet, and defendant promised to have it repaired, the toilet remained clogged and mechanically inoperable throughout the period of plaintiff's tenancy. . . . Plaintiff also discovered that water leaked from the water pipes of the upstairs apartment down the ceilings and walls of both her kitchen and back bedroom. Again, defendant promised to fix the leakage, but never did. As a result of this leakage, a large section of plaster fell from the back bedroom ceiling onto her bed and her grandson's crib. Other sections of plaster remained dangling from the ceiling. This condition was brought to the attention of the defendant, but he never corrected it. Fearing that the remaining plaster might fall when the room was occupied, plaintiff moved her and her grandson's bedroom furniture into the living room and ceased using the back bedroom. During the summer months an odor of raw sewage permeated plaintiff's apartment. The odor was so strong that the plaintiff was ashamed to have company in her apartment. Responding to plaintiff's complaints, Rutland City workers unearthed a broken sewage pipe in the basement, but defendant failed to clean it up. . . . [63]

When I discuss this case in class, I begin by asking how it smells. The pervasive fecal odor, particularly in combination with the tenant's

[63] *Hilder v. St. Peter*, 478 A.2d 202, 216 (Vt. 1984).

"shame," works with admirable economy to convey the message that human dignity has been affronted. The legal issue is whether the deteriorated condition of rental premises is relevant to a tenant's obligation to pay rent. At common law, a tenant owed the full contract rent regardless of the condition of the premises. *Hilder* is the case that changed that common law rule in Vermont. Note the imagery of children in danger: of plaster falling into cribs, of jagged windows slicing little hands. The underlying message is that, even if rental contracts generally should be enforced, this one should not because blameless children were placed at risk. The subtext is that we do not want to live in a society where property rights are extolled above the crushed heads of innocents.

The brilliance of *Hilder* lies in its ability to take this particular case out of the general run of cases (where, it implies reassuringly, contracts should be enforced). Its forcefulness also stems from its smooth, untheoretical surface. The work of an accomplished trial lawyer, it conveys the liberal dignity theme in an intuitive way, without stumbling into "inappropriate" religious language or high-blown phrases like "human values." In property law the dignity theme can so easily sound like religion, sentimentality, or socialism, but *Hilder* evades explicit political judgments. All the reader has to sign on to is that landlords should not be able to require tenants to live in excrement.

Submerging the dignity theme is the least risky strategy because of the current understanding that property involves issues of common sense. In this context the best strategy is to submerge the assumptions of the liberal dignity strain, much as the nature narrative submerges the assumptions of economic liberalism. This is precisely what *Hilder* does: it translates a highly charged moral choice into an issue of "common sense."

The alternative is to surface the values and assumptions in each vision, including those that present themselves as objective science or common sense. This approach allows judges to open up a conversation on social ethics without privileging those views that bury their normative assumptions beneath claims of objectivity. This strikes me as better than relying on clever arguments designed to hide our divergent views. We need to "see normative argument as encompassing the creation and elaboration of both competing social visions and forms of moral persuasion."[64] I do not hold out the promise of a comforting consensus or an

---

[64] Joseph William Singer, "Legal Realism Now," *California Law Review* 76 (1988): 533. The "continue to talk" formulation is from James T. Kloppenberg, letter to author, 17

easy conversation. Incommensurability is very real in a society where the richest 1 percent of households own more than 40 percent of the wealth: we live in one of the most economically stratified nations in the world.[65] But, considering the alternatives, we should continue to talk. Identifying our divergent, incommensurable "truths" is a precondition to constructing strategies and moments of coalition.

Judges' competing moral visions provide the conceptual underpinning of their decisions. We should change the existing taboo on admitting that. I have argued in favor of an open admission that judicial decision-making—not only about constitutional law but also about property and other common law topics—involves questions of social ethics. This shift will not undermine the rule of law, compromise judges' legitimacy, or raise the spectre of *Bowers v. Hardwick*. It will change our view of the social visions that present themselves as common sense or science. Putatively objective claims based on science or common sense will be seen as different *styles* of moral discourse rather than as alternatives to it.

February 1995. As Joseph Singer has pointed out, we disagree not only on our substantive social visions but also on "our conceptions of a mature moral conversation" (543–4).

[65] Lester Thurow, "Why Their World Might Crumble," *The New York Times*, 19 November 1995, 78–9.

Further readings

Abelove, Henry, and MARHO: the Radical Historians Organization, eds. *Visions of History*. New York: Pantheon, 1983.

Addams, Jane. *Twenty Years at Hull-House*. New York: Macmillan, 1910.

Adorno, T. W., et al. *The Authoritarian Personality*. New York: Harper and Row, 1950.

Altman, Andrew. "Pragmatism and Applied Ethics." *American Philosophical Quarterly* 20 (1983): 227–35.

Anderson, Elizabeth. "John Stuart Mill and Experiments in Living." *Ethics* 102 (1991): 4–26.

———. *Value in Ethics and Economics*. Cambridge, Mass.: Harvard University Press, 1993.

Appleby, Joyce, Lynn Hunt, and Margaret Jacobs. *Telling the Truth about History*. New York: Norton, 1994.

Arendt, Hannah. *Eichmann in Jerusalem: A Report on the Banality of Evil*. New York: Viking, 1963.

Behar, Ruth. *Translated Woman: Crossing the Border with Esperanza's Story*. Boston: Beacon Press, 1993.

Bell, Daniel. *Communitarianism and Its Critics*. Oxford: Clarendon Press, 1993.

Bellah, Robert, et al. *Habits of the Heart*. Berkeley and Los Angeles: University of California Press, 1985.

———. *The Good Society*. New York: Knopf, 1991.

Berlin, Isaiah. *The Crooked Timber of Humanity*. New York: Vintage Books, 1992.

Booth, Wayne C. *The Company We Keep: An Ethics of Fiction*. Berkeley and Los Angeles: University of California Press, 1988.

Boswell, John. *Same-Sex Unions in Premodern Europe*. New York: Villard Books, 1994.

Brown, Karen McCarthy. "Alourdes: A Case Study of Moral Leadership in Haitian Voudou." In *Saints and Virtues*, edited by John Stratton Hawley, 144–67. Berkeley and Los Angeles: University of California Press, 1987.

———. *Mama Lola: A Vodou Priestess in Brooklyn*. Berkeley and Los Angeles: University of California Press, 1991.

———. "Systematic Remembering, Systematic Forgetting: Ogou in Haiti." In *Africa's Ogun: Old World and New*, edited by Sandra T. Barnes, 65–89. Bloomington, Ind.: Indiana University Press, 1989.

Carter, Stephen L. *The Culture of Disbelief: How American Law and Politics Trivialize Religious Devotion*. New York: Basic Books, 1993.

Clausen, Christopher. *The Moral Imagination: Essays on Literature and Ethics*. Iowa City: University of Iowa Press, 1986.

Clifford, James, and George E. Marcus. *Writing Culture: The Poetics and Pol-*

itics of Ethnography. Berkeley and Los Angeles: University of California Press, 1986.

Coles, Robert. *The Call of Stories: Teaching and the Moral Imagination*. Boston: Houghton Mifflin, 1989.

Covington, Dennis. *Salvation on Sand Mountain: Snake Handling and Redemption in Southern Appalachia*. Reading, Mass.: Addison-Wesley, 1995.

Downs, Donald. *Syndromes or Self Defense? Battered Women at the Crossroads of Criminal Law*. Chicago: University of Chicago Press, 1996.

Dupré, John. *The Disorder of Things*. Cambridge, Mass.: Harvard University Press, 1993.

Dworkin, Ronald. *A Matter of Principle*. Cambridge, Mass.: Harvard University Press, 1985.

Edel, Abraham, Elizabeth Flower, and Finbarr W. O'Connor. *A Critique of Applied Ethics*. Philadelphia: Temple University Press, 1994.

Elshtain, Jean Bethke. *Democracy on Trial*. New York: Basic Books, 1995.

Eskridge, William N., and Philip P. Frickey. "Foreword: Law as Equilibrium." *Harvard Law Review* 108 (1994): 26–69.

Etzioni, Amitai. *The Moral Dimension: Toward a New Economics*. New York: Free Press, 1988.

———. *The Spirit of Community: Rights, Responsibilities, and the Communitarian Agenda*. New York: Crown, 1993.

———, ed. *New Communitarian Thinking: Persons, Virtues, Institutions, and Communities*. Charlottesville: University of Virginia Press, 1995.

Flanagan, Owen. *Varieties of Moral Personality: Ethics and Psychological Realism*. Cambridge, Mass.: Harvard University Press, 1991.

Friedman, Barry. "Dialogue and Judicial Review." *Michigan Law Review* 91 (1993): 577–682.

Galston, William. *Liberal Purposes: Goods, Virtues, and Diversity in the Liberal State*. New York: Cambridge University Press, 1991.

Geertz, Clifford. *Local Knowledge: Further Essays in Interpretative Anthropology*. New York: Basic Books, 1983.

Haan, Norma, et al., eds. *Social Science as Moral Inquiry*. New York: Columbia University Press, 1983.

Haberman, David L. *Journey through the Twelve Forests: An Encounter with Krishna*. New York: Oxford University Press, 1994.

Haines, Nicholas. "Responsibility and Accountability." *Philosophy* 30 (1995): 141–63.

Hare, R. M. "Descriptivism." In *Essays on the Moral Concepts*, 55–75. London: Macmillan, 1972.

Harpham, Geoffrey Galt. *Getting It Right: Language, Literature, and Ethics*. Chicago: University of Chicago Press, 1992.

Havel, Václav. *Open Letters*. New York: Knopf, 1991.

Herzog, Don. *Happy Slaves: A Critique of Consent Theory*. Chicago: University of Chicago Press, 1989.

———. *Without Foundations: Justification in Political Theory*. Ithaca, N.Y.: Cornell University Press, 1985.

Himmelfarb, Gertrude. *On Looking into the Abyss: Untimely Thoughts on Society and Culture*. New York: Knopf, 1994.

Holmes, Stephen. *The Anatomy of Anti-Liberalism*. Cambridge, Mass.: Harvard University Press, 1993.

Hooks, Benjamin. *Go Tell It!* New York: NAACP Press, 1979.

Kovesi, Julius. *Moral Notions.* London: Routledge and Kegan Paul, 1967.

Longino, Helen. *Science as Social Knowledge.* Princeton, N.J.: Princeton University Press, 1990.

Macedo, Steven. *Liberal Virtues: Citizenship, Virtue and Community in Liberal Constitutionalism.* Oxford: Clarendon Books, 1990.

MacIntyre, Alasdair. *After Virtue.* Notre Dame, Ind.: University of Notre Dame Press, 1981.

Marcus, George E., and Michael M. J. Fischer. *Anthropology as Cultural Critique: An Experimental Moment in the Human Sciences.* Chicago: University of Chicago Press, 1986.

Marsden, George M. *The Soul of the American University: From Protestant Establishment to Established Nonbelief.* New York: Oxford University Press, 1994.

Massey, Irving. *Find You the Virtue: Ethics, Image, and Desire in Literature.* Fairfax, Va.: George Mason University Press, 1987.

May, Larry. *Sharing Responsibility.* Chicago: University of Chicago Press, 1992.

Milgram, Stanley. *Obedience to Authority: An Experimental View.* New York: Harper and Row, 1974.

Mill, John Stuart. *On Liberty.* 1859; reprint, Indianapolis: Hackett, 1978.

Minow, Martha L. "Judging Inside Out." *University of Colorado Law Review* 61 (1990): 795–801.

———. "Partial Justice." In *The Fate of Law,* ed. Austin Sarat and Thomas R. Kearns, 36–45. Ann Arbor: University of Michigan Press, 1993.

Moontz, Francis, III. "Is the Rule of Law Possible in a Postmodern World?" *Washington Law Review* 68 (1993): 249–305.

Morson, Gary Saul. *Narrative and Freedom: The Shadows of Time.* New Haven, Conn.: Yale University Press, 1994.

Murphey, Murray G. "On the Scientific Study of Religion in the United States, 1870–1980." In *Religion and Twentieth-Century American Intellectual Life,* edited by Michael J. Lacey, 136–71. Washington, D.C., and New York: Woodrow Wilson Center Press and Cambridge University Press, 1989.

Nash, Gary, and Charlotte Crabtree, project co-directors. *National Standards for United States History: Exploring the American Experience.* Los Angeles: National Center for History in the Schools, 1994.

Nelson, Lynn. *Who Knows? From Quine to a Feminist Empiricism.* Philadelphia: Temple University Press, 1990.

Newton, Adam Zachary. *Narrative Ethics.* Cambridge, Mass.: Harvard University Press, 1995.

Novick, Peter. *That Noble Dream: The "Objectivity Question" and the American Historical Profession.* New York: Cambridge University Press, 1988.

Obeyesekere, Gananath. *The Work of Culture: Symbolic Transformation in Psychoanalysis and Anthropology.* Chicago and London: University of Chicago Press, 1990.

Palmer, Frank. *Literature and Moral Understanding: A Philosophical Essay on Ethics, Aesthetics, Education, and Culture.* Oxford: Clarendon Press, 1992.

Parker, David. *Ethics, Theory, and the Novel.* New York: Cambridge University Press, 1994.

Perry, Michael. *Morality, Politics, and Law.* New York: Oxford University Press, 1988.

Putnam, Hilary. *Reason, Truth, and History*. Cambridge: Cambridge University Press, 1981.

Quine, W. V. O. *From a Logical Point of View*. Rev ed. New York: Harper and Row, 1963.

Rawls, John. *A Theory of Justice*. Cambridge, Mass.: Harvard University Press, 1971.

Redish, Martin H., and Theodore T. Chung. "Democratic Theory and the Legislative Process: Mourning the Death of Originalism in Statutory Interpretation." *Tulane Law Review* 68 (1994): 803–81.

Rorty, Richard. *Contingency, Irony, and Solidarity*. Cambridge: Cambridge University Press, 1989.

Rosaldo, Renato. *Culture and Truth: The Remaking of Social Analysis*. Boston: Beacon Press, 1989.

Rosenstone, Robert A. *Mirror in the Shrine: American Encounters in Meiji Japan*. Cambridge, Mass.: Harvard University Press, 1988.

Sandel, Michael. *Liberalism and the Limits of Justice*. Cambridge: Cambridge University Press, 1982.

Sanders, Lynn. "Against Deliberation." *Political Theory* (forthcoming).

Schacter, Jane S. "Metademocracy: The Changing Structure of Legitimacy in Statutory Interpretation." *Harvard Law Review* 108 (1995): 593–663.

Schama, Simon. *Dead Certainties (Unwarranted Speculations)*. New York: Knopf, 1991.

Scheper-Hughes, Nancy. *Death without Weeping: The Violence of Everyday Life in Brazil*. Berkeley and Los Angeles: University of California Press, 1992.

Selznick, Philip. *The Moral Commonwealth: Social Theory and the Promise of Community*. Berkeley and Los Angeles: University of California Press, 1992.

Sharpe, Eric J. *Comparative Religion: A History*. 2d ed. LaSalle, Ill.: Open Court, 1986.

Siebers, Tobin. *The Ethics of Criticism*. Ithaca, N.Y.: Cornell University Press, 1988.

Singer, Joseph Williams. "Legal Realism Now." *California Law Review* 76 (1988): 465–544.

Smart, J. J. C. "Free Will, Praise, and Blame." *Mind* 70 (1961): 291–306.

Smiley, Marion. *Moral Responsibility and the Boundaries of Community: Power and Accountability from a Pragmatic Point of View*. Chicago: University of Chicago Press, 1992.

Smith, Jonathan Z. *Imagining Religion: From Babylon to Jonestown*. Chicago: University of Chicago Press, 1982.

Sowell, Thomas. *Compassion versus Guilt and Other Essays*. New York: Morrow, 1987.

Stout, Jeffrey. *Ethics after Babel*. Boston: Beacon Press, 1988.

Strauss, Leo. *Natural Right and History*. Chicago: University of Chicago Press, 1953.

Taylor, Charles. "Neutrality in Political Science." In *Philosophy and the Human Sciences*, 58–90. Cambridge: Cambridge University Press, 1985.

———. "Social Theory as Practice." In *Philosophy and the Human Sciences*, 91–115. Cambridge: Cambridge University Press, 1985.

———. "What Is Human Agency?" In *Human Agency and Language*, 15–44. Cambridge: Cambridge University Press, 1985.

————. *Sources of the Self: The Making of Modern Identity.* Cambridge, Mass.: Harvard University Press, 1989.

————. "Explanation and Practical Reason." In *The Quality of Life*, edited by Martha Nussbaum and Amartya Sen, 208–31. Oxford: Clarendon Press, 1993.

Tiles, Mary. "A Science of Mars or of Venus?" *Philosophy* 62 (1987): 293–306.

Todorov, Tzvetan. *The Morals of History.* Translated by Alyson Waters. Minneapolis: University of Minnesota Press, 1995.

Ulrich, Laurel Thatcher. *A Midwife's Tale: The Life of Martha Ballard, Based on Her Diary, 1785–1812.* New York: Knopf, 1990.

Walker, Lenore. *Terrifying Love: Why Battered Women Kill and How Society Responds.* New York: Harper and Row, 1989.

Wallace, Jay. *Responsibility and the Moral Sentiments.* Cambridge, Mass.: Harvard University Press, 1994.

Waring, Marilyn. *If Women Counted: A New Feminist Economics.* San Francisco: HarperCollins, 1990.

White, Hayden. *The Content of the Form: Narrative Discourse and Historical Representation.* Baltimore, Md.: Johns Hopkins University Press, 1987.

Williams, Bernard. *Ethics and the Limits of Philosophy.* Cambridge, Mass.: Harvard University Press, 1985.

Williams, Joan. "Rorty, Radicalism, Romanticism: The Politics of the Gaze." *Wisconsin Law Review* 1 (1992): 131–55.

Wilson, James Q. *The Moral Sense.* New York: Free Press, 1993.

Wolfe, Alan. *Whose Keeper? Social Science and Moral Obligation.* Berkeley and Los Angeles: University of California Press, 1989.

Wolin, Sheldon. *Politics and Vision.* Boston: Little, Brown, 1970.

Worster, Donald. *The Wealth of Nature: Environmental History and the Ecological Imagination.* New York: Oxford University Press, 1993.

Wuthnow, Robert, ed. *Rethinking Materialism: Perspectives on the Spiritual Dimension of Economic Behavior.* Grand Rapids, Mich.: Eerdmans, 1995.

About the authors

Elizabeth Anderson is associate professor of philosophy and women's studies at the University of Michigan. She is the author of *Value in Ethics and Economics*.

Wayne C. Booth is professor of English emeritus at the University of Chicago. He is the author of *The Company We Keep: An Ethics of Fiction*.

Karen McCarthy Brown is professor of anthropology of religion in the Graduate and Theological Schools of Drew University. She is the author of *Mama Lola: A Vodou Priestess in Brooklyn*.

Jean Bethke Elshtain is the Laura Spelman Rockefeller Professor of Ethics at the University of Chicago. She is the author of *Democracy on Trial*.

Owen Flanagan is James B. Duke Professor of Philosophy, professor of psychology, and neurobiology, and an affiliated professor in the Graduate Program in Literature at Duke University. He is the author of *Self Expressions: Mind, Morals, and the Meaning of Life*.

Richard Wightman Fox is professor of history at Boston University and the author of *Reinhold Niebuhr: A Biography*.

Jane Kamensky is assistant professor of history at Brandeis University and the author of *Governing the Tongue: The Politics of Speech in Early New England*.

Robert A. Orsi is professor of religious studies and adjunct professor of anthropology and history at Indiana University, and the author of *The Madonna of 115th Street: Faith and Community in Italian Harlem, 1880–1950* and *Thank You, St. Jude: Women's Devotion to the Patron Saint of Hopeless Causes*.

289

Marion Smiley is professor of political science at the University of Wisconsin—Madison. She is the author of *Moral Responsibility and the Boundaries of Community: Power and Accountability from a Pragmatic Point of View.*

Robert B. Westbrook is professor of history at the University of Rochester and the author of *John Dewey and American Democracy.*

Joan C. Williams is professor of law at American University and the author of *Reconstructing Gender* (forthcoming).

Alan Wolfe is University Professor at Boston University and the author of the forthcoming *One Nation, After All.*

Index

contingency (*cont.*)
142–8; vs. pure rationality, 58, 62–7,
76; vs. universalism, 12, 14, 17, 26–8,
49, 54–6. *See also* knowledge: as perspectival
contractarianism, 11, 12–13
contract law, 138
conversation. *See* dialogue
cost-benefit analyses, 12, 13
Covington, Dennis, 201–4, 218–24
critical intelligence. *See* reflection
critical race theorists, 137–41, 254
Cronon, William, 122
Crown Heights riot, 70, 82
cruelty, 38, 239–41
Cuban missile crisis, 87
culture (and morality), 7, 186
The Culture of Disbelief (Carter), 209
"culture wars," 2, 114, 231, 250. *See also*
identity politics
curses, 128

Dahl, Roald, 170n28
Darley, J. M., 98–9
Davis, Natalie, 142
Davis, Walter A., 173n32
Dead Man Walking (Prejean), 170n26
death penalty. *See* capital punishment
deliberation, 35–7
demarcation, 86
democracy: deliberation in, 35–7; and education, 145; and elections, 261–3. *See
also* "culture wars"; "incommensurability"; pluralism; relativism
Demos, John, 119
Derrida, Jacques, 48
description vs. evaluation (or norms). *See*
fact-value split
Dessalines, Jean-Jacques, 193
Dewey, John, 4, 6n5, 9, 15, 94, 206, 249
dialogue (and ethical justifications), 12,
265n32, 269, 281–2. *See also* relationships
difference: cultural, 181–200; and fairness,
81; between past and present, 126–48;
religious, 201–26. *See also* boundaries;
pluralism; self: and other; storytelling
discourse ethics, 47
disinterest, 228
Dr. Jekyll and Mr. Hyde (Stevenson), 162
Dole, Bob, 150n2, 158n15
domesticity, 275–6. *See also* "housework"
Dostoyevsky, Fyodor, 84, 110
doubt (skepticism), 8; as aspect of postmodernism, 4, 118, 237–8; among historians, 116–19; Hume's, 165; as part

of modern life, 50–1, 55; of pragma-
tists, 15. *See also* contingency; moral
confidence
Downs, Donald, 35
drug addiction, 73, 78
D'Souza, Dinesh, 184
Dupré, John, 26
Dürer, Albrecht, 53
Durkheim, Emile, 227–9, 234
Duvalier, Jean-Claude, 189n
Dworkin, Andrea, 141n68
Dworkin, Ronald, 231

Easton, David, 41n3
economics: attempts to avoid ethical judgments in, 10; and gender, 182–3; normative enterprises in, 23, 26–7, 30–4;
and property, 271–2. *See also* liberalism:
economic
education, 229, 245; assimilationism goals
of, 206; contingency in moral, 144, 146–
7; irony in, 108–9, 144, 147; Kohlberg's
moral stages popular in, 93; pluralism's
distrust of, 243; storytelling's role in
moral, 150–2, 155, 175
Eldridge, Larry, 136n
elections, 261–3
Eliot, George, 106
Ellis, Bret Easton, 149
Elshtain, Jean Bethke, 4; on battered
woman syndrome, 74, 75; on moral inquiry, 6, 8, 40–56; on separate spheres
doctrine, 32n; on "testimony," 37n
emotivism, 45–7, 85–9
empirical psychology, 91–111
empiricism. *See* experience
The End of Racism (D'Souza), 184
Enlightenment, 20–1, 84–5, 87–9, 147
environmental concerns, 121–4, 276
Eskridge, William, 263–4
ethical inquiry. *See* moral inquiry
ethnography. *See* anthropology
Etzioni, Amitai, 250
evaluative concepts. *See* fact-value split;
self: strong evaluation of
evil (in Vodou), 198
experience (empirical evidence): importance of, to ethical norms, 6, 11, 12, 14–
22, 25, 29–34, 37–9, 58–61, 76–111.
See also abstraction; contingency;
knowledge: as perspectival; self; storytelling
expressivism, 89n
Ezili Dantò, 194
Ezili Freda, 194

Other books in the series (*continued from front of book*)

Theodore Taranovski, editor, *Reform in Modern Russian History: Progress or Cycle?*

Blair A. Ruble, *Money Sings: The Changing Politics of Urban Space in Post-Soviet Yaroslavl*

Deborah S. Davis, Richard Kraus, Barry Naughton, and Elizabeth J. Perry, editors, *Urban Spaces in Contemporary China: The Potential for Autonomy and Community in Post-Mao China*

William M. Shea and Peter A. Huff, editors, *Knowledge and Belief in America: Enlightenment Traditions and Modern Religious Thought*

W. Elliot Brownlee, editor, *Funding the Modern American State, 1941–1995: The Rise and Fall of the Era of Easy Finance*

W. Elliot Brownlee, *Federal Taxation in America: A Short History*

R. H. Taylor, editor, *The Politics of Elections in Southeast Asia*

Šumit Ganguly, *The Crisis in Kashmir: Portents of War, Hopes of Peace*

James W. Muller, editor, *Churchill as Peacemaker*

Donald R. Kelley and David Harris Sacks, editors, *The Historical Imagination in Early Modern Britain: History, Rhetoric, and Fiction, 1500–1800*